The
Missiological Implications
of the Theology of
Gerhard Forde

Mark Lewellyn Nygard

Lutheran University Press
Minneapolis, Minnesota

LUTHERAN UNIVERSITY PRESS DISSERTATION SERIES

The Dissertation Series is designed to make available to libraries and individuals the scholarship and research of those pursuing advanced academic degrees. The final editing is that of the author, and the publisher assumes no responsibility for errors of fact, interpretation, or attribution.

The Missiological Implications of the Theology of Gerhard Forde
by Mark Lewellyn Nygard

Library of Congress Cataloging-in-Publication Data

Nygard, Mark Lewellyn.
    The missiological implications of the theology of Gerhard Forde / Mark Lewellyn Nygard.
        p. cm.
    Originally presented as the author's thesis (doctoral)—Luther Seminary, 2009.
    "Chronological list of Forde's published works": P.
    Includes bibliographical references (p.).
    ISBN-13: 978-1-932688-55-9 (alk. paper)
    ISBN-10: 1-932688-55-2 (alk. paper)
    1. Forde, Gerhard O. 2. Missions—Theory. 3. Evangelical Lutheran Church in America—Doctrines. I. Title.
    BV2063.N95 2010
    266—dc22
                              2010037485

Lutheran University Press, PO Box 390759, Minneapolis, MN 55439
www.lutheranupress.org
Manufactured in the United States of America

Table of Contents

LIST OF ABBREVIATIONS

LW   *Luther's Works*, American Edition

WA   *Luthers Werke*, Weimarer Ausgabe

CHAPTER 1

The Problem and the Approach

A. The Appearance of Incongruence

It seems safe to say that Dr. Gerhard Forde (1927-2005) has exercised a significant influence on the life of the Lutheran church in America and beyond over the past several decades. During a teaching career of thirty-four years, twenty-nine of them at Luther Seminary in St. Paul, Minnesota, it is estimated that he taught theology to over three thousand pastors.[1] My personal experience at pastors' gatherings in the Midwest off and on over the past thirty years suggests that Forde has become something of a household word among clergy of the Evangelical Lutheran Church in America, and that if one doesn't know something of what he represents, one is simply an outsider to the theological conversation.

But Forde's substantial theological work brought him to the attention of the church far beyond the circle of his students. His literary production includes over one hundred books, articles, reviews, and cassettes. He contributed two of the twelve loci of a major church dogmatics that was virtually required reading in Lutheran seminaries across the nation in the '80s and '90s and is still in use today. A confirmation text he co-authored instructed a whole generation of youth. His *Where God Meets Man* was translated into German, Norwegian, Japanese, and Slovak. His contributions to the Lutheran-Roman Catholic dialogues brought him ecumenical attention. Still unprinted materials, ranging from class preparations and sermons to articles requested by the national church offices, provide the basis for continuing publication after his death. In these works Forde engages the thought of leading theologians of our time—people like Barth, Bultmann, Moltmann, Jenson, and Braaten in the twentieth century, Hegel, Schleiermacher, von Hofmann, Ritschl, and Herrmann in the nineteenth—and all of this in a way that makes a characteristic contribution to the theological conversation.

Forde's emphasis was what has come to be called "radical Lutheranism." In short, Forde argues that the God of the scriptures is an electing God, Godself doing through Christ and the proclamation of Christ all that is necessary to claim his own. In this action there is no contribution by humankind, for we are bound in rebellion and unable to do, think, or believe anything that might help us. Through the law and the gospel God puts to death the rebel and brings to life a new person that lives in the freedom of faith in God's unconditional assurances. Through these emphases Forde is most closely associated with the fields of Luther studies and Christian dogmatics. Here is where he is treasured.

Less frequently is Forde connected to the missional task of the church. My experience is that folks are mildly surprised at the mere suggestion, as if Forde might even be against it. One can propose several possible reasons for this. One prominent expression of mission is a pietistic variety that emphasizes invitation and human response. These would be the very elements that Forde found so disturbing and against which he sought clarification. Another phenomenon in late-century missiology has been what is sometimes regarded as a clouding of the field caused by a broadening of missional concern, so that the evangelical edge of the task is dulled. Forde often complains that the church seemed to be losing clarity in its task. Yet another reality is the fact that Forde himself rather infrequently uses the word "mission," never writing an article on it as such. It would be possible to read a significant slice of Forde's work without being conscious of mission, and thus conclude that it is an area that does not particularly concern him.

I once assumed this was the case myself. Having come to seminary out of a sense of calling to overseas ministry, and being confused by the mixed reviews I heard about Forde, I successfully avoided him as a professor for two years, as I often say, tongue-in-cheek. But a reading of Regin Prenter's *Spiritus Creator* in my middler year opened me to a strong view of God's initiative, and Forde suddenly became very interesting to me, if still provocative. I took a class from him every quarter of my senior year at seminary and two of the three quarters of my master of theology year. He was simultaneously fascinating and irritating, and it seemed I could not get enough of him.

Forde's hermeneutical approach came to affect my fundamental attitude toward preaching. I grew to look upon every sermon as a moment when God might—just might—choose to use his Word in my mouth to create the death-and-life faith that was so essential to life in Christ, now and afterwards. That moment was not mine as proclaimer to control, and the faith was not my gift to give. Neither were they my parishioners'. It seemed clear that the faith in question was really not an option that my listeners might choose, even when they themselves might have understood themselves to have done so. The implications of this hermeneutic for the way people could be expected to come to faith, and thus for the ministry and mission of the church, were striking for me then and they remain so now after a career that has included nine years in two American parish ministries that I considered missionary and eighteen years in two West African ministries that everyone else considered missionary. Forde was simply a central component in the way I understood myself to have approached my task.

It should be noted at the outset, then, that this thesis is, first of all, to borrow a sociological term from the methodology of Cooperrider and Srivastva, an "appreciative inquiry."[2] That is, it is undertaken by one who felt a net positive effect of the theology of Gerhard Forde upon his missionary career and wondered if that effect should not have a wider impact. The expectation is that careful research could identify more precisely the insights in Forde's work that are helpful to the missional enterprise and allow them to make their contribution to the wider missiological conversation. Of course this reflects my experience, and I wouldn't be attempting the thesis if it didn't.

On the other hand, the apparent lack of public conversation between Forde's thought and the world of missiology suggests that the research include a corresponding "critical inquiry," as well. This means that we seek to be alert for elements of the theological conversations important to mission that Forde might have missed, misunderstood, neglected, or rejected. It means further that one might propose reasons for the haitus and imagine areas around which further missional conversation with Forde's work might be profitably pursued.

B. Methodological Approach

The thesis is woven around two poles, the shape of Gerhard Forde's theology and the character of ecumenical missiology as it presents itself today. Each of these poles is approached with an appropriate but unique methodology before an effort at relating them is attempted.

Approach to Forde's Theology

When dealing with an internationally acclaimed theologian who has had much time to write, it is not uncommon, out of considerations of sheer volume of material, for the researcher to find it necessary to define the limits of the literature to be included in the study.[3] Forde did not have the luxury of that much time. Not only was his writing produced on the run amidst intense day-to-day demands by his seminary and his church, it was cut short by a premature illness and death. With over a hundred published works to his credit, it would be misleading to call his literary remains modest in any sense of the term. Nevertheless, an inventory of his work suggests an initial methodological strategy of comprehensivity— that it would be possible to include Forde's entire published literary remains in the survey of his work. This is an asset that might allow Forde's writing to define its own scope and focus, whether it seemed related to the concept of mission or not.

Secondly, an effort was made to examine these works chronologically for the possibility that Forde's theological position developed over time. The books and articles were organized, not alphabetically, but chronologically by date of publication (see Appendix A), and they were read and data was recorded on them, for the most part, in that order. Allowing for the uncertainties surrounding publication date, as, for instance, the delay between delivery of a lecture and its publication or between the preparation of an article and its collection into a summary dialogue report, it was hoped that in this way significant broad tendencies might still be noticeable. The reader will sometimes be aware of this approach as material is identified as earlier or later in Forde's career. The results were, however, for the most part negative; the research left the impression of a deepening consistency in theological approach rather than a significantly changing perspective—and the references to time of writing in the thesis usually demonstrate this consistency.

Thirdly, since Forde's career sought to serve the proclamation of the church, an effort was made to include as many of his actual sermons as possible. One hundred forty-three were finally identified, of which only thirty-one are published and only twenty-one are dated to include the year. A few others are dateable based on references to historic events within the sermon itself, and still others may be assigned probable approximate dates based on the kind of paper on which they were written or the texture of Forde's argument. For the most part, however, no firm date may be discerned and no chronological order may be assigned to Forde's preaching. They thus required a different approach from that chosen for the articles, and, for lack of a better system, the sermons were considered in order of their biblical text (see Appendix B). As it became clear that deepening consistency was the character of Forde's books and articles, this seemed less of a disadvantage. Occasionally in the thesis, I will venture observations referring to earlier or later sermons, but these are relatively less sure and in any case, again, tend to support the claim to consistency more often than change.

Fourthly, most of the data were recorded in gradually developing categories of thought, eventually two hundred ninety-two in all, that collected references to subjects interesting to Forde or to my thesis.[4] Some of the data from the larger works, were, for the sake of time, simply gathered in separate documents of their own with reliance on the locating functions of the computer to find it. The way the data were collected invites four remarks. First, my choice of categories, though purposely broad, is not exhaustive, and it certainly reflects the perspective and interest of this researcher as I entered into the material. I propose, however, that, based as they are on some prior experience with and reading of Forde, they do justice to Forde's concerns while serving the goal of this thesis as laid out above. Secondly, it seems to me that the collection tends to represent Forde's thought more like representation in the

Senate than in the House of Representatives. That is, its comprehensivity gave a voice to every printed document and sermon, no matter how important, offering the smaller articles and sermons relatively more visiblity than they might have under a different method. I would argue that the effect is an assurance that we are viewing the whole theologian diachronically throughout his career rather than some favored phase of the theologian at some chosen moment, maybe some predetermined "apex." This is, of course, an asset because of the relative consistency of his thought. If Forde had demonstrated major shifts or development, this comprehensivity would pose problems. Thirdly, though intended as a cross-referencing tool enabling access to a large number of texts and their contexts, it has a tendency to turn the eye to the assertion rather than the argument. It is hoped that an awareness of this tendency together with an attempt to construct a broad structure that is faithful to Forde's approach will counter the possibility that such an approach could "tidbitize" Forde's thinking, isolating elements and running awry with them. Consequently, and fourthly, the method makes relatively more important the choice of systematic structure by which to understand Forde's thought. This structure arose almost intuitively out of the researcher's career-long familiarity with Forde's work and out of the comprehensive reading itself. While other things certainly might be said about his work, I have reason to argue the faithfulness of this representation of Forde's thought in the context of this conversation.

The analysis of Forde's theology is preceded by a brief account of his life and the more prominent influences that shaped his thought. At a superficial level this helps us to know in a more satisfying personal way Gerhard Forde as an individual and a theologian. But at a deeper level, it helps us make sense of his theology and imagine how it could take the shape it does. For instance, his high view of God's initiative would be a natural heritage of a son of the old Norwegian Synod. On the other hand, his remarkable hermeneutical accomplishment comes from a child of a precritical tradition who had to wrestle his way through modern viability and scriptural issues. We notice his proposals for more essential ecumenical conversation follow two decades of personal participation in the renowned Lutheran-Roman Catholic dialogues in the United States. And we marvel that his christology, bold and innovative as it is, has roots in parish presentations of Handel's Messiah in a rural Minnesota church when he was a boy! In these and other cases we not only get to know Forde better, but are enabled to make connections between his theology and his history that enhance our appreciation of his work.

Approach to Missiology

An assessment of the missiological implications of anyone's theology needs to take place with respect to some recognizeable standard of current missiological conversation. How may we say what constitutes the shape of missiology today? Given the vigor and complexity of this conversation in our time, this has become a daunting task. We attempt it here, after an introduction to scriptural and historical roots, by a survey of four recent missiological resources to construct a kind of atlas of late-twentieth century missiological concerns. First, Timothy Yates' *Christian Mission in the Twentieth Century* (1994) demonstrates the rapid evolution of missional thought through the course of the last century. Secondly, David Bosch's widely referenced *Transforming Mission* (1991) sketches thirteen elements of an "emerging ecumenical missionary paradigm." Thirdly, Bevans and Schroeder in *Constants in Context* (2006) propose a broad synthesis of the assets of three missional typologies using six recurring missional concerns. And finally, in a slight change of pace recognizing Forde's affinity with Luther studies, the trajectory of the opinion of Luther studies on mission in Luther is briefly traced through the twentieth century from Warneck's damning *Outline of a History of Protestant Missions* (1901) through Ingemar Öberg's *Luther and World Mission* (2007).

It is not our goal to assess the respective efforts, create some new synthesis, or redefine the field. This is simply a roadmap, reflective of a breadth of goals and destinations. Yet it is, we hope, a generally recognizeable roadmap that would offer few surprises and few omissions for the modern missiologist. Complex though it be, it offers a kind of measuring stick by which the interests and insights of Forde's theology might be judged or entered into the conversation.

Approach to the Comparison

After an initial assessment of Forde's own use of the word mission and related terms, the various emphases raised by the four missional approaches are revisited with Forde's work in mind. Where possible, connections are made. Sometimes the connections are substantial, as when Forde's emphasis on vibrant and faithful theology as a primary tool for proclamation and as a primary mission of the Lutheran church bears a strong correlation to Bosch's twelfth element, "mission as theology." At other times the connections are weak, as when Yates' first paradigm, "mission as expansion," is related to Forde's awareness and occasional excitement over a global scope for the gospel. Sometimes, there seems to be little correlation at all and thus little to say, as when Bosch's third point explores missiology's work on a broader definition of salvation. At still other times, there seems to be almost a negative correlation, as when the first of the three Bevans and Schroeder portraits seems to use the doctrine of the Trinity for a missiological basis in a way that Forde might find unwarranted. The goal is to discover areas of congruence and incongruence between the fields of Forde's theology and missiology.

The three most significant areas of congruence are summarized as contributions that Forde's theology might make to missiology, and these are restated with respect to mission. Three areas of apparent incongruence are also identified and attempts were made to probe the disparity. Three problematic areas from chapter three are also revisited as "missional issues in Forde's theology," areas where we would expect missiology to engage Forde in further discussion in response to its concerns.

Since missiology is such a practical field, it seems necessary not to leave the matter as theoretical conclusions, but to finish by relating a particular mission situation to Forde's work in light of them. My missionary experience, especially my years in Senegal, provide a basis for attempting a coherent missiological model that takes into account both "the reality on the ground" as I experienced it and Forde's missiological insights. By articulating the possibilities and limitations of Forde's theology in such an effort, the goal is to enflesh the work of this thesis and invite others to do the same.

C. Statement of the Thesis

This thesis is being written in the hope of furthering the conversation between Forde's theology and modern missiological thought. If Forde is, as I believe, a reservoir of remarkable missional insight and provocative missional conversation, his work should be more widely referenced among missionally-concerned people. In the pages that follow I will seek to demonstrate that the theology of Gerhard Forde brings powerful, if unplummed, contributions to the church's conversation concerning its missional task. In particular, I will suggest strong missional connections with Forde's emphasis on the eschatological act nature of the proclamation, his concern for the viability of the theological effort and the proclamation that follows, and his insistence on the freedom of the new person in Christ that may express itself in care of the neighbor and the earth.

In the process we will explore some of the discontinuities between Forde's theology and some current manifestations of missiology. These include differences in the function of the doctrine of the Trinity, in the universality and urgency of the commission to share the gospel, and in the breadth of the missiological self-definition itself. In addition, we will explore some issues that arise in Forde's own theology as the missiological task is considered, namely the herementucal tension in the role of the interpreter in Forde's system, a uniformity of anthropology that seems not to address the full spectrum of human situations, and a focus on the accusing action of the law in such a way that cooperation with people of other faith traditions for the good of society at large seems compromised.

We will attempt this in six chapters. This first explains the apparent haitus between Forde's theology and missiology, proposes to demonstrate a connection, and explains a methodology for accomplishing it. The second chapter presents Gerhard Forde's life and theological career with special attention to the influences that shaped him and the concerns that occupied him. The third chapter attempts a comprehensive *summa* of his theology with an eye to identifying elements that invite further missional attention and to formulating some critical questions based on them. The fourth chapter seeks to create a standard of definition for contemporary missiology that would be recognized by missiologists today through an examination of the concerns of four selected missiological approaches. The fifth chapter relates the theology of Forde to the missiological standard just created, noting affinities and contributions as well as incongruities and tensions. And the sixth chapter fleshes out the relationship of Forde and mission just obtained through a living demonstration in a concrete situation.

CHAPTER 2

The Life and Context of Gerhard Forde

Since Forde was not wont to talk about himself, the sources to get at his life story are not abundant. Thankfully, at the repeated urging of Ted Peters, Forde wrote a theological autobiography for *dialog* magazine, the winter of 1997, with the specific intent of sharing his understanding of how the events of his life affected his theological development. In this it is unique among published sources, and is far and away the most important resource in reconstructing his life. It may be said to have a brief unpublished counterpart in the short "Autobiographical Sketch" available under his name in the ELCA Region 3 Archives. This was written in his youth, after his year in Madison, and has the texture, perhaps, of a statement required of him for admission to Luther Theological Seminary. Also important are a number of memories preserved in an article on the Norwegian Synod that he wrote for *Striving for Ministry*, a centennial book celebrating the streams of tradition that had flowed into Luther Theological Seminary. Apart from these, data comes in snippets: a paragraph here on his difficulty in the interfaith dialogues, a sentence there on his favorite passage in the Book of Concord, a phrase in a sermon about reading the sports page, and so forth. Forde's death is recent enough that the impressions from these sources could be corraborated with those who knew him, especially with his wife, Marianna Forde, who still works with the Lutheran International Library Assistance Project at Luther Seminary as this thesis is being written.

A. Forde's Life

Family Background

On September 10, 1927, Gerhard O. Forde was born near Starbuck in Pope County, Minnesota, the son of Rev. Gerhard O. Forde, Sr. (1884-1964) and Hanna Halvorson Forde (1877-1928), grandson of Rev. Nils Førde (1849-1917) and Nora Otilia Erickson. On his father's side, Gerhard's aunt Laura was a student (1917-1918) and then teacher (1919) at the Lutheran Ladies School in Red Wing, his aunt Agnes was a voice teacher in New York and was honored by the Norwegian embassy for her years as organist at the Norwegian Seamen's Church in Brooklyn, and his aunt (Amanda) Magdalene married a pastor, the Rev. O. J. H. Preus who eventually became president of Luther College in Decorah, Iowa,[5] so that it may be ventured that the life and service in the church was important for the Forde family as a whole. Gerhard's own father,

Gerhard O., Sr., was a pastor of the Norwegian Lutheran Church in America and, before the merger of 1917, the Norwegian Synod, that immigrant church with the closest ties to the state Church of Norway (more on this below, pp. 23-29). He served congregations in the Starbuck area for a period eventually totaling forty-four years, the same congregations that Gerhard's grandfather had also served for twenty-five years before him, so the Forde name was well established in the parish.[6] One of those congregations was Indherred Lutheran Church, two-and-a-half miles north of town, the congregation in which Gerhard was baptized.

Strong Norwegian influence was a fact of life in Starbuck then as it is today, and no less so in a congregation that was what Gerhard called a "cultural center" for the area.[7] Pastor Gerhard, Sr., it is remembered, preserved his command of his forbears' particular nineteenth century Norwegian dialect so fluently that linguists from Norway came to him in Starbuck to document what, in Norway, was passing away.[8] Young Gerhard, only a second generation American-born, would eventually be sent to a college that emphasized its Norwegian heritage, there to take no fewer than eight semesters of Norwegian.[9] Years later he and his wife would visit the Førdegaard near Voss, Norway, from which the family had come.[10]

Early Years

When Gerhard was only six months old, his mother was killed in a car-train accident. Though he would not later remember this, he attributed to it a certain independence, aloofness, and skepticism that kept him from trusting others completely and required him to find solutions himself.[11] To help in the crisis, his aunt and uncle, Ralph and Ausilga Forde, and their children came to the Indherred Lutheran parsonage to live with them until his father remarried Astrid Oliva Flack (1908-2009) in 1939. With two families in the house, there were at one point five children under the age of three underfoot. These were good and busy years and Gerhard would in later years dream of them. It was a physically active life that included milking the cow before school, playing football, and skiing.[12] He attended a rural school, District No. 3, for eight years and then Starbuck High School, apparently enjoying the challenges of academic life, "trying to find out who I was" by "grappling with the material put before me in school," as he would later reflect. He enjoyed especially poetry—his father had mastered "reams of it" by memory—and he read classics like Dickens, Hugo, and Hawthorne that he found in his father's library. During this time he had "no intention of becoming a pastor or a theologian. But then," he wryly remarks, "I recall at this stage no particular intentions at all."[13]

For Christian education Gerhard attended parochial school every single Wednesday of his grade school life, Sunday school on Sundays, and Vacation Bible School and Bible camp during his eighth grade year.[14] The curriculum began with Bible stories and catechism memorization in the earlier years and culminated in two years of catechetical instruction before confirmation that included Luther's *Small Catechism*, an explanation to the catechism, more Bible history, and hymns. Here basic dogmatic affirmations were supported by proof-text verses to be memorized. Forde later reflected how these verses would still come to him "out of the blue" during systematic discussions: "Say what you want about the perils of 'proof-texting,' it is certainly preferable to having no text in mind at all!" Cultural events at Indherred Lutheran included a choir, an orchestra, and an annual presentation of Handel's *Messiah* in which Gerhard sometimes soloed. Forde later credited this as a significant source of his Christology and his view of the atonement.[15]

The Search for Direction

After high school Gerhard immediately enrolled at Luther College in Decorah, Iowa, since the military draft of World War II was still in effect. After one semester he enrolled in the Army Medical Corp and spent eighteen months stationed at various hospitals across the country. Discharged from this service in 1947, he returned to Luther College, completing a B.A. in chemistry, mathematics, and German in 1950. He pursued an additional year of graduate study in organic chemistry at the University of Wisconsin in Madison, part of the search to synthesize cholestrol. The sciences were attractive to him, he says, because they "appeared to me to be rigorous, solid, and logical." The "calm, judicious, thoughtful and careful confidence" of his professors in the sciences contrasted favorably with "the more strident opinions of other professors," especially some religion professors in a day of "considerable strife and defensiveness in the church over against the threat of biblical criticism, liberalism, and other pernicious twentieth-century evils."[16]

In the spring of 1951, looking out the window of the organic lab at the people hurrying by, Forde was suddenly struck by the question, "What am I doing here?" and realized that he was not sufficiently invested in chemical research to devote his life to it. Soon after, during a visit to his older brother at Luther Theological Seminary, a chance encounter with the "patriarch" of the seminary, Thaddeus Franke Gullixson, brought Gullixson's call, "Were you looking for me?" and Forde's stammered response, "Yes, I guess I am." He later reflected, "If there has been anything like a call from God in my life, that was probably as close as you can get!"[17] He enrolled at Luther and graduated in 1955 with a Bachelor of Theology degree.

The Search for a Better Case

Forde has several critical reflections on his seminary experience. In the first place, as a science major, he had to learn a new philosophical vocabulary which he found fascinating, but which he felt never became his "native language." His language was "the ancient catechetical tradition" of his youth, and he was always suspicious of the possibility of flights of fancy with the new talk. But secondly, he observed a kind of controlling instruction that implied, even when it didn't say it, "Don't ask questions." Given Forde's independence of thinking that has already been remarked, it is not surprising that he would recoil from such authoritarianism. "Luther didn't tear the whole church apart just for this," he would later remark, and it became one of the impetuses for him to pursue Luther studies. And thirdly, he experienced teaching that seemed to him a compromise of the view of the gospel that he had received. On one level he felt the *heilsgeschichtlich* approach so current at the time left disturbing historical questions, and on the other hand he instinctively rejected a professor's suggestion that human responsibility and divine election had to be held in tension. As he later wrote, "There are no doubt some things we might hold in tension, but not this thing, not the question of human salvation!"[18]

His trajectory over the next decade may be understood in terms of this quandry. Though he was truly an heir of what he likes to call the "ancient tradition," "grasped by the gospel content," yet he was "not convinced by the scholastic method and trappings," and was thus caught up in "a search for a better case." He writes, "I was looking, I think, for something deeper and more compelling, a gospel authority that establishes itself by its own power and attractiveness, not a legal authority that simply demands submission."[19] In his search for this authority Forde launched into a doctoral program at Harvard that spanned more than a decade, from his request for enrollment during the 1955-1956 school year to his graduation in 1967 and his thesis publication in 1969. This time of his doctoral study was punctuated by several teaching assignments: St. Olaf College in Northfield, Minnesota, 1955-1956; Luther Theological Seminary, 1959-1961; Luther College, Decorah, Iowa, 1961-1963; and a permanent return to Luther Theological Seminary in 1964. It was also marked by a year of study in Tübingen, Germany, 1958-1959, through a Lutheran World Federation scholarship; associated travel in Europe (Italy, England, Germany, and Norway are mentioned in his letters); his marriage to Marianna Carlson, a New Jersey-born French professor at Wellesley College, on June 20, 1964 (they eventually had two sons, Timothy and Geoffrey, and a daughter, Sarah); and a tutoring position at Mansfield College at Oxford, England, 1968-1970. The Lutheran World Federation assigned him duties as chaplain to Lutherans in the Oxford area while he was there, for which he received ordination as an American Lutheran Church pastor before his departure.[20] Through it all his doctoral pilgrimage continued, and eventually the reflection it produced positioned him to offer his proposal for his case "deeper and more compelling" to the wider church.

Theological Career

Forde's Luther Seminary career began with that first post-Tübingen invitation by Eugene Fevold, Clifford Nelson, and Alvin Rogness to lecture for two classes on the history of Christian thought through the Reformation for one year, and this was renewed a second year. When he returned to the seminary in 1964, he was named instructor in church history, but moved to systematic theology in 1971. In his mind "[t]his did not present any major transition in my thinking or teaching. . . . It did mean, however, that I have always taught systematics from a historical base—as it ought to be taught!"[21] In 1974 he was named professor of systematic theology, a position he held till his retirement in 1998. During this time, he was highly regarded in the classroom as these words of Lloyd Svendsbye, seminary president after Rogness, attest:

> Dr. Forde is a very influential classrom teacher. His classes always draw a high number of students. If one talks to many graduates of this institution, as I have done, those graduates invariably refer to Dr. Forde as one of the most profound influences in their lives. His influence appears to be a lasting influence as over against a form of passing intellectual entertainment.[22]

It is the experience of this student of Forde's (1975-1976, 1984-85), as well, that this was the case. It was not a dynamic pedagogical approach or flamboyant personality that won our hearts; his bearing was actually quite reserved and outwardly unspectacular—I once affectionately used the word "crumpled"—though his wry wit could be very winning and his coy smile showed that he was enjoying the conversation immensely. It was rather the thrust of his message itself—"the fundamental death/life structure . . . intimately connected and indeed structurally identified with the thoroughgoing 'dialectic' of Lutheran theology in general," as he puts it,[23] repeated and defended from every possible attack—that pressed its way into the hearts of even those of us who were originally "second form" Lutherans and made us grapple with it all our lives.[24] Among Lutheran clergy and lay students late-century and in the opening years of the new millenium, it has seemed to me from pastorates in the upper midwest, if one cannot do business with the theology of Gerhard Forde, either appreciatively or critically, one is simply left out of the conversation.

Forde's first published material is a 1962 book review for *dialog*, three years after his return from Germany, discussing *Dogmatics*, a newly translated work of a "particularly" helpful professor at Tübingen, Hermann Diem.[25] His first article was "Law and Gospel as the Methodological Principle of Theology" for the Luther College Press in 1964. His first book was perhaps his most scholarly—his own doctoral thesis, *The Law-Gospel Debate: An Interpretation of its Historical Development*, published in 1969. His second book was probably his most popular, *Where God Meets Man: Luther's Down-to-Earth Approach to the Gospel*, still read in four languges by pastors and laity alike.[26] From these early beginnings Forde's literary production continued unabated throughout his career, despite his regular teaching load and other commitments to the wider church. In all, it totals, by my count, 19 book reviews, 63 articles in journals or books, 11 books or major book portions, and 14 audio or videocassettes, with unpublished works remaining.

Because of his calling as a seminary professor, Forde's preaching tended to be occasional rather than regular: seminary chapel in scheduled rotation with his colleagues and students, a Lenten or a Sunday morning service at the invitation a local congregation, the observance of a special event like a centennial or a wedding. It means that his sermons are not many by parish pastor standards: there are in his personal papers by my count only 143 extant sermons in all, of which 31 have been published posthumously by Mark Mattes and Steven Paulson. It also means that he probably never preached on most pericope texts, and, of those he did, on only sixteen did he preach more than once. It makes the texts singled out for repeated preaching the more striking: three times for Ps 51:15, Matt 22:1-14, Luke 11:24-26, Luke 15:1-7, Rom 3:19-28, and the "Father, forgive them" of Luke 23:32-38; four times for Jesus' cry from the cross in Matt 27:46; and no fewer than seven times for the "It is finished!" of John 19:28-30. (See Appendix B for a listing of Forde's sermons.) Since, ironically enough, this church historian didn't date or mark the occasion of most of his sermons, they are ordered by biblical text or, where there are several sermons on a given text, alphabetically by title or by first line where there is no title.

Forde took his preaching seriously as evidenced by his careful preparation. This often took the form of a handwritten manuscript, heavily edited, sometimes even unto the back side, followed by a typewritten manuscript, itself usually edited yet again. The sermons are faithful to his classroom theological emphasis on proclamation as actually doing the act of the electing God. Yet the manuscripts often convey a passion not always evident in his reserved professorial manner and an expectancy that incarnates his eschatological theology. They illustrate the difference Forde himself remarks between the "second order" discourse of the classroom and the "first order" discourse of the proclamation.[27]

The church called Forde to many tasks besides teaching and preaching. Perhaps most notably he served as a Lutheran participant of the Lutheran-Roman Catholic Dialogue from 1974, and his name appears on the participant lists of four of its reports: *Teaching Authority and Infallibility in the Church* (1978, 1980), *Justification by Faith* (1985), *The One Mediator, the Saints, and Mary* (1992), and *Scripture and Tradition* (1995) (see below, pp. 40-42). Also significant for the Lutheran church at large was his service on the Commission for a New Lutheran Church (1982-1988) that proposed the shape of the Evangelical Lutheran Church in America, a commission on which he exercised strong leadership "especially in the formation of the statement of faith and purpose."[28] Among the committees and task forces of his seminary he is perhaps most remembered for his contribution to the curriculum committee (1991-1992) when his proposal for a three-step approach to curriculum planning was effectively adopted as the agenda moving into the new millenium.

In his last years Forde was afflicted with a form of Parkinson's disease. His last book, *The Captivation of the Will: Luther vs. Erasmus on Freedom and Bondage,* was dictated to Steve Paulson when he himself was unable to write, and published the year of his death. Gerhard Forde died on August 9, 2005. He is buried in Indherred Lutheran Cemetery north of Starbuck, Minnesota.

B. Forde's Theological Heritage

We have already noted the regard that Forde has for what he calls "the ancient catechetical tradition" that he received during his growing-up years. This would be the pre-1917 doctrinal position of the Synod for the Norwegian Evangelical Lutheran Church in America, also known as the Norwegian Synod, also known in Norwegian as the *gamle synode,* "the old synod." The thrust of this tradition and its role in the Norwegian Lutheran Church in America in which Forde grew up must be the starting point of any understanding of Forde's theological trajectory.

But beyond the "ancient tradition" there were other theological ideas and moves that were instrumental in Forde's development. In his theological autobiography Forde singles out a handful of theologians as being particularly influential: the father of neo-orthodoxy, Karl Barth, particularly in his first *Epistle to the Romans*; theologians of the Luther renaissance, particularly Hans Joachim Iwand in his essays in *Um den rechten Glauben*, but also Lauri Haikola and Gerhard Ebeling; and Gustav Wingren, "perhaps as a counterbalance to Barth" and especially in *Theology in Conflict*. He also cites Dietrich Bonhoeffer favorably, especially earlier in his career.[29] A look at the contributions of these theologians, too, then, however brief, is thus necessary for an appreciation of Forde's mature theological approach.

The Tradition of the Old Norwegian Synod

Forde was baptized into the Norwegian Lutheran Church of America (NLCA), renamed The Evangelical Lutheran Church (ELC) in 1946 to better reflect the increasing American identity of the immigrant stock that constituted it. It joined in the formation of The American Lutheran Church (ALC) in 1960, and eventually flowed into the current Evangelical Lutheran Church in America (ELCA) in 1987. The NLCA of Forde's youth was still a young body, the fruit of a 1917 merger of three predecessor churches that represented two significant variations of Lutheran thinking. On the one hand, the Hauge Synod and the United Norwegian Church emphasized the importance of faith as a defining aspect of the Christian life. That is, they shared a characteristically pietistic concern for the subjective experience of trust within the believer brought about by the gospel. On the other hand, the Norwegian Synod emphasized the announcement of the objective Word of forgiveness as the critical factor without unduly pondering the character of its reception. That is, the reality of Christ's work for the world was declared to be sure and true whether it was believed or not. The fact that the two positions had been able to come together into one church indicates that their respective emphases, in E. Clifford Nelson's words, "could be understood in a way satisfactory to the other side and as not being mutually exclusive."[30] At the same time, the fact that they had been forty years in the process of doing so and that the road to union had been rocky and fragile explains the persistence of a consciousness of the difference within the new church. That is why, for a theologically astute pastoral family like the Fordes, the tradition of a Norwegian Synod that no longer existed was still the dominating theological reality, and this in poignant contrast with the opposing view.

A Search for an Assurance to Count On

Forde himself characterizes the Norwegian Synod, or affectionately the "Old Synod," or sometimes simply "the Synod," as a "a search for objectivity . . . amid the confusing and often conflicting claims, demands, and needs of the immigrant situation."[31] To quote E. Clifford Nelson,

> In additional to their formal instruction [at Christiania], the Synod's leaders had been strengthened in their confessionalism by their negative reaction to the American religious scene. Plunged from the relative theological security of a state church into a situation where pastor and members of a church seemed altogether free to choose their own theology they reacted strongly towards a heightened confessionalism.[32]

One aspect of this search was the return to "objective truth of God's Word, which knows whereof it speaks and can bear witness with conviction and authority."[33] The motto inscribed in the seal of the Synod was *gegraptai*, "It is written," and the motto of the official periodical was John 8:31-32, "If you continue in my Word . . . ."[34] The commitment to the Word was such that the Synod devoted three synodical conventions in a row, 1869-1871, to the issues involved in proper biblical interpreta-tion and adopted sixteen principles to that end to be used in the Synod.[35] The result according to Fevold was two-edged—unifying within the Synod and alienating without:

> The Synod pastors were so dogmatic and unyielding in their orthodoxy because they were convinced that in all theological disputes in which they were involved their position was the only correct position because it was based on the Word which had been interpreted literally according to the exegetical principles which would permit only one interpretation. Their theological opponents, although believing themselves as fully loyal to the Formal Principle, objected to what they regarded as a too mechanistic and wooden use of Scripture, fearing the substitution of an intellectual acceptance of a logically developed theology for an experience of faith.[36]

Forde, as we will see, while appreciating the Synod's aspirations to ob-jectivity, would find it necessary to modify his hermeneutical approach in light of modern awarenesses (see below, pp. 46-51).

Another aspect of the search was the deepening confessionalism itself. Feeling its way forward on the new ground, the Synod soon sensed a kindred spirit in the Missouri Synod, and from 1858 it began to send its pastoral candidates to their seminary in St. Louis. This continued until 1876 when the groundwork was laid for a Norwegian-speaking seminary of its own. In St. Louis the future leaders of the Synod were formed within a confessional commitment of Missouri which included the Formula of Concord, a Lutheran confession to which the Church of Norway did not officially subscribe and of which most Norwegians had never heard. Given the role that Article XI of the Formula was to play in the future definition of the Synod, it seems in retrospect like a fateful move, but Forde suggests that Missouri's influence should not be over-played. He proposes that the issues involved were significant enough that they would eventually have had to be faced by Lutherans in any case, with or without Missouri.[37]

A Definition of God's Election

During the 1880s the growing Norwegian Synod had experienced a sharp dispute known as the Election Controversy. At issue was a proper understanding of conversion and salvation: how to affirm that salvation was from God alone, yet, at the same time, to account for the fact that not all persons were saved without resorting to the idea of some human responsibility in the matter. Calvinism had an easy answer in predestina-tion—God simply chose some for salvation and others for damnation—but Lutherans who began by acknowledging the love of God for all people could not go there. How God's love could be general but God's election specific was simply an intractable intellectual problem. If God alone were responsible, it was hard to see why God was not responsible for eternal human loss as well, not to mention the multitude of worldly woes, so that his universal love seemed in question—what appeared to Lutherans to be an error on the Calvinist side. On the other hand, if God alone were *not* responsible, then it was hard to see why humankind didn't play a role in some way, however small, but apparently decisively so. In that case, human salvation must ultimately be seen to rest at least to some extent on human endeavor—a decidedly syncretistic option. For Lutherans focused on the Reformation "*sola*"s, an assurance of salvation based in the slightest degree upon a proper human response looked like an error on the Roman Catholic side.[38]

Norwegian Synod theologians sought to avoid errors on both sides using two different sources. From before the immigration, Norwegian Lutherans had been familiar with Bishop Erik Pontoppidan of Bergen's *Sandhed til Gudfrygtighed*, or *Explanation of the Catechism*. Question 548 in the explanation asked, "What is election?" and Pontoppidan answered, "God has appointed all those to eternal life who He from eternity has forseen would accept the offered grace, believe in Christ, and remain constant in this faith unto the end."[39] This was predestination *intuitu fidei*, in view of the faith forseen, a widely accepted interpretation among German theologians in the period after the Reformation and generally, but not officially, accepted in Norway at the time of the immigration.

A second source, Article XI of the Formula of Concord, mentioned earlier, was the basis of the teaching by C. F. W. Walther (1828-1887) in St. Louis. Here, human participation is clearly rejected: "Therefore, it is false and incorrect to teach that not only the mercy of God and the most holy merit of Christ but also something in us is a cause of God's election, and for this reason God chose us for eternal life. For he had chosen us in Christ not only before we had done anything good but even before we were born . . . ."[40] Here salvation is clearly through *sola gratia* without any reference to faith whatsoever.

In 1881 H. G. Stub, a Norwegian Synod professor, offered a clarifying address to his Madison, Wisconsin, congregation, in which he named election based on the Formula of Concord "first form" and election based on Pontoppidan's explanation "second form." Fevold summarizes Stub's position:

> Although an advocate of the first form, he refuses to label the second form as false. The second form is inferior to the first, he argues, because synergists and Semi-Pelagians can more readily hide behind it than the first form. The latter, on the other hand, provides a great intellectual cross, whereas the

second form represents an attempt to clarify and understand a great mystery. It is possible to hold to either form of election without attributing any merit to man in his conversion, and the important consideration is to ascribe conversion wholly to the grace of God.[41]

His approach from the "Missourian" side favored first form while not excluding the second.

An example of the "anti-Missourian" position would be that of Norwegian Synod professor F. A. Schmidt. In a series of articles in 1883 he proposed that "election in view of faith" reflects the basic scriptural teaching of justification by faith. Again, by Fevold's summary of his position,

It is the presence or absence of faith which determines whom God justifies. One is justified because he has faith; another is lost because he does not have faith; the possession of faith makes the difference. The elect are those selected by God to enjoy eternal salvation. Since it is impossible to please God without faith, God elected to eternal salvation those whom He foresaw would accept Christ in faith. There must be complete harmony between the doctrine of election and the doctrine of justification. This occurs when one holds fast to the teaching that the election of certain sinners to salvation to the exclusion of others takes place in view of faith, or more correctly 'in view of the merit of Christ grasped by faith.'[42]

Schmidt believed that the Missourian approach to election resulted in a Calvinist failure to make the critical connection with faith. He thought such a connection should be possible if they were to use the word election "in the broad sense" that "includes under that category the whole *ordo salutis*, all of the provisions that God has made for man's salvation."[43] Faith then would be the factor that rendered it effective.

It is not the purpose of this thesis to trace the historical details of the Election Controversy, but two results must be noted. First, the controversy eventually resulted in a significant schism in the founding of a separate anti-Missourian seminary at Northfield, Minnesota, from 1886 and an exodus of no less than a third of the membership and congregations of the Norwegian Synod in 1887-1888. As traumatic as this was for the hitherto thriving church body, the 1890 synod president, Herman A. Preus, was able to represent it in its best light as *en Renselse*, a cleansing, in which the synod was purged of anti-Missouri viewpoints.[44] In fact, the Norwegian Synod would henceforth be so unified on the matter that it could be identified with a "first form" approach to salvation. Certainly coming generations of pastoral families like the Fordes would tolerate nothing less.

But secondly, the controversy left "deep scars in the body of Norwegian American Lutheranism that even time could not readily eradicate."[45] The dispute reached an intensity such that charges of heresy and betrayal left an abiding suspicion on both sides of the integrity of their opponent's faith. Congregations had been torn apart, congregational property was disputed, sometimes in court, and the heart of many a believer was left bitter for a lifetime. A generation had passed since the trauma of the schism, but the fact that the Fordes shared its memory is evident in Gerhard's recollection that the explanation to the catechism used in his confirmation instruction was a respectable first form edition, "*not* Pontoppidan's, that was second form!"[46] Surely the reason Gerhard had such a viscerally negative reaction to his only experience of Bible camp was the practices there designed to enhance the awareness of faith: "all sorts of 'goings-on' which were strange to the son of an Old Synod parish—emotional songs which I had never heard, testimonies, tears and what not. I didn't know what was going on. I couldn't believe it! I never went back."[47] And if a young Gerhard might use a second form expression in his biography for an application to a seminary that perhaps asked for it or expected it, this, too, was certainly not his native language.[48]

A Commitment to Unity

Given this context, it is an astonishing fact of history that the Norwegian Synod was, within a generation, able to participate in an organic union with the United Lutheran Church and the Hauge Synod. Paradoxically, the schism increased the natural yearning for fellowship that the Norwegian laity had always felt. The departing third of the Norwegian Synod responded in 1890 when they merged with the Norwegian Augustana Synod and the Norwegian Danish Conference to form the United Norwegian Church. But even among Synoders who stayed, disappointment was expressed that the merger was not including them. For example, the 1890 Minnesota Conference of the Synod passed a memorial expressing "deep regret" that "the Norwegian Synod, without any reason whatever [sic], has been excluded from the so-called work for union which is now being carried on" and acknowleged an "obligation to work for unity among the Norwegian Lutheran church bodies here in this country."[49]

These feelings drove repeated intersynodical gatherings in search of union such as those in Madison, Wisconsin, in 1891, Willmar, Minnesota, in 1892, Lanesboro, Minnesota, in 1897, Austin, Minnesota, in 1899, and St. Paul, Minnesota, in 1901 with the Norwegian Synod often leading the way.[50] These turned serious with the reengagement of the Hauge synod in 1905, and a series of eleven meetings of a union committee of the Norwegian, Hauge, and United synods were held in Minneapolis between 1906 and 1910. They began "in a spirit of friendliness and genuine goodwill" including common prayer in which the Norwegian Synod, too, participated.[51] Sheer persistence of purpose drove the work through anxious moments in 1908 and 1910-1911 when discussions reached the familiar deadlock concerning election. To attempt to overcome it, elections were held in the synods for new union committee members in 1911. The newly-elected committees got acquainted at a St. Paul meeting in November, appointed a subcommittee to work on the differences in December, and met again at Madison, Wisconsin, February 14-22, 1912, spending no fewer than five of the days discussing Article XI of the Formula of Concord. The resulting doctrinal agreement, known as the *Øpgjör*, or "Settlement," or "Madison agreement," acknowledged Article XI of the Formula of Concord as "pure and correct doctrine" not seeming to require more elaborate theses of faith, but also acknowledged instruction that has won "acceptance and recognition within the orthodox Lutheran Church," including that of "recognized teachers of the Church" including Pontoppidan.[52] Thus the agreement "unanimously and without reservation" accepted "that doctrine of election," described with the singular, "which is set forth in" the two documents, described with the plural.[53] The signing of this "Madison Agreement" was heralded with the ringing of church bells across the nation as the news reached one Norwegian congregation after another, and after five further years of careful and sometimes delicate ecclesiastical preparations, led on June 9, 1917, to the formation of a united church, the Norwegian Lutheran Church in America. To this remarkable drive to union with other Lutherans, sought as steadfastly by the Norwegian Synod as by the United Lutheran and Hauge synods and culminating only ten years before Gerhard's birth, the Fordes were certainly heir.

The Influence of Modern Theologians

Of course Forde grew in many ways beyond the articulation of his own Lutheran church tradition, and we have named some of the leading theologians of his day that contributed to his theological maturing. Without attempting an exhaustive analysis of these theologians' work it seems useful to look briefly at their influence on Forde as well.

Karl Barth: On the Act Character of the Word

Whatever else needs to be said, it is a fact that, page for page, Forde has more to say about Karl Barth than any other theologian except Martin Luther himself. He calls Barth "one of the best conversation partners for Lutheran theology because he raises the right questions," and those Lutherans who listen to Barth, however critically, "the most interesting."[54] One gets a sense for his admiration in a 1994 *Word & World* article, "Does the Gospel Have a Future? Barth's Romans Revisited":

> I like Barth's *Romans*. In some ways I like it better than the *Church Dogmatics*. It is always so deliciously nasty and fresh

and exciting. When I teach Barth, I always begin with *Romans* simply because it is, for one thing, so much fun. . . . I soon get suspicious of theologians who worry overmuch about whether Barth might have gone too far in his relentless attacks on every sacred oak in sight. *Romans* is still the great thunderhead that looms over it all, threatening ever and again to blast our flimsy theological constructions with divine lightning and awesome thunder.[55]

As early as his doctoral thesis, Forde calls the thrust of this thunderhead "the act character" of the Word of God:

In Barth, the Word of revelation is no longer a mere report about a past event, nor is it a timeless truth, but it is an eschatological address carrying in itself that which it has to give as demand and gift, form and content. Barth has attempted to restore the act character of the Word by making it more 'exclusive,' by removing the possibility of understanding it in terms of some system of 'natural theology.' The Word is the eschatological address which breaks in upon man.[56]

We have seen in Forde's biography how abrasive the authoritative assertions of dogma were to him during his seminary years, and we have remarked his search for a hermeneutical principle other than that offered him by the Old Synod. The act character of the Word, or later, of the proclamation, would become a central response to these epistemological issues and a major contribution of Forde's to the hermeneutical conversation. It appears that in Barth's paradigm-shattering stress on the discontinuity between God's self-revelation and human thinking about God, Forde found a valuable approach congenial to one raised on a first form emphasis on the objectivity and certainty of God's definitive action on behalf of humankind and congenial to one suspicious of fanciful flights of human philosophy.

It is not that Barth gets it all right. There is plenty that Forde will criticize: a depreciation of the critical law-gospel distinction before Barth's overwhelming Word of God-word of humans distinction;[57] the reversal of the law-gospel order and a consequent misunderstanding of the law as the form of the gospel and the role of the law as permission;[58] Barth's Calvinist rejection of the *communicatio idiomatum* in reaction to the perceived danger of a wider human divinization, an idea congenial to the facist thought of Barth's era;[59] the search for objectivity in a *Gottesgeschichte* in eternity rather than in the reality of space and time—a manger, a cross, and ultimately proclamation—so that the significance of the historical act, even in the pulpit, is minimized;[60] and a consequent christology that invites consideration of the confrontation rather than the identification of the two natures in a approach implicit with Nestorianism.[61] Forde is no Barthian, strictly defined. He is rather an appreciative Lutheran critic of Barth who affirms the thrust of Barth's central insight against nineteenth century liberal theology and who proceeds to do his own Lutheran construction on the basis of it.

Hans Iwand: Peerless Defender of Justification by Faith

Where in his "Theological Autobiography" Forde acknowledges his debt to Barth and leading theologians with a sentence or two each in a section named "Others," he splashes his appreciation of Hans Joachim Iwand (1899-1999) across two sections of the article, including the entire central section, "Discoveries." True enough, Forde never wrote an article on Iwand as such, but he reserved the highest praise for him: "my favorite interpreter of Luther" and "the most important fruit of my year in Germany" and "peerless defender of the doctrine of justification by faith."[62] The spirit of Nestingen's assertion that Iwand is the mature Forde's most referred to source in his *Christian Dogmatics* articles seems accurate with Iwand citations widely strewn throughout the articles "setting the frame of reference within which Forde makes his argument."[63] And in his *The Law-Gospel Debate* Forde uses Iwand as a defense against the venerable Barth himself in maintaining the distinction of law and gospel as more critical for the doctrine of justification by faith than the distinction of God's word and human word. The Luther scholar, Iwand, it would seem, was understood by the mature Luther scholar Forde in a class apart as a critical influence upon his theology.

Iwand himself is mostly untranslated and thus virtually unknown to the English-speaking world.[64] In Timothy Schueler's unique English summary of his theology,

> Iwand's burning concern is to avoid a trivializing of the doctrine of justification. He does so through his life by stressing that what happens in the Word of God really does something to the hearer. It kills and makes alive. It binds and looses. It casts down and raises up. It speaks of sin and grace, Law and Gospel, faith and works. . . . Like Luther, Iwand's driving concerns are to rightly distinguish the Law and Gospel in order to enable the Church's clear proclamation . . . . [65]

If this summary is not unduly influenced by Schueler's own knowledge of Forde himself, the vocabulary and its use suggest striking appropriation by an appreciative Forde.

Schueler proposes that Iwand was "a systematician who did not care too much for systems when it came to Protestant theology." For both Iwand and Forde, it was not the doctrinal system that describes justification, but the reality of the new birth itself, the new human existence that characterizes it, that was the important thing. For both of them one drove towards God's effecting of the important thing through the proclamation of the law and the gospel.[66]

But beyond such similarities, Forde points to the heart of his appreciation when he affirms the consistency of Iwand's commitment to the primacy of God's will.

> Iwand is the only interpreter I know who was able to swallow Luther's view of the bondage of the human will whole together with all the theological presuppositions and consequences entailed in that view. He is the only one I have found who accepts the Lutheran *decretum horrible* that the *deus absconditus* has not bound himself to his word but kept himself free over all things.[67]

Here this son of an Old Synod pastor heard purest gospel and claimed an ally. Where "even among the staunchest Lutheran theologians" an obligation was sensed to "hang on to some bit of human choice and responsibility over against the God of election," Iwand recognized that this is "precisely our problem" and held firm. "The compulsion, the claim to freedom vis-à-vis God, *is* the bondage." It is "not *theoretical*, but *actual*."[68] It must be renounced, and renounce it Iwand does so cleanly that Forde is deeply appreciative.

Lauri Haikola: Clarity about Law and Gospel

The imprint of Finnish theologian Lauri Haikola (1917-1918) on Forde's theology is most overt in Forde's 1969 doctoral dissertation where his critical eleventh chapter, "Interpretation of Law by Lutherans," cites him no fewer than seventeen times in twenty-four pages. Other appreciative mentions of Haikola occur once in Forde's 1976 article on the Formula of Concord Article V and three times in Forde's two substantial contributions to the 1984 *Church Dogmatics*,[69] all in discussions of the law. Nestingen calls him "Forde's principal partner in his exposition of Luther's understanding of the law."[70] Forde, looking back in his *Theological Autobiography*, calls him "vital for the development of my understanding of law and gospel."[71]

Works by Haikola quoted by Forde include *Gesetz und Evangelium bei M. Flacius, Studien zu Luther und zum Luthertum,* and *Usus Legis,* but none of these are translated into English. It appears that only a 1960 lecture for the Second International Congress of Luther Research, "A Comparison of Melanchthon's and Luther's Doctrine of Justification," has been rendered into English for the journal, *dialog.*[72]

Perhaps the most consequential of Haikola's research occurs in *Usus Legis* when he argued that Luther did not subscribe to the concept of a *lex aeterna,* an eternal order based on law. Nestingen calls this proposal of Haikola's "a critical breakthrough not only for Luther studies but also in Lutheran confessional scholarship." Subsequent examination of Melanchthon's approach to law in comparison with Luther's enabled him to make significant distinctions between the the ways Luther and Lutheran orthodoxy talked about justification. In Forde's description of Haikola's view,

> [L]ater Lutherans failed to make the distinction between law and gospel in as thoroughgoing an eschatological fashion as Luther made it, with the result that Luther's theology simply falls apart into confusing and contradictory segments. The general result of this failure was to return to the purely significatory understanding of the terms law and gospel. This means that for the most part Lutherans came to look upon law not as the preserving and accusing letter of the Old Age, but rather, as an eternal ontological reality, an objective order, a way of salvation which is then legalistically satisfied by the work of Christ.[73]

This has implications for Haikola's view for atonement. If law as an eternal order of the universe is overthrown, then fulfillment of the law cannot be construed as mere satisfaction of its demands, but as its very end. God's wrath is real, not merely an eternal standard to be fulfilled, God's mercy is unfathomable, not merely a required satisfaction, atonement becomes actual, not merely an objective fact to be known, and the proclamation of this actually realizes its happening, not merely passes on information.[74] These insights become integral to Forde's own approach in his doctoral work and beyond.

Gerhard Ebeling: A Broader, Existential Law

In his *Theological Autobiography* Forde acknowledges that Tübingen and Zürich professor, Gerhard Ebeling (1912-2001), through his "interpretation of Luther and early preoccupation with hermeneutical questions," stirred in him "a constant concern about questions of interpretation."[75] Nestingen in his *Examining Sources* remarks that "some Lutheran ecumenical scholars have claimed that Forde is dependent on Gerhard Ebeling," though he doesn't say who those scholars are and he seems to have some reservations about the assertion—"[c]ontact, even correspondence, does not necessarily equal influence, however."[76] In any case Forde himself quotes Ebeling no fewer than eighteen times widely scattered over the last four chapters of his doctoral dissertation, twice in the second of the *Church Dogmatics* contributions, and occasionally in articles earlier in his career. Most of the citations are from *Wort und Glaube*, translated into English as *Word and Faith* in 1963.[77]

In Forde almost all of these contributions bear on a proper understanding the law. Ebeling makes the point that there are different understandings of law functioning in the theological world.[78] In contradistinction to Barth's narrow view, Ebeling sees it as a reality of fallen humanity, a broad term describing human existence in any religion and situation.[79] It is not useful to distinguish between its essence and office, because it is not permitted an independent status.[80] For us there is no law but an accusing law, and that, only in this age, and only until Christ ends it.[81] This happens when an eschatological event in the present brings freedom.[82] Law does not survive this event for the believer, and a third use of the law is countermanded, for it is only God who uses the law; humankind only misuse it in lack of faith.[83] By his citations Forde draws on the work of Ebeling at points most significant to his work.

At the same time Forde can be critical of what he considers Ebeling's limited approach to history. In a 1967 book review of his *Theology and Proclamation: Dialogue with Bultmann*, Forde confesses frank admiration for Ebeling's wrestling with the historical issue: "Few theologians on the contemporary scene have wrestled so strenuously with the problem of the relationship between faith and historical knowledge as Gerhard Ebeling," yet he criticizes his conclusion.

> [W]hen one evaporates the resurrection by denying it any sort of facticity and making it instead merely a Christological affirmation, then one courts the danger of falling into a *theologia gloriae* . . . the negative *theologia gloriae* of the old mystics. . . . . [A]s long as it is impossible to speak of the resurrection as God's act based in his freedom for which we can hope, and for which Jesus has given us the right to hope, so long will the cross remain only an example to follow.[84]

What bothers Forde is that the possibility of an eschatological event has been betrayed.

> Perhaps Ebeling is right in insisting that we do the *theologia crucis* no service by speaking of the resurrection simply as an historical event. But this means only that we shall have to find better ways to speak of it as an *eschatological* event, as the *end* of history, which cannot fail to leave its mark on history and to qualify the way in which we look at history.[85]

Gustav Wingren: A Lutheran Counterbalance to Barth

Though Swedish theologian and professor at the University of Lund, Gustav Wingren, (1910-2000) is relatively less quoted in Forde's writings, he receives a remarkable tribute in the *Autobiography*: "Wingren has been important, perhaps as a counterbalance to Barth. His little book on *Theology in Conflict* was decisive in my early struggles with Barth over law and gospel.[86] Nestingen guardedly agrees: "While not necessarily accepting Wingren's critique of Barth, Forde has followed Wingren in the overall shape of his thinking, particularly in matters of law and Gospel."[87]

Perhaps the most focused attention Forde gives Wingren in his writings is two pages in *The Law-Gospel Debate*. Here, indeed, Forde portrays Wingren's critique of Barth's approach to gospel and law. Reacting to "the anthropologically centered theology" of the previous century, Barth seeks to turn it around, but in the process maintains the selfsame "structural antithesis" of God versus humankind. Where Barth's problem is a lack of knowledge of God and the solution is revelation, Wingren argues that the biblical approach sees the problem as guilt and the solution as justification. It is then not human knowledge of God through revelation that saves, but God's acts for human redemption from "the hostile forces which are arrayed against him," an aspect lacking in Barth's work.[88] Forde summarizes:

> Wingren believes, therefore, in spite of all assertions to the contrary, that the center of Barth's theology is *man and his question* rather than God and his acts. This means that the Word of God is "imprisoned in an anthropology that is constructed independently of the Word of scripture," and that God loses his freedom.[89]

The impact on an understanding of law and gospel is significant. Law as Barthian revelation would be a source of mere "knowledge about God" and thus guidance as if for some "political order or a social program." As the form of the gospel, it would turn the gospel into a new law.[90] These will be seen to be positions almost polar opposites of Forde's. Forde's statement about Wingren's counterbalancing effect would seem to credit him with an important role in making that happen.

Dietrich Bonhoeffer: Appropriate Life for the World

Forde never ceased to be rankled by the attack of Dietrich Bonhoeffer (1906-1945) on cheap grace.[91] "Grace is indeed not cheap. It is free!" Forde delighted to proclaim,[92] and perhaps for this reason Bonhoeffer is not a theologian widely associated with Forde's thought. He is nonetheless favorably cited by Forde a number of times in works including two book reviews (1963, 1965), the concluding chapters of *The Law-Gospel Debate* (1969), a reference in "The Work of Christ" in *Church Dogmatics* (1984), and in three references in *Theology Is for Proclamation* (1990).

In the first of the book reviews, reviewing *The Place of Bonhoeffer*, he summarizes the work of the contributing theologians in this way:

> They seek to answer the question that Bonhoeffer himself asked at the end of his life, "Who is Christ for us today?" from Bonhoeffer's own theological work. By doing this they have concentrated on Bonhoeffer's main concern, that Christ become a concrete reality for our time in and through the church.[93]

He sees their work as very successfully avoiding the extremes of an un-critical hero mystique and a "misreading or mishandling of his demand for a non-religious interpretation of biblical concepts."[94] Forde makes clear in the second book review that he himself considers this "mishan-dling" unwarranted. He argues that secular theologies of meaningfulness that try to do this "depend precisely on the idea of religion [emphasizing outward effects] and an immanent God which Bonhoefffer rejects."[95] Rather,

> Bonhoeffer's call for a "religionless Christianity" was a call to reinterpret Christianity so as not to make religion a precondition for faith and thus to allow the "thing itself," the Word of the Gospel, to confront man and to give meaning to man.[96]

This is reminiscent of Forde's own emphasis on an active and effective word.

Years later, Forde, in an anti-Hegelian move, cites Bonhoeffer in an argument against "attempting to assimilate the death and resurrection of Jesus to an immanent rational scheme: infinite Spirit going out from itself and returning to itself, understood as the necessary unfolding of its own nature." He affirms Bonhoeffer's naming this the "ultimate deceit" of the human *logos* aimed at resisting the claim of the *logos* of the cross.[97]

Similarly, Bonhoeffer in his *Christ the Center* provides Forde with the catchword so congenial for *Theology Is for Proclamation* that it is cited twice: "There are only two ways possible of encountering Jesus: Man must die or he must put Jesus to death."[98] Both scandalous possi-bilities are lifted up by Forde at various moments in his theology.

Perhaps most significantly for our purposes, Forde sets Bonhoeffer against Barth's dialectic as "influenced too much by Kantian transcen-dentalism and by a purely formal definition of God's freedom." Agreed, there is a "two-membered" dialectic, but that dialectic should be "*exclu-sively* determined by the nature of the eschatological revelation itself," not by "other concerns." A true simultaneity of the ages for the commu-nity of faith—"*total* judgment and *total* grace"—means "that man can be content to allow his acting and thinking to remain as it is, totally in this age," not claiming for it more than it deserves; and "he can trust in Christ entirely for the gift of the new age." Only in the church does the "act" of revelation take on "'being' appropriate to it in this age." In this unique situation a useful distinction between the church and the world is made "which is meant to 'heal' and 'save,' not to divorce and separate," certainly a missional reflection here about how the church relates appro-priately to the world.[99]

C. Forde's Vocational Context
The Tradition of Luther Seminary

During the years when Forde attended Luther Seminary, it was the one and only seminary of the Norwegian Lutheran Church in America. According to Roy Harrisville, seminary president Thaddeus F. Gullixson had but recently "hauled the school into the 20th century" with such moves as the hiring of speech instructor and future seminary president Alvin Rogness to help children of Norwegian immigrants with English pronounciation, and the calling of the first non-Norwegian professor, John Milton, a Swede.[100] Latvian refugee professors Janis Rozentals and Edmund Smits were added after the war. These scholars brought a first introduction to the historical critical method to a school that had had other things to think about in pioneer America. Its arrival was stormy for people who took their faith seriously—Milton himself renounced its more radical aspects in later years—and charges that the seminary was becoming heterodox under the "deeply imbedded heresy of higher criticism" persisted into the 1970s. The deeply ingrained habits of a more literal approach to scripture may help explain Forde's dissatisfaction with the scriptural hermeneutic that greeted him as a student (see below, pp. 46-48) and he would become part of the new wave of seminary professor that integrated the new scriptural methods into his theology.

The issues that so troubled the merging bodies of the NLCA before 1917 did not just go away in the years that followed, the "Settlement" notwithstanding. Gullixson, though a staunch son of the Old Synod, was concerned to maintain the balance that the Madison agreement had established for the good of the united church. In 1936 Herman Preus of venerable Old Synod heritage had been called as systematics professor, and he firmly held the Article XI, first form, position on election. It therefore seemed right to Gullixson in 1938 to arrange the call of George Aus to the seminary to maintain the other side that emphasized Pontoppidan's foreseen, second form, human response of faith. The friction between the two quickly became so great and the arguments so public that, in Harrisville's words, "Gullixson, aghast at the carnage, summoned the chief protagonists and ordered them to cease and desist." Outward peace was restored, but "an entire generation of pastors took their theological orientation from that noisy, percussive, explosive, raucous period" and went into their parishes with a renewed sense of the old issues.[101] Forde was part of that generation, and with his Old Synod upbringing clear in his mind, it was not hard to predict where his sympathies would fall (see above, p. 28). Forde later became widely regarded as the heir to Herman Preus' position, though with a significantly updated hermeneutical and theological contribution and in an age when the memory of the historical conflict itself was on the wane.

Kent Johnson has described the tremendous transitions that the seminary experienced from 1976 to 1996—organizational, ecclesiastical, financial, demographic, and social. Particularly interesting for this thesis is the following point:

> [T]he seminary began the era very much aware that American society and the world were changing in significant ways which touched on how it saw its mission, and ended it with enlarged programs dealing with global missions, cross cultural studies and a curriculum that focused on mission.[102]

After David Tiede's 1987 election as seminary president, a plan for "Excellence in Ministry" was developed that called for approval of a new curriculum by 1992, though its use was not actually inaugurated until 1993. The four-year development process was a comprehensive task for the seminary, involving considerable investment of time and thought on the part of the faculty. The result had a missional emphasis that included a paper on the seminary's "Mission in a World of Many Cultures," and a new flow of coursework that moved towards a missional goal.

Rollie Martinson, chair of the curriculum development committee, asserts that Forde's own contribution to the process was substantial, even one of the decisive elements.[103] In a document presented to the committee in August, 1990, "The Minister as Ambassador," Forde laid out a proposal and the rationale for the approach that, after considerable discussion and revision, was eventually adopted. A three part educational plan had the first year focusing on the biblical story and its significance "for the exegesis of human life *coram deo*," the second year focusing on confession, "what the faithful are impelled to say and do when their lives are transected by the story," and finally a third year focusing on "Mission," including "courses on Church and Ministry, Pastoral Theology, Proclamation, Evangelism, perhaps World Mission, and so on" and stressing "the actual doing of the divine deed as public office through the church and its ministry in all its forms."[104]

It is true that Forde was distressed with the way the second part of his proposal was eventually modified to become "Interpreting/Confession." He saw it as a lack of consensus in the faculty on the way movement from story to mission was understood and a reversion to traditional departmental structures rather than fresh presention of some "desparately [sic] important matters: hermeneutics; truth and meaning; the truth claim of the christian faith; the relation between the testaments; canon; ecumenical creeds; confession; the critical tradition; to mention just a few." In his mind the lack of consensus endangered the missional goal his proposal was designed to foster. "[H]ow then, pray tell, are we to get from the story and its interpretation to a solidly based concern for mission?

And what, precisely, is the mission? Even if we succeed in reading the audiences, how will they read us?"[105] At stake in Forde's words seems to be not whether mission ought to be undertaken, but the identity of the mission that the church will undertake.

The Theological Journal dialog

During Forde's first year of teaching at Luther College, 1962, the first issue of a theological journal, *dialog*, was published. Forde is listed as a one year member of the first editorial council and, as it turned out, he was reelected continuously until his death. His service to *dialog* put him in editorial collaboration with what is now an impressive array of theologians from across American Lutheranism—Braaten, Jenson, Lazareth, Harrisville, Burtness, Knutson, Marty, Quanbeck, and others— as well as distinguished colleagues from Europe—Brunner, Lønning, Pannenberg, Nygren, Pinomaa, Prenter, Thielicke, and others.[106] During his lifetime Forde contributed no fewer than thirty-six articles to *dialog*, spread rather evenly over a thirty-eight year span, making it the primary vehicle for his public theological reflection.

Those gathered at McCarthy's restaurant in Minneapolis on January 15, 1961, to found the journal tended to be younger theologians, often still in graduate school and not yet part of the ecclesiastical structures of their day. A later board member would call theirs "a loyal and yet critical voice" of "the Church (the Christian Church in general and the Lutheran Church in particular)."[107] They were unified in a kind of confidence that they could bring "the fertile soil of the reformation tradition" and "the towering theological teachers of our century" to bear on the the pressing issues of the church of their age. They considered the effort their "existential participation" in "that original primary dialogue between God the Creator and men his creatures," patterned "after the analogy of the eternal-temporal dialogue with all the accompanying features of contrast, controversy, even contradiction."[108]

As the journal matured, there was less emphasis on "bringing the important fruits of twentieth-century theology to the Church" and an increased sense of "responsibility to do its own theology and thereby assist the Church in the task of constructing a theology for the next decade." The critical perspective was still valued, but, as *dialog*'s contributors gained positions of authority in the church, it would have to come "as a vigorous and prophetic voice within the Christian community and not a comfortable echo of entrenched positions within the institutions of the Church."[109] There would be more diversity of opinion than at first, when editorials did not even bear the names of their authors. On the thirtieth anniversary edition of the journal, the name of Forde would be one of seven featured as examples of different approaches and directions in the contemporary Lutheran heritage. That is to say, among *dialog* editors and Lutheran theologians at large, he had become a household word for all that he stood for.

The Lutheran-Roman Catholic Dialogues

Lutherans and Roman Catholics were not speaking to each other publicly when Forde was growing up, at least not on a serious theological level. Hardened stereotypes of more than four centuries meant that theological encounters had to be attempted underground, as Forde's first experience with dialogues apparently was. As early as 1961, with Alvin Rogness' quiet permission, Jack Eichhorst and others organized a theological encounter between selected participants from Luther Seminary and their counterparts at St. John's Seminary in Collegeville, but it had to be absolutely discreet. In light of his later ecumenical work it seems significant that Forde, then in his first year as an instructor at Luther Seminary, was invited and accepted to be part of that early, first clandestine seminary dialogue.[110]

The interfaith climate changed dramatically during the third and fourth sessions of the Second Vatican Council.[111] The presence of churches not in communion with the Roman Catholic Church were acknowledged by Rome as an "ecclesial reality,"[112] and for the first time Roman Catholic theologians could approach them as Christian communities, not just separated Christian individuals, and to do so hoping for convergence, not just capitulation.[113] Vatican II was "the signal" which led the U.S.A. National Committee of the Lutheran World Federation to seek dialogue partners, and perhaps also the National Conference of Catholic Bishops in the U.S.A. to establish a Commission for Ecumenical Affairs.[114] The resulting series of Lutheran-Roman Catholic dialogues that began July 6-7, 1965, are now moving into their eleventh session.[115]

In 1979 one of the original Lutheran theologians in the conversations, Warren Quanbeck, died suddenly, and Gerhard Forde was selected to replace him. Over the course of two decades he participated in four rounds of dialogues, comprising no fewer than thirty-four separate sessions in locations ranging from Burlingame, California, and Biloxi, Mississippi, to Princeton, New Jersey, and his own Minneapolis, Minnesota. Forde himself delivered veritable flurries of prepared presentations to the committee, eight in all, including "Infallibility Language and the Early Lutheran Tradition" (1974), "Agreement on Justification? Some Reflections on the Systematic Problem" (1978), "Forensic Justification and the Christian Life: Triumph or Tragedy?" and "*Usus Legis*; The Functional Understanding of Law in Lutheran Theology" (both in 1979), "Review Critique of V. Pfnür" (1981), "What Is a Saint? Notes on a Lutheran View" (1985), "Could Invocation of the Saints Be Considered an Adiophoron?" and "Nature, Creation, and Grace: Some Preliminary Observations for Discussion" (both in 1986). Some of these remain unpublished.

Despite his long tenure on these, perhaps the most visible of American interfaith dialogues, Forde was frankly critical in his judgment of them. As early as 1982, after only three years as a participant, he remarked,

The results of such exercises, though helpful and encouraging, are rarely very satisfying. The agreed upon formula or position seems to many to be some sort of *Mittelding* with which neither communion is entirely happy and which has the effect of blunting the sharp edges of what each really wants to say. What most often happens then is that every one goes home and carries on as before, still having grave suspicions about one another's thought and practice. The ecumenical "consensus" turns out to be largely foreign policy which has little real effect on domestic practice.[116]

Six years later he complained about the constraints on free discussion imposed by the goal:

The constant drive for consensus, particularly in this instance [justification by faith], deters understanding by attempting to minimize the differences and thus inhibits discussion and, finally, genuine understanding. I expect that only a more frank and open discussion of the *differences* will lead to progress on these matters.[117]

It's not that he didn't appreciate the promise and the accomplishments of the dialogues. It's just that he expected so much more from conversations based on their achievements:

We have, I think, come a long way in our dialogues, and I do not wish to discount that. After centuries of acrimony and misunderstanding, we have been able to discover and affirm what we do hold in common. But that should also mean that we have arrived at the point where we can discuss openly and candidly the matters that still seem to divide us. We have to ask ourselves now whether the determined pursuit of consensus has not arrived at the point where it begins to inhibit rather than promote such genuine dialogue.[118]

Near the end of his career, Forde more broadly criticized the ecumenism practiced generally by the ELCA, calling it blurring and confusing in its effect:

When one steps back and takes a look at the whole, one sees that the drive towards consensus has created a kind of mythological middle kingdom in which deliberate ambiguity is practiced, blurring the lines and turning all theological cats gray. One puts together this-worldly adjective [sic] and eschatological substantives like 'visible unity' or 'full communion' and so quite thoroughly confuses rather than sheds light on the issues and problems before us. *A policy statement ought not to do that. It ought to define and clarify issues so we know who we are and where we intend to go.*"[119]

Once again, it must be said that he had high expectations of interfaith conversations, expectations worthy of his Old Synod forebears who were as persistent as they were uncompromising in the dialogue that brought together Norwegian Lutherans in America. Marianna Forde remembers him having good moments in his participation in those dialogues as well, such as his sparkling camaraderie with George Tavard and others of the Roman Catholic participants.[120] But, generally speaking, over the period of his career, his hopes seem to have been disappointed.

To review, we see in Gerhard Forde a theologian deeply influenced by "the tradition," as he called it—that is, the tradition of Christian faith as expressed in the old Norwegian Synod that merged into the Norwegian Lutheran Church in America. Yet the precritical shape of that tradition almost turned him away from ordained service to his church. The "search for a better case" for the tradition brought him through a decade-long doctoral effort and into a teaching career concerned with clarity on the church's proclamatory task. In the process he was influenced by significant twentieth century theologians, particularly Barth, Iwand, Haikola, Ebeling, Wingren, and Bonhoeffer, and exercised his influence in turn through such institutions as Luther Seminary, the theologial journal *dialog*, and the Lutheran-Roman Catholic dialogue in the United States.

CHAPTER 3

Forde's Constructive Theology

In the last chapter we examined briefly some of the historical data that describe the unfolding of Forde's life and theological development with the expectation that it would deepen our appreciation for Forde's constructive theology. In this chapter we attempt to create a faithful *summa* of that theology. We do this in order to place it into conversation with the concerns of contemporary missiology. This means, on the one hand, we seek to construct a representation of Forde's theology that is arguably true to his work and that would be generally recognized as such. On the other hand, it means we remain conscious of the task to come, the comparison with missiological concerns and the subsequent conversation. To accomplish this, we proceed critically alert for elements that invite further missional conversation, and hope to conclude the task with a list of points for further discussion once a missional standard has been established.

A lifetime of reflection is rich beyond measure, and the shape of an overview of that reflection will be determined in large measure by the foci chosen to attempt it. It seems evident from the whole span of Forde's writings, as an initial consideration, that the foci should not stray too far from the question of the nature of the encounter between God and humankind. His first widely read book, for instance, *Where God Meets Man*, considers the direction of the encounter. A classic mid-career volume, *Justification by Faith: A Matter of Death and Life*, invites thought on how the sinful person is brought to its end by the word of justification and how a new person comes forth. His *Theology Is for Proclamation* in later years considers the real life event through which this happens: proclamation. Almost every journal article can be related to this question. And in his sermons Forde never shows more obvious delight than when he announces the electing act of forgiveness as the basis for the relationship. At such moments one hears from this rather reserved theologian exclamations like "It's wild," and, "Preposterous,"[121] and, "Far out!" and, "Outta sight!"[122] From Forde's major works, supporting articles, and surviving sermons it seems clear that the death- and life-dealing encounter of the human with his/her God is the fundamental concern of Forde's theology.

We choose four themes with which to develop this central concern: 1) his hermeneutical principle; 2) the function of the law; 3) the eschatological act character of the revelation; and 4) the freedom of the new person. The first will explore his epistemological and interpretive approach that leads to this concern. The second, based upon Forde's own doctoral thesis, will show how a fresh approach to the question of the function of the law opens the way to a basic reconfiguration of its understanding. The third will explore his understanding of the proclamatory moment as an event that creates it, an endtime moment where new life in Christ is evident even now in the present. And the fourth will elaborate on the free character of the new life that flows from it. It is expected that the resulting theological portrait will be recognizably Fordean, and that chosen elements of it, when placed in conversation with twentieth century missionary thinking, will offer fruitful insights for the missional enterprise.

A. A Hermeneutical Principle

In summing up the introduction to his Seventh Locus of *Christian Dogmatics*, "The Work of Christ," a mature Forde lays out a methodological and hermeneutical strategy for the work that will follow:

> The questions we have put [for exploring the work of Christ] set for us the procedure to follow: first, investigation and evaluation of the tradition; second, an attempt at reconstruction which seeks to avoid the hazards and to state the work of Christ in a form true to Scripture and viable today.[123]

Perhaps nowhere in all of Forde's writings does he so clearly articulate a guiding hermeneutical principle for a piece of constructive theology. Although he states it with respect to the locus he is introducing, the work of Christ commonly called atonement, its strategic clarity invites the researcher to wonder if it may not be considered more generally applicable in describing the way Forde comes to the theological task.

The statement suggests three aspects that need to be explored in the wider context of Forde's writings. First, there is an awareness of and interest in the witness of "the tradition," a concern, both positive and critical, of historic understandings within the church and their potential "hazards." Secondly, there is the effort at a reconstruction that will articulate the matter at hand in a way that is "true to Scripture," a concern for faithfulness to the scriptural sources. And thirdly, there is a desire that the theological reconstruction be "viable today," a concern that the result be coherent to the worldview of his contemporaries. By using Forde's wider writings to investigate his approach to these aspects, we will go far toward an understanding of his broader hermeneutical approach.

The Tradition

As one might expect from the son of a synod known for its orthodoxy, Forde had a high regard for church tradition. "I found the answers to my [theological] questions," he says in his theological autobiography, "not in nineteenth- and twentieth-century attempts to transcend or re-model the tradition but rather in a probing of its depths."[124] Certainly, personally, it must be said, Forde experienced a positive net contribution to the theological task from church tradition, even when he viewed it critically.

He voices this at different times and in different ways. "I think," he says in a 1992 article addressing sexual questions of the day, "we dare not neglect the tradition of the church. The tradition, after all, is simply a record of how the faithful have read and sought to honor the scriptures in the past. Even though we are not legalistically bound to it, it deserves to be honored and ought not be changed without compelling argument."[125] Here the tradition is defined derivatively in terms of its dependence upon and attention to the Scriptures. It is for this reason, Forde says, that it merits our unobliged respect.

In another article published at the very end of his life, Forde writes, "The tradition, perhaps it could be said, is an account of what the company of hearers has diachronically heard, what we believe and confess, the intent of which should be to summon us to the task of listening ever more carefully and exactly, asking: Is this not what it says? As such it is to be taken seriously and even given a primary place in the discipline of listening."[126] Here the definition is based on the perception of the message by the believing community over time. Its history of confession becomes interesting to us because we claim to be part of that confessing community, and their faith is also truly our faith. We explore the expression of their faith with the hope that their articulation of it will be helpful, if not authoritative, for our own.

While he thus stood in a position of positive regard for the tradition, Forde held a reserve toward it as well. Certainly it could not come to regulate scriptural interpretation, as, for example, in the Roman Catholic Church:

> Tradition understood as an extra-scriptural institution that is to preside over the process of interpretation and put a check on the *sensus proprius* of the interpreter really leaves that *sensus proprius* basically intact. . . . [T]he subjective *sensus proprius*, in concert with the collective *sensus proprius*, finds a 'meaning' in the text convenient to its own concerns. The subject remains the interpreter of the text; the text is not allowed to become the interpreter of the subject.[127]

The great danger for tradition, as for theology in general, according to Forde, was that the human mind would, while yet basically unchanged by an alien word of God, proceed to assign its own convenient understanding to a text and thereby make the text impotent, dependent upon the will of the interpreter.[128] This is not the last time that he will voice such a concern, and the question for Forde of the proper work of an interpreter in the face of such danger is a question to which we must return.

It's almost as if one of the positive values of tradition is a negative one. It "does not exist to call attention to itself, or to insert itself between us and scripture . . . , but rather to clear the way, to point us toward a proper hearing of the text." It helps warn us of pitfalls, the "hazards" mentioned in *Christian Dogmatics*. Forde calls it a "hearing aid," the better to listen to scripture, and a "*norma normata*," a "normed norm," reflecting the norming call of scripture, not itself the message or of itself an authoritative "*norma normans*," a "norming norm."[129] That higher role is reserved for scripture itself.

Scripture

So it comes down to scripture, then. After having evaluated the tradition, Forde proposes to do some theological reconstruction, avoiding the hazards but being true to scripture, the *norma normans*. This means the Bible, "God's Word, preached and set down by inspirited prophets and apostles,"[130] and Forde can voice strong respect for the book itself. We find ourselves committed to preaching on its texts.[131] "It is 'inspired' scripture. It is canon. It can't be changed. It will always be there waiting for us."[132]

Some passages obviously hit us harder or more directly than others. Yet we must ask whether something is not to be retrieved from even the most obscure passages. In any case, it would seem that if we are to honor scripture we can only proceed on the premise that at least within the perspective of scripture there is a reason for things, and we cannot rest until we are satisfied that we have done our best to see it.[133]

This is a preliminary point. Forde has much more interesting and pressing things to say than this, but a high regard for the scriptures themselves as an alien voice from without is evident at the outset,[134] and this voice must be "honored."[135]

Search for an Adequate Epistemology

Whence comes this high regard? Certainly not through an acceptance of an infallible scripture based on a doctrine of inerrancy, and this for a number of reasons. First, logically, it seemed to Forde a poor starting point for apologetics. In his earliest printed article, he argued that if you were to go to the mission field, say, to make a case for the gospel from the ground up, you most certainly would not begin your witness with a doctrine of verbal inspiration, as though this were the cardinal point and it were necessary to believe this point before anything else.[136] But more than that, epistemologically, it was simply inadequate. The historical-critical methodology and the new understandings of historical record that had burst upon Forde's church required new reflection about the claims for the biblical witness. In his theological autobiography, he writes of his own approach: "Older views of biblical inerrancy were not an offense, they were just intellectually offensive. I was looking, I think, for something deeper and more compelling, a gospel authority that establishes itself by its own power and attractiveness, not a legal authority that simply demands submission."[137] Thirdly, dogmatically, it was dangerous. Though Lutherans in the era after the reformation had "flirted" with such an idea as a basis for asserting the veracity of the required doctrine gleaned from scriptures, "they have had some anxiety and suspicion that it might be contrary to a gospel appropriation of the scriptural message."[138] And for good reason. On the one hand it was used to establish standards for "heroic self-denial and sacrifice in obedience."[139] "The moral absolutisms that this brought reduced the state of [Christian] freedom to captivity."[140] On the other hand it was broken down into equivalently revealed pieces of information to be explored and analyzed, "a mine for dogma, . . . a source book for the history of salvation."[141] The treasure of information bites that it thus provided could then be assembled into dogmatic beliefs that would be required of believers, even into some "biblical concept of God"[142] that could be manipulated by the religious person to suit one's spiritual needs. Forde warns against this as an unhealthy use of scripture, a "legalistic biblicism."[143]

At this point, given the importance of correct assembly and proper manipulation of the scripturally gleaned data, the critical question becomes, not only what scripture says, but who is doing the interpreting. For, it is the interpreter who has become the subject of the exercise and scripture is merely his or her object of study. In this scenario "[t]he interpretation yields doctrine and practical mandates. Faith equals acceptance of such doctrine and practice. The problem immediately engendered by such a model is the subjectivity or potential arbitrariness of the exegete."[144] The obvious answer is a return to tradition for a definition of the exegetical point of view, or, in the case of Rome, a magisterium capable of deciding the issue. Thus, from an ecclesiastical point of view as well, the solution to an inspired data-bite scripture gives rise to troublesome hierarchical problems.

In reality, a recognition of a Word of God in scriptures or anywhere else, according to Forde, comes not through a prearranged assurance of infallibility, but through one's existential experience of its present effects on oneself. It is "because of the way in which it works on me . . . ."[145] It is "the experience of reaching the end of one's rope and then being rescued, of being killed and then made alive."[146] It is "the short word" which "cuts off all attempts to escape."[147] It can actually do this because "[t]he

Word of God is not a thing, not a proposition; it is an event." When it is proclaimed, "*something happens.*" "And that which happens, that which *actually occurs* in a very concrete sense, is the action of the living Word."[148] In short,

> The authority, sufficiency, and revelational quality of the scripture is due, according to Luther, quite unpolemically and *a posteriori*, to the experience that Scripture imparted to him, life, salvation, comfort, freedom—i.e., a new being in faith.[149]

For Forde, therefore, it is this experience of the real effects of an active Word in the present that calls forth the confession that this is nothing less than the Word of God. That is, through the proclamation, the alien message of scripture becomes so much a part of the inward experience through its effect on the hearer that its divine and ultimate nature begins to seem self-evident.

When this happens, it is not due to the machinations of some confident interpreter comfortably handling and exploring the scriptural object, though exegeted and proclaimed it must be, and Forde will have things to say about the interpreter's role. Rather, *scriptura sacra sui ipsius interpres*: sacred scripture, suddenly making itself abundantly clear, rises up over against the hearer to threaten or to comfort as if from elsewhere, from outside the world of the hearer, as if from God's own self. This is the kind of talk that makes Forde's blood run red, the prospect of the ministry of a living encounter with the living God through the "present tense, the creative address character of the word, the proper *usus.*" Here, "[t]he word is to be used not merely to convey information but to do something to us."[150] When Forde speaks of "honoring scripture," he is most interested in this active function of a vital word of a living God. The whole purpose of theology for him is not an intellectual field trip, however interesting, nor a methods class on relations with God, however useful morally and spiritually (or not!), but a preparing of the ground by the proclaimer for the moment of the hearing of that active word actually delivered in preaching and the sacrament.[151]

A Law-Gospel Approach

Forde locates the scriptural key for this hermeneutical approach in 2 Corinthians 3:4-6:

> Such is the confidence that we have through Christ toward God. Not that we are competent of ourselves to claim anything as coming from us; our competence is from God, who has made us competent to be ministers of a new covenant, not of letter but of spirit; for the letter kills, but the Spirit gives life.[152]

Here we find the basis of the work of the minister of the Word described in terms of action in two kinds: a killing kind and a life-giving kind. At issue is not what is symbolized for the benefit of the hearer's imagination and subsequent belief and conduct, but what is actually done to the hearer. Symbolization of meaning results in a dead letter of no ultimate consequence, but a living word is pregnant with possibility, can put an end to a person's self-seeking aspirations and efforts, and can bring one to an essentially new realization and approach to life.[153]

The law and gospel are the theological names for this killing word and this life-giving word that address the hearers in the present and actually do God's work on them, and we characterize them briefly in Forde's own words. "Law is an accuser," he writes in an article on forensic justification and the law. "That is its chief function."

> The law does not open the future, it closes it. . . . To love under the law is always to be attempting to repair or atone for yesterday; thus yesterday always controls tomorrow. The law kills and brings death, not life, for yesterday is always yesterday. . . . Grace . . . is humanity's tomorrow. Since that is the case, the law *must* function to cut off every human attempt to create its own tomorrow. The law and its office or function is therefore strictly limited to this age.[154]

In accomplishing its this-agely task, "law has no compassion and, indeed, always turns to accuse and to worm its way into the conscience."[155] It holds its burden on us "ultimately not because it is written in law books or even in the Bible, but rather because it is written 'in the heart.'"[156] This means that we cannot do away with it. "[The law] will sound *even if we attempt to silence it by altering or abolishing the laws that attack us.*"[157] Its goal is to bring about the end of the sinners' striving to justify themselves before God.

By contrast, gospel takes the because-therefore form of "unconditional promise."[158] Forde defines it in this way: "just the sheer and unconditional announcement . . . the uncompromising insistence that there is nothing to do now, that God has made his last move . . . . It is all over! . . . Conclusion? You can now only consider yourself dead to sin and alive to God in Christ Jesus."[159] Concise definitions of the gospel like "the account of Jesus" or "the inbreaking of good news" such as Forde offers in one of his earliest articles, he even then considers inadequate because they don't sufficiently convey the action that was done to the hearer of it.[160] For the gospel is better proclaimed than explained. That is, the hearer properly realizes what the gospel involves when it is "done to" that hearer so as to be experienced by him or her much more than when it is logically defined and talked about so as to be intellectually grasped and "understood" by him or her.[161] Forde regularly gives examples of gospel proclamation in his sermons that reflect its existential, present hold on him and the hope he has that it might gain such a hold on his hearers. Consider the following:

> I can only say: Repent, for you have stumbled onto [the treasure] today, here and now. For I say unto you, your sins are forgiven for Jesus sake. There it is! Did you hear me? Your sins are forgiven! Jesus entered into the blackness, the nothingness of death and rose triumphant for you! There is the hidden treasure! The kingdom of heaven comes to you today in that.[162]

Or,

> That's the way it is with God's grace—it's wild! . . . You *are* God's own! . . . *I declare unto you the forgiveness of your sins!* There it is! Isn't that preposterous? Something absolutely novel? . . . You have heard it, there it is! How do you know there is a God? Through this![163]

Or,

> For the kingdom of heaven is like a great feast! Everything is prepared; everything is ready! And the only response to such an invitation can be to celebrate! To enter into it wholeheartedly and with joy. That is what we are called upon to do when we come here to worship; to celebrate![164]

The critical hermeneutical approach for Forde in using and "honoring" the scriptures is the discernment of this law and this gospel. It's not about infallibility; it's not about information bites. It's about distinguishing between what is law and what is gospel, about understanding the shape of the action of the words upon the listener, how they function and what they do, and then "learning what to do with the words."[165] In short, as Forde writes in an article on infallibility for the Lutheran-Roman Catholic dialogue, "The important question (*a la* Ebeling) is not merely what the words signify, perhaps infallibly [or perhaps not], but what they do and how they do it. The important question for Luther, is how the words are used."[166] This a matter of the highest consequence, and its centrality cannot be minimized:

> The Church is the body of believers that has been called into being *by the gospel.* Its primal doctrinal *datum* is thus precisely the difference between law and gospel. The Church knows this difference and has as its primary doctrinal responsibility the custodianship of this difference. Indeed, this is the canon by which purity and rectitude in doctrine is to be measured.[167]

In Forde's mind as in Luther's, this two-sided action of the Word best happens in oral or sacramental proclamation.[168] "Proper preaching . . . is therefore the goal and the solution to the problem of interpretation." For, "[o]ne cannot interpret one's way out of death. Thus the final move, and the final solution to the problem left by interpretation, has to be the move to preaching. This entails, for Luther, the transition from talk *about* letter and spirit to the preaching *of* law and gospel."[169] Forde calls this "first order discourse:" the use of the second person in the present tense to confront the listener in the name of a present God. This contrasts with what he calls second order discourse, the use of the third person in the past tense to remind the listener of a God who once was.[170] Second order discourse is critical for theological reflection and confessional formulation, which serves to clarify the message in terms of the current worldview and prepare for the proclamation. But that proclamation should then, finally, take a first order form, as he writes, "[T]he church needs to stop lecturing *about* God and then appealing for acceptance in one way or another, and to begin speaking a word which in itself creates faith."[171] Proper preaching, therefore, must proceed sharply aware of this distinction in speaking, lest the past tense of most biblical texts remain simply past tense and dead letter, and not the present tense and active character necessary to make them viable today.[172]

Viable Today

The Random House Dictionary's first definition of viable is "capable of living." Applied to a message, one might propose in a preliminary way that it is the capacity of that message to live in the life of its hearer, to be so "vivid, real, and stimulating" (fourth definition) that it might not only be understood, but "grow, expand, develop" (sixth definition) with effects of its own.[173] Forde's own concern for viability is sprinkled across the full breadth of his works. He uses a form of the word as early as his 1967 "The Newness of the Gospel" and as late as his 1997 *Christian Century* article, "On Being a Theologian of the Cross." The term itself occurs at least forty-two times in at least ten works over those years, thirty-two of them in a single article on the viability of Luther, but his concern for it seems evident in many other expressions in other works as well, such as "difficult to hold today,"[174] or "convey better in our time,"[175] or "in a vital and living manner,"[176] or "a living tradition,"[177] or "a gospel I believed I could preach to the twentieth century."[178] The discerning reader will discover others. In almost every case it is a highly desirable quality.[179]

Theological Viability

While Forde uses the viability concept to describe a variety of antecedents—the church,[180] the church's witness in the world,[181] exegetical integrity,[182] and the sacraments,[183] he most frequently reserves it for theology—the formulation of doctrine,[184] its presentation in a systematic structure,[185] a particular understanding of the gospel,[186] the theology of Martin Luther,[187] a statement of the work of Christ[188] (as in the hermeneutical formulation we are considering), and so forth. That is to say, in terms of the kinds of discourse briefly alluded to above, when Forde speaks of viability, he is usually speaking of the viability of second order theological discourse. In fact, nowhere, apparently, does he seem to use it directly of preaching as such, a first order discourse, though such is surely implied by the rarer usages, as of the church's witness or the sacraments. This is surely not because he is less interested in the viability of proclamation! All the weight of Forde's writing shows his deep conviction that proclamation is the proper goal and outcome of theology and that it, too, should be what one might call viable, actually "doing the text to the hearers"[189] in an actual, real-life, "viable" phenomenon, one might say. But such proclamation is served by theology, as he says many times,[190] and viable theology is for Forde the most critical element—though perhaps not the only element, we will propose—for viable proclamation.

What would this significant quality of viability mean to Forde in terms of second order constructive theology? Nowhere does he propose a clear definition, so we have to look for clues in the way he talks about it. In his own autobiography it seems to mean intellectually satisfying answers to the troubling theological questions that touched off his own theological "quest" concerning such concepts as "divine election, bondage of the human will, and being a theologian of the cross."[191] In an article on the meaning of confessional subscription, he wants interpretation of historic documents to be consistent with current historic methodology as applied in historical criticism.[192] In his first published article he writes, "As far as I can see, it is absolutely imperative that we operate today with a method which enables us to face the world and to enter into meaningful conversation with it."[193] If we do not, we run the danger of losing a genuine engagement with those who think in the current worldview by retiring into thoughtforms no longer used:

> [T]he greatest temptation for all of us, I fear, is simply to fall back unreflectively into the old traditional ways, the old cliches, and expect to be carried along *by* the tradition, rather than becoming someone who carries and transmits the tradition in a vital and living manner. . . . What [God] really wants, what he really demands is men who know how to respond to the new thing he is doing, . . . living men who can pass on a living tradition, not merely petrified adherents of a past that is dead."[194]

Forde shows he wants theology to make sense, to be coherent in the prevailing *Weltanschauung*, to live in the minds of the people who do it, for the sake of the hearts of the people who will eventually hear its proclamation. He wants the "'real man' of today" to be "confronted by a real theology"[195] in order that a "real event" might eventually occur.[196]

If this "real theology" must be viable "today," what would the "today" of Forde's particular theology look like? We have already remarked that Forde was a twentieth century modern, thoroughly influenced by the Western scientific worldview. Perhaps the early death of his mother, as he proposed, gave him the independence of spirit that made him a questioner, if not a sceptic. As he matured, his preference for the intellectual certainty offered by his science teachers over the defensiveness of his religion teachers in the face of Enlightenment challenges brought him to graduate studies in chemistry before it did to seminary. He required a biblical approach that was "not embarrassed by human advancements in science, history, or other disciplines."[197] He found he could not hold to a verbal inspiration theory that "is unable to deal with facts gained both by research into the Bible and the world around us." One simply cannot "retreat from the world and refuse to face those things which one finds uncomfortable."[198] Theology that is viable "today" for Forde thus requires reasoning that takes account of the historical and scientific methodology used and relied upon in the twentieth century West.

This means that validity of the metaphysical thought of the ages is thrown into question. It is not helpful, Forde proposes in a sermon, when we develop "a kind of religious or theological split vision" and look "elsewhere, into the realm behind the scenes somewhere, the realm of ideas and theories . . . looking for the lost pieces of the puzzle which supposedly make 'sense' of this strange event . . . ." As he continues later, "I am afraid sometimes that the main reason we ask [how someone could die for us]   is . . . that we are always off somewhere in some cloud-cuckoo land, lost in the maze of our theories."[199] That is, rather than looking at the cross itself, for instance, we end up considering artificially conceived structures of meaning like an Anselmian sense of honor or a Aulènian cosmic victory. "[A] motif which speaks of victory over demonic forces on a grand cosmic scale," for instance, "is too 'objectifying' in a mythological sense to carry much weight today."[200] It's simply not coherent to a modern sense of historical and scientific reality. This is true even when considering the work of one as important to Forde as Luther himself: "[T]he powers attacking the Christ . . . seem still to have much too abstract and mythological a coloring for contemporary eyes. If anything Luther's formulations still have too much of the traditional metaphysical and mythological freight."[201] Clearly, a theology viable "today" for Forde means a theology that keeps in close touch with current categories of time and space and shies away from some "abstract exercise,"[202] or "heavenly transactions,"[203] or "celestial machinery,"[204] however conceived.

One aspect of reality that certainly does not seem mythological or metaphysical to moderns is the sense of the self, a focus of lively philosophical debate from Kant through the present. Theological reflection on the life of the self is omnipresent in Forde's work. For example, in a characteristic passage describing the plight of the self, Forde asserts we are *curvatus in se*, all turned inward upon ourselves. We have a desparate [sic] time getting out at all. [L]ike the nervous ground-hog I will be frightened, perhaps by my own shadow . . . . All it takes is some little word, some slight mistake, some nuance, glance, gesture. . . . My internal self constantly defeats or swallows up the word coming from without.[205]

Or, in another characteristic passage describing the freedom of the self in Christ,

[a]ll the space in the "inner world," the conscience, is occupied by Christ. There is no room for a self that wants to feed only on its self. One is turned inside out. The law cannot get in there any more. It can only be turned back to the world where it belongs, to be used to do what it is supposed to: take care of people not tyrannize them.[206]

These are unabashedly existential reflections. So much of Forde's work on the Old Adam, atonement, death and new life, faith, serving the neighbor, and so forth is concerned with the life of the self in this manner that it seems clear that, without saying so, he assumed its evident viability for the modern.

How he conceives this viability is made clearer in his 1984 *dialog* article, "The Power of Negative Thinking."[207] Here, using a veritable swarm of fifty-three occurrences of "self" and its synonyms over only five pages, he makes connections between the thought of Luther and the thought of significant nineteenth century philosophers concerning the self. His thesis is that the last two centuries of thought have been intent on preserving what Kant called the "autonomous self" by negating God in various ways: by bringing God's law within oneself (Kant), by love's overcoming and negating this law in human thought (Hegel), by making God a human projection, thus preserving divine predicates for human beings where they belong (Feuerbach), by further preserving these predicates against individual death by attributing them to the human species (Stirner), and finally by projecting the enemy, the old self that needs destoying, upon someone else—the capitalist (Marx). Forde builds on the idea of preservation of the self as something that would make sense to modern thinkers in light of this historic philosophical struggle. By putting Luther's insistence that the cross ends "any possibility for a positive synthesis between human religious striving and divine grace"[208] in the context of this discussion, he seeks to lift up negation of the self (Old Adam) as a viable solution of the modern problem of self. This is very close to a central proposition of Forde's entire system, and the importance of its connections to the contemporary struggle should not be underestimated.[209]

Proclamatory Viability

Thus far, we have considered "viability today" primarily in terms of a theological understanding that could make sense in terms of the presuppositions of the prevailing worldview of Forde's time. We dealt with theology first because Forde himself seems to give it a priority when he raises the issue of viability. Nevertheless, as we have noted, he occasionally uses the term in a way that suggests proclamation as well, as noted above, and there are internal reasons as well to believe that he was intensely concerned for viability of the first order discourse, the proclamation. We will attempt to demonstrate this on two levels.

First, almost on a rhetorical level, it would appear that Forde shows that he values practical efforts to translate his message into the linguistic and cultural idiom of his hearers. Already in his articles he uses imagery from modern science to illustrate points to persons who could be expected to appreciate them: "[L]aw 'resonates,' to use an image from chemistry, between two poles."[210] Or again, "[t]o use an image from atomic physics, [the church] have always tried to put rods in the reactor to get some kind of controlled energy flow . . . ."[211] His carefully chosen theological language regularly uses colorful images for the sake of effect: "sacramental or hierarchical high jinks,"[212] or "the questions are [the old Adam's] 'death rattle,'"[213] or "poking around in the wreckage for the black box."[214] When one considers his preaching, the effect is considerably heightened as he works his thoughts into modern vernacular that might almost be called street language. In one sermon on John 19:28-30 he has Jesus saying, "If fighting were the name of the game my Father would send legions of angels and we would have a real donneybrook [sic]!"[215] In announcing the Easter gospel, he expresses astonishment over Christ's resurrection: "Who ever heard of such a thing? Gone! Escaped! Flown the coop!"[216] In the sermon entitled "God's Rights," he helps his listener approach the eschatological event with the words, "Is it not wild? Don't you see? All our little games are over."[217] These are not expressions that would be widely or quickly understood in international English, nor are they standard theological terms that would appear in a theological dictionary. Clearly, Forde has chosen particular, vivid idioms known to his particular audience for the sake of the raw existential impact of the message upon them. Like every effective missionary at the boundary of the eschaton, he has strained all conventions of the vocabulary and grammar of his culture to create new combinations of meaning and useage that will make the message heard afresh.

The point is that Forde is demonstrating linguistic and cultural as well as philosophical concern to do cognitive business with the people of the time and place he addresses. He is not uninterested that his message be heard clearly by those to whom he is speaking—in fact, there are moments in his preaching when he seems positively urgent to be understood by them—and he takes appropriate steps accordingly. He uses not only their philosophical worldview, but also their linguistic and cultural habits of expression within it. In this sense of this-worldly communicability he wants the message of the proclamation to be "viable."

But, secondly, his concern goes beyond using the worldview and the cultural and linguistic idioms of the age to catch a culturally-formed ear or mind. In light of the forgoing discussion of a living and present Word of God, this viability must be understood in a deeper way as well. It's not just any word that must get through; it's the eschaton-bearing Word of God that must arrive in the heart of the hearer. Forde has confidence that through a law-gospel hermeneutic that allows the text to do its work in the present, the Word of God will demonstrate a vigor of its own—almost an alien power—to make its own way in the world, viable through its own integrity of life from within, as it were. In, with, and under all efforts at interpretation, translation, and mediation, Forde would argue that, finally, the proclaimer's job is to make way for the message itself. Viability in this deeper sense is not so much something the proclaimer *gives* the text as something he or she *discovers* in the text itself in order to *permit* it to express itself. We catch the spirit of this appeal in a Good Friday sermon: "[Proclamation] is the art of learning how to get out of the way of the message. Because the message has got wings. The point is to let it fly, man, let it fly. It is finished, and nothing can stop it."[218] Put another way, the proclaimer is one who is cognizant of the inner vigor and integrity of the message and does the proclaiming task in the manner, described earlier, that allows its death-and-life address on the hearer, its viability. So informed and acting accordingly, the proclaimer will bear a vital tradition forward to do its vital task on a new generation. The way in which Forde understands that to happen will be considered more carefully during the course of this chapter.

We need to mark what seems to be a paradox in Forde's understanding of the role of the proclaimer at this point. On the one hand there is an appeal for a certain restraint or respect—"get out of the way,"—as if before an alien power that is not under the proclaimer's control in the confidence that the Word of God has its own fulfilling dynamic. On the other hand, there is a call for proclaimerly initiative—"carries and transmits the tradition in a vital and living manner"—as if the proclaimer, too, had a vital part in the passage of the message to the new time and place by insuring that the intrinsic dynamic might occur. The theological groundwork of the proclaimer must somehow address this paradox. We will to return to the question how Forde might understand the proclaimer both to *permit* and to *enable* the Word to have its say.

If Forde comes to express the intention that a theological understanding be "viable today," he would not want that confused with what he usually calls relevance. With only a very few exceptions, the idea of relevance receives Forde's strong censure, sometimes quite sarcastically so—"a horrible, usually misunderstood and misused word."[219] He sees it is a ploy of the old Adam to defend its wayward turf:

> In all our fussing about 'relevance' we have tended to make the fatal mistake of thinking it was possible to make the word attractive to fallen beings . . . . We may as well face it. The Word is not relevant to the 'Old Adam' as such. It is an attack. It cuts off. It puts to death so it can make new."[220]

What is relevant to the old Adam is not the killing word but the human "wisdom of survival" that helps us *avoid* the killing word.[221] Relevance has to do with continuity and survival of the old, not with discontinuity, not with death and resurrection of a new. "I have come to believe that the idea that the gospel should or could be made 'relevant' to old beings is one of contemporary theology's greatest miscalculations," Forde asserts in his theological autobiography.[222]

In a possibly unique effort to reconfigure the term, Forde proposes that "[t]oday we tend to confuse relevance with topicality. If something is relevant, it transcends that which is only of passing fancy or interest, and is thus lifted above a particular time or place to the level of universality. If it is relevant, it is always so."[223] In this sense it is the gospel that is the relevant thing and the world's enterprises that turn out not to be. But since this is not the general useage of the word, it is better avoided and preachers should not waste their concern on it:

> So when you come home and ask yourself whether anything was really said about the text, the answer most likely would have to be that the preacher was too preoccupied with being relevant and so never really got around to it! Better luck next time![224]

And not just the word, but the spirit it suggests:

> When we operate on the assumption that our language must constantly be trimmed so as not to give offense, to stroke the psyche rather than to place it under attack, it will of course gradually decline to the level of greeting-card sentimentality. . . . It has lost its theological legitimacy and therefore its viability as communication.[225]

In light of what has been said about viability, this harsh judgment on relevance might at first seem confusing. After all, how can an irrelevant word be viable? As we have observed, a word that does no linguistic, cultural, or intellectual business can hardly be expected to be effective theologically or eschatologically. We would argue here that Forde's negative concern about relevance here is best understood as a backhanded way of expressing the positive desire for viability noted above. If the proclaimer is to permit and enable the word to do what it needs to do, he/she cannot limit that work on the basis of what is comfortable or congenial. If viability should happen to require a task hard for the human spirit to bear (bringing an end to false hopes and dreams, for instance), that viability is not helped by requiring the task to coincide with perceived human needs or solutions. Such coincidence might even be found to stand in the way of the vitality of the word, which is Forde's point. In fact, when that Word is God's, he thinks it probably will.

To summarize Forde's hermeneutical approach, then, we see a theologian heir to a rich history of theological conversation, respectful of that tradition of thought and strongly identifying with it, interested in probing its attempts at theological understanding but not bound by them, and willing to learn from its hazards as well as its insights. Higher is his regard for scripture as a source of faith. Scripture is not viewed as a font of infallible information, a position which leaves one with problems intellectual and theological, most tragically, the possibility of remaining unmoved by scripture's address. Instead, scripture is experienced as the Word of God when a proclaimer using a law-gospel dialectic brings its message to bear in a killing and life-giving word in the present according to 2 Corinthians 3:4-6. This occurs in first-order proclamation through preaching and the sacraments.

The concern for viability is already implicit here. Forde's concern for the capacity of the message to live is usually directed towards a coherent theological formulation in terms of the worldview of his age. We identified three aspects of this worldview that seem important to his sense of viability: a respect for current historical and scientific presuppositions, a corresponding reticence to rely on the abstractions of metaphysical structures however conceived, and heavy engagement with modern conceptions of the self. Though Forde doesn't use the term viability for the proclamation, his urgent concern for its clarity invites its consideration at two levels. First, he demonstrates a proper missionary concern for linguistic and cultural address that communicates meaning effectively, for proclamation as well as for theology. And secondly, he invites the proclaimer's openness to the Word's own purpose and power that enables the law-gospel dialectic to do the text's intended task. Negative concerns about relevance must be seen in light of this positive concern for a viability not cut short by the convenient or the comfortable.

B. The Theological Function of the Law

With the law-gospel distinction so pivotal for Forde's hermeneutic, it is not surprising to discover in his doctoral thesis, *The Law-Gospel Debate*, an effort to clarify it. He does this through an exploration of the role that law has played for several generations of theologians, and he repeatedly remarks the confusion evident in its reinterpretation. A brief review of the more significant of these theologians will set the stage for increased clarity about Forde's understanding how the law actually does and does not function in an eschatologically lively life of faith.

Forde's Critique of Traditional Approaches

Law in Lutheran Orthodoxy

Forde sees the orthodox theological system of his own heritage as fundamentally structured around the idea of the law, and this almost as a defense mechanism. God is confessed as, by God's very nature, omnipotent and free to do as God pleases with humankind as with all creation. This utter freedom of God strikes the human heart as dangerous, since God might turn out to be arbitrary or capricious. In response to such a thought, Forde marks a steady tendency of successive generations of Lutheran confessors to add that God surely only acts according to God's nature, "the inner law of his own essence." If God's claims on us could be seen as consistent with this law, it not only would take the edge off the unpredictability of a God on the loose, but also set forth "the ideal to which human life must attain in order to find favor with God." In this system law is "an eternal, objective order, a *lex aeterna*." Forde calls this "the static-ontological concept of divine law," because it is "rooted in the divine being as an eternal and unchangeable standard."[226]

The system based on the law in this way determines a whole array of theological constructs—in particular, Anselmian atonement, where "vicarious satisfaction of the demands of the law" are central.[227] In its broad strokes Lutheran orthodoxy follows Anselm, but views the punishment itself *as* the required satisfaction. The atonement theory "provides the rational framework for understanding what takes place in atonement."[228] It is speculative because it attempts a description of what happens from a divine perspective, concluding what satisfaction of God's nature might be. And it is rational because the faith it seeks is an intellectual acquiescence to the description it proposes. That is to say, it is the material content of its propositions that have to be "believed" if one is to be "saved." This content comes from the Bible, and it thus becomes important that the Bible become the infallible sourcebook of the propositions that faith must accept, the course that Lutheran orthodoxy actually chose.[229]

Forde cites E. W. Hengstenberg (1802-1869), professor in Berlin from 1828-1869, as a classic example of this use of the Bible.

Hengstenberg sought to use the scriptures as an objective source of information something like scientific data, outside the observer and subject to investigation by the observer. Since revelation was contrary to human reason, scriptures functioned independently of it, and the threat of historical criticism was avoided. Upon such a renewed biblicism the orthodox distinction of law and gospel depended.[230]

Despite the renewed life it gave the church in the early nineteenth century, Forde concludes that the position had no future. "[F]or those who really took historical criticism seriously and who could not simply dismiss the developing historical world view as something antithetical to Christianity, Hengstenberg's biblicism could hardly be a viable alternative" (see the discussion on viability, pp. 51-55). "To attack this biblicism, though, meant to attack the entire system of which it was a part,"[231]and that meant that the conception of the role of the law had to change.

Law in Hofmann's Heilsgeschichte

Working in the aftermath of D. F. Strauss' 1835 attack in *Leben Jesus* on the historical reliability of the Gospel accounts, J. C. K. von Hofmann (1810-1877) sought fresh ground on which to confess the faith. Where Hengstenberg insisted on a legalistic subscription to something that must be believed—the biblical narrative— Hofmann proposed that the basis of faith was the Christian experience itself. The influence of pietism and Schleiermacher is obvious here, yet against pietism and Schleiermacher, he emphasized this not as a subjective existential awareness, but as a corporate historical phenomenon shared by the Christian community and corroborated with the scriptures. That is, "God's action in history continues in the present through the church," and "[w]hen faith is created, this means that God's historical activity has reached its appointed *telos* in the believer."[232] This faith is a "self-authenticating" historical fact in the present and upon it a system of theological understanding can be built.[233]

Hofmann's methodology for accomplishing this is "an unfolding the content of the experience" from a vantage point within the experience. This means one can't think *about* the experience, as if one were an outsider, so as to produce doctrinal opinions, but rather "*in* the actual situation of being a Christian." From within, there is a kind of "evolution" of the content of the corporate experience of "God's dealing with mankind in history," in a way simple enough and general enough to be recognizable by all Christians. All this is accomplished in the awareness, as Hofmann himself summarized it, of "the personal communion of God and mankind mediated in Jesus Christ."[234] The change in approach was striking. In Forde's words,

It was a thoroughgoing departure from the orthodox system. It has a different way of validating the facts of Christian experience, it understood the nature and function of theology differently, and it established a different relationship to scripture and tradition. At every point it tried to avoid any suggestion of a legalistic understanding of faith.[235]

Where in orthodoxy the basic content of faith was propositional, here it was historical, *heilsgeschichtlich*. The Christian experience had to be understood as "the result of a chain of historical events issuing from God and culminating in the creation of faith." It was all part of a "continuum of historical cause and effect."[236] Unfolding the content of this continuum from within according to Hofmann's methodology provides a basically new system for articulating Christian theology.

The new system permitted Hofmann to work out an understanding of Christ's work that was virtually free of reference to law. It happens as part of a larger history of God's effecting a relationship with humanity. This includes the family of Abraham, his descendants, and the nation of Israel prefiguring the relationship before Christ, and the church of Christ into which the Christian is included afterwards. But Christ himself is "the climax of the scheme,"[237] and his work may be understood as the entry of the "archetypal-world *telos*" into human nature "to be the mediator of a new relationship." The explanation is thus not in terms of satisfaction of the law but of restoration of a relationship:

> In the incarnation God makes himself into the antithesis of God the loving Father and God the Son subject to the divine wrath. What occurs therefore will have to be that the Son preserves his personal relationship with the Father to the end—in the face of all that results from sin—and in so doing removes the contradiction in his own person. Jesus endured to the end in that he suffered in the most extreme manner the full force of the opposition focused on him because of sin (the activity of the contra-divine forces acting through man). His act was the preseverance in the attitude towards God which made good what sin had corrupted. In this act reconciliation is accomplished *in* mankind, and thus in him true righteousness is realized.[238]

Law is not mentioned in this *heilsgeschichtliche* approach. Jesus didn't fulfill the law. Rather he realized "the divine will to love mankind." He "established a *new humanity*, a new righteousness in which the eternal will is realized." He made possible a "transfigured existence" wherein "a new and unconditional relationship between God and man can be realized." And "[t]o be a Christian is to be conscious of one's participation in this new existence, to be included in the body of Christ, the church,"[239]not to know oneself liberated from the law by the work of Christ.

"What Hofmann did," Forde concludes, "was to replace the law with *Heilsgeschichte*."[240] Law there is in Hofmann's history, but it is a national law for Israel alone to help distinguish her from the nations. That national law was "superseded," "supplanted," a "between the times" phenomenon only.[241] Law doesn't determine human righteousness; rather, "acceptance of God's action in history" determines human righteousness. Even "the task of ethics, for Hofmann, is to *describe* the reality of the new life and not to *prescribe* what ought to be according to a set of laws."[342] It can be seen, then, that the orthodox concept of *lex aeterna* as the determining force was everywhere contested by a fundamentally different structure. And even if Hofmann's new structure itself was mostly forgotten in the years that followed, the debate it opened up took on a life of its own as the role of the law in theology was considered and reconsidered.[243]

Law and Wrath in Theodosius Harnack

Hofmann's conclusions appeared to Theodosius Harnack (1817-1889) contrary to Luther's own views. In setting out to prove it, and to claim Luther's views for orthodoxy, Harnack provided a major systematic impetus for modern Luther research, though there was nothing unbiased about his research itself.

Forde notes a number of contributions of Harnack's Luther research. There is the discovery of vicarious satisfaction talk set right beside dualistic victory language without an apparent sense of conflict for Luther. Harnack sometimes remarked on Luther's comment that vicarious language was "too weak,"[244] but he never followed up on the observation and continued to affirm it as the primary paradigm in interpreting Luther. There is also the discovery of "twofold knowledge of God," God in creation where "an active and retributive righteousness" prevails, and God in Christ where one finds "pure grace." Both of these pictures of God are true as one is "in Christ" or "outside of Christ."[245] In Luther Harnack found a dialectical God of wrath and love "in sharp contrast with the monistic tendencies in Hofmann and Ritschl and the entire 19th century."[246] Harnack's formula for relating the two poles was that "[t]he knowledge of God as wrath gained through the law is objectively valid, but 'only conditionally and not of the same stature' as the knowledge of God gained through the gospel."[247]

Perhaps most significant for this conversation is Harnack's discovery that Luther had a broader concept of law than Hofmann. Whereas Hofmann had reduced law to a mere phase of Israel's history, rejecting its wider claims to which he attributed a false basis for atonement, Harnack found it essential to Luther's understanding that the knowledge of law was natural as well as revealed.[248] That is, it was present and effective in creation before revelation in Christ and Christ's work could be related to it. It was this discovery that permitted Harnack to revert to orthodoxy with its fundamentally law-based structure.

Law in Albrecht Ritschl

Albrecht Ritschl (1822-1889), by contrast, is an example of a variation of Hofmann's position. Backing off from early friendly criticism of Hoffman, Ritschl held his work in high esteem according to Forde, depending only on Schleiermacher more than him, according to Seeberg.[249] The chief point of difference that remained between the two had to do with the role of the community in experience:

> Whereas Hofmann understood the Christian experience more in terms of the direct relationship of the risen Christ to the individual as something prior to the historical community as such, Ritschl thought more strictly in terms of actual mediation through the historical community—what has been termed his revelational positivism. For Hofmann, one might say, the experience had mystical and pietistic overtones, whereas for Ritschl it had to be more concrete and historical. For Ritschl the object of theological science was not the religious consciousness but revelation as objectively given and mediated in and through the historical community.[250]

It is almost as if Ritschl is the fulfillment of Hofmann's anti-subjective move to link Christian consciousness to the historic community of faith. Instead of simply corroborating the veracity of individually "thought-in" faith with that of the historic community, Ritschl actually based its reality upon it. For Ritschl there simply is no prior independent "thinking in;" for him it is rather all about "thinking about" the faith of the community in comparison with other religious expressions.

This meant that Ritschl, even more dependent than Hofmann upon the historical reality of Christian community, had to offer other guidelines, "a conceptual scheme," on how that reality revealed God's acts to the believer. Forde proposes he used "his own particular synthesis of Luther and Kant" for this purpose rather than the orthodox system and its legal structure. From Kant he took the idea of freedom of spirit. Christians are free from outside "causality" when they spontaneously respond out of love through the redemption of Christ. And from his understanding of Luther he took the concept of justification by faith and faith defined as trust in the *pro me*.[251]

Ritschl regarded all of these parts of the synthesis the more highly for their practical, as opposed to some theoretical, value. One would expect practicality and a concern for the ethical from a community of people who had to live together. If the community is the source of revelation, its value judgments should be made, not *dependent* upon some "theoretical value system," some metaphysical principle or intellectual theological structure, but *independent* of all but the life of faith within the community.

And so the doctrine of atonement, for instance, could be understood only in relation to the historical Christian community. It was not a "once-for all objective act in the past upon which forensic justification is based." That would make it a metaphysical abstraction. Neither is it "Christ in us," as Osiander argued. That would open it to charges of subjectivism. Instead, the community experiences both aspects in a moment of time. Ritschl proposes that "the unity in time between the objective justification and the subjective consciousness of it which has its place *in religious experience* must be surrendered *in the theological view* of the matter."[253] Forde observes a critical juncture here:

> In making a distinction between religious experience and theological exposition, Ritschl gave up the attempt to define *theologically* the simultaneity of objective justification and subjective consciousness. The simultaneity is given in religious experience but cannot be expressed in a theological system.[254]

That is to say, in considering atonement, at least, theology as such must ultimately be abandoned for the sake of the religious experience of the historic community. That is, the reality of atonement is knowable only through the experience of it in the community Jesus established.

Then the critical work of Jesus is the establishment of this community where atonement takes place. This is his proper "calling," and he was faithful to it.[255] Atonement is not about Jesus' death. The thought that his death brings about atonement is an "intrusion of non-Christian naturalistic metaphysics." God is a God of love, and this is known through God's revelation. Justification by this God comes "from God's absolutely free judgment," and not through some "satisfaction of divine wrath." This happens through "the religious influence of Jesus in the historical community," described in practical, present tense terms of sin, guilt, and the realization of forgiveness and trust. Sin causes "a barrier to man's approach to God," not metaphysically conceived as natural or inherited, but as "a moral and religious inhibition" through "the feeling of guilt." Christ's work breaks down these barriers, not by metaphysically conceived substitution, but through "the drawing near to God of the separated sinner through the priestly act within the context of covenant—within the established community." This brings about not a metaphysically conceived satisfaction, but a real-life community of love and trust despite sin. To say more about the link between Christ's work and forgiveness is not possible. Even Hofmann's use of a dramatic victory motif is unwarranted. It is sufficient "that the awareness of forgiveness comes through the influence of the life and death of Christ and its peculiar working in the community throughout all ages.[256]The force of this is a present ethical concern for the congregation, since the influence of Jesus brings about the moral reign of God's love where people are in Kantian fashion moved to do the love that is in them. Anything less is abstraction.

The concept of law for Ritschl is interpreted in this context. Since outside the community sin cannot even be known as sin—there, it is only ignorance—so law is not really law, against Harnack and Luther. And within the community the determining factor is the rule of God which is a rule of love, not law. Here, freely expressing God's love within them, members of the community spontaneously do what is within them, following an "internal moral law," "the moral imperative of the kingdom of God." The influence of Kant is evident. Theologically, it results in what Forde calls "a synthesis or perhaps even identification of law and gospel."[257]

> For Ritschl, then, redemption involved a change in disposition or mind. It was this adaption of Kant which allowed Ritschl to take law within the kingdom and unite it with the gospel. There is no dialectic of law and gospel, rather a synthesis in the kingdom of God.[258]

This blurring of the law-gospel distinction led Ritschl to "reverse the normal order of law and gospel" in repentance."[259] For repentance to be genuine, it must arise from a heart that already loves the good. This cannot happen apart from faith that participates in the loving reign of God that comes through community. Repentance thus arises from gospel, not law. Ritschl read Luther in such a way as to find a young Luther discovering this and an older Luther, perhaps influenced by Melanchthon, forgetting it, a portrait that has not been sustained by later research. Ritschl was not the last to reverse law and gospel in a struggle for understanding; half a century later Karl Barth would do it again, but with such a transforming new eschatological edge as to make it virtually a new idea.

Law in Karl Barth

For various reasons—theological in the nineteenth century and sociopolitical in the twentieth—the driving theological concern for Karl Barth (1886-1968) came to be a clear distinction between the Word of God and the words of humankind. Since both law and gospel belong to the former rather than the latter, their common character as the address of God in Barth's system reorients his thinking about them in terms of unity rather than difference. That is, sharing their character as speech of a gracious God, they *both* must convey grace, for "[t]he very fact that God speaks to us at all is in itself grace, and this is true whether he speaks through gospel or through law."[260]

Barth used the concepts of form and content to help explain this. Gospel speaks of God's action on our behalf in Christ, the content of the revelation. This action does not end with itself, but awaits responsive action by us. It would be "not only dangerous but perverse" to attempt to understand this responsive action that God awaits in any other way than through Christ. The law is therefore established in Christ, that is, we understand what we are to do through our understanding of God's grace towards us in Christ. In this way the law is the "*form* of the gospel," the "shape of existence which the gospel creates in this world."[261] Law and gospel therefore go together, united as form to content, but the proper order is content, gospel, followed by the form, law, that the gospel will take in our lives and world; thus, gospel and law.

The function of this united Word of God is, however, affected by its encounter with sinful humanity, both negatively and positively. Negatively, the law which is the form of the gospel gets distorted because it is misused by sinners intent on establishing their own righteousness. Likewise, the gospel is distorted when it is turned into a stopgap measure to complete what the sinner couldn't finish under the law. In this context the good but abused law, which remains God's law despite the abuse, turns on the sinner to express God's wrath. Then, positively, the gospel does its proper work, coming "as a rescue from apparent condemnation under the misunderstood law."[262] Only in this scenario of human abuse it is possible to say that law, the misused law, precedes gospel. Its proper order, Barth repeats, is gospel-law, in which law is "the expression of God's will which follows the gospel."[263]

Thus both natural law and natural knowledge that may have preceded the coming of the Word are excluded. So is Kantian natural religion. The force of Barth's construction is to emphasize the awful discontinuity that comes with God's address, and that discontinuity cannot abide prerevelational contributions. This is what sets Barth a world apart from Ritschl, outward similarities notwithstanding. No longer "a command to love, as the practical moral imperative at the root of religious life," Barth's law comes as "the concrete and particular form in which relevation comes to men at a particular time."[264] It was not there, in "religion," beforehand. It came from without, revealed by God. As such it is not a general law, widely perceived and commonly understood as something self-evident. It is rather "the particular and concrete demand" one would expect of a divine address of a revelatory moment.[265] Thus is this Barthian concept of law firmly attached to the Barthian Word.

Coming as a good gift from a good God, indeed, as the form of the gospel itself, the Barthian law is blessing, in contradistinction to all other laws. Used aright in the context of the gospel, it doesn't condemn; it gives permission, and so it grants freedom:

> Other commands in every respect are a 'holding fast, a binding, a fettering'; they create and maintain a sphere of distrust and fear. The command of God, however, which has its basis in the

claim made upon men by Jesus Christ, orders man to be free, and it secures obedience by in fact setting men free.[266]

There is simultaneously order and gift in this concept. God commands and God also makes it happen. This is not a basis for ethics as commonly understood. This is a description of a basically new situation, "law *in* the gospel, the law of freedom . . . grasped only through faith." Forde summarizes Barth's position: "Law is the very specific unity of authority and freedom which is given in Jesus Christ and apprehended only by faith."[267]

Barth traces a delicate distinction in the relationship of this divine law to all the normal human and creational laws encountered in the world. On the one hand, Barth wants to say they are all different from God's law because they all bind rather than free. They all are of this earth while God's law comes from God. On the other hand Barth wants to connect them to it, too: God's command "'without prejudice to its particular form'—*always* wears the 'garment' of another claim of this kind," so that an earthly command "'can actually be the command of God veiled in this form.'"[268] This is truly a delicate distinction. Forde proposes that "[f]aith, apparently, will be able to recognize it as God's command in that it will bear the marks of freedom—the specific conjunction of obligation and permission."[269]

Related to this is another nuanced point: Barth's dependence in his system on the misused law to set the stage for the rescue of the gospel on the one hand, and his denial that that is the purpose of God's law on the other. "The misused law, even though it derives its authority and power from God and apparently is in some sense a revelation of sin to man, is not a propaedeutic to the gospel; it is, for Barth, simply the law of sin and death."[270] God's law, rather, is to be connected with "the law of the spirit of life in Christ Jesus." Forde describes Barth's position in these words:

> The law of God . . . is not the sum and superlative of the 'infernal assault' of the law of sin and death, nor is it even the 'infinitely multiplied' intensity of this assault. The assault of the law of sin and death leads to death, no doubt, but it does not produce the death which leads to life. Only the command of God does that. The command of God assaults and seizes man indeed, but it does this not like an enemy but rather like a friend. This assault is radical precisely because it is the command of our true, best friend. It is radical because it is the law *in* the gospel.[271]

So the assault of the misused law is God's assault because it is still God's law reflecting God's power. The situation this assault creates has a positive result in that it sets the stage on which the gospel "operates 'fully for the first time' as 'the really glad tidings for real sinners'"[272] But the death it produces does not lead to life. "Only the command of God does that."[273] This would be the law *in* the gospel which gives form to the content of the good news. But the gospel would not have delivered its content if the law *outside* the gospel had not exercised God's own authority. It is a fine line.

One hears in this conversation rather violent characteristics attributed to the law: "assault" and "sieze." These are not terms that we have remarked before in Forde's review of theologians on the law. They constitute a part of what Forde calls "the act character of the Word," and he credits Barth with an attempt at its restoration:

> In Barth, the Word of revelation is no longer a mere report about a past event, nor is it a timeless truth, but it is an eschatological address carrying in itself that which it has to give as demand and gift, form and content. Barth has attempted to restore the act character of the Word by making it more "exclusive," by removing the possibility of understanding it in terms of some system of 'natural theology.' The Word is the eschatological address which breaks in upon man.[274]

It means that the law is not in Barth a neutral object to be examined and commented upon. It shares with the gospel the capacity, as from God, to do things to the hearer: to assault and to sieze, even, although, for Barth, in a paradoxically friendly way. This act character constitutes a significant new aspect to the debate that Forde, even as he strongly disagrees with Barth's gospel-law scheme, will develop further in his own way.

Law in Modern Luther Research

"The current [1969] interpretation of law among Lutheran theologians is a result, mainly, of Luther research," Forde begins in his final chapter of analysis of theologians, and he integrates the work of three of them in his overview: Lauri Haikola (1917-1987), Gerhard Ebeling (1912-2001), and Gustaf Aulén (1879-1977). He chooses them not because they reflected some consensus in Luther studies by that time—disagreement persisted and work remained to be done—but because these men "claim to find in Luther an interpretation of law which runs counter to the interpretation we have found in the development from Hofmann through Ritschl to Barth." Forde is looking for alternative approaches, and these men seem "to set forth a definite advance in the debate about law" that has found a responsive chord in Lutheran systematics. Forde attempts to summarize their view of law.[275]

First, according to Haikola, a significant difference between Luther's and later orthodoxy's views of the law was the extent of its revelation. Orthodoxy approached law almost as if it were a complete, given manuscript, "an objective scheme of demands and prohibitions which must be fulfilled"[276] and which in substitutionary atonement *were* fulfilled. Here, law is virtually a known datum. Luther, while sometimes himself using the term *lex aeterna,* is much more reserved about its knowability:

> At no time, according to Luther, does man possess full knowledge of the divine will, but only a knowledge of the law appropriate to his actual historical situation. . . . The will of God is not made known to man in once-for-all fashion, least of all can man capture this will in the form of eternal principles. Rather man must learn to know God's will anew in each new situation.[277]

This means there's a certain hiddenness about the law in any context, just as there is about God. There is no human control over it. It can appear in diverse forms—anything that attacks or accuses humankind, from the ten commandments to the rustling of a leaf—so that its capacity actually to confront us by surprise is preserved.

"Law is not therefore an idea or a collection of propositions" as something to be misunderstood, "but the reality of fallen humanity." It is "an existential category," describing the threat of what is. As such, it is "that which terrifies the conscience,"[278] even if it be words that outwardly seem like gospel. However God "confronts man in judgment," that is law. This happens at the level of the heart, and not just "technically or materially . . . or gramatically." There it "sounds, . . . exhorting, piercing the heart and the conscience until you do not know where to turn."[279]

Distinction of this practical accusing function, its office, from some neutral eternal essence of the law is beside the point. The question for the sinner is what it does to one, and the answer is that it always accuses. There is no law for the sinner to consider besides the accusing law. The law ceases to accuse only at the eschaton when sin ceases to be a problem. "[F]or man as sinner, the 'essence' of the law is the 'office.'"[280] It's function may be eternal from the sinner's point of view, but Luther backs off from admitting that its existence or essence is. For him it's all about function. And the function of the law will end when it is fulfilled.

There's no situation from which humankind can look at law objectively. Luther says it is never *lex vacua,* an empty or neutral law to be examined, because humankind is never above the law to examine it. It is always in our face, threatening, killing, and the only response to the law is to die, an eschatological event. "This means that in place of a one-membered eternal scheme, a two-membered dialectical scheme governs the system. Only by participation in the eschatological event does the law come to an end for the believer."[281]

Although Forde is aware of Swedish theologians who hold that Luther held to an "Anselmic" atonement theory, he focuses on Gustaf Aulén's position to the contrary:

Aulén, opposing the Latin theory, insists that however one looks at the matter, one thing is certain: for Luther atonement means the abolition of the judicial order (*Rechtsordnung*), the removal of all legalism from one's relationship to God. Atonement through Christ means the casting off of the religiosity of the judicial order, the setting aside of the power and tyranny of the law. In Luther's view, Aulén admits, the law indeed must be fulfilled, but it is fulfilled in order to be *removed* and *cancelled*, not because it is the eternal standard of justice according to which God *himself* must be satisfied.[282]

Given the results of Luther research on Luther's understanding of the law, Forde proposes that the language of Luther that harks back to Anselm may nonetheless be set by Luther in a quite structurally different model. "For if the law is understood in a different way, then it follows that such terms as satisfaction and fulfillment will have to be understood quite differently."[283]

Haikola uses the terms quantitative and qualitative to explore this point. It would be an objective conception of the law that would permit the kind of quantitative measurement of its fulfillment that vicarious satisfaction implies, and this Luther did not entertain. Rather, Luther envisions "a qualitative subjection of man to God in faith and love" such as the First Commandment that sums up what the entire law requires.[284] It is under this demand that Christ died, according to Luther, not satisfying by buying off God's wrath (a quantitative understanding), but satisfying by totally identifying himself with humankind, bearing their punishment, and dying their death "in their place" (a qualitative description). Both scenarios use satisfaction language, but the qualitative approach of subjection gives quite a different sense than the calculating *lex aeterna* approach. It gives, in fact, a death in preparation for a new rising from the dead.[285]

This approach has several advantages for Haikola, according to Forde. First, "God's wrath against sin retains its character as real wrath," not having been integrated into a scheme that, in effect, disarms it. Secondly, "God's love retains for Luther its character as pure, unfathomable mercy," not something that was calculated and bought by a sacrifice. Thirdly, "atonement retains its perpetually actual character" with power that "attacks man in his own life situation," so that the subjective and the objective aspects always go together. That is, in the same moment one subjectively experiences what objectively comes upon one. And fourthly, "the problem of history is more easily handled," since there is a presentness about the event. "The Word, the proclamation of Christ's victory, is not merely intellectual information about an objective transaction but is itself the bearer of ongoing atonement." There is temporal ending and beginning in this event, rather than just a timeless legal structure to be understood and appreciated.[286] Clearly, the law precedes, not follows, the gospel in this event.

Again, with Barth, these theologians remark the present-tense effects of the law upon the hearer. Forde lists the adjustments in understanding that will be required to bear this "eschatological understanding." First, the orthodox concept of *lex aeterna* is set aside, as Hofmann said. But, secondly, the law is not displaced by "an objective historical dispensation" as Hofmann proposed. It always afflicts the conscience in the old age. Thirdly, against Harnack, it is not only "outside of Christ" that it afflicts, but also includes "God's judging action in Christ." And Harnack's distinction of an essence as opposed to an office of the law is rejected as lending itself too easily to a return to *lex aeterna*. Fourthly, the Ritschlian concern for actuality is more effectively fulfilled by the eschatological framework of old and new than by opposing the theoretical to the practical. Likewise, a strong treatment of wrath fulfills this same concern in a way that an attempt to erase the law cannot. "The reality and actuality of the divine love is rather asserted most strongly when it is seen as the power that breaks in and overcomes wrath." In these and other ways Forde sees the proclamation of the eschatological Word strengthened by this dialectic.[287]

In this cacophony of voices about the role of law Forde marks two divergent trends that exacerbate the difficulty of conversation and understanding on atonement. First, there is a trajectory of voices ending in Barth that represents a narrowing of the concept of law. It began with orthodoxy where it was closely connected with natural law. Hofmann reduced it to a Jewish historical dispensation, and Ritschl subsumed it into the kingdom as the internal law of love. Barth, at the last, rejecting the idea of law apart from the Word, understood law solely to mean following the gospel from the eschatological moment of death and life— that alone. All else was not truly law.

By contrast, there is a trajectory of voices following Luther research that represents a broadening of the concept of law. Here the natural element has been expanded so that law comes to mean anything that threatens the human conscience, from the commandments to a rustling leaf to the life of Jesus itself. Here, it's not so much the content (essence) of law that is important, since any threat will do, but the function (office)—the accusing effect that will not be explained away. Where the Barthian line of development is a "particularization of the law" down to the precise moment of God's revealing, the Lutheran line is a "generalization," a broading as general as the accusing shape of human "existence in this age."[288]

The difference between the two approaches was cause for considerable confusion in the law-gospel debate of Forde's day. Forde looked to Luther research for "its contribution to the solution of the problem of law and the act character of revelation."[289] The coming subsection will offer a more precise presentation of Forde's own understanding of law in light of this history of thought. And the next section will examine Forde's understanding of that act character of revelation.

Forde's Own Approach to the Law

The closing chapters of Forde's *Law-Gospel Debate* summarized his concerns and conclusions in light of his extensive historical survey, but that didn't end the matter. The role of the law remained a primary concern for Forde the rest of his theological career, and his writings as a whole are a rich resource for understanding his position. Using the conclusions of his doctoral thesis, then, but supported by other statements at other times, we attempt to summarize Forde's teaching on the law.

A Functional Understanding

There is nothing theoretical about the concept of law in Forde's mind. The very idea is itself misleading, if not dangerous, as if law could be rationally defined and controlled. It is "much more immediate, dynamic and actual" than that, and so it must be understood functionally by what it does rather than materially by what it is or of what it consists. "[A]rising from the sum total of human experience in this age, up to and including the cross," it is "a voice demanding that we fulfill our humanity under God."[290] Again,

> "The law" in this sense is demand, that voice which "accuses," as the reformers put it, arising from anywhere and everywhere, insisting that we do our duty and fulfill our being. Anything which does that exercises the function or "office" of the law. Law is not a specifiable set of propositions, but is one way communication functions when we are alienated, estranged, and bound.[291]

Rejected here is orthodoxy's essential and eternal law, *lex aeterna*, the being and content of which can be analyzed and made the structure of a system where it remains nonfunctional. Rejected also is Hofmann's *heilsgeschichtlich* appraisal of law as an ethnic dispensation in history, interesting archeologically, as it were, but valid only for a bygone age. Rejected also is Ritschl's experiential approach where law is known only as a religious phenomenon within a community of believers. While Forde grants valid concerns for each of these approaches, he finds them all unwarranted and ultimately useless attempts theologically to render the law benign. Forde finds he must look to Barth, though with serious reservations, and to modern Luther research to get the expectant and active language he requires to describe the action of law. He wants to make room for a real and alien action by the law in the present.

For the law is "an existential category. It designates the manner in which God confronts sinful man in judgment."[292] It "accuses the sinner."[293] It "exposes sin."[294] It "attacks the lost."[295] It "terrifies the conscience."[296] It "always turns to accuse and to worm its way into the conscience."[297] Through the conscience it "makes us refugees and exiles with no place to rest."[298] Ultimately, it "kills and brings death, not life."[299] It *must* function to cut off every human attempt to create its own tomorrow."[300] It "has no compassion.[301] "Law authority works by coercion, pressure, fright, threat, and force."[302] The dynamic act character is evident in the piling up of verbs; the existential character is clear in the menace the verbs present to humankind.

It might be protested that these fearsome verbs may seem to relate primarily to what Luther called the second use of the law, the theological condemning use that drives the sinner to Christ, and neglect the first use, the civil ordering use that maintains creation till the eschaton. As a matter of fact, the uses of the law are a distinction that Forde knows in Luther but almost never raises as such. In one of the very rare mentions of it in the corpus, raised under some theological duress, he urges caution even as he brings it up. He thinks it may be too easily abused, wrongly assigning different spheres of operation, "the civil having to do with politics and the natural, perhaps, and the theological with 'religion' and the sacred." Such a separation "cannot be rigidly maintained in practice," he thinks.[303] And in any case, God is the one who uses the law, not humankind.[304] "The doctrine of the uses of the law is simply an attempt analytically to discern what law actually does."[305]

After all these qualifications, we may turn to what Forde prefers to call its "proper use,"[306] a "civil use" the fundamental concern of which is "the care of the social order" (see below, pp. 80-81 and 122-124). Its purpose is indeed positive, and the ordering it accomplishes is indeed beneficial. Nevertheless Forde prefers to state it negatively: "It sets limits to sinful and destructive behavior, usually by some sort of persuasion or coercion—ultimately by death itself."[307] He admits that more positive statements might be possible but he himself usually declines to do so for fear of antinomianist tendencies, lest the law be "tamed" and "its coercive and accusing function forgotten."[308] Thus it turns out that the accusing nature of the law is maintained for Forde, even under terms that remind of the traditional distinctions about the law's "use."

It may also be protested that the fearsome verbs may be applied by Forde more universally than is warranted, since they seem to relate more to the proud than to the broken. Is it really so that law must function uniformly upon humankind, even upon, in Forde's words, the "downtrodden and defeated who have lost a sense of self-worth"[309] in the same way that it does upon the "autonomous self"[310] in its pride? Forde often discusses the plight of the poor and oppressed—often discusses the value of the impulses by which his generally non-poor and non-oppressed hearers might care for them. Yet, it would appear that Forde rarely addresses them directly, possibly because the shape of his particular ministry did not give him occasion to do so. What would he have said to them? Would he have allowed the fearsome verbs access to the broken and defeated as well?

An article on the viability of Luther for today is one of the very rare occasions when he seems to address these questions:

> A sense of self-worth is always a subtle matter. It doesn't grow on trees, not even theological ones! From the perspective of the gospel, however, a sense of self-worth is lost because the self is in bondage to the causes and projects of this age which it cannot manage or surmount. The self is told that it ought to succeed, ought to find happiness, perhaps even deserves to make it, but cannot. Preachers of optimism attempt to buoy up the self in its attempts to make it according to the given systems but thereby simply leave the self in bondage and so end by just adding to the problem. The despair only goes underground. The self is like an addict who tries to save self-esteem by telling himself he can quit any time. Meanwhile he can't. He hides his habit under the cover of the 'official' optimism. But despair and loss of self-worth only become more secret. To regain a sense of self-worth one must be delivered from bondage. Theologically speaking, presumption and despair are manifestations of the same disease. The gospel which declares the death of the old and the rebirth of the new through faith by its very nature at once puts down the mighty from their seats and exalts them of low degree. It brings a new creation. The proclamation must be radical enough to do that.[311]

What is unusual, here, is that Forde seems to be allowing for a victimization of individuals by a culture that feeds them unattainable aspirations of success and holds them in bondage to these aspirations, even when they fail, under an optimistic and encouraging word. Yet, these people are still responsible, because, "like an addict," they buy into it. It seems that this understanding of victimization is not broad enough to include all of "them of low degree" that need to be considered: the enslaved, the plundered, the raped, the beaten. It might be argued that it is not aspirations that hold these in bondage, but the systems and powers and the mighty of this world. Or, alternatively, it might be argued that they, too, by their yearning to be free, express the same will to power that will, as Reinhold Niebuhr says, oppress in the same way when they have the chance. It is interesting that Forde connects despair and presumption here as manifestations of the "same disease." Presumably, that disease is the desire of the Old Adam or Eve to survive, or, in philosophical terms, the will of the autonomous self to power. It seems, then, that Forde finds all, high and low, susceptible to the same terrifying verbs of the law. It is a point to which we shall have to return.

Human Engagement with the Law

So, no friendly verbs are possible to describe the action of the law. A law with a bite like this is never a friend, but always and only a mortal enemy to a humankind seeking continuity and control: continuity with a sinful past and control over a self-willed future.[312] This is the humankind of "the fall," and Forde's understanding of human engagement with the law has everything to do with the way this is portrayed. Too often, it is the wrong portrait:

> We talk about ourselves as "fallen creatures." And by that we give the impression that our trouble is that we started out somewhere higher up on the way to God and have "fallen" to some lower place, so that now there is some kind of a gap that has to be made up somehow. Either we have to go to God, or he has to come to us and help us back up. . . . [I]t is into this gap that we pour all our theological nonsense, all our investments in piety. We engage ourselves not in *bearing fruit* befitting repentance, because that after all is only secondary. First we have to get to God."[313]

Here, our proper humanity is interpreted as some lost, higher level of being. The human task becomes to reascend to this level. This is variously understood, but, however so, Forde sees the law used by humans as a critical means of this reascent, "a scheme by which God supposedly rewards those who live up to it and punishes those who don't."[314] It becomes the basis for human striving, progress, and projects in the name of self-improvement:

> We try to arrange things in our systems in some way so that God can have his freedom and we can have ours too. We claim that we are free, responsible, moral and all those nice things and then we adjust God to our claims. But it is difficult to see how all this amounts in the end to [more than] holding God at arm's length so that he can't interfere too much in our affairs. . . . God is necessary to us as the final guarantee of our enterprises, but he can't be allowed to interfere.[315]

Here is the control—in the way humans manipulate the law to seek to keep their fate in their own hands and out of God's. Human resistance to a loss of control is fierce, and Forde loves to expose and review what he considers the standard human objections to it. In his chapter in *Christian Spirituality: Five Views of Sanctification*, he lists thirteen objections in one paragraph alone:

> Is it really true? Can one announce it just like that? No strings attached? Don't we have to be more careful about to whom we say such things? . . . But surely we have to do *something*, don't we? Don't we at least have to make our decision to accept? Isn't faith, after all, a condition? Or repentance? Isn't the idea of an unconditional promise terribly dangerous? Who will be good? Won't it lead perhaps to universalism, libertinism, license and sundry disasters? Don't we need to insist on sanctification to prevent the whole from collapsing into cheap grace? Doesn't the Bible follow the declaration of grace with certain exhortations and imperatives?[316]

"'Death rattle' questions," he calls them, because they resist the death of the old Being.[317] "All those boring questions," he says in another place, because they are so predictable in the resistant old Being.[318] Without the gospel humans are bound to diminish the law so as to control it and to bring it to heel.

The End of the Law

But the law by its active accusing nature still hounds the calculating sinner, and manipulation and performance are no ways to be free of the accusations. Law is "the only voice that will be heard as long as the sinner lives," and "[t]he only escape from it is death."[319] "The patient can't be cured on his or her own terms, but must die to be raised."[320] Or again, "If we are to be saved by [Christ], we must somehow be ready to receive what he comes to give. But that will take some dying."[321] By talk like this Forde means not a physical death of the body, but a death to all hoping and trying to attain the former humanness by one's own contribution or efforts. It is a despair of any self-help, any "positive synthesis" of human action with God's actions, any accomplishment through the law.[322] For Forde, calling it death is not a figure of speech. There is reality about this death: "The self does really come up against an end, a stone wall, through which it cannot see. Negation is not merely verbal, not a self-evident or automatic dialectical process. There is a real death at stake, and the outcome hangs in the balance."[323] We will consider the cause of this death that ends the law more carefully in the next section, but for the moment we mark Forde's insistence that nothing less than a real death will do.

What can be said now, however, is that, in any case, theology is certainly not able to bring about the end of the law, though it goes to great pains to that end. In effect, that is what the various positions Forde surveyed above attempted to do: "remove the threat of the law theoretically by means of systematic construction."[324] Theology as commonly practiced does this to spare humanity the direct attack of the law that is part of a sinner's encounter with God. "Most of modern theology," Forde argues in an article on evangelism, has been "a rather frantic attempt to avoid really encountering God."[325] It works hard to "tailor God to fit my convenience":

> As a consequence, theology becomes the quite abstract exercise of making God over to fit our alienation, our skepticism. Theology, you might say, becomes the business of holding God at arm's length so that he can't do any harm. . . . We have quite literally theologized him to death.[326]

But it doesn't work. Since it is, as shown before, an existential reality of human life, the law gets around human efforts to repress it and inevitably returns with a vengeance. "It only gets worse," is a favorite Forde motif usually used in this context.[327] "Thinking to lighten the load *for ourselves* and *by ourselves* through our own theological cleverness or reductionism we more often than not succeed only in making the burden heavier."[328] That is, the existential threat, momentarily thwarted by a systematic reorientation, finds another way to reassert itself with more virulence than ever.

Antinomianism is an historic move in the church "to get rid of, to change, to water down 'the law'" in an effort to diminish its impact on the sinner's life and to avoid the death.[329] Forde distinguishes two types, overt and covert. In the former the law is simply declared irrelevant after the gospel and an effort is made to remove it: a frontal approach. This is of less concern to Forde because he sees it growing out of a high regard for the gospel. Of much more concern to him is covert antinomianism which is dangerous because it sometimes unwittingly tries to change the law to reduce it to manageable proportions or to make it sound more like gospel. Forde sees it being done in a number of ways: distinguishing between ceremonial and moral law, postulating the third use, contextualizing and relativizing the law, seeing the Torah as a blessing for Israel, linguistic word change to make it sound like gospel, and metaphorical language to make it sound like parables.[330] In a classic Forde way, he concludes, "Antinomianism of all sorts succeeds only in making matters worse. The law does not go away by theological arrangement. It comes back, though unrecognized, in worse and more devastating form."[331] The end of the law must happen in another way.

Law from the Perspective of Faith

The question arises how Christian faith changes one's relationship to the law. While a deeper investigation of Forde's understanding of faith is reserved for the next section, several things need to be said here about the relation between faith and law.

It is widely proposed that the law ought to be a helpful guide for the faithful, a "third use" of the law by faith for the life of faith. If the strength of his insistence that death be the only end to the law is not clear enough, Forde's repeated denunciations of third use should make it clear that Forde has no time for it. The very existential force of the law's attack mitigates against it; its sharpness will never be friendly, but always dangerous for the sinner. In Forde's mind third use can only be "a watering-down and blunting of the impact of the law. Instead of ordering and attacking, law is supposed to become a rather gentle and innocuous guide."[332]

In fact, the idea has a number of problems. It threatens the cleanness of the law-gospel dialectic, confusing law with gospel; its history in orthodox thought links it to a *lex aeterna* structure with the implicit legalistic possibilities that suggests; it gives the impression that the believer has somehow already entered the eschaton and escaped from the real force of the law, a dangerous perspective given the old Adam and Eve still struggling for survival; it diminishes the effectiveness of the proper use of the law, discussed below; and it calls into question the law-gospel theological order.[333] The delicacy of Barth's attempts at taking law as a form of the gospel enduring after gospel has already been noted. To hold out for an eschatological encounter wherein the law is permitted to exert its proper function and force, Forde believes that the proclaimer must not compromise with notions of law that lead to lesser expectations.

If the faithful have no special privileges in the use of the law, neither do they have any advantage in understanding the *content* of the law, or even that "its formal possibilities of knowing" are improved. The law precedes faith, after all, and its accusations respect no ethnic or religious boundaries. The Christian faithful has no reason to think that an unbelieving neighbor might not have as helpful angles on the law as any believer in a given culture or situation. There's no room for superiority with respect to the law here; quite the contrary, Forde proposes that faith "drives home to [the believer] his solidarity with all mankind" in matters of the law.[334]

Though the law is not more congenial to faith through a third use, and though its content is not more obvious to faith than to nonfaith, it does appear that the function of the law is more clearly understood by faith. The law was generally known before faith, as we have seen, in something so small as the rustling of a leaf, but there was before the coming of the gospel no basis for putting law into its proper perspective. We have mentioned Forde's understanding of fallen humankind's perception of the law—granting it a role in regaining of lost status and of salvation itself. The burden that the law brings in that context is great, so crushingly great that it is modified as we have seen to make it bearable. And still the voice haunts humankind. A great deal changes when that role is firmly taken away from it. Forde says, "Only a faith that knows of [the law's] true end, both its goal and its cessation, will be able to let it stand just as it is and begin, at least, to gain some insight into the way God the Spirit puts the law to proper use."[335]

That is, if it is not looked to for salvation, it need not be dumbed down for the sake of human survival and can be permitted to stand in all its uncompromising force. "Where there is no forgiveness we have to take steps to absolve ourselves by reducing the law to managable proportions or by getting rid of it altogether," Forde writes.[336] But "[b]ecause we are justified by faith, there is neither any need for nor point to changing it, toning it down, indulging in casuistry, or erasing it."[337] "It is because Christ and Christ alone is the end that I can let the law stand *just as it is*."[338] The driving need to make it reasonable passes, and the integrity of the law for now, until the promised end, is established. Only such a faith is in a position to let law be law.

Another way of saying this is that only faith knows the distinction between law and gospel. In an early book review Forde writes, "It is only because of the gospel that law is finally recognized as *law* at all (because prior to the gospel men invariably try to make a gospel out of 'law.')"[339] Where gospel is defined as "the entire doctrine of Christ," it includes that which accuses therein, and gospel is confused with law even as Christ is preached. But where gospel is perceived by faith as the grace and comfort in the doctrine of Christ, then the difference between accusation and comfort becomes striking. "It is in . . . this glimpse of the goodness of God, that the *proper* distinction between law and gospel is made," Forde writes, and praises it as "the deepest experience of faith to arrive at a position where one can allow law to be law precisely because one has heard the gospel as gospel."[340]

The Proper Use of the Law

Where the force of the law need not be feared for its judgment, it can be applied to the preservation of human society. Forde calls this its proper use, in contrast with the illegitimate use by the sinner concerned to justify the self. "Proper use of the law comes through a faith which accepts Christ as the real and personal eschatological limit to one's existence." If it is known that Christ is the end of the law, then one doesn't need to strive for an ending oneself. "Faith opens up an entirely new sphere of possibility and action, *this* world bounded by the end. Here law can be viewed in a positive way." For the first time, in this civil use, "actions here and now could be judged as *good*."[341] Freed from other striving by his hope in Jesus Christ, "man can live in faith in this world and apply himself to being a proper steward of God's law."[342] It's a new prospect made possible by a faith that experienced the death of the old impossibility.

This proper use of the law is all about the care of the neighbor rather than the preservation of the self. The world around us becomes "God's other realm" where the law becomes "God's other way of fostering justice" for the time being. "[T]he proper use of the law in that realm" is "a purely *political* use, for the care of the neighbor and the world rather than a soteriological or perhaps even ideological use of the law."[343] It is not to save us, or to bring us into the assurance of the gospel. It is rather the "first use of the law" in Lutheran dogmatics, the "civil use," and "the fundamental concern of the civil use is the care of the social order." Here, in the daily world of economics and politics and human welfare, the law "sets limits to sinful and destructive behavior," and this for the sake of justice.[344]

This is so much the case that the law in its civil use is actually changeable. When justice for this world demands a revision of the law, it not only can but must be changed, because "[w]e are not called merely to be law-abiding, but to take care of this world, and law must be tailored to assist in that task,"[345] and Forde quotes Luther, "We must write our own decalogue to fit the times."[346] This is possible because of the broad Lutheran understanding of the law as an existential category. A follower of Barth with his narrowly-defined law as very specific revelation could not imagine it. But if the law properly understood serves to preserve society, then its articulation must do that. And since law is always an accusing phenomenon, it must be articulated attackingly so. The law must be brought to bear upon the sin that threatens society in new forms daily, not to accommodate it, as words like "contextualizing," "interpreting," "reinterpreting," "relativizing," "declaring obsolete," and so forth suggest.[347] It's not, after all, that the basic content of the law will change, but that it "may indeed be *applied* variously according to the situation."[348]

It is possible for the law to be abused in an overbearing way, too. Tyranny is a favorite word of Forde's to describe the consequences of this civil misuse of the law. Tyranny is what happens if "this use of the law is overextended, . . . if one begins to take the law into one's own hands in order to bring in one's own version of the kingdom."[349] It occurs when the eschatological limit of "human schemes and quests for justice" is forgotten and the worldly powers absolutize their relative success.[350] "Wherever law is used to tyrannize men for the sake of the state or for personal aggrandizement, wherever men are sacrificed for an ideology, wherever earthly power of any sort becomes an end in itself, there law is being misused . . . ."[351] This can also include the church, if it should claim more for herself than she should.[352] "Whenever [the law] oversteps its bounds, as it inevitably seems to do, tyranny is the result and someone is sacrificed."[353]

In his doctoral thesis Forde made the case that the church "has the responsibility of bearing witness to the proper use of the law."[354] Because of the eschatological act that brought it into being, the church understands the difference between law and gospel. It knows that the fate of the law in Christ exposes its eschatological limits in the world, limits that could not be expected to be clear to anyone else. Where the law is abused for tyranny,

> there the church has both warrant and responsibility to bear its witness. The church must bear witness to the fact that the law ultimately is God's, that *he* is the one who "uses" it, and that his use of the law has its End in the gospel. In the light of the gospel, the church is called to eternal vigilance over the use of the law.[355]

Forde notes here the "great possibilities" this vigilance portends for a positive engagement by the church in social justice, and referred to it repeatedly throughout his career.[356] Though it never became the focus of his message, and though he could be sharply critical of the way the church handled it, it appears that an awareness of the church's responsibility in assuring the proper use of the law on behalf of society never left his consciousness.

C. The Eschatological Act Character of the Revelation

In the last section we attempted to trace the main lines of Forde's understanding of the law, the difficulties it poses to the old Adam, and the consequences of its end for faith. While we alluded to the kind of faith that this might be and the way the end of the law happens for it, we reserved more careful treatment of it for this section. Here, using especially his Seventh Locus of *Church Dogmatics* but also other writings, we want to examine Forde's critique of the tradition of atonement theory and explore his own exposition of Luther's position on atonement. Then, by looking at how Forde understands it actually to happen and how it might actually be permitted to happen, we hope to make clear Forde's investment in the idea of the eschatological act character of the revelation.

Forde's Critique of Traditional Atonement Reflection
The Cross of Christ in the Scriptures

In reflecting on Christ's work in the Seventh Locus of *Church Dogmatics* Forde starts by reviewing the tradition of Christian reflection on atonement theory beginning with the story of Jesus itself. Jesus of Nazareth lived a life manifesting the love of God, but he ran "roughshod over the laws and traditions that keep earthly life in shape," and "[h]e had to go." It was an offensive death, but "the very folly and offense of it is the stuff from which the theology must start." And, in God's raising of Jesus from the dead, "God put his stamp of approval on the one humiliated and degraded. God ratified the action of the one who had the audacity to forgive sins."[357] One starts at the simple story.

Forde remarks that the earliest sources for the Gospels seem united on no particular interpretation of Jesus' work and fate. His death was understood as part of "the usual fate of God's prophets," and this reflected "the unrepentant, unbelieving, and guilty stance of God's people," but this was not unique to Jesus. True, there are references to the value of his death as a ransom such as in Mark 10:45, or to the "blood of the covenant, which is poured out for many" in the passion stories, or the passion predictions themselves, but these are usually considered the work of later redaction. But "even in their final form," the Synoptics "afford little explicit interpretation of Jesus' work."[358]

More significant is the implicit interpretation achieved at the redaction stage. The passion predictions attributed to Jesus show that the redactor saw it, not as "the result of mere human caprice," but as "part of the divine will, . . . played out according to the apocalpytic timetable, . . . part of the apocalyptic drama." In short, Jesus' life and death "have eschatological import." It was "an end-time event" and "one through which final judgment was exercised." In this judgment Jesus brings salvation, so that there is a "soteriological significance," as well. Mark made the cross central in this significance, and the other Gospel writers followed Mark so that "[t]he cross assumes a paramount position for interpreting the work of Jesus, the risen Christ."[359]

The Christian tradition has ever since wrestled with how this could be understood. Under the influence of Hellenistic Judaism there arose the idea, apparently very early, that Jesus' death was somehow "an atonement or expiation for sin." This is evident occasionally in the Synoptic passages mentioned above, the Johannine literaure, Romans and certain Pauline-dependent materials, and in a most sustained way in the Epistle to the Hebrews. While this train of thought was later used by Anselm and many in the West to speak of vicarious satisfaction, Scriptures never speak of God's being satisfied by Jesus' death as the object of his propitiating action. They do, however, speak of the cross as "for us" in a "substutionary" or "representative" sense. A substitutionary reading would have it mean "instead of us" along the lines of such Old Testament motifs as the ritual sacrifice or the suffering servant.[360] This understanding seems to have lacked currency in Jesus' own day, however, and current scholarship tends to interpret the "for us" passages "more in the sense of 'on our behalf,' 'for our good,' or 'for our benefit,' rather than 'instead of us.'"[361] Here the emphasis would be on the future rather than the past, not covering old mistakes so much as lifting up the example of Jesus for the days to come.

The apostle Paul seems to be the most centered on the cross and its offense as historical realities to be dealt with in his proclamation, not as elements of an underlying intellectual system of meaning like sacrifice or ransom. "Paul is . . . adamantly opposed to every attempt to avoid, stop short of, leap over, or detour around the cross in its reality and offensiveness." For him it is a "crisis, the eschatological crisis, the absolute end and the new beginning."[362] Precisely the cross is the catalyst for the occurrence of faith that transforms reality and makes all things new. There's a connection between cross and faith:

> When Paul wants, therefore, to describe the new flowing from the work of Christ [sic], he can simply say that faith has come, faith born out of the shame, offense, and weakness of the cross, where the love of God for all is hidden from the wise of this age, but revealed to those who believe.[363]

The fact that the way of the cross, for all its offensiveness, was vindicated by God through God's resurrection of Jesus from the dead is the "shattering fact" for Paul. In the faith thereby created comes the end of an old way of thinking and "a new beginning."[364] Here, with Paul, Forde ends his account of the work of Christ according to the scriptural tradition.

Law-Based Atonement Theory

Forde proposes that prior to Anselm in the eleventh century, knowledge, or *gnosis*, was the paradigm for understanding salvation. One was saved because one *knew* the eternal *logos* in a way superior to the way the gnostics speculated. He argues that the paradigm was unable to do justice to the life or death of Jesus, spiritualizing the history and rendering it secondary to "allegory or the appearance of the transcendent gnosis."[365]

Sensing a weakness in the *gnosis* approach, Christian theologians attempted to make the history itself significant. There were "various pictures of the atonement" including simple teaching images like "ransom paid to the devil" or "reconciliation through sacrifice," but in Forde's view, "solid dogmatic treatment" fell into three camps. Those who made of Jesus an example ended up with a "martyr theology" in the effort to follow Jesus to the death. Those who focused on the joining of the divine logos with the flesh emphasized a sacramental participation in the "God-man" and the reception of "the medicine of immortality." And those who, Irenaeus-like, "read a kind of inner logical order out of—or into!—the historical facts themselves" arrived at a "true gnosis." Forde sees a "split vision" of these efforts that continued to lift up the ideal behind the history. That is, they shifted from God's action in Christ to God's being. In a significant summary statement, that he repeats elsewhere, Forde writes, "When one systematizes the history, one sees through the scandal of the cross, and history is in fact transcended by gnosis."[366]

Anselm of Canterbury (1033-1109) is a watershed in the effort at articulation. By asking why the event of the cross had to happen, he became "the first to pose the soteriological question as a specific theme in itself" and to attempt to answer it through "a rationally deduced *a priori* necessity."[367] Forde's summary of Anselm's theory follows classic lines: In an effort to be coherent about the necessity of the God-man, Anselm pushes the question into God's own being, discerning there "a necessity laid on God in relation to the fallen creation." God's problem was how to deal with human disobedience. Faced with a debt of unfulfilled obedience in the past, sinful man is obliged not only to obey God in the present but make up for the past lack of obedience, an impossible situation. Simple forgiveness of this past lacuna is "not possible or fitting for God," since its arbitrariness would cancel justice and order and attack the distinction between sin and justice. The only solutions that preserve the honor of God are punishment for the offense or satisfaction of the debt. Punishment of the creature would end the problem unfavorably in the distruction of humankind, so God looks to satisfaction. Since the creature cannot do this, the God-man as a sinless one must. Only he can offer to God a satisfaction more than the sinner is obligated to give, and this he voluntarily does. Not needing the merit thereby gained for himself, he can give it to those for whom he became incarnate, providing those who receive it with salvation.[368]

Forde calls Anselm's work "an acute juridicizing of Christ's work."[369] Setting it in the legal framework of the courtroom, he removes sin from the realm of personal relationships and makes it a matter of judicial bookkeeping. Forde sees in this an effort to take the actual cross event seriously, and he appreciates that. Nevertheless, he charges that the questions remaining are formidable: God's mercy is drawn into question by the insistence on honor and God's freedom seems infringed upon since God cannot do otherwise. Forde concludes, "The result of the attempt to prove necessity is inevitably the elevation of justice over mercy."[370]

In response to its own doctrine of justification and the challenges of its day, Protestant orthodoxy of the seventeenth century codified Anselm's legalism with renewed vigor. We have already remarked on orthodoxy's "concept of law as a fixed, eternal way of salvation" where "an objective schema of commands and prohibitions" forms "a checklist of what must be done and not done to be saved." In fulfilling this checklist for us, "Christ as the substitute fulfills the law instead of us," an objective justification "outside of us."[371] The stringent requirements of God's penal code are satisfied in a scheme, not where satisfaction by

Christ replaces punishment for us as with Anselm, but where Christ's punishment *is* the satisfaction.

The Protestant formula has several advantages. First, its equation, as it were, of punishment and satisfaction means that the personal willingness of Christ (his freedom) to make satisfaction through the sacrifice is not contrasted quite so obviously with the systematic necessity of the punishment—simply, "Jesus suffers the punishment due and . . . since he is also divine, his suffering is of infinite worth." Punishment and merit are one action. Secondly, it recognized that "Christ's work was not only a passive suffering under the law and wrath," but also "an active doing of the law for us in his life." In so doing it included "his life as well as his death" in the saving deed, though that meant that the legalizing pall was cast there as well. Thirdly, it entered the ecumenical conversation of dogmatics, gracing Catholic as well as most Protestants with a common vocabulary concerning "the three-fold office of Christ" in which, as Prophet, High Priest, and King, Christ brings salvation through his life, death, and eternal rule.[372]

Love-Based Atonement Theory

Aspects of Anselm's theory have proven so abrasive over the years that it has been challenged a number of times, and Forde looks at some of these challenges. The first was Abelard of France (1079-1142) who in Anselm's own lifetime successfully raised embarrassing questions about God's mercy and freedom in the theory: why God's mercy must be dependent upon God's justice, whether forgiveness didn't precede Jesus' death, how a cruel death could in anyway be deemed not only acceptable, but reconciling by a merciful God, and so forth.[373] In this context Forde highlights the irony that an explanation that is supposed to help coming to God actually hinders it:

> Abelard shows clearly how the vicarious satisfaction doctrine recoils on God. It restricts the freedom of God and leads to a gruesome and forbidding picture of the deity. This remarkable outcome of the dogmatic enterprise must be noted carefully. The very attempts to construct a neat theory about the reconciliation to God leads to the exact opposite: It alienates from God by creating a forbidding picture of God.[374]

In the sixteenth century the Socinians continued Abelard's challenge on several points. God's freedom was not limited by God's rights. The idea of God's satisfaction of God seems absurd. So does the thought that sin might be somehow transferred from a guilty one to an innocent one. In any case the finite suffering of a single person would seem unable to balance the sins of the whole world.[375]

Forde argues that both protests ended up with "a complete moralization of Christ's work." Abelard's Christ was primarily one whose faithfulness unto death shows us, too, who are attached to him, how to be faithful to the death in love. And for the Socinians, just as Christ's suffering was rewarded by God in the resurrection, we, too, may hope for such a reward. In either case, for all their protest of Anselm, they follow him in finding theological meaning in a legalistic structure.[376]

Resistance to this structure in the name of God's love came to be a pattern of the liberal theology of the nineteenth century. Friedrich Schleiermacher (1768-1834) used the idea of the "actual historical community" to seek a resolution between vicarious satisfaction and moral influence:

This could be done, he thought, by seeing the redeeming activity of Christ as establishing a new life common to us and to him—original in him, new and derived in us. The historical activity of Jesus is not mere example, it is the establishment of a new corporate life in an actual historical community.[377]

Here Forde sees an earnest effort to get away from a soteriology based on a legal apparatus. The new life created in us is based not on satisfaction of the law, but on "the feeling of absolute dependence," on "the idea of God-consciousness." Sin is defined in terms of the impeding of this dependence and conciousness. Christ's work is defined in terms of Kantian-style, moral excellence—perfection, no less—which is communicated to us through his personal working in us. "The perfection radiating from him convicts of sin at the same time it draws under his influence." The cross itself adds little; it merely demonstrates how this "religious virtuoso" remained faithful to the end. In effect, "protected from the terror and disaster of his own death by [his knowledge of] the system," Jesus does not really die; he rather demonstrates his "absolutely potent God-consciousness."[378]

Albrecht Ritschl, as we have seen in the section on law, followed in Schleiermacher's emphasis upon the historical community, but rejected that which he considered to be too metaphysical—the "absolute dependence upon God" and "abstract monotheism." More insistently than Schleiermacher, Ritschl asserted that the experience of the community is the essence of atonement, because here, God's love is known:

Jesus reveals God as Father, the God of love to whom we can draw near with confidence. Wrath is replaced by love; wrath pertains only to life outside the kingdom. Christ draws people into this community of confidence and trust in the God of love who in creation and redemption has set the true *telos* for human existence: a kingdom where all are united to God in love in spite of all hindrances of a natural, physical, or metaphysical sort. One is saved from false conceptions of God by being drawn into the community of love by Jesus.[379]

As we have seen, Jesus' calling here is best understood in terms of the establishment of that community of love, and Jesus' death was simply faithfulness to his calling.

We have already remarked the futility of theological exploration of the connection between Christ's work and forgiveness in Ritschl's view. The experience of the communion itself is what is important, and Jesus acts in Schleiermacher fashion in his heroic but subjective influence through the community. Jesus' cry from the cross expresses his closeness to God, not the experience of God's wrath. Ritschl's system doesn't deal with wrath, Forde remarks. Like Schleiermacher's, it doesn't do eschatology at all. Its realization of scripture's *pro me* comes from a sense of affirmation from within rather than an electing declaration from without. Citing Iwand, Forde generalizes, "Any *pro me* apart from the radical *extra nos* (outside us) is mistaken and a fatal methodological error. All christological assertions are indeed *pro me* assertions, but also all *pro me* assertions must be christologically interpreted."[380] By their reduction of the cross to a demonstration and by their emphasis on Jesus' heroic influence, both Ritschl and Schleiermacher have in Forde's mind compromised the connection.

P. T. Forsyth (1848-1921) is Forde's example of a theologian who "took the tack of deepening the idea of love to include divine holiness." That is, it is not the liberals' sentimentalizing love, but a "*holy* love, a love shaped by morality and justice, a revulsion against sin."[381] God's identity is to be located in his holiness, and from this flows the faithfulness upon which the believer depends. A permeating awareness of this holiness was the basis for what Forsyth called "the moralization of dogma," where God's actions are understood in the context of his holiness and the moral order that they give creation. In particular, Christ's work is "the justification of God's holiness." Christ reflects perfect obedience to God's holy, unchangeable will. The reconciliation that God seeks is accomplished "only in such a way that divine holiness be perfectly maintained, confessed, and satisfied." When Christ is "'made to be sin for us' so that the treatment due sin actually falls on him," he accepts the judgment it draws. The critical thing here is not the dying with our sins, but Christ's acceptance of the judgment, thereby witnessing to the divine holiness confronted by sin. This witness is redemptive because it has "a sanctifying effect:" "The cross gives holiness its due, and when humans see this they are made new creatures, drawn into the actual kingdom of holiness in Christ." Here, the cross is technically not necessary for God to forgive repentant sinners; rather, it "brings the world to its knees before God," a subjective effect. But Forsyth argues it is also objective, because it is "representative," "creative of a new order," "surety for the fallen race," "creating the holiness that is lacking," actually altering the world and those who are in him, not by the forgiveness of sin but by the honoring of God's holiness.[382]

Forde sees Forsyth's system as similar to Ritschl's, except that "holiness tends to replace divine love as the decisive factor." That is, "what Jesus is obedient to is not love but the vision of the holiness of God which must be confessed among humankind." The connection with God's love is that "*God* does it. God sends Jesus to do this for us and for the world and to reconcile us to himself."[383] One might say that love stands behind the system, but it is the witness to holiness that drives it.

Emil Brunner (1889-1966) also spoke of a love beyond "mere sentimentality," a "holy love." But this could not be just general revelation, just a good idea. It needed to be the holy love of "a *special* revelation, a special act of deliverance on the part of the God who is holy love." It had to be eschatological, "a revelation that actually changes the situation." Atonement must be so closely associated with this kind of revelation that they become the same thing. While Forde appreciates this contribution, he is concerned that "a theological distinction," that between general and special revelation, "is once again made to do the work of the eschatology itself and threatens therefore even to displace the cross and resurrection."[384]

Victory Atonement Theory

The victory motif of Gustav Aulèn (1879-1977) seemed at first poised to break the theological stalemate between supporters of the objectively inclined vicarious satisfaction approach and the more subjectively inclined approach based on divine love. The motif pursued the picture of a contest of cosmic forces in which God faces off against the demonic and wins. Its context is dualistic, but not metaphysically so, portraying the "radical opposition between the forces of evil and the creator God, even though evil does not have eternal existence." Its dramatic action is continuous, God acting positively towards the demonic defeat throughout rather than actively first and passively later as in Anselm's theory. It is an ancient motif; "essential features of this view are to be found in Irenaeus' theology of 'recapitulation.'"[385] And it takes the resurrection seriously, unlike the other theories which tend to be able to neglect it without losing their coherency.[386]

But this theory, too, has its problems, Forde points out. It has the same difficulty as the other theories in explaining the necessity of Christ's death: why could God not have won his victory in some other way? It finds itself explaining the action in terms of a demonic opponent principle, much as vicarious satisfaction used a legal principle, only with defeat rather than satisfaction as the goal. As with many narratives, the logic is not tight, so that Aulèn argues that it is actually not an atonement theory at all, but rather "a dramatic picture defying systematization." Yet he makes systematic analogies based on it as if it were indeed coherent.[387] And most seriously of all, Forde fears that this theory, like the others, by its systematization, obscures the visceral impact of the cross itself:

> In sum, the dramatic-dualistic imagery can also misdirect our attention away from the Jesus who was crucified for us under Pontius Pilate to a mythic figure who was paying a ransom to the devil and deceiving the devil at the same time. Why the cross? . . . The "victorious" Jesus can all too easily be portrayed as one who does not finally die."

Forde regrets that the net effect of the atonement debates is a relativizing one. "Carved up in bits and pieces atonement becomes the plaything of human 'need'—the modern equivalent of 'making a wax nose' out of scripture."[388] The theories become pictures, facets of reality, all useful, none exhaustive, human experiments in thought.[389] The effort of understanding, at least partially, in a variety of ways, overwhelms the expectation that God is actually at work here, and Golgotha risks becoming "a precious jewel one examines at leisure"[390] rather than the judging event it is.

Forde's Own Approach to the Atonement
The Paradigm of the Accident

In contradistinction to the atonement conversation outlined above, Forde pursues the direction Luther charted in seeking to be a "theologian of the cross." By these words Luther meant letting the cross of Christ be the scandal it is and do the work its scandal does. The systems for understanding atonement reviewed by Forde, by contrast, all fit the cross into some scheme or other that, in effect, seeks to reduce the scandal and "put roses on the cross."[391] Each in its own way found a way for the theologian of glory to call the cross good when what is needed is the clarity to see it for the darkness it is. Forde seeks rather to start here in the apparent nihilism before the resurrection and call a thing what it is: evil and tragedy and despair.

In a 1979 article for *dialog*, revised for his 1984 Locus VII in *Christian Dogmatics*, Forde lays out a fresh approach to the atonement that he hopes might not "revert to our old protective games."[392] He begins with "one of the most offensive images in all of scripture," the Hebrews 13.11-13 comparison of Jesus' suffering outside the gate with the garbage heap outside the gate where the leftover refuse from the priestly sacrifices were burned. Here, at the conclusion of Hebrews, the cross is considered not within the "in-house" system of temple atonement by ritual sacrifices, but with reference to the polluted place of meaninglessness and curse, "the real altar." Here the important thing is not "the conceptual scheme," but "a real event, which radically questions and puts any given scheme in its place even if it draws upon it."[383]

To stay here and experience the scandal of the cross, Forde proposes using the paradigm of the accident. How might it affect us if we consider the cross in terms of an accident? Three advantages of accident language pose themselves immediately. 1) Since accidents "just happen," subsequent events are spontaneously rearranged in response to them. 2) Since accidents are opaque, effort is not wasted in plumbing their meaning. 3) Since accidents are "up front," in one's face, the luxury of determining their relevancy and whether to risk exposure to them is absent. They are simply there.[394] These are characteristics Forde would like to make part of any conceptualization of atonement.

The accident story Forde proposes is as follows: "A child is playing in the street. A truck is bearing down upon the child. A man casts himself in front of the truck, saves the child, but is killed himself in the process. Accident."[395]

Here it surely may be said that the man offered himself as a sacrifice: "He gave his life for another." But no more than that is required. It doesn't need to be further systematized in a metaphysical or cultic understanding answering irrelevant questions like "to whom." All that can be said has been said. It was simply an accident.

But it cannot as surely be said that we are "the more or less innocent child playing in the street" who was saved from death by the victim's sacrifice. Forde proposes that would be too close to the victory motif and its tendency to treat sin too lightly. There are scriptures neglected by the other atonement theories that lay the blame for the crucifixion not on the law, nor on the evil one, but on human rejection.[396] What if *we* were the drivers of the truck, he asks, and the child were not us but our neighbor:

> Suddenly there is someone who casts himself in our unheeding way and is splattered against the front of our machine. If the atonement is to be seen as actual event, the cross must have that kind of direct, immediate, shocking impact. . . . It cannot be brought back "inside the camp . . . ." It remains outside, a permanent offense.[397]

Here, clearly, "we did it," a realization missing from most atonement theorizing. "Jesus throws himself in *our* path. And just so does he 'bear our sins in his body.' There is no strange metaphysical transference, it is actual and public fact."[398]

The Role of the Resurrection

But, Forde asks, how can the historical story be universalized so that it impacts us today without the use of some system? How can it be preserved from becoming "an idea, a frozen 'universal'"?[399] The answer is the resurrection of Christ, yet another aspect generally neglected by the various atonement theories.

This resurrection for Forde must be real, and Forde preaches it with a historical vigor:

"He is not here; see the place where they laid him!" Who ever heard of such a thing? Gone! Escaped! Flown the coop! Not where he is supposed to be—safely dead and laid to rest like everyone else. Not here! Where can he be? Where is he gone?[400]

Or, again, in another sermon:

He who was one of us is not here. He has escaped. We didn't get him after all and we shall never get him now. He has fulfilled all righteousness; He is the end of the law. There is, indeed, some cause for trembling, astonishment, and fear in that. For now he is no longer at our disposal, not available for our choosing, not catchable in any of our news.[401]

In a 1967 review of Gerhard Ebeling's *Theology and Proclamation*, Forde criticizes Ebeling's approach which "evaporates the resurrection by denying it any sort of facticity and making it instead merely a Christological affirmation." Mythification of the resurrection invites one into a theology of glory of the ancient mystics where "the *resignatio* leads more or less automatically to the participation in the divine,"[402] and the eschatological tension in faith is lost. "Theology will have to find better ways of handling the problem of the resurrection than this," Forde avers. If he grants Ebeling's point that perhaps history is not the best way to handle it, he is loath to leave the matter adrift of history:

[W]e do the *theologia crucis* no service by speaking of the resurrection simply as an historical event. But this means only that we shall have to find better ways to speak of it as an *eschatological* event, as the *end* of history, which cannot fail to leave its mark on history and to qualify the way in which we look at history.[403]

We need to be able "to speak of the resurrection as God's act based in his freedom for which we can hope, and for which Jesus has given us the right to hope;" otherwise Jesus becomes a mere example to follow.[404] It appears that for Forde the deciding point of view for talk about resurrection is not the historical in a historical continuum, but rather, perhaps we may say, the historical in an eschatological event that ends history. This is another way of saying that while Forde is not unconcerned about how the resurrection is described, he is much more concerned that the resurrection *do* what it needs to *do* to the one who hears of it.

How is this to be understood? This resurrection of Christ has a vindicating effect for his work. The one "universally rejected" was raised from the dead and doesn't go away. The resurrection prevents the crucifixion from fading in our memories as only an unfortunate event that simply had to take place for the sake of the higher good of our "religious, social, juridicial, and political systems." The encounter with the risen Lord signals that God stands on the side of the crucified against us and our sinful systems. We are thereby judged by God. Our systems have to go. Christ's word of forgiveness in the face of the systems is what is validated and vindicated by God's raising him.[405] Paradoxically, the presence of the risen Lord is thus law and death to the old Adam:

> Within the confines of our little affairs, there was nothing to be done. He had to die. . . . He didn't fit. He had to go. Of course we didn't *intend* to kill the Son of God, but how were we to know? Accident. But God vindicates him—the one we rejected. The tables are turned. Now it is not the little misdeeds or mistakes but the entire enterprise we are engaged in that is called into question—the grim inertia of all our religious, social, juridicial and political systems which cannot swerve aside no matter who gets crushed. Accidents will happen, you know! But he is raised. Then we are judged—in the sight of God.[406]

But not only is it judgment; it is also grace. "The one splattered against the front of our machine returns to say 'Shalom!'"[407] "The presence that judges us also offers us reconciliation, and this, directly, without any intervening metaphysical structure. Since Christ has been raised, there is no more sin, death, or curse, for those in faith are grasped by the resurrection. . . . The believer has everything from Him who has triumphed over death."[408] Or again, "Jesus comes to bring something *entirely new*, something quite beyond all our attempts to enlist him in some cause or other. Put most simply, he comes *to heal*, to bring salvation . . . ."[409] We will return to this in the next section.

As the fact that Christ is risen dawns, Forde proposes, faith sees revelation in the "accident." It is to faith as if God himself placed him in our path, for here God can "get through to us to express who he himself is." Here we can come to realize that there "was no room for him in *our* enterprises," so God made room by Christ's dying at our hands. "God slips into the world in the crack of the accident, softly, lightly, but with the ultimate authority of absolute grace. There he can be *for* us."[410]

Forde sees the resurrection as central in the event of death and new life, yet without detouring around the cross: "His death is our death; his resurrection is our life—grasped in faith."[411] These are not to be understood in isolation from each other, it seems to me, as if they were two events. Christ's death would not be our death without the vindication of Christ's resurrection as discussed above. And Christ's resurrection would not be new life for us without the impact of the cross. Rather they come upon us with the force of one event. "If this event, the 'accident,' breaks into our lives with the impact we have been trying to describe then it will involve a full stop and a new beginning; a death of the old and a resurrection of the new in faith."[412] We will return to this idea of death and new life in the coming subsection on the eschatological event itself.

The Direction of the Action

It is true that we, viewed as drivers of the truck, become actors in the accident story and the force of that fact accounts for some of the critical work Forde is interested in. Nevertheless, Forde would see the primary action in the story as *God's* action upon *us*, because God is the one who, through his word of forgiveness in Christ, placed himself in our way. This primarily divine initiative and action is a significant reversal of the usual direction in the atonement theories, a reversal Forde traces back to Luther.

Although there are examples aplenty of Luther's use of atonement language in what seems like the classic Anselmian tradition cited above, and in fact some scholars like Althaus take Luther's approach to be Anselmian, Forde notes that the evidence is mixed. As a matter of fact, "Luther often and explicitly attacks the idea of satisfaction as at best too weak and at worst an abomination and the source of all error."[413] While some have attributed the resulting tension to theological ineptness (or richness!), Forde proposes that Luther has made a breakthrough. Might it be that Luther has "somehow transcended the differences [in the atonement theories] so as to point the way to something quite different, enabling him freely to use the various terms without contradiction"?[414]

Forde thinks so—in the idea of reversal. For Luther the change is as basic as the direction of action. Atonement is not Godward, as in Anselm, as if something had to be offered to God, but humanward in God's gift of salvation to us:

> The question is not whether there is blood precious enough to pay God, or even the devil, but whether God has acted decisively to win us. The question is whether God can actually give himself in such a way as to save us. For God is not the problem, we are.[415]

By the incarnation, by placing himself in a position to do the reconciling deed with all the crucifying risks it involved, God in Christ made the humanward address.

Luther gives shape to the divine action with the idea of a "happy exchange" of natures: "Christ, through his actual coming, his cross and resurrection, takes away our sinful and lost nature and gives us his sinless and righteous nature." This, indeed, is the whole point of Christ's truly human nature: the taking upon himself of the sin which resides in our nature. The happy exchange can take place

> . . . only if Christ actually takes our place, takes our sinful nature, 'has and bears' our sins. He cannot just take human nature; He must take sinful human nature and come under the curse of the wrath of God. To give us his life he must take our death.[416]

Only so can "the law and sin attack him and damn him" as he becomes "the object of the just and terrifying onslaught of the curse."[417] The cry of dereliction shows that "Christ feels himself in his conscience to be cursed by God and really and truly enters into eternal damnation from God the Father for us." It is not a calculated "active offering" to God by one who is above it. It is all a "passive suffering" with "nothing to do under wrath, death, and so on but to suffer it and to die" as a sinful human being, really, with the outcome hanging in the balance.[418] Such is the initiative that God takes in Christ.

Actualization of the Atoning Action

Forde appreciates this "happy exchange" formula from the tradition, and affirms that the revolutionary reversal of direction in the idea marks "a great advance." Nevertheless,

> If Luther is to be criticized, it will have to be that he did not go, or perhaps was not able in his context to go, far enough. The weight of the tradition was still too heavy. . . . [T]here are still vestiges of something quasi-physical about such an exchange. Natures and sins seem to be shifted around too much like quantities. . . . If anything, Luther's formulations still have too much of the traditional metaphysical and mythological freight.[419]

Forde would take Luther's insight and actualize it. It "cannot be an abstract metaphysical transaction. . . . If it is to be a 'happy' exchange, our hearts must be captured by it,"[420] and this, actually, through an living proclamation with a real effect upon the listening self in the present. This constitutes a "radically different perception of our relationship to Christ,"[421] not a mental image cast upon an artificial structure, but an event that is experienced in the life of the hearer.

It makes atonement talk quite a down-to-earth affair. The theologian's conversation must be turned away from the speculative, about what might happen to God's wrath "up there" when the payment is made, and towards the actual, about what really happens in the listener, "down here" as it were, when God's action impacts him or her:

> [W]rath cannot be placated in the abstract by heavenly transactions between Jesus and God. Nothing is accomplished for us by that. God's wrath against us is placated only when God's self-giving makes us his own, when God succeeds in creating faith, love, and hope.[422]

The question, then, becomes an actual one: "how God can succeed in giving himself to us so as actually to take away our sin, to destroy the barrier between us and God."[423]

The answer, too, if it is to be "viable today," needs to be an actual one, not a metaphysical one, however venerable. It will not do to say that we have "an unambiguously spotless Lamb, a sinless Christ to offer God as a substitutionary payment" according to some mythical scheme of transcendent debt and its satisfaction. Such payment would be "abstract"—an artificial and imaginary construction unrelated to present existential reality of sin and alienation from God. No, we must say that "Christ must be one who has and bears our sins; he must actually become a curse for us to set us free from the curse of the law."[424] Our sins must actually pass over to him and he must actually die with them, a sinner, accursed. Forde insists on real action, here, in each human life in the present.

A New Approach to the Communicatio Idiomatum

In this actualization, a corresponding change occurs in the way we speak concerning Christ's divine nature. For Luther Christ's truly divine nature is evident for Luther in the victory that follows the crucifixion. Only after taking the cross of Christ so seriously is it meaningful to add, "Yet in the resurrection the divine power overcomes even death, and thus conquers, kills, devours, destroys, buries, and abolishes death, sin, the curse, the law, and all the tyrants."[425] This victory was real, "not simply a foregone conclusion."[426] Its very reality points to the divine nature of Christ, since nothing but divine power could have won such a victory.

We have already observed above that Forde, while taking the history of the resurrection with all seriousness, interpretes its force in a different way. Rather than victory language, Forde uses vindication language as the primary idiom. This permits him to discuss the impact of the resurrection without resorting to poetic imagery or metaphysical concepts. Because of the resurrection, in Forde's view, the cross is not an isolated event that can be put away and forgotten, but rather God's judgment in the present upon us who caused Jesus' death and Christ's subsequent approach to us in the present to make peace.

These observations provoke fresh thought by Forde on the natures of Christ. In his 1990 lecture on Karl Barth and Lutheran Christology, Forde offers that the force of the doctrine of the *communication idomatum genus majestaticum* is not metaphysical, "that human nature is somehow infinitely extended in space and time abstractly," but that rather,

> . . . as even Luther liked to insist, [God] has all time and space present to himself; that as a human story, [the story of Jesus] does God to us always and everywhere as it is proclaimed; that God pours himself out into this story, does himself, conquers all distance, and thus communicates divine attributes to it.[427]

The doctrine of Christ is redefined here, not on the basis of being, but on the basis of doing. It is not so much a Chacedonian reflection about how the human and the divine natures are present in one life of Christ, but rather how Jesus, through his suffering at our hands, experiencing the result of our sins upon him, and by being raised from a death we brought upon him, reveals who God is for us by what he does to us in the present. This is for Forde a fruit of Christ's work for us proclaimed. He thinks it is a much more fruitful approach for faith than efforts to understand the ontology of Christ's person:

> Without this hermeneutical turn [of using the words so as to *do* the event to the hearer] attention will likely be concentrated on the *identity* and *being* of the 'reconciler' rather than on his work. This results again in a strong pull away from history as well as the tendency to express the soteriological significance of Jesus in terms of participation in his *being* rather than in what he does to and for us.[428]

In a 1992 exchange with James Nestingen, Forde writes that he considers this a potentially significant christological contribution that should be considered carefully. As a move "from the more static language of 'being' which tends just to get in the way by setting itself up as the means of mediation, to a more direct language of doing through proclamation,"[429] he hoped that it would serve a renewed theology of the cross and the "doing" of it to us.

The Eschatological Event Itself

Forde comes at the eschatological event itself from several angles. Here we will trace his understanding of it by considering his work on justification by faith, on death and new life, and on the shape of faith when it occurs.

Justification by Faith

Definition

Justification by faith is not a uniquely Lutheran, or even Protestant article, Forde remarks as he begins a 1988 article for *dialog* journal. It is, after all, a biblical concept— raw data for the tradition, as it were—and so justification as such actually attracts a kind of broad consensus as a self-evident Christian teaching. At this level "[e]ven Pelagius considered himself a champion of justification by faith," Forde points out.[430]

What is this doctrine that, on a formal level, is so widely accepted? In *A New Handbook of Christian Theology* (1990), Forde offers a definition:

> Justification is a primary biblical and dogmatic concept denoting the action of God in reestablishing a proper relationship with fallen creation. This is accomplished through the cross and resurrection of Jesus Christ and its subsequent proclamation. Justification means, therefore, that through Christ sinners set against God are "set right" with God, the source of all justice and the final judge of all.[431]

Justification uses a "moral or legal metaphor"[432] to understand this set-right-ness. The righteousness is not earned by our uprightness, but reckoned for Christ's sake. It is "forensic:"[433] it comes as a courtroom decree that declares a legal justice where no moral or personal justice may be presumed. "Justification language means being addressed by an absolutely unconditional affirmation and promise,"[434] as through a judge's decree. Not only so, by the addition of the *sola* Luther made explicit what seemed to him evident and implicit: that justification is not by faith in such a way that it is by faith and by other ways at the same time. Justification by faith is clearly justification by faith *alone*.

A Resisted Doctrine

In light of Forde's aversion to building a soteriology around a legal structure however understood and his movement to death-and-new-life language, we might expect him to devalue this kind of talk, but this is not the case. Multiple affirmations of it in a 1999 response to the *Joint Declaration on the Doctrine of Justification*, cosigned by Forde, are evidence to the contrary. It is "the fundamental doctrine of the Lutheran Church." It is "the 'basic reality' for all of Christian life." "[J]ustification by faith alone is *the* criterion by which all is to be judged." "As Luther was wont to claim, get the doctrine of justification wrong, you got it *all* wrong."[435] In fact, as in Forde's 1988 *dialog* article, "there is no point in perpetuating the church at all, however united it might be, where that article is not its aim and goal."[436] Legal and forensic etymology notwithstanding, it has a "radical eschatological nature"[437] that actually "brings with it a break in continuity with existing systems of law and progress . . . ."[438] Forde sees this epitomized in a passage from the Smalcald Articles that is, he says, "just about my favorite statement in the Book of Concord": "This then, is the thunderbolt by means of which God with one blow destroys both open sinners and false saints. He allows no one to justify himself."[439] It's the "creative act of God which ends all previous schemes and begins something absolutely new."[440]

> It is . . . a flat-out pronouncement of acquittal *for Jesus'* sake, who died and rose for us. As precisely that kind of unconditional decree it puts the axe to the root of the hegemony of legal language. Paradoxically, if not perversely, it seems to attack and destroy the very language on which it depends.[441]

Here the link in Forde's mind between the justification and the death-and-new-life languages is already evident.

Thus, it is not Forde who resists the forensic language of justification, but a whole spectrum of others—all formal adherents of the doctrine, to be sure. These opponents range from modern Roman Catholic dialogue partners who would speak of it as "an" and not "the" *articulus stantis et cadentis ecclesiae*[442] to "virtually all theologies opposed to Lutheran orthodoxy—pietist, biblicist, moralist liberal, even some strands of neo-orthodoxy."[443] They do this, usually inadvertently, not because of legal language but because of the dazzling sharpness of the *sola*—"by faith alone." They do it because "the unconditional pronouncement for Jesus' sake" is "a word which reduces to nothing all the deeds of the flesh at the same time as it creates, calls into being, the new life of faith in the Spirit."[444] Something about this unconditional disregard for human efforts in matters relating to salvation is sufficiently alarming that it garners a broad defensive response, Forde remarks. It's a retreat from the *sola* behind a façade of support for justification, and the uniformity of this retreat draws into question the uniformity of the support. Perhaps the support was just the old Adam's lip service after all.

An Electing God

The other side of the human impotence in the *sola* is the divine omnipotence. If *sola* means that no human act has the slightest effect in justification, then God's act has complete effect. "It is an absolutely unconditional decree, a divine decision, indeed an *election*, a sentence handed down by the judge with whom all power resides."[445] God may do as he pleases "with no apologies," and Forde often and in many ways emphasizes the scandal of it all. For example, in a 1998 baccalaureate sermon, of all moments, he preaches:

> The God who meets Moses and tries to kill him [Ex 4:21-26] brooks no explanation, and neither asks for nor needs any. With Moses we need to realize that this is all God's affair, and that God will do as he pleases and that we had best stand in awe.[446]

We are faced with what Forde in another sermon calls an electing God, "a God who is running the show. . . . It's all true, you know," he continues. "God, is God; the place where the buck stops. The God of scripture is an electing God."[447] And again in a 1990 *dialog* article: "The God of the Bible is an electing God. Nothing is so offensive to us and our hopes to control our own destiny as that."[448] Nevertheless, with justification's *sola* around, the idea is not only biblical; it is necessary for our salvation, never clear without a God who can assure it. As Forde says, "[T]he doctrine of predestination [is] a doctrine vital to soteriology."[449]

This predestination is for Forde tightly connected with the historic cross of Christ. This contrasts with the more common, Barthian version where the divine decision in the heavenly realms before all time renders the cross a mere implementation, perhaps even an illustrative postscript for the divine letter already written.[450] The justification Forde has in mind takes the cross with utter seriousness. For Forde the cross of history is the simultaneously justifying and electing event in which God is discovered to be a gracious God.

But such a purely historical victory puts "tremendous pressure on the doctrine of God."[451] If we cannot, like Barth, propose that the matter was solved in a prehistoric decision in God's heart, but must insist, with Luther, that that happens only at the historic cross of Christ, it is almost as if there were two Gods, a God of wrath and a God of grace. For God understood apart from a prehistoric atoning decision is ambiguous, even dangerous, even satanic, stewarding apparently random suffering and death in wrath:

> God is hidden to fallen creatures who will not have him as a God of mercy. By the same token, God is timeless and immutable abstraction . . . to those who will not have God clothed in the concrete event—a sheer terrifying abstraction that merges indistinguishably into Satan, the accuser and destroyer. And one should make no mistake about it. That is the way God *is* outside of Jesus Christ.[452]

Luther calls this God *deus absconditus*, as opposed to the *deus revelatus* in Christ, and apart from some prehistoric mechanism for "gracifying" God, it is not clear outside of Christ that they are even the same. Forde says Barth is not unusual in seeking theologically to "remove the threat," "lift the burden," "penetrate the mask," "bring God to heel." He also says it doesn't work. "Only the revealed God can save us from the hidden God"—only Jesus Christ and him crucified.[453]

Forde addresses the question of God's wrath and God's mercy in terms of absence and presence. If God's wrath is a sign of alienation from God and God's absence from us, then the answer is a drawing nigh and God's presence with us. If human terror before the *deus absconditus* comes from the "naked abstraction," God must clothe himself in "concrete event."[454] Jesus is all about presence in concrete event: "in the manger; at his mother's breasts; on the cross; appearing beyond the grave. God present for us is the only solution to the absent God. Faith in the present God alone will save. There is no other way."[455]

The Bondage of the Human Will

This consideration of the electing God, so important for the doctrine of justification by faith alone, makes the resistance to the doctrine noted above all the more comprehensible. As fallen creatures in the old realm, we find we do not like God to be God over us. The thought is terribly offensive.[456] We find we would rather be in control ourselves; we would rather be God. In Luther's words, "The natural man . . . wants himself to be God, and God not to be."[457] This is less a dogmatic assertion than it is a daily human experience. Luther calls it the bondage of the will; Forde at the end of his life tried "the captivation of the will."[458] The term describes "the inescapable reaction of the alienated sinner to the very idea of God, . . . a confession of our disaffection, our recoil from God's 'godness,' from God's being above us."[459] In our recoil we vigorously assert that, nevertheless, we *are* free, however qualified that freedom might be. Surely, we may do as we want. "And that is just the trouble!" Forde replies. "We are bound to do what we want."[460]

> [T]he root assertion on bondage is that we do not have to do with force. We are not dragged by the scruff of the neck into doing something we really do not want to do. That is what we begin to see when the light of the gospel dawns. We do what we want. And that is just the trouble. We are bound to do what we want. That is why there is no such thing, really, as a free will.[461]

And again,

> The very assertion of freedom—the only thing I can do—is the bondage. The bondage is not something I am forced into. It is a bondage of *the will*. I do what I want. That is just the problem. I *can* do only what *I* want. I cannot do anything else— because *I do not want to*. It is not that I have no will. Indeed, I do. I am not a puppet. The question is of the way things are: of what in fact I do will.[462]

Every religious thing we as sinful alienated beings think or do this side of the grave is subject to this bondage. We "aspirants for heaven, straining to achieve the prize," are determined save ourselves by our projects, and only need God's help "to a greater or lesser degree, depending on how conservative or liberal we are. It is a sham. The one thing we cannot stand about God is that he is God."[463] And we are bound to feel so.

No, not humans, but God, Forde affirms, the God of scriptures, is free. The God revealed in scriptures is a God who may choose, if he will, to be a God of mercy instead of a God of wrath, who may choose a cross in order to be that God of mercy, who may by that cross choose a people to be his own. On this basis the critical doctrine of justification by faith alone is established.

Death and New Life

The Missing Metaphor

At the beginning of his 1982 book *Justification by Faith—A Matter of Death and Life,* Forde à la Barth likens the ecclesiastical, doctrinal, and confessional "remains" of the Reformation—including the doctrine of justification by faith alone itself—to a bomb crater. It is clear from the crater that there was once a great explosion in the church, and it is interesting and useful to investigate the remains. But that is not enough:

> [W]e have to get beyond the research as such and somehow to recapture the explosion. . . . [W]e have to get beyond the research as such and put it to work in trying to grasp the explosion itself, recapture it so that it can be set off again and again in the life of the church. What once shook everything to the roots can do so again today.[464]

Academic understanding may be valuable in its own way, but, clearly, beyond that, Forde has an evangelical passion for the rekindling of the world-shattering force of the gospel message in the church today. He is looking for "the fire, the passion" in those who hold the Reformation statements of faith, and too often he doesn't find it.[465] Something is missing.

The problem is not the Augsburg Confession itself with its doctrine of justification by faith alone—Forde affirms it as a faithful witness to the faith of the Reformation. What's there is fine. The problem is what is *not* there: "at least half of the Reformation story is missing. One of the vital ingredients that makes the Christian 'power' so explosive has been left out or forgotten." That ingredient is "death and new life in the crucified and risen Christ," a second metaphor necessary to stand alongside the "moral or legal" metaphor of justification by faith in order to render the message potent. For "[t]he legal metaphor cannot stand alone."[466] This may be considered a central theme not only of this particular book, but of Forde's theological posture generally:

> My basic thesis is that the explosive character of the Reformation's confessional message can come to light once again if the death-life languge is recovered and restored to its proper place. When such language and *the reality it represents* is revived and made complementary to the legal language, the theological explosion can take place once again.[467]

Forde's goal is thus not a more adequate theological structure for its own sake; he is aiming at nothing less than the reality of a renewed Reformation explosion in the church, and he thinks he has his hand on the key to that reality in the death-life language.

The language itself Pauline. It comes from two passages in particular: Romans 6:1-11 and Galatians 2:16b-21. In these verses, when people protest the cheapness of grace-and-faith talk, as if morality would be lost by it, Paul answers with strong death and resurrection talk: Our death with Christ is already a fact, he says, and that has freed us from sin for new life with Christ.

> [J]ust at the crucial point, the point where justification by faith has destroyed the whole legal scheme and we are getting terribly nervous and beginning to back down, dampen the explosive message, put rods in the reactor, Paul steams ahead and shifts almost imperceptibly to death-resurrection language without even breaking stride.[468]

The legal language allowed the possibility of a misguided hope of continuity and fulfillment under the law: perhaps, after all, it could be the old self as old self that is the one justified in God's eyes. Now, the introduction of death language cuts off the hope of such a prospect, and the resurrection language offers hope on a radically new basis. It constitutes the end of old striving that was our life and an expectation vested in God's new initiative in Christ.

Death

Forde's writings are filled with references to this death. They occur in the context of sinners bound by the law we have already discussed. We have seen that this is a functional understanding in which the old nature in us is bound to hear the accusing action of the law in every rustling leaf, bound to hear only law there and everywhere, bound to hear it as long as the sinner lives.[469] Faced with the accusations of the law at every turn, our anxiety grows. "We are perishing, that becomes the first principle of our thinking, and the conviction that this is so is accompanied by the certainty that we are surrounded by enemies, human, natural, political, even spiritual . . . and that all these forces are bent on our extinction." We do what we need to do not to die. We develop "the wisdom of survival," and "we fight to survive."[470]

> We set up neat systems and we think we have always got the final word, we think that we have got God, or at least maybe the world all figured out. We have a system, a plan whereby we think that we can reach our goal . . . . And we tell ourselves that if only people would live up to it, everything will be fine . . . . But that, of course is the problem.[471]

Or, again,

We, however, possessing all our faculties, . . . must embark on greater quests, we must search for meaning and truth, we must talk of glory and majesty, of eternity and transcendence, we must seek out the infinite. . . . [F]or ours is a noble task.[472]

Once again, we seek to enter into "positive synthesis" with God,[473] we doing the best we can, God helping us out as we need it. When the law still continues to accuse despite all our manipulations, we seek a marvellous array of ways of damping it or silencing it theologically, as we have seen in the last section.

It is in this situation that death is required. That death is first of all, as we have seen, the death of the Crucified. God had no way to get through to people with their own systems, plans, quests, and goals than to be killed by them as the one who got in the way, as Forde proposed in the image of the accident. Only the awareness of the murder—the sight of the shed blood—has a chance of bringing a sobering, a loss of hope in the systems, plans, quests, and goals constructed under the law, an awakening to their murderous futility, a death to the life lived in chasing them. "His death becomes our death. He dies 'for us.'"[474] Note well: "Jesus' death is not a substitution for our death; it *is* our death."[475]

What is that death? . . . When the word of forgiveness comes to a world bent on its own survival systems, that world is suddenly robbed of its whole reason for being. The death is suddenly having nothing to do. If Jesus lives after we have killed him, then we have died. To die means to be reduced to nothing, to be able to do nothing but wait. . . . We are thrown out of the stream that usually protects us. If Jesus lives, then we as old beings are through.[476]

Once again, this death is a real death and no mere figure of speech. In his 1982 *Justification by Faith*, Forde cites Luther from *Bondage of the Will*:

Baptism thus signifies two things—death and resurrection, *that is, full and complete justification*. . . . This death and resurrection we call the new creation, regeneration, and spiritual birth. *This should not be understood only allegorically as the death of sin and the life of grace*, as many understand it, *but as actual death and resurrection*. For baptism is not a false sign.[477]

Forde argues that Luther should be read here to see a priority in the death-resurrection language. Both are evident in baptism, but the death and new life are "the primary reality." It is, in fact, "more than a metaphor, a symbol, an allegory, for something else, some 'profound transformation' of some sort or other, some 'rebirth' which means only 'giving in' at last to law and 'conscience.' It is the reality itself."[478]

In a 1985 exchange of articles between Ted Peters and Forde, Peters proposed that the death in Christ is not real, but just metaphorical. That is, the individual believer does not really physically die, but only experiences a disillusionment that can be compared to death. Forde's reply is quite sharp:

> About all I have to say to that is that such objections are best not raised lest one's unbelief become too apparent. Peters persistently obfuscates the matter by confusing the real death of which I speak with what he calls 'literal' death, and consequently mangles the eschatology of the locus."[479]

Forde counters, here, that allegorizing that happens in the eschatological moment of faith is tantamont to minimizing it, to charging that it is not real, to making it penultimate. His response must be understood to mean that, although not necessarily physical (though it probably will have physical manifestations), the dying of the eschatological moment is incomparably more real and more significant than physical death itself.

New Life

Newness is an often used concept for Forde. Whether in preaching or in writing, examples abound. "God is doing this new thing every day! For the gospel is the only really new idea there is. It is new every day and it must be received as something new or not at all," he proclaims in one sermon.[480] "There is a different world, a new one, just around the corner, just on the other side of all your calculations, your scheming, your pious or impious games. You are forgiven for all that—*all* of it."[481] "[T]he newness consists in the fact that what has happened is something completely new, the breaking in of the new order of things altogether, the coming of the new age . . . ," he writes in an article entitled "The Newness of the New Testament" for *Word & World*.[482] And, in the article on human sexuality, "all we have to offer finally is not loopholes, but absolution and newness of life. If that is not the end of our conversation, I fear it has no end at all."[483]

Forde likes the concept of newness because it expresses the kind of complete discontinuity with the old order that he would have us expect from an eschatological event. He prefers newness as the paradigm of life in Christ in contrast with a number of weaker words such as conversion, transformation, reorientation, movement, progress, or growth. These words he is able to use in a strained sort of way, but only with considerable qualification, and some not at all later in his ministry.

Conversion talk, for example, does have a place, Forde affirms, and he is, as a matter of fact, not unconcerned that it happen. In the 1973 article criticizing the Key 73 evangelism effort, he asks, "How can there be an 'evangelism' not concerned with convincing – even converting (it does have a place, after all, in spite of misuse!) others?"[484] In an undated sermon on Matthew 3:1-10, more likely to be earlier than later in his career, he asserts, "Repentance means change. The Greek word for it means change of mind, but in the NT much more is involved than just change of mind. It means a whole reorientation of one's life, a turning about, what we sometimes refer to as conversion,"[485] again a guardedly positive use reflecting pastoral concern for its occurrence. In a late-career videotaped lecture, "The End of Theology," the term has definitely taken on negative overtones because of its connection of the old and the new:

> [In Christian gnosis] [s]alvation is shifted from the eschatological hope to some sort of ontological continuity. [W]e come to look upon ourselves as continuously existing beings to whom only minor or what Aristotle would call 'accidental' changes occur. Fall is an accidental change . . . and consequently so is redemption. 'Conversion' we call it, or perhaps some kind of 'transformation." Always some continuity must be preserved, usually in the understanding of free will. It can't be completely lost in the fall, and so it must be considered partly operative in conversion, and then of course come into full and glorious display in sanctification. And so on and so on.[486]

No, if the word is to be used at all, it must submit to redefinition in the context of the wider death and new life language, as he writes in a posthumously published article: "[T]here is no way this authority [of the gospel] can be imposed upon me by a power[,] move, force, or even argument. To be grasped by it is to be reborn or converted to it. That rebirth of conversion is a death to the old and a resurrection to the new."[487]

Likewise, with the rather rarely used concept of transformation, its use withers away before the need for the more radical dialectic. In an early sermon typed on the back of St. Olaf stationary, Forde was indeed able to speak of transformation of life:

> What is presented to us in the New Testament is a radical transformation of life, a whole new level of being. It is a new life, not a new set of rules. It is a step upward to a new kind of existence, a kind of existence in which morality is transcended, in which we no longer live to serve the self or its rules, but in Christ to serve all men. It is a level of existence in which one desires for himself no advantage, in which he should be ready to give everything, perhaps even his morality if need be. It is a level of existence in which we are set free to play the whole game, to spend, literally to spend ourselves, for the sake of others.[488]

But notice how, at every opportunity, the concept is radicalized, with new life already being used as a defining concept. Even so, Forde was apparently not satisfied with it, because he effectively left off using the term for most of his ministry. When it reappears in 1992 it occurs in a decidedly negative light in an article on invocation of the saints: "What takes place for the sinner is not, therefore, a transformation as such, but a death and a resurrection in Christ."[489] Five years later he mentions it again in a dark correlation with conversion: "some kind of transformation."[490] And in a posthumously published article we see it once more: If the word doesn't kill and make alive, "then either the old being reads it as an excuse for license or the death of which it speaks becomes (à la Marcus Borg) just a metaphor for 'spiritual transformation.'" The term is simply too weak to express the vigorous eschatological discontinuity necessary.

Likewise movement, progress, or growth are counterproductive words for Forde in talking about the eschatological event. In the first place they are hard to reconcile temporally with the event-like imputation of justification:

> If justification comes at the beginning of the movement, it is a legal fiction. One is declared something one is not. If on the other hand it comes at the end of the movement, it is superfluous. If one has made the movement, one need not be declared just, one *is* so. . . .[491]

In the second place they are dependent upon morality based on the law for their normal functioning. "Since righteousness comes by divine imputation only and is synonymous with forgiveness of sin, all thinking in terms of law and movement from vice to virtue is simply impossible."[492] As with conversion and transformation, Forde can conceive of a guarded use of these words, but it will have to be defined in light of the eschatological break. After all, the progress is not ours but the kingdom's:

> That is why it is a growth *in grace*, not a growth in our own virtue or morality. The progress, if one can call it that, is that we are being shaped more and more by the totality of the grace coming to us. The progress is due to the steady invasion of the new. That means that we are being taken more and more off our own hands, more and more away from self, and getting used to the idea of being saved by the grace of God alone.[493]

The new being in Christ, then, is, in Forde's mind, to be considered eschatologically distinct from the old Adam. Without reviewing the meaning of the death of the old being and its aspirations considered above, we may say that the new is not to be compared quantitatively with the old. In particular, the new cannot be said to be more moral or less sinful than the old, since the justification was made on other grounds. "The *simul iustus et peccator* is . . . a conclusion drawn from the divine action, the divine imputation and forgiveness," not "a conclusion drawn from a bad conscience under the legal system."[494] This is not only so for the present, but the new may not be expected to be getting morally any better in the future this side of the eschaton, either. The new life of the new being is simply not a progressive affair in terms of the old struggle for morality:

> Rather each moment, each encounter with the shock of divine holiness, could only be at once both beginning and end, start and finish. . . . Anyone who has ever been overwhelmed by the magnitude of the divine imputation knows that it is always a matter of beginning again.[495]

Instead, the life of the new being must be understood in terms of the eschatological event, the encounter. If sanctification may be taken as the shaping of the new life, then it is helpful to consider Forde's definition of sanctification:

> Sanctification is what happens when the unconditional and eschatological event of justification breaks into one's life. Sanctification is what happens when one acts out of faith in the gift of total and complete righteousness, when one simply takes God at God's word. Faith issues in good works—that is, neither in laxity and vice, nor in rigorism and the lust to be a virtuous person—done for the sake of the other.[496]

Attention is turned away from the old schemes of achievement and towards the declarations of God's imputed righteousness. Life lived apart from the need to pursue the old schemes will have time to serve the neighbor.

Faith

We have already seen in Forde's treatment of the law how major theological effort has been invested in ending the reign of the law. When this happens, when the law is "disposed of theoretically," then faith is seen as "man's 'understanding' how this has taken place." In this scenerio "the paradigm for faith is the act of recognition."[497] This is a kind of gnosticism where esoteric knowledge saves one. Forde's move from this static legal framework to a dynamic death-and-new-life event perspective invites a fresh concept of faith consistent with the eschatological experience.

Forde offers several connected approaches to faith, all with the eschatological event much in mind. Perhaps his favorite approach is to connect it with death: "Faith in Christ is a death."[498] "For simply to believe is to share in his death."[499] "To believe is precisely to be crucified."[500] "[T]he faith we preach, if it is anything at all, is dying—dying [to] the world to live to God."[501] "The death [to the old, the 'universal truths of reason,' the abstractions, the law] is simply faith."[502] To use another word, "[Luther] said that true faith was born out of despair—when man finally comes to that point where he despairs of himself, of his religion, of everything he has to offer God—then he is at that point where God can do something with him."[503] In this approach we see faith in Christ described as the experience of the decisive break with the past, described negatively as a state that ends one's attentions to an old way of life, and described passively as something that happens to one exactly as death happens.[504] From observations of frequency of occurrence alone, it seems clear that this negative and passive description is the first and most insistent thing that Forde needs to say about faith, perhaps the thing that he most fears won't get said. Faith is the experience of a death.

But it seems just as clear that Forde is not talking about any old death—the death from which there is no rising, for instance.[505] When he speaks of faith, he has a particular death in mind—the death that is followed by new life in Christ:

> To look on that death, . . . to see that all the old business with God is over, is to die and to be made new, to be made something entirely different, to begin a new kind of life. That is what it means, I think, to believe—to die that death so that new life can arise.[506]

There's a critical connection, even an organic unity, for faith in Christ between its experience of the death and its experience of the life. It means that it "is not just a death; it is also the hope of resurrection, a being grasped by a new life of love, hope, and care."[507] Therefore,

> There is nothing to do now but to die to the old and be raised with [Christ] to the new—that is what it means to believe. For simply to believe is to share in his death, it is to put the old Adam to death and thus to be made one with him as he is one with the Father. That is atonement.[508]

To define faith in such manner is to give priority to the eschatological event and to speak of faith in terms of the event. It's an event that gives new life after the death, and faith is the experience, not only of the death, but of that new life as well.

Forde also considers faith in terms of the way in which the eschatological event comes to pass—that is, through the creative Word that formed it. For instance, "[f]aith here, of course, is not simply the acceptance of doctrine but the trust engendered by that word from God."[509] Or, "[f]aith is the state of being grasped and captivated in the Spirit by the proclamation of what God has done in Jesus."[510] Or, "[t]o hear and believe the divine imputation is to become a sinner justified by faith."[511] Or, "the Word of God authenticates itself in grasping and claiming believers through faith,"[512] and such a Word "is not believed because the Church attests it but because one senses it is God's word."[513] It is "the joy in God and the divine creation evoked by the proclamation of Jesus Christ."[514] Perhaps we may say that for Forde faith is the shape of the encounter—being grasped, trusting, claimed, joyous—with the will of God through God's word when it kills and makes alive. To say it is the *fruit* of the encounter is less useful because it might seem to reduce the encounter to history, not Forde's idea of the actuality of the event.

In particular, faith is the response elicited by the unconditional promise of God. This promise is the gracious God's promise of mercy, as Luther said, making the thought of his wrath false for those who believe it.[515] The promise is simultaneously the decree of the electing God "who plans to have his way with us at last."[516] The two aspects are connected: the unconditional promise of the gospel is "guaranteed by the immutable will of God."[517] The promise of this gracious and electing God comes to us in the "absolutely unconditional affirmation and promise" of justification language.[518] It is not a generic promise, such as love for all people, but a specific and concrete promise such as is offered to each person in the moment of absolution and the sacraments.[519] "Faith is being grasped by that promise, by that future."[520]

It is important for Forde that these promises come to us as from without, so that they are clearly distinguished from subjectivity and human reason, so that their very externality may elicit trust.[521] For instance, in an an *Interpretation* article, "Something to Believe: A Theological Perspective on Infant Baptism," he considers baptism, before which faith is "the trust that this 'external' event, this washing with water, is the act of the electing God. It is the belief that this happening, at a specific place and time, is the will of God 'for me.'"[522] The externality of the promise in the sacrament connects with a belief in divine necessity—that all things happen according to the divine will—to give a sense in the recipient of the promise that the promise was divinely intended for the recipient and in that moment for the recipient alone, thus engendering trust in the truth of the promise as offered to the recipient. In Forde's words, "faith is precisely the trust called forth by such occurrences of grace in the 'external' world as baptism in the confidence that they reveal the will of almighty God 'for you' according to his Word and promise."[523]

Although not a primary idiom of his in describing the Christian believer, Forde can join others in speaking of faith in terms of a "relationship" to God through his promise. Forde was one of six Luther Seminary faculty who signed *A Call for Discussion of the "Joint Declaration on the Doctrine of Justification."* Here, faith is "a 'right' or 'just' relationship to God which is awakened by God's eschatological promise."[524] This relationship "*is* faith—i.e., trust—in God and God's Word: crediting God as truthful." It can be seen that the "relationship" here is entirely defined by the posture of the believer towards the word of promise. This is not surprising, since some of the characteristics of faith just noted as response to the Word (p. 109) —terms like "being grasped, trusting, claimed, joyous"—are in fact characteristics of a relationship. By not choosing relationship as his primary definition, Forde appears to prefer considering faith in terms of its source in God rather than its result in humankind, yet not exclusively so. There seems to be room for definitions that make reference to human responses.

At rare moments Forde indicates what such faith might look like by proposing, almost doxologically, examples of confessions or prayers of faith. In his sermon on John 10:22-30, for example, he reviews the petulant objections of the old Adam resisting death and the preacher's insistent affirmation of the gospel through them all. At the conclusion, he writes, "The answer, you see, is yes, yes, yes, always yes, until at last we die of it as old beings and finally begin to whisper Amen, Amen, so be it. Lord. Can you hear it?"[525] This prayer evidences all the aspects of Forde's approach to faith that we have considered thus far. There is the death of old resistance to an end of controlling cooperation with God. There is new life in the positive acquiescence to God's way and the acknowledgment of God as Lord. It is all shaped by an encounter in the present with God's insistent external word of unconditional promise: "yes, yes, yes, always yes." The word of forgiveness itself creates a relationship of trust that affirms God's "yes" as true. It is, to use the bondage-of-the-will language discussed above, "to surrender control of one's own destiny."[526] It is, to risk language that resembles contemporary "evangelical" language, faith that "accepts Christ as the real and personal eschatological limit to one's existence."[527] To return to Forde's preferred idiom, this faith "cannot be simply a metaphor for transformation or a change of heart. There must be a real savior, a real death, indeed, one in which we are involved and implicated, i.e., put to death, and consequently a real resurrection from the dead."[528]

Proclamation as the Vehicle of the Event

The Nature of Proclamation

Since Forde is so interested in the death-and-life *boulversement* of an actual eschatological event rather than mere assent to a static body of knowledge, he invests careful attention to the way the event might be understood to be brought actually to happen in the world today. Just as event is distinguished from knowledge, so what Forde calls "proclamation" is to be distinguished from teaching. It's the difference between "talk about God" and "God speaking to us."[529] Teaching, talk about God, is "indispensible for proclamation," of course; but it "must be such that it makes room for and clears the way for the proclamation." That is often not the case in modern preaching, in Forde's view. Teaching is mistaken for proclamation on such a massive scale, in fact, that "[t]he most dangerous enemy of proclamation is teaching."[530]

In a 1990 *dialog* article Forde gives the following careful definition of proclamation: "In its essential or pardigmatic form proclamation is present-tense, first-to-second-person, unconditional promise, authorized by Jesus Christ according to the Scriptures."[531] The definition has four parts. First, it is present tense. It is not, as is so much preaching, concerned about teaching or explanation of past realities, but is concerned with the actual state of things right now. It is concerned to "do again in the present what the text authorizes the preacher to do."[532] Secondly, it is first-to-second-person. It doesn't talk about what some third person might be up to, or what others have done; it is an address from "I" to "you," as if God's own self is actually speaking to the listener. Thirdly, it is unconditional promise. We've discussed this in some detail in the last section, but it bears repeating: in proclamation the merciful and electing God decrees the future that God in his mercy wills for us at last, not generically, but specifically and concretely for the one who hears it in order that it might be believed by that one.[533] This distinguishes it from moral schemes or historical reflection or theological constructions from the pulpit.

And finally, the proclamation is "authorized by Jesus Christ according to the Scriptures." Sometimes, and maybe primarily, Forde seems to be thinking of the commission implicit in the vindication of Christ's ministry by the Father when he raised him from the dead.[534] It is as if the resurrection of Jesus bears its own authorization for all witnesses of it, and in a special public way for those ordained by the community of witnesses to the resurrection. But other times, Forde refers to Jesus' specific words of commission, as in his sermon "You Are My Witnesses" based on Luke 24:44-49:

> Before Jesus, in the Old Testament especially, everyone knew that God was loving and forgiving in general. But Jesus came to say that word *in particular*. He had the nerve to say it: "I forgive you your sins." The result was that he got killed for it . . . . But God raised him up. God put his stamp of approval on Jesus' preaching of forgiveness in particular. And it is he, the risen Lord who speaks the words of our text to us, telling us and giving us the unheard-of authority to go and say the same thing for God.[535]

Ministry is the result. It is simply "the concrete carrying out of the divine election now authorized and commissioned by the crucified and risen Lord Jesus," or again, it is "obedient service to the revealing of the mystery of God's election through Jesus Christ in a fallen world." [536]

The Function of Proclamation

Nevertheless, though useful in making distinctions, there is something static and ontological about these definitions. Perhaps more useful for our purposes is the functional definition of his 1999 article, "The Word That Kills and Makes Alive," already cited:

[P]roclamation should be the attempt to *do the text to the hearers, to do once again in the living present what the text records as having been done of old.* Proclamation is doing once again what the biblical text authorizes and mandates us to do together.[537]

The thought of "doing the text" to his listeners is a formulation of a theme that was a favorite idea of Forde's: that the proclamation would "do" something to the listener. As early as his doctoral thesis in the '60s, he was concerned about what was necessary to insure the "act character of revelation."[538] In 1980 he was interested in a "particular use of language" where words "*do* what they *say.*" He wanted a language that was "performative" with words that "do not just talk *about* or *describe* salvation, they actually give it."[539] 1981 may be the first time he uses the phrase "doing the text:" "We must develop an understanding of preaching which involves what might be called *doing* the text to the hearers, not just *explaining* it."[540] In 1984 he admonished preachers, "[T]ake what the text authorizes you to do and do it to the hearers."[541]

In his 1990 book *Theology Is for Proclamation* he elaborates:

Just as in Christology we were impelled to move from the language of being to the language of doing, so also the proclamation must move from explaining to doing the text. The proclaimer should attempt to do once again in the living present what the text once did and so authorizes doing again.[542]

Here the task of the preacher is not primarily exegetical reconstruction of the ancient meaning, nor is it interpretive translation of that meaning to make it relevant for the present. Rather, the preacher is "to inquire what the text did to the hearers and prepare to do that again."[543] It is as if the text gives the preacher this authorization by the account of what once happened. By a self-conscious move on the part of the preacher,[544] he or she serves, attends to, enables a present event as understood to be God's saving will in the present because it was God's saving will at the time of the text.

Forde calls this doing the text "an adaptation of the old law-gospel method."[545] That is, it basically requires a recognition by the preacher of the force of the textual words as potentially killing and life-giving and a willingness to allow them to have their way. Seeing these possibilities of law and gospel in the text, the preacher needs courage and wisdom: courage ("guts") to believe that this is the moment for which the killing and life-giving words are intended, and wisdom to get out of the way. "[I]n spite of our reluctance and timidity, it isn't some herculean task we are being asked to do. It has all been done. All we have to do is say it; just let the bird fly!"[546]

Forde gives some fairly specific suggestions for preachers seeking to do just that. He invites the preacher to watch for the offense in the text and start there "instead of some cute story." When one has dwelt on the offense intently enough for it actually to do its offensive task to the hearers, then "one can subsequently turn it over as life-giving Spirit," looking at God's vindicating work in it such a way that the hearers are given life. In such manner the preacher allows the proclamation to "be a Word of the cross," once again, not just to offer "lots of talk about the cross" but to "cut in upon our lives to end the old and begin the new."[547]

The Call to Faith

In the eschatological drive of Forde's actual preaching, he commonly though not always brings the death-dealing and life-giving action to focus in a kairotic moment when he hopes or expects that faith might be born. These are moments when the old way stands discredited, when the new life has been portrayed as compellingly real, and when the hearer is invited into the new reality in a move that, if the word has done its work, will seem by this point utterly self-evident. The moments are characterized by the overwhelming promise of the new reality, by Forde's own passion for the goodness of that reality, by shortness of phrase and incompleteness of grammar, and by imperatives and invitations to enter that are steeped in the gladness of the moment. It would appear that these moments are a homiletical phenomenon, not required by the theological basis for Forde's preaching, but a recurring practical feature in its service. For the sake of this discussion I name them "calls to faith," though the dangers of misunderstanding in identifying and isolating them as such is real. There are dozens of examples from all parts of Forde's career.[548] Here we will consider three.

In an earlier sermon on Matthew 22:1-14, actually dated September 26, 1966, and preached in St. Olaf chapel, Forde's last paragraph includes these words:

> For the Kingdom of heaven is like a great feast! Everything is prepared; everything is ready! And the only response to such an invitation can be to celebrate! To enter into it wholeheartedly and with joy. That is what we are called upon to [do] when we come here to worship: to celebrate . . . So above all, come prepared to celebrate![549]

In considering the man without a wedding garment Forde portrays the kingdom of heaven as such a celebratory event that guests will *want* to come to it, not one that they should feel obligated to attend. After the passionate exclamation-point-studded portrayal of this feast prepared, Forde uses yet another exclamation point to emphasize our invitation, as well, to enter in. The closing imperative is used to create expectancy. Certainly the response hoped for is evident, not a matter for consideration or discussion. To the faith that is anticipated here, the eschaton has broken into the present and is at hand.

A second example is his sermon on John 1:18 and 5:19, typed on the typewriter that he often used in his early to mid-career. His last paragraph reads:

> And now we meet today around his table to receive what he has done. For he is doing today what he did of old, doing what he sees the Father doing, giving himself absolutely for you. For he says: here I am for you. Think on that, and tremble! And, repent and believe![550]

In this communion setting Forde is making strong statements about Jesus as the "doing of God among us," now "doing today what he did of old," "giving himself absolutely for you." In a first person address at the conclusion of it all, Jesus offers himself to the hearer: "Here I am." The immensity of the news and the offering brings passion to Forde's imperatives as he once again uses exclamation points to invite the listener to "think on that" and "tremble," and then "repent" and "believe." The possibility of the creation of a responding faith makes it an eschatological moment.

Yet a third example from later in his ministry comes from the last paragraph of Forde's sermon on Matthew 8:28-34, written on a word processor:

> What shall we do with Jesus? What is left to do but repent? For he comes to save us from our sins and to cast out the demons. What is left but to begin to stammer, somehow, *Maranatha*, come Lord Jesus.[551]

This paragraph follows an account of the "strange" and "marvelous" persistence of Jesus despite our resistance. "The more we try to get rid of him the more tightly he closes in with majestic constancy." Even after we crucified him, he rises from the dead, announces our shalom, promises another comforter, and says he will never leave us. In the context of this persistence our repentance is literally the only remaining possibility, and Forde calls us to it: "What is left to do but repent?" It's not a choice; it's more like the last remaining option. This is one of the rare moments we noted earlier when Forde risks proposing what that repentance might look like in a prayer of faith: "What is left but to begin to stammer, somehow, *Maranatha*, come Lord Jesus. Amen." That prayer of faith marks the arrival of the ultimately significant moment of the death and new life of the hearer.

These moments are surely not "preaching faith." This is the mistake of the past: "exhorting, describing, cajoling, or threatening." "Preaching faith is like trying to make flowers grow by pulling on them.

The very thing one wants to promise is killed." The moments are rather "arousing faith to be grasped by its heritage."[552] I take Forde to mean by this so letting the killing and enlivening word do its work that faith happens and that the "heritage" of unconditional justification in Jesus' name actually grasps the hearer in the living present.

A Sacramental Shape for the Proclamation

The idea of proclamation as a present-tense-doing of the text to the hearers helps one understand how the sacraments may be considered a form of proclamation. In this case the elements of the sacraments actually impact upon the bodies of the receivers with the unconditional promise. Forde sees complete accord between Word and sacraments: "It must be apparent that the spoken and the visible Word complement each other perfectly, supporting and reinforcing each other so that together they save us."[553] The task of proclamation by word is precisely the task of proclamation by baptism and the Lord's supper. There's no room for competition.

Thus, what has been said of the force and goal of proclamation as an eschatological act may also be said of the sacraments as well. In terms of death and new life, "If sacraments . . . leave the old subject intact we could not . . . put such confidence in sacraments. Either we must preach them so they kill the old Adam and Eve or we better forget them."[554] "Baptism," for instance, "signals the end of old beings incurably turned inward upon themselves, who use even their own religiosity as the last line of defense."[555] One hears such defense in the common protests against the grace in baptism. "Why should supposedly stalwart believers in the unmerited grace of God get so upset when that unmerited grace is given freely?" It is "a permanent offense"[556] that such lowly elements might be bearers of such a great promise apart from our striving:

> The elements themselves participate in the attack on our pride . . . . It is, to sum up, a great and mighty offense that I, great religious being that I am, should be reduced to depending for my eternal salvation on eating a bit of bread and drinking a sip of wine. . . . [T]he elements help to bring the words down to earth.[557]

Here the religious old Adam is being put to death at the moment free and unmerited forgiveness of sins is offered.

Likewise, in terms of faith, "the sacraments save us because they work on us to create faith just as the audible word does. They give us something to believe . . . . The sacrament, that is, works to create the faith which receives it."[558] What Forde calls the "indubitable alienness" of the elements does this because they are so outwardly evident that the promise joined to them becomes evident as well, and faith thereby engendered cannot be confused with an inward or ambiguous piety. As such the sacraments become bearers of that "new eschatological reality that comes *extra nos* and breaks in upon us bringing new being to faith, the death of the old and the life of the new."[559]

Reserve before God's Proclamatory Act

Something about this analysis of proclamation as a vehicle for the eschatological act moment may suggest that the proclaimer thereby gains control over the action. This would be to misunderstand Forde. Indeed, this is precisely the temptation in preaching that Forde seeks to resist. "[I]f . . . preaching steps in to *domesticate* the alien, to attempt merely to return sovereignty to our threatened subjectivity so as to leave us in control, then all is lost."[560] At all costs the action—if there is any at all— must not be seen as the preacher's; the action itself is and remains God's. "It is what God does."[561] Making the preacher in control reduces God to one idea among others to be juggled for effect. "No, my friends, God is not an idea. He is one who acts."[562]

A stronger sense of Forde's affirmation of God's initiative in the proclamation comes through his assertion of reserve for the proclaimer. The action of a sermon is never sure. He reveals his heart when he says, in his sharp critique of the Key 73 evangelism campaign, "Of course we all hope that somehow the Holy Spirit can make use of our efforts, how- ever distorted, wherever the name of Christ is preached." Yet the fact that the Spirit is not bound by our work at proclamation is clear. In his 1976 discussion of the origin of repentance in the Phillipist controversy, he writes,

> [I]f the distinction [between law and gospel] on the deepest level is a functional one, how can the preacher or the theologian ultimately control that? Does this not finally make the distinction meaningless as far as the preacher is concerned and leave it ultimately in the hands of another, the Holy Spirit, who alone can preside over what the words do?[563]

Forde is not advocating abandoning the distinction or turning the prob- lem over to the Holy Spirit without further preacherly effort. But he is advocating that the proclaimer must stand respectful before the sover- eign Word and the Spirit that uses it.

There is a tension here. On the one hand, "we are 'outsiders' and without the Holy Spirit will not understand a word of Scripture," as Forde quotes Luther approvingly, "not that Scripture is unclear, but that *we*, as human beings, are 'unclear' and internally confused."[564] On the other hand, the Holy Spirit that does this cannot be detached from the Word, as so much tradition has attempted. "The Reformation . . . in- sisted that the Spirit comes through the Word as the gospel's enlivening and liberating voice. This occurs when the letter (the law) puts the old being to death and raises up the new in the Spirit."[565] As Luther writes, says Forde, "the Spirit is in the *use*, not in the object as such."[566] Thus the proclaimer must use the law-gospel distinction with confidence, hoping for the Spirit's working in the effective dividing of the Word. Yet the proclaimer must do it with humility, knowing that it is not he or she who is in control, but rather an electing God who may or may not choose to make of that proclaiming moment the only moment that ultimately matters in the life of a particular listener.

D. The Freedom of the New Person

Certainly, it may be argued that the thrust of Forde's work involves a proper understanding of the eschatological act character of the revelation, as the disproportionate space we have used exploring it suggests. Nevertheless, it remains to be considered where that leaves the new person in Christ and how the life that new person lives may be understood. In answer Forde points to a particular understanding of freedom, the concern of this section.

The Shape of the Freedom: The Froms, Fors, and Ins

In considering the law in section B of this chapter, we traced Forde's functional understanding of the law and its effects on humankind. We found it is not simply a set of requirements, but "one way [that] communication functions when we are alienated, estranged, and bound."[567] As a persistent, accusing voice from anywhere and everywhere, the law insists that we "do our duty"[568] and "fulfill our humanity under God."[569] For a humanity bent on continuity and control, such a law becomes the basis for human striving, progress, and projects in the name of self-improvement. We set up systems whereby we may use the law for our own self-preservation and keep God and his power at bay, lest our situation get out of hand. This consumes our time, our energy, and our lives. It is a bondage. Yet, despite all our efforts, the law still hounds the calculating sinner who finds that neither manipulation nor performance stills the incessant voice.

Forde argued that the only end to the law is death—a despair of any self-help, any "positive synthesis" of human action with God's action.[570] This death is real, not allegorical, with real consequences, and most theological effort is a frantic but futile attempt to avoid it. This death actually happens in that encounter with Christ where the death-dealing aspects of the crucifixion are not covered over, but permitted to do their work. When the listener realizes that it was through his or her striving under the law that Christ died, and that God has validated the cause of Christ, not that of the busy listener, through the resurrection, then the whole life of such striving is exposed as not only useless, but devastating.

At the same time the unconditional promise of the electing God in Christ engenders trust in the truth of the promise. The sacraments join the witness of the preached word in a present tense, first-to-second person proclamation that makes the promise tangible and compelling. They create a faith that grasps at the promise and builds life and hope on it. Such faith counts exclusively on the decisive work of God in Christ and flies quite free of the structures of the former existence imposed by the law.

In the first place, then, Christian freedom is defined over and against the former system. This is freedom "in the larger sense of being grasped, set free, turned around, saying, 'Look, forget about yourself . . . .'"[571] It is freedom "from bondage to this age"[572] in which one was constantly calculating how one was doing. It's an interior freedom of conscience where one is released from the hounding voice within, as Forde affirms using Luther's reflections on Galatians 5:1:

> The freedom which Luther championed was the freedom of faith, the freedom for which Chirist has set us free (Gal. 5:1), liberation of the conscience from the power of law, sin, and death. We are set free, Luther says, "not from some human slavery or tyrannical authority but from the eternal wrath of God." Such freedom "comes to a halt" in the conscience, "it goes no further." Indeed, for Luther, this is the highest reach of freedom. "This is the most genuine . . . freedom; it is immeasurable."[573]

So Forde can, at a certain point, describe what Christian freedom is "freedom *from*"—freedom from the power of law, sin, and death, freedom *from* the wrath of God, freedom *from* the bondage of concern for and service to the self under the system of the law.

In this context one might expect Forde to add a positive side to his definition, some "freedom *for*"—perhaps a freedom *for* a new life that becomes possible through faith in the promise, or some such thing. Indeed, there are a number of examples of situations where he uses the phrase or language that implies it. We are free to apply ourselves "to being a proper steward of God's law,"[574] to take care of "the whole world,"[575] "to take care of human beings and to fight for their proper care,"[576] "for such concrete questing for justice,"[577] "to spend ourselves for the sake of others,"[578] and so forth.[579] Yet, Forde punctuates the use with a caveat massive enough to qualify them all: they can look like an effort to predetermine the shape of the life of freedom in Christ. He is concerned that the old Adam's sense of scandal before true freedom will result in a covert reassertion of the law upon the freed conscience—covert in the guise of a pre-defined freedom. As Forde points out, "Luther's idea of freedom is itself radical enough to engender an anxiety which sends us scurring to do damage control."[580] One of the ways we do this is, ironically enough, to attempt to define in a counter-freedomly manner what the freedom must look like.

As early as a 1976 article, "Bound to be Free," for Eric Gritsch's book *Encounters with Luther*, Forde expressed this:

Personally, I get rather uneasy over the way freedom is often handled in the church. Usually it is said, when we get nervous about the excesses of 'freedom' today, that we are, of course, *not* only free *from* something, but also free *for* something. True enough! But often such talk becomes simply the excuse for laying the law on us again . . . .[581]

The "true enough" grants the possibility of truth in talking like this. But the danger of such talk lies in the possibility of forcing the hand of freedom, a danger serious enough that it demands immediate qualification.

In the last decade of his career in his 1993 lecture, "Called to Freedom," to the Eighth International Congress for Luther Research at Luther Seminary, Forde repeats the complaint:

We always seek the comfort . . . that we must not only think of freedom as freedom *from* something, but also as freedom *for* something. Freedom is never the last word, the ultimate goal. A vast defensive rhetoric builds on the foundation of anxiety that reduces Luther's vision to the banalities against which he directed his scorn. The offense is leeched [sic] out of freedom and it dies a lingering death.[582]

By this time the use of the "for" and the "from" raises so many warning flags ("a vast defensive rhetoric" built on "the foundation of anxiety") that Forde really doesn't condone using them at all. Even if they don't immediately snuff out freedom, we ought to fear its "lingering death" under their influence.

No, better than a focus on "freedom *for*" something, or even on the "freedom *from*," perhaps, one does well to follow Galatians 5:1 and assert "freedom *in*"—that is, freedom in Christ. In Christ there is a setting free that transcends prescriptive concerns:

One need not ask, for Luther, what such freedom is for. It [is] as St. Paul pronounced, for freedom itself. [Forde cites Gal 5.1.] It is a freedom *in* Christ, not from or for something. To retreat from freedom is simply to make Christ of no effect. . . . Luther unlike virtually everyone believed that what the fallen world really needs first and foremost is more freedom, not less. What is distinctive about Luther's view is the *hilaritas*, a certain fearlessness, even recklessness, in setting forth the claims of freedom.[583]

Here, bold words of cheerful abandon and openness to the future replace words that position freedom with respect to the bound past or define freedom with respect to an expected future.

Fresh Paradigms for the New Life in Christ

Exploration of these words give a better sense of the idea of the freedom that Forde understands here. *Hilaritas* is a word Luther used for the joy and spontenaity that faith engenders, a joy Forde celebrates: "After the bondage to sin comes spontaneity, the *hilaritas*, of faith and its good works."[584] This is the end of theology, "both the *finis* and *telos*": joy and freedom—"the new age held fast in the joy, the *hilaritas*, as Luther could say, of faith."[585] There's no obligation or duress here. "[W]hat God wants is not a creation which 'needs' him, but a creation which loves him and enjoys him in absolute freedom and spontaneity for, we might say, the 'fun of it.'"[586] Fun suggests a basic disregard for sin: If one doesn't protest that sin may abound, "one probably hasn't yet grasped the radical *hilaritas*, the joy of grace."[587] Fun even suggests lawlessness: "If the thought of an anarchy inspired by eschatology doesn't bring a smile to your face you probably can't be saved anyway. We are reaching out here, you see, for the joy, the hilaritas, of faith."[588] To the old morality-conscious Adam this is not necessarily good news: "It appears wild and dangerous and reckless to us, just as it did to Jesus' contemporaries."[589] In general, he wonders how the world can survive "if mercy and forgiveness are just *given* unconditionally." "Actually *doing* it, giving it unconditionally just seems to us terribly reckless and dangerous. It shatters the 'order' by which we must run things here."[590]

In his sermon on Psalm 74:22-23 Forde admires Luther as a man of the gospel in terms just like these. "There is about the man a kind of reckless and tempestuous hilaritas, the joyousness of a faith willing to risk anything for a cause."[591] In his 1994 *Word & World* article on Barth's first Romans commentary, he admires Barth in the same terms:

> It is precisely the recklessness and abandon with which Barth goes at the task that is so hopeful. . . . Important about Barth's *Romans* is that it didn't only talk about the future, it actually made one. Perhaps the secret is precisely in the recklessness. After all, what more is a preacher to do?[592]

This is the very language Forde uses of the resurrection itself, as the first draft of his Easter sermon on Mark 16:6 proposes: "He is not here, he is risen. What shall we say of these words? These words which seem to shatter the grammar of earth so rudely, so boldly, so recklessly [with double underline beneath recklessly]?"[593] It is the spirit with which Forde waxes passionate in many of his sermons:

> Isn't that fantastic! Isn't that wild! Isn't it somehow divinely comical! . . . There is a new world, a different world, just around the corner, just on the other side of all your calculation, your scheming, your pious and impious games. You are forgiven for all that—*all* of it."[594]

It's Forde's portrayal of sanctification: "free, uncalculating, genuine, spontaneous."[595] The most compelling portrayal of Forde's sense of freedom in Christ comes through words like these.

What the words have in common is an attitude of openness to and excitement for the future—just what one might expect from an event of the magnitude Forde claims for the death-and-rising experience. One can hear this attitude beneath the surface in many of Forde's sermons—for example, in his sermon on the ten maidens in Matthew 25:

> The point is that the Christian life is meant to be something different. We do not worship a static God of the past. We worship a Lord who in his death and resurrection has overcome the world and who is still on his way, still to come in all his glory. It is possible, therefore, indeed, we are admonished to see in upheaval and devastation not just destruction and despair . . . but also the possibility of the new, of something better, to look for the dawning of a new day, to be prepared for change. . . . This is not, of course, to say that everything that happens to change things is good, or even that any change is a change for the better. . . . But it is to say that the Christian attitude can never be one of settling down and being cozy with the way things are.[596]

The words make the prospect of change a positive possibility. "[W]e have nothing to lose from change," he preaches in an early sermon. "[I]n most instances we ought to welcome it . . . ."[597] The short-term future is never sure, but the promise of God is, and the resulting confidence is the basis for the "*hilaritas*" and the "recklessness" that accompany the attitudinal openness to the possibilities.

To sum up and connect, the freedom of the new self is a corollary of the newness that comes with the risen Christ, with the proclamation of the vindication of the forgiveness that the Christ offers, and with the promise of God that is grasped by the faith it brings forth. While there may be some use in defining this freedom in contrast with the bondage of the old self that dies, or even by imagining the shape of the life of the new self that emerges, this must be done with reserve lest the law reassert itself and the self be bound again. Instead, freedom is most properly defined by its "in-Christ-ness," where faith is born by the forgiveness of Christ and the promise of an electing God, and where no thought is taken again of the tyranny of the law.[598] So much is this the case that the resulting life of freedom may be best described with modifiers that emphasize the unpredictability of the phenomenon—spontaneous, joyful, wild, reckless, and dangerous—all to the consternation and dismay of any surviving old selves. Quite in contrast to the old self's move to safety and control, the new self finds itself open to the future, just what one might expect from the ultimate eschatological event.

Expressions of Freedom: Caring for the World and the Neighbor
There is considerable tension in Forde's theology at this point. On the one hand, as we have seen above, he is determined to let freedom be freedom and not to prescribe the way it must work itself out. The modifiers rightly emphasize its unpredictability and openness to the future. The newness is real and no one knows where it will lead.

On the other hand Forde expects that the newness will bring the new self to find its way, somehow or other, to service to the world. He finds himself constrained to say it again and again, never as his primary message, but as an abiding corollary and fulfillment of that message. It's as if he finds it necessary to share his vision[599] of the reality while insisting on the importance of its spontaneous nature. Conscious of the points just made on the spontaneity of freedom, we explore Forde's vision.

Especially in the earlier half of his career, Forde draws repeated attention in various ways to the social problems confronting the world of his day and the church's responsibility before them. As early as his doctoral thesis (1969) and located in as strategic a place as the second to the last paragraph, Forde writes,

> Wherever law is used to tyrannize men for the sake of the state or for personal aggrandizement, wherever men are sacrificed for the sake of an ideology, wherever earthly power of any sort becomes an end in itself, there law is being misused, and there the church has both warrant and responsibility to bear its witness. . . . It is not my task here to attempt to outline fully what this would mean, but I do want to suggest that in the much neglected concept of the use of the law there are great possibilities for understanding the *positive* relationship of the church to the problems of social justice."[600]

The following year in an article based on a speech at Augustana College in Sioux City, South Dakota, he describes the turmoil of the era:

> What is going on in Vietnam today if it is not to a large degree simply the sacrificing of thousands daily on the altars of our mythologies? Not only that but here at home we tyrannize our fellow men, shut the black man out of our society, beat down the underprivileged, tear up the earth, deface it and turn it into one vast garbage dump.[601]

His sermon on Luke 16:10-13, datable to 1976, is conscious of a survival ethic in the face of "the stench and peril of our pollution and exploitation on a planet with multiplying trash heaps and rapidly dwindling resources."[602] In his inkjet-era sermon on Matthew 11:2-5 he says, "Abject, cruel, grinding, hopeless, unjust poverty is constantly before us and ought to be heavy on our consciences. And we must do something about it."[603] As late as 1984 he can write,

Does not this ultimate comfort [that God is for us] discomfort us about the world we see around us? Can we eat this bread and still look away from those for whom bread is too high priced? Can we eat this bread without price and still tolerate the liars and cheaters who traffic in people's lives?[604]

Clearly, Forde is concerned about the state of the world and ready to call the church to engage its problems.

At the same time, and perhaps increasingly later in his career, Forde can be critical of the wrong kind of attention to these social concerns. In a 1993 chapel sermon entitled "On Losing One's Life," Forde warns of premature activity, since the old nature, too, can invest itself in such activity:

The old being in us, of course, thrills to hear the uncompromising summons to dying for whatever great cause is worthy enough for attention—even if it has no intention of actually doing it![605]

Such activity is dangerous if it gives the impression that it is itself eschatological, bringing in the reign of God. In a 1987 *Word & World* article Forde reminds us,

The Kingdom of God indeeds [sic] comes by God's power alone, and thus one is turned back into the world for the time being to serve the neighbor. But such turning takes place only to the degree that one believes in the eschatological Kingdom of God, and is thus freed to do so. . . . If the movement is not one of freedom, all is lost. Moralists, social reformers, ideologues, revolutionaries, and even just plain zealous religious people may no doubt find this frustrating and maddening, but is of the very essence of the matter.[606]

The activity is deadly for the church if it leads to a confusion of purpose and priorities. "Is [the church] here to ratify the world's causes or to foster the freedom and spontaneity of faith?"[607] The options are not exclusive, just prioritized: it's not that the church cannot be involved in the world's problems; it is just that the attention to the freedom and spontanaeity that come from the gospel energizes and makes possible churchly attention to those problems. In Forde's words, "When such causes are espoused, it cannot be at the *expense* of freedom, but rather the means through which freedom expresses itself."[608] Otherwise, the activity of the church blends undifferentiatedly with that of all the other old age institutions, and the church has nothing to offer.

Here are words to address the tension: Forde speaks of *means* by which freedom *expresses* itself. What might those means be? "Having a foretaste of things to come in justification by faith, the believer hopes and serves in this world,"[609] a first "means of expression." And what might such hope and service look like?

The Christian vision leads into the world, to suffering for and with others in the expectation of God's will being done on earth as it is in heaven. The aim is not to gain one's own holiness or to bring in the kingdom by force or tyranny, but to care for God's creatures and God's creation.[610]

It looks like the cross. It looks like expectant suffering for and with the world and the neighbor. It looks like doing whatever is necessary, not for oneself nor for a forced rule in God's name, but for others: God's creatures and God's creation. This is an oft repeated pair in Forde's vision of a life of freedom: care for our world and care for our fellow human beings, stewardship of the earth and love for the neighbor, ecology and justice.[611] It becomes possible only because attention is freed from the self under the law. God has broken the tyranny of the law. A favorite question of Forde's was, "What are you going to do now that you don't have to do anything?"[612] In the tension of preserving a space for freedom to be freedom, Forde risks his vision: freedom will express itself in caring: for the world and for the neighbor.

To review briefly the findings of this chapter, then, there are good reasons to understand Forde's theology as a concern for the shape of the encounter between God and humankind. This encounter is rooted epistemologically in the scriptures, authoritative not because of some prior required definition of infallibility of information, but because their action and effects have actually been experienced in the life of the hearer. This happens when their message is offered with such viability in terms of worldview, culture, and communication that its inherent force may accomplish its purpose.

In one way or another, the esteemed tradition of the church has made the law the definitive matrix around which to understand the work of Christ on behalf of the encounter. This is unhelpful. Law is not the fundamental, eternal reality which must be satisfied and fulfilled, but rather an accusing and terrifying voice that must be silenced and ended. This functional definition leaves it out of control, to our distress. Human efforts to "bring it to heel" through morality or through theology are inadequate. Only God's action through Christ can end the reign of law so that its limits are evident and it may serve its useful functions in society.

The esteemed tradition never agreed upon exactly how the work of Christ should be understood. In light of a critical analysis of the various atonement theories and a consideration of the ways each diminishes the cross, Forde proposes a different approach. If the death of Christ could be viewed in terms of an accident in which we caused the death of an innocent victim, efforts would not be wasted on explanations that take our eyes from the death. Attention remains where it belongs—on our culpability and on God's vindication of the victim through the resurrection of Jesus. With attention fixed here, a real action may actually happen, not just in some metaphysical world of debt payments, demonic defeats, or happy exchanges but in the present, in the life of the person who hears the law-gospel word in a way that brings to life a new trusting person.

Forde calls the action an eschatological event and describes it in at least three ways. First, justification by faith is the "moral or legal metaphor" most used in church dogma. Here, an electing God declares an otherwise completely bound and helpless person forgiven and free for Christ's sake. Secondly, and for Forde perhaps preferredly, there is death-and-new-life language, where the old Adam or Eve actually dies to the law and its efforts at salvation and a new person comes forth trusting in the word of forgiveness. This emphasizes the discontinuity between the old and new and creates expectancy of new creation. And finally, there is the appearance of this trust, or faith, in the life of the believer. This faith is first treated negatively and passively, as a description of an experience like death, but it is also discussed in terms of the Word that created it, the unconditional promise and decree of God, and in terms of relationship with God.

The way in which this eschatological event is brought forth in the world is proclamation—the "present-tense, first-to-second-person, unconditional promise, authorized by Jesus Christ according to the Scriptures."[613] Just as law was defined functionally on the basis of what it does, proclamation of the gospel in both preaching and sacrament is best understood functionally—by what it *does* to the one who hears it when it pleases God. What it *does* is the giving of new life described above, and Forde offers advice and calls for preacherly nerve to wield proclamation in such a way and with the hope that it might actualize these effects of eschatological import.

The freedom arising from the eschatological event is a real freedom in Christ, and Forde guards it jealously against hasty impulses to define it and direct it. It is possible to speak of freedom *from* the law, sin, death, wrath, and service bound by the law, and freedom *for* good stewardship, care of the world, care of the neighbor, and so forth. But Forde is concerned that such suggestions will snuff out the new freedom before it has a chance, and he offers a new set of descriptors that invite an open horizon—*hilaritas*, recklessness, spontaneousness, uncalculatingness, and the like.

Among the issues that arose in the course of the review of Forde's work, the following especially invite further missiological attention in chapter five. First, Forde holds what is perhaps a higher than usual tension between a strong assertion of the inherent dynamic of a Word of God from without and an insistence that the theology that undergirds that word must be viable today. This is an interesting tension for persons with a high regard for the Word seeking to communicate a message across divisions of worldview and culture. Secondly, Forde uses a common approach for the diversity of people to whom the Word must come. The question of human similarity and diversity within Forde's anthropological system invites further conversation especially in the world missional context. And thirdly, the emphasis on the accusing role of the law stands in some tension with the proper civil function that even permits the law to be called a friend, even allows the law to be rewritten to better serve society. Further delineation of the civil function of the law for the sake of justice and ecology becomes pressing in moral deliberation with the non-Christian neighbor.

CHAPTER 4

The Context of Contemporary Missiology

Having examined carefully Gerhard Forde's theology, it now becomes necessary to take a look at the concerns of modern missiological thought. If we intend to address Forde's thought missionally, we need some missiological definition with which to relate it. In broad strokes we need to sketch what mission has meant for past generations and what it means for missiologists today in the first decade of the third millennium.

A hundred years ago this would have been a much easier task. Then, the field of missiology was still coalescing. As recently as the first half of the nineteenth century the Protestant Friedrich Schleiermacher (1768-1834) accorded mission studies a place in a theological system for the first time, attaching it to practical theology. As recently as 1867 the first chair of evangelism was established at Edinburgh, Scotland, and Alexander Duff was appointed to it. And as recently as 1892 Gustav Warneck (1834-1910), the father of Protestant missiology, began defining his "Protestant doctrine of missions" in the *Evangelische Missionslehre*.[614] A hundred years ago it was a young science with a limited history of reflection.

That has changed. The twentieth century has witnessed a veritable explosion of missiological conversation. With Edinburgh in 1910 the great tradition of missionary conferences that had emerged in the last half of the nineteenth century began not only to be inspirational, but also productive of creative thought. The establishment of the International Missionary Council in 1921 set this trend on a more sure organizational footing, resulting in the regular, influential, and wide-ranging reflection of the World Council of Churches and, indirectly, the Lausanne Movement. As the world situation changed dramatically through two world wars and a post-colonial transition, so did the opportunities and challenges for mission. All of this has led to a complexity and richness of missional thinking unprecedented in world history.

In sixty pages we cannot do justice to the breadth and depth of missiology. What we can do is to sketch its parameters sufficiently to propose some contributions of Forde's work in a way connected to the contemporary missiological conversation. From various sources we will review briefly what mission has meant through the earlier history of the church. We will follow Timothy Yates through some developing mission paradigms of the twentieth century. We will examine two recent attempts to summarize the current situation of missiological thought: David

Bosch's influential *Transforming Mission* and Bevans and Schroeder's more recent *Constants in Context*. And, since Forde was a Luther scholar, we will conclude with a review of missiological reflection on Luther from Gustav Warnack (1901) to Ingemar Öberg (2007).

A. The Origins of the Concept of Mission

Etymological Origins

The word mission derives from an old Latin word for "sending," *missio*, or, equivalently, *missus*, both participles of the Latin verb *mitto*, "to send."[615] The term itself was not applied to work of the church until relatively recently in church history – as late as the 16th century by Ignatius Loyola to characterize the calling of the members of his order, as late as 1729 to describe the task Jesus gave in the great commission, and as late as the 19th century in the plural to describe outreach by Christians to non-Christians or to still developing Christian communities.[616] Nevertheless, the reality behind the term is as old as the scriptures themselves, where sending is an important and recurring concept.

Mission in the Old Testament

Of the more than eight hundred times that the Hebrew *saleh*, "to send," is used in the Old Testament, over two hundred of them are predicated of God's own self according to Ferris McDaniell. His word study reveals that this sending is a purposeful act, reflecting the will of the sender. To accomplish these purposes the sender exercises his/her authority through a messenger who accepts to go forth, obediently or sometimes reluctantly, out of deference to that authority. In going they bear an "authorized communiqué," spoken or written. It is in the context of this understanding that the OT identifies thirty prophets who speak on behalf of Israel's God. The word that God gives to them "almost takes on a force of its own," as in Is 55:11, working the will of God for punishment and for benefit in Israel and among all people.[617]

Given such sources in the Jewish scriptures, it is not surprising, as Bernard Bamberger writes for *The Universal Jewish Encyclopedia*, that "[a] missionary element was from the start implicit in the Jewish religion, with its message of a universal God."[618] Until recently, there had been broad scholarly consensus on this. Jeremias is a nuanced example of this consensus. While he would not call Judaism a missionary religion until after the Maccabaean period, he notes a growth that "reached its climax in the lifetime of Jesus and the apostles" when, with "intense zeal" the faith met the "deeper religious longing" of the age and "made every possible effort to facilitate the passage of Gentiles from heathenism."[619] McKnight's more recent study, on the other hand, proposes that missionary intentionality was lacking, and that the flow of conversions in the intertestamental period must be attributed to the attractiveness of the truth and values that it bore "as a light among [not to] the nations" rather than to "aggressive attempts to convert Gentiles or in the sense of self-identity."[620] There seems to be some disagreement in missionary definition, here, whether by inner nature, intent, or result. Clifford Bedell proposes that even if intent were lacking, Judaism would still have to be considered "'missionary' *in its effect*—and therefore participating in 'mission'—without sending out missionaries!"[621]

Mission in the Life of Jesus

The writers of the Septuagint chose the Greek word, *apostello*, to translate three-quarters of the occurrences of *saleh* in the Hebrew Bible.[622] In the New Testament, this word occurs 132 times in 13 books, 51 of which are ordinary daily human activity, but 81 of which have God, the Father, Jesus, or the Holy Spirit as the acting subject. It is not the purpose of this thesis to analyze these occurrences in detail, but to remark in a general way the extent to which this *missio* permeates the New Testament witness.[623] I identify at least ten different categories of sending in the New Testament beyond daily and mundane human-to-human sending: references to the Father sending Jesus to the world as in John 17:18, God sending Jesus specifically to certain persons as in Acts 3:26, God sending an angel as in Luke 1:26, God sending chosen persons as in Matt 11:10, God sending a message or salvation as in Acts 28:28, the sending of the Holy Spirit or the Spirit's gifts as in 1 Pet 1:12, the Spirit sending people as in Acts 10:20, God sending spirits out into the earth as in Rev 5:6, Jesus' sending his disciples in ministry as in Mark 6:7, and witnesses of Jesus sending word of him to others as in Matt 14:35. No doubt other nuances of sending in the New Testament could be discerned.

Over a third of these sendings are the Father's sending of Jesus, "the primal missionary," as Martin Hengel calls him.[624] Before one considers Jesus' teaching and sending of his disciples, the biblical witness asks us to consider how Jesus is portrayed as understanding his own sending. According to John Harvey's summary of the material, the Father is the initiator of the sending and Jesus' task as the one sent is to "faithfully discharge the mission entrusted to him." This he does with an authority so closely identified with that of the sender that the church came to confess their common divinity. The task was salvific: "He sought men and women with the explicit intent of calling them to repentance, and he gave his life as a means of obtaining deliverance for them."[625]

The gospels offer confusing signals on Jesus' understanding of the scope of his mission, as Jeremias makes clear. On the one hand, Jesus "pronounces a stern judgment upon the Jewish mission" (as in Matt 23:15), "forbade his disciples during his lifetime to preach to non-Jews" (as in Matt 10:5f), and "limited his own activity to Israel." On the other hand, Jesus "removes the idea of vengeance [upon the Gentiles] from the eschatological expectation" (as in the modification of Is 61.2 in Luke 4:19), "promises the Gentiles a share in salvation" (as in Luke 4:25-27), and speaks of his authority in such a way that it is universal. Jeremias resolves the apparent contradiction by proposing "we have to do with two successive events, first the call to Israel, and subsequently the redemptive incorporation of the Gentiles in the Kingdom of God."[626] By tending to the first, Jesus was opening the way for the second, and the early church would understand that time had now come for the mission to the Gentiles.

Even during his earthly ministry Jesus expressed the intention of preparing his disciples to participate in his mission (Matt 4:18-22 and parallels) and was sending his disciples out on mission trips, perhaps even twice: the twelve (Matt 9:35-10:42 and parallels) and the seventy (Luke 10:1-20). The task he gave them on these trips resembled his own work completely in terms of authority (to cast out demons), activities (preaching and healing), message (the approach of the kingdom of God), target group (only to the house of Israel), and results (submission of even the demons). As John Harvey remarks, "Their task was, in short, identical to that of Jesus."[627]

All four gospels and Acts include some form of a commission by Jesus giving his followers a missionary task, though the Marcan commission is surely an addition. These commissions are variously described as making disciples, baptizing and teaching (Matt 28:18-20), proclaiming the good news (Mark 16:15), proclaiming repentance and forgiveness of sins in Jesus' name (Luke 24:47), forgiving and retaining sins (John 21:23), and being witnesses to Christ (Acts 1:8). Bosch shies away from the notion of a Great Commission, arguing that the Matthean commission has to be understood against the background of Matthew's gospel as a whole" lest it be misunderstood.[628] This is undoubtedly true for all the commissions, and generalization of their call may be unhelpful. Yet, the point remains that every evangelist's account of Jesus (with the possible exception of Mark's) ended with the impression that the life of Jesus implied and called forth a sending of those who followed him.

Also, in every case, the commissions are set after Jesus' death and resurrection. Jesus is portrayed as referring to the future worldwide mission of his followers before his death (Matt 24:14, for instance), but he has rather little to say about it. Bosch can argue that the entire gospel of Matthew was written with the closing commission in mind. In other words, the whole book is an evangelical focusing of his community's faith and future, now already some forty years after Jesus' earthly life, in the call to make disciples in a new age. In the case of Luke it is the Holy Spirit sent by the risen Lord Jesus after his ascension who directs the church to its missionary task.[629] It is therefore on the basis of Jesus' authority that the church ventures out to its work.

Despite some continuity with mission during the life of Jesus, there was a basic shift in the substance of the proclamation after his resurrection. Where before it had been that "the kingdom of God was near," now it became specific testimony to Jesus' death and resurrection. "It is the risen Christ and the salvation blessings bestowed by him that take center stage."[630] The message came to focus on Jesus himself.

Mission in the Ministry of Paul

Apostolos, or sent one, was the primary self-understanding of the writer to whom almost half the New Testament documents are attributed, Paul. Only once in the New Testament is Jesus himself called an apostle (Heb 3:1). Most of the rest of the occurrences refer to the twelve, or those added to their number in one way or another, like Mathias or Paul. Only rarely does it refer to other sent ones like Andronicus and Junia (Rom 16:7) or Barnabas along with Paul (Acts 14:4, 14). Howell distinguishes a derivative, nontechnical sense, "sent ones," in the latter case, from a technical, primary sense in the former as referring to "representative spokesmen commissioned by the risen Lord to carry out the task of extending and establishing the church under authoritative tradition."[631] Apostolic authority, both in terms of content of message and the range of its sharing, is given directly by Christ through the commissioning. Even if, descriptively and functionally, as noted above, others participated in the apostolic task, Paul claims that primary, authoritative designation for himself and his message.

The mission of Paul may be analyzed from many perspectives. It had a unique origin in Paul's conversion. It had a strategy and pattern that reflected "contextualized proclamation" aimed at conversion and spiritual maturation in "emerging churches." It had an inner dynamics that included reliance on the Holy Spirit, early transfer of his work to trusted colleagues, and continuing intercessory prayer. But the determining core of his mission, Howell argues, is the message, the gospel of God's righteousness apart from the law, that brought about the "theological and experiential realignment" in Paul's life and, Paul hoped, in the lives of others.[632]

While admitting its complexity and its untransferability directly to the modern context, Bosch attempts to characterize the Pauline paradigm of mission under six headings: 1) the church as a new community where Jews and Gentiles find themselves non-negotiably united; 2) tremendous tension between God's ultimate salvation for the Jews and a converting mission to them; 3) an eschatological awareness of God's victory that must be maintained; 4) a tension between involvement in the world based on what Christ has already accomplished and eschatological hope for the future beyond anything we may be able to do; 5) the weakness and consequent suffering in mission that expresses Christian engagement with the world; and 6) a cosmic aim of mission that transcends the church and looks for the redemption of the world.[633] These may be said to characterize more or less the primitive church with its Jewish base, its minority status, and its apocalyptic vision.

An Ever Changing Shape for Mission

We will not attempt here to write a history of missionary awareness in the church. Nevertheless, lest mission be mistaken for a monochromatic phenomenon, it is useful to draw attention to some of the diversity of shape that it took in succeeding centuries. Bosch uses Hans Küng's characterization of Christian history to offer six paradigms of missionary awareness and activity.[634] The first is that of the primitive church, already sketched in the consideration of Paul, above.

The second is the Eastern Church mission paradigm, where the primitive apocalyptic character was replaced with a timeless gospel made manifest in *theosis*-anticipating lives. These Christian lives witnessed by lifestyle and sometimes in a martyr's death to the truth of the gospel as articulated in Greco-Roman intellectual concepts against heresies to the contrary. The corporate church is the aim and fulfillment of mission which cannot be attempted without it, and the church's liturgy is a critical vehicle for it.[635]

A third paradigm is that of the medieval Roman Catholic Church, where mission operated within an Augustinian focus on the individual in penance and on salvation. This salvation was administered within a unifying church structure dominated by "specialists" and often linked to the state. Within this linkage, a mission was pursued corporately that was ready to use force and advantage in crusade and colonialism. By contrast a monastic element, while "not *intentionally missionary*," was yet "permeated by a missionary dimension."[636]

A fourth is the Protestant Reformation paradigm, where the reformers put forth "an essentially missionary theology" in justification by faith, rediscovered through a focus on the scriptures, and applied subjectively, "for me." While an intellectualization of this insight impeded mission in Lutheran orthodoxy, mission flourished in Pietism's warm concern for both body and soul, still often in close linkage to the state. In fact, consistent with the concept of the priesthood of all believers, the Anabaptist wing of the Reformation made the missionary mandate "mandatory for all believers."[637]

A fifth is the post-Enlightenment mission paradigm. Here Bosch remarks, "[T]he entire modern missionary enterprise is, to a very real extent, a child of the Enlightenment," as a "new expansionist worldview . . . paved the way for a worldwide Christian missionary outreach."[638] An initial impulse of love for those who had not heard gave rise to a sense of spiritual superiority over them, not unconnected with a Western sense of cultural superiority. The resulting paternalism became a stumbling block to the maturing of the emerging churches. Most mission agencies were critical of colonialism, yet their European backgrounds benefited from its protection and participated in its advance. Characteristics of the mission of the church at this time include a recurring millennialism that linked mission with the end of time, a voluntarism that permitted church or mission society members to contribute to the cause without consideration of church office or vocation, a pan-confessional character that, at least initially, transcended denominational convictions, and a spirit of practical and optimistic confidence.[639]

Bosch's final paradigm, the postmodern, is our own new situation. The current fall of confidence in Western culture and progress draws the mission project of the past age into question and opens the world to new approaches to experience, meaning, eschatology, and interpretation, Christian or not.[640] The shape of mission in this new time remains to be defined.

Aquinian Mission

In the midst of all this reflection on what we today call mission, it is not inconsequential in light of contemporary conversations that the first theological use of the word mission referred to actions of persons of the Trinity, not humankind at all. Thomas Aquinas (1225-1274) initiated its theological use in his *Summa Theologica*, Book I, Question 43, on "the mission of the divine persons." He reflects on the apparent incompatability of divinity and sending, since 1) sending seems to imply a greater sender and a lesser sent one; 2) sending seems to imply separation; and 3) sending seems to imply nonpresence at the place left for new presence at the place arrived at, all ideas contrary to our understanding of the divine. But since Scripture insists that the Son was sent by the Father (as in John 8:16), the sending must be understood differently for divinity "in the sense that on the one hand this implies procession of origin from another, and, on the other, a new way of being present somewhere." In the case of the Son, the presence would be "in a visible way," though as God he had always been there. In the case of the Holy Spirit it would mean that the Spirit is "newly present in someone." Though linked to the idea of eternal procession from the Father, the sending refers to the historical event of Christ's earthly coming or the historical coming of the Spirit to an individual. "A mission is a procession in time."[641]

Although the Father gives himself and so might be said to send himself, Aquinas reserves mission for "a going forth with respect to origin." While it is true that "[t]he entire Trinity abides in the soul by reason of sanctifying grace . . . , being present through grace and being from another person belong to both Son and Holy Spirit" but not to the Father, so that sending should not be applied to the Father at all.[642]

Missions are connected not only with new presence but with "sanctifying grace." "No other effect but sanctifying grace . . . is the explanation of a divine person's being present to the intelligent being in this new way," and "there is no mission or temporal procession of a divine person except by reason of grace." This gift "empowers the intelligent being . . . for loving union with the divine person." Though the Son's and the Spirit's missions are distinct and unique, they are both rooted in this common grace. And where there is grace given, there is an invisible divine mission to the recipient of the grace, as among the Old Testament fathers, or in the growth of virtue, or in advancement to a new act or stage of grace, or when the sacraments are given.[643]

In all this carefully nuanced presentation of mission, or indeed, anywhere else in his entire *Summa*, Aquinas makes not the slightest connection of mission to the human sending we have roughsketched from Judaism through the present time of the church. Given contemporary mission debate, this is really quite striking, and suggests a strong sense of the uniqueness of the mission of the Son and the Spirit to the world.

B. Yates' Rapid Evolution of Missiological Paradigms

As noted in the chapter introduction, missiological thought has undergone such a growth of perspectives and nuances in the twentieth century that it is almost beyond description. Timothy Yates attempts to summarize the century with a sequence of characterizations of new missionary approaches as the century progressed, and we will use these as a streamlined and simplified outline of that thought, finally adding a characterization of our own.[644]

Given the worldwide geographical expansion of the faith in the preceding four centuries it is not surprising that the twentieth century should open with an emphasis on mission as expansion. The vision of the Matthean commission, "Make disciples of all nations" (28:19), seemed to find an enthusiastic echo in the Student Volunteer Movement's watchword, "the evangelisation of the world in this generation." Warneck might warn that "the non-Christian world is not to be taken by assault," that it is not for us "to specify a time when the evangelisation of the world is to be completed,"[645] but new missionaries left Europe and North America by the thousands to see it accomplished. Out of the Christian student movements came the ecumenical statesmen like John Mott (1865-1955) who led to the the great 1910 Edinburgh Missionary Conference. One sees the expansionist expression of mission in four "directions for the future" resulting from the conference: 1) fear of advancing Islam and anticipation of engagement and "battle" on the African continent; 2) a longing for Christian unity and an awareness of the detriment to expansion that disunity could bring; 3) rising nationalism in mission lands that might help or hinder the expansion; and 4) a sense of need for "'a comprehensive plan for world occupation,' expressed often in militaristic metaphors" such as "world conquest" and "aggressive policy."[646] The geographical overtones are unmistakeable.

Yates assigns to the second decade of the century a growing emphasis, particularly among German missionaries, on the development of the *Volkskirche*, or ethnic church deeply reflecting the history and social characteristics of its members. From the time of Karl Graul (1814-1864) and Wilhelm Löhe (1808-1875) there was concern that mission be about more than individual conversions, that it include a church life that maintained "as much of the 'natural' and national custom as was possible," that was *"bodenständig,"* "truly rooted in the soil."[647] Gustav Warnack in attempting to mediate between individualistic and corporate goals of mission proposed that "the folk church [is] the school in which mankind [as] ethnic groups is brought to the discipleship of Christ."[648] For Bruno Gutmann (1876-1966) among the East African Chagga, it meant organizing the church around a tribal understanding of elders as an example of God's prevenient and good activity in created community.[649] For Christian Keysser (1877-1961) in New Guinea it meant, not individual and lonely baptisms, but persuading believers to return to their ethnic group to bring the entire tribe to baptism, thus affirming God-given family solidarity.[650] For Karl Barth such talk was a deadly compromise of the gospel with the natural theology that gave rise precisely to the *"Volk, Blut, und Boden"* paganism of the Third Reich.[651] But Johannes Hoekendijk (1912-1975) concluded his study of Gutmann and Keysser with these words: "[S]o long as the approach is treated as one of the possibilities [of mission] there is nothing sinful in talking about *Volkskirche.*"[652] As Yates himself summarized, "[T]here will be times when the approach to the group is very much more productive than an individualism which ignores the social contexts to which the gospel is addressed."[653]

Yates consigns the '30s and the '40s to chapters he calls "Mission appraised," one and two, in recognition of the soul-searching that the mission enterprise experienced after the war. Already before this time, Roland Allen's *Mission Methods: St Paul's or Ours?* (1912) proposed that reliance on long-term missionaries diminished opportunities for the Spirit's work and the natural giftedness of new local congregations.[654] And Daniel Johnson Fleming (1877-1969) in his *Whither Bound in Missions?* (1925) had attacked "missionary or Western 'superiority,'" challenging "the old-time vocabulary of conquest and condescension."[655] A conference document prepared for the International Missionary Conference (IMC) in Jerusalem in 1928, *The Relations between the Younger and Older Churches*, reflected these kinds of critiques when it called for the Chinese church to be "the chief center of responsibility" with missions and missionaries relating to the church in their tasks and duties.[656] The seeds that would culminate in independent, indigenous churches in the second half of the century were thus already sown.

The question of the role of social involvement in mission came to a head with the report of an IMC Commission of Appraisal, the Laymen's Foreign Missions Inquiry in 1932-33. Its seven volumes were the basis for the book, *Rethinking Missions* by W. E. Hocking (1873-1966) and others, "the Hocking report" as it came to be known in heated debate. "Jesus as teacher and example" was lifted up as more relevant to the situation of the younger churches in modernizing societies than was the dogmatically correct Christ the Son of God, and the development of a rural community life was portrayed as more critical than development of the rural church.[657] That is, the well-being of the wider society outside the church was seen as an ultimate goal of mission. Kraemer asserted that the kingdom of God "can never be the direct object and achievement of our labours, because it is in the hand of the Father."[658] Nevertheless, such thinking flowed into conceptions of "holistic mission" later in the century.

If the first of Yates' soul-searching chapters considered missionary reevaluation of its accomplishment of its own work within, perhaps it may be said that the second considers its reevaluation of its attitude toward the remaining task without: the world religions with which it dealt. This is reflected in another major document prepared for the Jerusalem conference, entitled *The Christian Life and Message in Relation to Non-Christian Systems*, addressing Christian relations with Hinduism, Islam, Buddhism, Confucianism, and secularity. Its approach explored a more positive assessment of these ways. One of its authors, for example, Nicol Macnicol, suggested that there was much that was gracious and beautiful in Hinduism, and that Christ came not to destroy this but to fulfill it—a sympathetic rather than superior or confrontative approach.[659] The achievement of mutual understanding with other faiths that might grow out of this paradigm was viewed as "the ultimate object of all missionary enterprise" by some and as betrayal and syncretism by others.[660] Continental missions, for example, were sufficiently upset by Macnicol's proposal that Mott found it expedient to arrange a pre-conference in Cairo in 1927 to discuss their reservations.[661] Hendrik Kraemer's *The Christian Message in a Non-Christian World*, prepared for the IMC at Tambaram in 1938, argued for the importance of the recognition of the discontinuity between Christian claims and those of other religions, so that "conversion and regeneration were better terms to express the unexpectedness of God's fulfillment of human aspiration."[662] And yet, as Knak noted, quoting Hartenstein, "the seeking for God in the non-Christian religions is a proof that man is designed for communion with God."[663] These kinds of conversations explored that statement.

Yates marks the '50s as the epitome of mission emphasis on presence and dialogue, almost in response to the renewed respect and acknowledgment for other religions before the war. Max Warren (1904-1977) "encouraged an expectation of finding Christ already present in the alternative traditions," so that we find "Christ present before he is proclaimed." Not only so, but Christian witness is "hinged on Christian presence," so that "our first task in approaching another people, another culture, another religion is to take off our shoes for the place we are approaching is holy."[664] Stephen Neill (1900-1984) extended this attitude to interreligious dialogue, "rigorous and uncompromising" engagement between participants who are "committed, resolute and uncompromising," considering "whether there may not be a whole dimension in Christian faith, of which the partner in the dialogue is unaware but to which perhaps he may be introduced," expecting "enrichment . . . as the participants have to rethink their faith in terms familiar to others, while remaining faithful to their own body of truth."[665] Kenneth Cragg (b. 1913), incarnating these insights with respect to Muslims, sought to help Christians penetrate the depths of Islam for the sake of nonagressive witness and "retrieval," that is, helping Muslims find the Christ they have missed.[666] Philip Potter (b. 1921) of the World Christian Student Federation warned that presence and dialogue could not be used to "avoid the element of confrontation and decision."[667] And Donald McGavran (1897-1990) warned that "a pluralism which resulted in co-existence for mutual edification" might end up betraying the Christian's distinctive witness.[668]

Liberation, one of a triad of emphases Yates marks for the '60s, is a direct result of Christian faith offering fresh thought on oppressive situations, especially in Latin America. The lingering heritage of dependency and oppression in these places from the colonial era made churches there impatient with the Western theological heritage they had received if it had no connection with action on behalf of the poor and suffering. In 1968 a gathering of Roman Catholic bishops in Medellín, Colombia, looked at the world situation as the arena of God's activity, making it the basis of subsequent Christian reflection and action.[669] Gustavo Gutierrez in *Theology of Liberation* (1974) agreed, but proceeded to define it politically and economically—a need for "a profound transformation of the private property system" that would give "access to power of the exploited class and a social revolution."[670] J. L. Segundo in *Liberation of*

Theology (1976) spelled out a new hermeneutic based upon suspicion of given ideological, theological, and exegetical ways of thought and openness to new data in the present situation. Here, "a profound human commitment," a partiality for humanity, needed to replace "scholarly neutrality, a state of total impartiality . . . , 'precisely the pretense of academic theology'."[671] For Hugo Assmann in *Practical Theology of Liberation*, the enemy was dualism. That is, "[t]o talk in ideal terms, to talk of abstract truth, very easily leads to the detachment of truth from the historical plane. Then historical reality can be 'manipulated by the powers that be' and used to maintain the status quo.[672] Since that status quo proved so destructive for so many people, the mission of these and other liberation theologians was transformation, and the thought leading to that transformation needed to be grounded in positive action.

Yates marks proclamation and church growth as characteristic of the '70s. As the World Council of Churches coalesced and dealt with radical new approaches to mission described above, conservative voices within evangelical churches expressed concerns about the implicit universalism in a church-minimizing approach where societal well-being took precedence over churchly evangelism. In 1974 these concerns led to an alternate missionary gathering, the Lausanne Congress, and its own statement of missionary understanding, the Lausanne Covenant. While concerns for social justice and unity were strong for Lausanne as well as the World Council, Lausanne is best known for its emphasis on the salvific uniqueness of Christ, the urgency of evangelism to make him known, and proclamation as the primary act of witness. Donald McGavran's "church growth movement" is not only one important expression of this concern, but a strategy for its accomplishment. Since "a people is not an aggregate of individuals," but rather "a social organism," evangelism must be attempted based on "homogenous units" of culturally alike groups rather than on individual conversions without respect to culture. That means that, initially, persons would come to Christ through association with their own ethnic group; only later, in a "perfecting stage," would they grow to experience the catholicity of the church.[673] The overriding goal is numerical increase in the church, and mission resources should be focused to maximize a numerical response.

Convergence between the World Council of Churches and the Lausanne movement in the '80s permitted common conversation about pluralism and enlightment, the last of Yates' paradigms of mission. In a mobile world where world religions found themselves side by side, pluralism was a new fact of life for many, and dialogue grew to be an accepted ecumenical approach by which to explore truth. Stanley Samartha (b. 1920) of the World Council expressed a more hopeful attitude toward pluralism when he said, "Pluralism does not relativise Truth. It relativises different responses to Truth."[674] For Wilfred Cantwell Smith (1916-2000), it's not as Radhakrishnan charged "that it was the Jews who had 'invented the myth that only one religion can be true,'" but rather, "what the Jews asserted was that only one God is real." Smith argued generally against "reification of religions" in which religions are defined abstractly in contrast with others, stressing instead "the faith which makes for humanity in whatever tradition it might be found."[675] If this is the way it is, then faith in a common God differently expressed and experienced by different individuals may be profitably shared, and mission becomes, in John Hick's (b. 1922) words, "interpenetration of positive values."[676]

The question of Christ's uniqueness is raised by such talk, and theories of inclusivity or exclusivity fought for acceptance. Are unique moments (such as the cross and resurrection) of ultimate significance for faith or not? John Hick proposed that it was not Christ, but God, who was central in theology, and that conceptions of a unique incarnation must be viewed as figurative.[677] Max Warren, on the other hand, mentioned above, held for "an inclusive uniqueness," that is, Christ is representative humanity before the Father for people of all religions and so is still the one who saves, whether or not that is recognized.[678] Paul Knitter, taking the side of Hick, ended up "deploying maximum theological weight" to "relativise the resurrection of Christ."[679] Leslie Newbigin, on the other hand, questions "plausibility structures" that stumble at so central a tenet of Christian faith. In his mind the post-Enlightenment consensus in the West on knowing the truth needs to be addressed to "allow for the central reality of the living God."[680]

Yates' analysis, published in 1995, offered no characterization for the last decade of the century. Now, thirteen years later, we may venture to supply the missing paradigm using the one that has shaped global mission in Forde's church body, the ELCA, as the century came to a close: accompaniment. Coming out of the Latin American Lutheran churches, this accompaniment is not merely a partnership, a term widely used in the second half of the century but which can still cover a contract between unequal sides. Rather, it is "a walking together in Jesus Christ of two or more churches in companionship and in service in God's mission," based on the biblical idea of *koinonia*.[681] Theologically, it is modelled on the God-human relationship in which God accompanies us in Jesus Christ through the Holy Spirit, and a powerful image of this relationship is the Emmaus text of Luke 24:13-35:

> In the walking together on the road to Emmaus, the Lord reveals himself to his companions. While walking together, each of the two disciples' and Jesus' stories become interlocked. Their three stories become intertwined. As the stories come together, God's plan in Jesus' resurrection becomes clearer. A

new community, the church, begins to emerge in Jerusalem. In sharing a meal the companions recognize the presence of Jesus with them.[682]

In several ways the accompaniment approach consciously resists the oppressive heritage of the colonial era. It recognizes that "each church has primary responsibility for mission in its area." Between these churches it "emphasizes relationship before resources," and values this "for its own sake as well as for the results." It focuses on "the mutual respect of the companions," treasuring this as "a primary reality." It binds the companions "more closely to their Lord and further informs their mission, as they "learn together in the journey."[683]

Critics of the accompaniment model feel it is weak, attentive specifically neither to the mandate to share the gospel nor to the command to love the neighbor. It is more practical than theological, it is charged, avoiding annoying questions about uniqueness and pluralism by tending to one aspect of the church's witness: respectful relations at the interchurch level.

Thus we see a rapid succession of related but differing missiological concerns rising to prominence through Forde's century, none completely replacing its predecessors, but each influencing the others and all piling up in a rich simultaneous interplay. Stephen Neill warned of unending expansion of the word mission in his famous 1959 proverb, "If everything is mission, nothing is mission."[684] Yet, it is clear that the course of our understanding of the *missio*, the sending, has taken an expansive direction, and no account of mission is complete without realizing something of its breadth and complexity. The following section examines two portraits of mission so portrayed.

C. Comtemporary Characterizations of Missiology

So what does missiology look like today? How do the twentieth century's contributions add up? Our attempt to answer this broad question will review briefly two recent attempts that will probably still be considered definitive for this era fifty years from now: David Bosch's massive twelfth chapter, "Elements of an Emerging Ecumenical Missionary Paradigm," in his *Transforming Mission: Paradigm Shifts in Theology of Mission* (1991) and Stephen Bevans and Roger Schroeder's *Constants in Context: A Theology of Mission for Today* (2006), Part III. Bosch's approach is a listing and discussion of thirteen elements of contemporary mission with the warning that they are interrelated and must be considered together, and Bevans and Schroeder use a complex methodology to arrive at a synthesis of three basic typologies. We begin with Bosch, numbering elements as we go.

Bosch's Thirteen Interrelated Elements

David Bosch begins with a discussion on the role of the church, a missionary element that impinges on all of the others. Where in an earlier generation an institutionally considered church was seen relatively disconnected from mission (witness the multiplication of independent Protestant missionary societies), now, as Vatican II's *Ad Gentes* proclaimed, "The pilgrim church is missionary by its very nature."[685] This move required rethinking the nature of the church: not so much divine institution as mystical communion of faithful in the body of Christ.[686] *Lumen Gentium* made the missionary connections: not societal in a worldly sense but sacramental and instrumental, not "imperious" community of "exalted souls" but humble, "a servant community." Truly, Bosch remarks, "LG's ecclesiology is missionary through and through."[687] The modern conversation on this church-mission connection is wide and includes voices as well known as Barth's and Newbigin's as its ramifications are plumbed. Bosch discusses it as his first element, "mission as the church-with-others."

The nineteenth century had been intensely concerned with mission as a human activity, but beginning with a 1932 paper by Karl Barth[688] and developing rapidly through the work of the 1952 International Missionary Conference at Willingen, the idea blossomed that Godself is the primary actor in mission. Human actors are simply privileged to be participants in this "mission as *missio Dei*," as it came to be called, Bosch's second element. Since it is God's mission and not our own, some like Hoekendijk even looked for it outside the church, a controversial approach that drew into question the importance or even helpfulness of the church's participation.[689]

There has been new thinking on the third element, "mission as mediating salvation." Bosch suggests that the *theosis* talk of the Greeks and the *satisfactio vicaria* language of the West had the effect of attenuating the definition of salvation and sundering ecclesiastical preoccupation with it from Christian vocation in the world. Twentieth century thought, by contrast, has at times ventured an optimistic identification of God's activity in this world with salvation, sometimes indistinguishable from simple well-being. More sober experience at century's end calls for the mediation of a salvation that preserves the eschatological tension between expectation and accomplishment, and that makes the *totus Christus*, all of Christ's story, available for the total human need, soul and body.[690]

This thinking calls for "two different mandates, the one spiritual, the other social,"[691] and this, after an almost two century-long emphasis on the spiritual as most important. As Bosch proposes, "[n]ever before in history has people's social distress been as extensive as it is in the twentieth century,"[692] and a strong "quest for justice," Bosch's fourth element of contemporary mission, responds to this crisis. A concern for justice needs balance, however, between reduction of the mission to "a simple temporal project" as concrete goals are attempted here and now, on the one hand, and a focus on otherworldly realities that diminish earth and its problems, on the other.[693]

The fifth element, "mission as evangelism," or evangelization in ecumenical and Roman Catholic use, answers to the second, spiritual mandate and constitutes the fifth element in Bosch's list. Unlike social justice, evangelism had always been a primary understanding in the evolving mission concept, but it experienced some fluidity of use and a multiplication of definitions during the century.[694] Bosch proceeds to give it lengthy and precise late-century definition, narrower than mission which is "the total task God has set the church for the salvation of the world," but "imbedded in this mission," and never done isolated from it. In short, "evangelism involves witnessing to what God has done, is doing, and will do."[695] It seeks a response in the hearers, but the way it seeks that response is always invitation, never judgmental, always modest about itself. It is not proselytism, nor church extension, nor membership recruitment, and it is not designed to hasten the day of the return of the Lord. It is made personally to individuals, but is not, itself, individualistic, because it relates contextually to the community of which the individual is a part and it includes a call to service as part of the evangelizing community. While the emphasis of evangelism is on the verbal, it includes deeds of witness as well.[696]

Where once theology was seen to have its own essence which mission simply transplanted into new locales, now the church is poignantly conscious of the contextual nature of every message. Every text is an interpreted text, as Paul Ricoeur emphasized, assigning its meaning "from below," and one should exercise a "hermeneutics of suspicion," as Nietzsche argued, toward Western revealed explanations "from above."[697] "Mission as contextualization," the sixth element, means that we are open to the refiguring of the message that happens when it interacts with a given situation, not merely explaining a textual story, but, more seriously, experiencing and acting upon the message in the context.

Two important expressions of mission as contextualization are "mission as liberation," seven, and "mission as inculturation," eight. Recognizing the context of "global structural relationships" of "dominance and dependence," liberation theology saw mission in practical avenues of concrete historical liberation from them. So central was this for the Melbourne conference of 1980 that it called the way the church affirmed the poor "the missiological principle par excellence" and "the missionary yardstick."[698] That is, the poor were to be the church's first focus of attention because they were God's focus of attention (the "preferential option" of Puebla, 1979), and some like Matthew Lamb went so far as to identify the voice of the victim with the voice of God.[699]

Recognizing the context of diversity of cultural expressions, on the other hand, inculturation speaks about the relationship of the gospel to them. In an unprecedented way, the local communities themselves, moved by the Holy Spirit, are looked to as translators and integrators of message and context. The kenotic and incarnational aspects of this are so marked that it is as if the church is not merely being expanded, but actually "being born anew in each context and culture" as it reworks the cultural material. Thus Bosch can speak of a "double movement": "inculturation of Christianity and Christianization of culture."[700]

The union of the IMC with the WCC in 1961 signalled publicly the integral unity of mission and the ecumenical movement, so that mission should be seen not as a precursor to churchly unity as in the past, but as its "common witness," the ninth element.[701] This makes mission as enduring as the church itself, not thinkable apart from the church, and certainly not about the business of proliferating churches. Disunity in this context "is not just a vexation, but a sin."[702]

Bosch's tenth element is "mission as ministry by the whole people of God." That is, today's church realizes its mission is accomplished by laity as well as the ordained in what Bosch calls "one of the most dramatic shifts taking place in the church today."[703] "The vertical, linear model, running from the pope via the bishop and the priest to the faithful (a model which has its parallels in Protestantism) is gradually being replaced by one in which all are directly involved." The sense of apostolicity, once reserved for the clergy, is now applied to laity as well, and it is the *community*, not the clergy, that is the primary bearer of mission.[704]

Eleventh is "mission as witness to people of other living faiths" like Hindus, Buddhists, and Muslims, faiths that Christians have been relatively unsuccessful in bringing to conversion. Where once these faiths were simply obstacles to conquer or displace, now missionary approaches are more varied: exclusivism, where other faiths are considered human fabrication; fulfillment, where Christian faith is seen as the completing or consummating of other faiths which may have prepared the way; and pluralism, where religions are seen as products of their diverse histories and reflective, more or less, of truth within those contexts.[705] Dialogue is lifted up as a missional approach in this situation.

As has been already observed, missiology is a relatively new phenomenon, with the very first instructor of mission, Charles Breckenridge, called to a theological school, Princeton, only in 1836.[706] How striking, then, to find missiology now established as a discipline with chairs and departments in theological institutions all over the world. Truly, "mission as theology," twelfthly, has come into its own. Bosch cites two main tasks. First, as "a missiological agenda for theology," it acts as "a gadfly in the house of theology," challenging theology itself to be faithful to the missional task. And secondly, as a "theological agenda for mission," it addresses the missionary praxis – "critically to accompany the missionary enterprise, to scrutinize its foundations, its aims, attitude, message, and methods."[707]

And finally, Bosch sees contemporary mission as focusing on "mission as action in hope," a thirteenth element. In recent centuries, eschatology has fallen into two unhelpful ditches: the utter non-eschatological historization of nineteenth century Enlightenment thought which focused on our best efforts and neglected God's coming reign, and the hyper-eschatological futurism of millenarians which made this world's needs superficial in the face of the future apocalypse. As Carl Braaten writes, "In every Christian tradition and in every continent we are still in the midst of a movement to reformulate a theology of mission in the light of an authentic eschatology."[708] The challenge is to find "an eschatology for mission which is both future-directed and oriented to the here and now,"[709] and its search characterizes mission today.

So ends a sketch of Bosch's comprehensive portrait of "an emerging ecumenical missionary paradigm." To venture a summary, mission may be said to be the privilege of participation by the church as the people of God in God's own venture, mediating an eschatologically coherent salvation through mandates that call for social justice and evangelical witness. In this mission the church is aware as never before of the contextualization task as worked out in liberation and inculturation. It attempts the task as church, united in common witness, inclusive of all the people of God in its efforts, yet respectful and interested in the insights of those whose faith is different.

Bevans and Schroeder's Synthesis

Bevans and Schroeder's more recent analysis offers three portraits of contemporary mission and concludes with their synthesis. The first, "mission as participation in the mission of the Triune God (*missio Dei*)," recalls Bosch's second element, "mission as *missio Dei*," but demonstrates a trinitarian probing of the term by the church not evident in Bosch.[710] For instance, if "the church is missionary by its very nature," the reason is "because it itself is the result of the overflowing love of God, expressed in the mission of the Son and the mission of the Holy Spirit."[711] Thus, the missionary nature of the church is not an accident nor a human decision; it is a reflection of its creation by a God whose missionary character is evident first of all precisely in God's triuneness. This triune character informs mission in a number of aspects: in a communal nature, as among persons of a trinity, that "aims at drawing humanity and creation in general into this communion with God's very life;"[712] in a mutual character, as of the persons of a trinity, that points "toward a community of equals related in mutuality;"[713] in a diverse character, as in differences between the triune persons, giving room for reflection on ways to consider other faiths during this time of vivid awareness of religious and cultural pluralism; and in a "dialogical" character of giving and receiving that reflects the perichoretic triune sharing.[714] The church bears such characteristics into its mission in the world because its mission is God's mission and the triune God who brought it forth bears just such characteristics. Mission is thus firmly grounded theologically in the very trinitarian being of God.

Bevans and Schroeder's second portrait, "mission as liberating service of the reign of God," is a reminder of Bosch's seventh element, "mission as liberation," here rooted in Jesus' proclamation of the kingdom of God.[715] This proclamation, affirms Pope Paul VI in his 1975 *Evangelii Nuntiandi*, "sums up the whole mission of Jesus," and "is so important that, by comparison, everything else becomes 'the rest' . . . ." Since the church's mission is "to prolong and continue Jesus' mission," its mission is thus defined by the kingdom that Jesus preached. This kingdom is understood in terms of salvation, that is, radical conversion and a healing inwardly and outwardly as people are drawn into the community of disciples. It is "liberation from everything that oppresses man" (a first official use by the Vatican) but also "openness to the absolute, even the divine Absolute."[716] In continuing this ministry the church's focus is directed, not on itself or its development, but on God's reign and the liberation from individual or corporate sin that goes with it. "Ultimately, it is not to the church that people are called, but to the reign of God."[717]

The third Bevans-Schroeder portrait of mission, "mission as proclamation of Jesus Christ as universal Savior,"[718] focuses on the uniqueness of Jesus Christ and the urgent need to proclaim his benefits that they may be assured to their hearers. Here one hears from diverse parts of the church that "[i]t is only in faith [in Jesus Christ] that the Church's mission can be understood and only in faith that it finds its basis,"[719] or, the commitment to mission flows "from a deep conviction regarding the uniqueness and all-sufficiency of Christ's person and work,"[720] or, "Jesus is the key to understanding God in God's full salvific, trinitarian reality."[721] At its best, this missiological portrait does not neglect trinitarian awareness, but the focus is Christological *within* that awareness.[722] Since knowledge of this Christ occurs in the church and comes to others only through the proclamation of the church, it becomes an urgent task for the church to get the word out, and evangelism is a primary task. For "evangelicals" it is nothing less than eternal salvation that rests on the resultant faith in Christ and one is simply lost without it. If Catholics hold out for the possibility that God's Spirit might mysteriously work it out for "women and men of sincerity and good will" in some other way,[723] they nevertheless hold that *the Church is the ordinary means of salvation* and that *she alone* possesses the fulness of the means of salvation."[724] This witnessing task of the church is given a certain priority. As John Stott said,

> Anything which undermines human dignity should be an offence to us. But is anything so destructive of human dignity as alienation from God through ignorance or rejection of the gospel? And how can we seriously maintain that political and economic liberation is just as important as eternal salvation?[725]

Yet, social justice and liberation remain a serious concern for most of those who identify with this portrait, and the search for proper balance between evangelism and social concern continues.

After affirming the validity of all three mission approaches, Bevans and Schroeder propose "that only a *synthesis* of all three will provide the firmest foundation for the model of mission that we are proposing as the most adequate model for these first years of the twenty-first century: mission as prophetic dialogue."[726] As dialogue, it is characterized by the communion that characterizes the interior life of God, "gift and reception, identity and openness to the other, communion in relationship and communion in mission," not only contributing in service, but growing and deepening in the process. It is "never about imposition, but always about persuasion and freedom-respecting love," always carrying out its work in humility. But it's also Bosch's "bold humility," participating in "God's unimaginable, unbounded love" through Jesus, as his Spirit-inspired mission proclaimed and embodied the reign of God and called forth justice. It witnesses to his death and resurrection which promise new life for all people and all creation.[727] In this the church's mission is *dialogue.*

But at the same time, it's *prophetic* dialogue, and this in three directions: "with the poor, with culture, and with other religions."[728] Raising its voice on behalf of the poor, against cultural encroachment or imperialism, and holding its faith in Christ while engaging other religions, the church maintains an over-against-ness that brings a fresh perspective to the world and opens the possibility of change.

Bevans and Schroeder propose "six essential components" to flesh out what this "prophetic dialogue" might mean practically. The first is "witness and proclamation as prophetic dialogue." Witness is "those acts and words by which a Christian or community gives testimony to Christ and invites others to make their response to him,"[729] and it is carried out in four arenas: personally, congregationally, ecclesiastically, and ecumenically.[730] Proclamation, on the other hand, is the gospel communication itself in such a way that those who believe it are invited to join in making it "audible and visible in the world." It tends to follow witness, always proposes, never imposes, usually responds to a question, and proceeds out of vulnerability and weakness.[731]

The second essential component is "liturgy, prayer and contemplation as prophetic dialogue." These occur at the center of Christian life, but constitute mission if they "participate in God's [boundary crossing] life at the boundaries."[732] Here liturgy is done sensitive to the cries of the world and prepares the community for ministry in that world. Prayer is "aligning oneself with God's purposes in the world, . . . opening ourselves up so that God's will may be done in us and in God's creation, . . . transforms us into more available partners with God's work."[733] And contemplation is relating to the world "on a deeper level of attention" leading to deeper involvement with its needs.[734]

Thirdly is "justice, peace and the integrity of creation as prophetic dialogue,"[735] esteemed in all its aspects on a level with evangelism and establishing congregations. This includes not only "the *alleviation* of human suffering and exclusion" as historically practiced in Christian circles, but also "the eradication of their roots."[736] As the good news of a just God is preached to the poor, they are themselves empowered to strive for justice in companionship with a church that acknowledges the "preferential option for the poor."[737] In actively promoting peace the church addresses the violent fruit of injustice at another level. And in actively promoting ecological responsibility the church addresses the related violence that human greed inflicts on creation. The holistic expectation is that Christian conversion should be intimately connected with these concerns.

Fourthly, there is "interreligious dialogue as prophetic dialogue."[738] In the context of "the church's teaching about the presence of grace and salvation outside the boundaries of Christianity" in the wake of Vatican II, Christians need to approach other religions open to the possibility of new depths of faith.[739] Their deepening discovery of the fullness of Christ, "as though Christ himself actually grows through the work of mission," no less,[740] is "'a complementary side' of explicit Christian witness and invitation to conversation."[741] Such dialogue is nonthreatening because it is truly mutually edifying, and may take place at levels of personal sharing, joint public action, theological exchange, or religious experience.[742]

Fifthly, "inculturation as prophetic dialogue"[743] gives a radical new depth to the culture-sensitive contextualization that missionary work has always included. Where European conceptions and expressions of Christian theology were once regarded as definitive, the new world scale of Christianity has given rise to a sense that these are only one set of contextualizations of the faith. "[W]here culture is taken as an empirical reality, a certain equality among the world's cultures is recognized, and so theology can be in dialogue not just with one normative culture but with any culture in the world," and especially so when that culture is considered to contain "seeds of the word" and to be "charged with 'immanent transcendence.'" This calls for a new humility among cultural outsiders, "listening, learning, and being evangelized by the context," a new confidence for the cultural insider as he/she ventures giving theological voice, and an openness to basically fresh translations of the faith.[744]

And finally, "reconciliation as prophetic dialogue" lifts up healing through Christ and his community as a missionary model after a particularly alienating century.[745] Personally, culturally, politically, and within the church, it permits victims to look back on brutal history from God's "perspective of grace and mercy." Such, the church may mediate, but only God can accomplish it, and so, though one might offer "elements" for its attainment, it remains more "a *spirituality* rather than a *strategy*."[746]

D. Missional Considerations from Luther Studies

Given the importance of Luther research in Forde's theology, it seems necessary to consider the assessment of the missional aspects of Luther's thought by the rising disciplines. This assessment underwent dramatic change during Forde's century, from decidedly negative to profoundly positive.

Gustav Warneck

In 1882 "the founder of modern missiology," Gustav Warneck (1834-1910), wrote the first edition of his influential *Abriß einer Geschichte der protestantischen Missionen von der Reformation bis auf die Gegenwart*. Its second (1884) and considerably expanded seventh (1901) editions were translated into English as *Outline of a History of Protestant Missions from the Reformation to the Present Time*. Here Warneck presents what came to be a widely influential position that the sixteenth-century reformers in general, and Luther in particular, lacked a missionary vision. Not only did they not send missionaries; they expressed no regret over the geographical and political circumstances of their day that prevented it. In Warneck's words,

> If . . . the Reformers and their immediate disciples have no word either of sorrow or excuse that circumstances hindered their discharge of missionary duty, while they could not but see that the Church of Rome was implementing this duty on a broad scale, this strange silence can be accounted for satisfactorily only by the fact that the recognition of the missionary obligation was itself absent.[747]

This is not a pleasant realization for Warneck, nor for Protestants in general, as shown by the many who sought to disprove it with quotes from Luther, yet only unsuccessfully in Warneck's eyes. Gustav Leopold Plitt, for example, proposes that Luther considered his reforming activities to be essentially missionary, so that one might speak of a "Reformation mission."[748] Warneck counters that Plitt's quotations of Luther attest only that "Luther's mission sphere was, if we may so say, the paganised Christian church," not "the non-Christian world," and that by so arguing Luther's sense of mission, "Plitt evades the question at issue by substituting an unusual conception of missions."[749] No, Warneck says, though aware of the scandal "amongst ourselves" of "Turks, Jews, heathen, non-Christians all too many," Luther doesn't see these as "the objects of regular missionary work." Instead, he always applies "ta ethna" to the "non-Jewish nations which constitute Christendom," as, for instance, in the meaning of the second petition to the Lord's Prayer, "We pray that the kingdom of God may come *to us*."[750]

It's not that Luther lacks a sense of the universality of Christian faith. Warneck quotes his conviction that the gospel must reach the whole world and his articulation of the missionary commission to that end. Yet, Warneck quotes Luther (without giving the reference), "Many say that that has not yet been brought to pass. I say, nay, the saying has long ago been fulfilled." While not specifically asserting, as later Lutheran orthodoxy did, that the twelve apostles personally reached the entire world, "for his own time he reckons the missionary proclamation proper as accomplished."[751] That is, it has been offered throughout the world, but not everywhere accepted. For Luther's definition that is enough.

Warneck grants that there are Luther sayings apparently to the contrary. He is aware of the 1522 Ascension Day sermon, for instance, where the newly discovered "islands" are mentioned as places where the gospel has not yet come. Yet, Warneck is disappointed with Luther's response to the observation: instead of a summons "to any systematic missionary enterprise," he likens the preaching to "when a stone is thrown into the water" and "it makes wavelets and circles . . . and the wavelets move always farther and farther away . . . till they come to the bank. So with the preaching of the Gospel."[752] Where is any kind of call to action? No, "[t]he systematic work of missions is, in his judgment . . . a work confined to the Apostles."[753]

It is the same with Luther's references to the hope that captive Christians might give meaningful witness to the Turks. Though they seem positive, Warneck judges these to be "the spirit of Christian testimony, but not missionary," for "[n]owhere does he recommend a purposeful sending out or a voluntary going out of preachers to non-Christians with the view of Christianizing them."[754]

How could this be? The political situation has already been referred to, above. But Warneck charges that two elements of Luther's own theology are also responsible for this lack of missionary awareness. First, Luther's doctrine of election precludes mission: "God, to be sure, has everywhere His elect, whom by divers means He leads to faith; but how He brings this to pass, that is a matter of His sovereign grace,—a human missionary agency does not lie in the plan of His decree." In fact, God might Godself remove the gospel from a people as punishment for their neglect of it, yet this will not stop its course in history. It will simply pass to other nations. "But this unhindered course of the Gospel is not effected by missions, but by the free activities of Divine grace."[755] God will tend to the growth of his kingdom, and "[w]ith missionary institutions this confident hope has nothing whatever to do."[756]

Secondly, there is Luther's sense of eschatology, a sense that he shared with virtually all the reformers, that the end of the world was near. Warneck proposes that, coupled with the fact that the heathen "lay quite beyond their sphere of vision," it "clearly explains" their lack of mission. He weakens this particular argument by a double qualification. True, this sense didn't hinder the apostles from mission, but then they weren't encumbered by a conviction that the preaching to all nations had already been accomplished. And also true, Luther himself "does not assign the nearness of the end as a reason for dissociating the duty of missions from the church in his day; but this is simply because, even without that eschatological view, he knew nothing of such a duty."[757]

When Warneck wrote, the Luther renaissance was yet to happen, and Warneck himself, while conversant in Luther's writings, was no Luther scholar. His verdict on Luther's missional awareness, however, gained wide currency through his premier missiological reputation and the prominence of Germany's first missions chair at Halle which he occupied. Paul Wetter lists thirty-six missional voices after Warneck's that negatively assess Luther's mission awareness, many cited with reference to Warneck—"completely in the way of Warneck," "even stronger than Warneck," "following up on Warneck," "still in the way of Warneck," "Warneck's interpretation found for a long time a line of representatives," "took hold again of the arguments of Gustav Warneck," "coincides also in large measure with Warneck's point of view," and so forth.[758] The list includes such significant names in twentieth-century missiology as Kenneth Scott Latourette, Karl Barth, Stephen Neill, and William Richey Hogg. Perhaps it may be ventured that, in large measure through Warneck, the borning field of missiology got off on the wrong foot with respect to the heritage of Luther.

Karl Holl

A period of renewed Luther research and reassessment that began with the publication of the first volume of the *Weimarer Ausgabe* on the four hundredth birthday of the reformer, 1883, reached maturity with Karl Holl (1866-1926). Beginning with his 1910 essay, "The Teaching of Justification in Luther's Lecture on Romans, with Special Reference to the Issue of Certainty of Salvation" and culminating with his 1921 volume of eight and later nine Luther essays,[759] Holl articulated thought that would rivet Luther researchers for a generation in a movement that came to be called "the Luther renaissance." Part of that thought touched mission.

In 1924 Holl published an article in *Neue allgemeine Missionszeitschrift* called "Luther und die Mission," that, without referring directly to Warneck, seems to address some of the very points he raised. Citing from the new *Weimarer Ausgabe*, Holl shows that Luther was not merely silent on the question of whether Germany had ever been visited by an apostle; Luther emphatically denied the idea. It was clear to him that Germany had been evangelized by later missionaries, not the apostles. Farther afield, Luther's awareness of newly discovered "lands and islands" proved to him that the gospel had definitely not yet been everywhere heard. In Luther's well-known "ripples in the water" sermon Holl sees in Luther an awareness of a mission task that will go on until the last day. That is, it is one that must be fulfilled in the present, not only in the Americas and East Asia, but also nearer at hand, among the Turks, and Luther chastises the pope for coming to them in crusades rather than with the gospel.[760]

Holl rejects the idea that Luther's eschatology hindered a mission interest. Did he not at great cost lead an entire reformation? Expectation of an imminent return never kept him from that task; surely it would not keep him from mission. No, it was a lack of opportunity, Holl asserts. It was the Catholic church, not the Protestant, that had access to the world through the burgeoning colonial power of its catholic lands:

> What could Luther actually have done to bring a mission about? . . . Where lay the regions to which Protestantism could have gone? Where should Luther have gotten the ships to send his missionaries over?"[761]

In the face of the impossibility, Luther turned his attention to building up the church at home, and we may say that it was pragmatic rather than dogmatic considerations that kept Luther from a wider mission.

If Luther was unable to attempt mission in a global sense, he was able to prepare his church for it theologically. If the church is the congregation of the faithful that looked directly to Christ as its head, then all missionary authority is decentralized. Mission can be done by any Christian anywhere. Though it is true that Christians should submit to church order in Christian lands, this restriction falls away completely where there is yet no gospel.[762]

Holl is impressed by the depth of Luther's insight that mission is God's work and Christ's work. Christ is not far off during mission, but very near at hand to empower it and enable it. "God and Christ create it; humankind are only handymen; they can only pass the gospel forward. But they are still as handymen indispensible and should find their honor in this, that God validates their service."[763] In this awareness it would seem that Holl is a precursor to the *missio dei* awareness that emerged in the following decades through Barth, Hartenstein, and the Willingen missionary conference.

Holl remarks that Luther offers considerable practical missionary advice. For instance, one needs to get to know those to whom one goes. This includes knowledge of the language, but more than that, knowledge of the religious and ethical views of those to whom one is sent. One ought to be able to appreciate the good side of unbelievers' culture, even in the face of a doctrine of original sin. The customs and laws of those evangelized should not be automatically abrogated, but should be explored for "*Anknüpfungspünkte,*" contact points for the gospel, and be deepened by the Christian law of love. The goal of mission for Luther is to help people put the relationship of God and man into correct order, as evidenced by such documents as the *Small Catechism*. Politics and compulsion have no role to play in it, for the gospel seeks only freely-hearing listeners.[764]

The contrast with Warneck's view of Luther is dramatic: here Luther emerges as a mission-minded reformer who is thwarted only by circumstances from attempting a wider witness. Wetter marks Holl as a watershed, after which positive evaluations of Luther's missional approach gradually gain number and weight.[765] The thirty-five names cited as referring positively to Luther after Holl include Werner Elert, Walter Holsten, Gustav Wingren, George Vicedom, Johannes Aagaard, Rolf Syrdal, and James Scherer.

Werner Elert

Professor of historical theology and later systematic theology at Erlangen between the wars, Werner Elert (1885-1954) is known as one whose synthesis of historical method and dogmatic faithfulness led him to witness for an essential agreement in the work of Martin Luther, the Lutheran confessions, and the historic Christian dogmatic documents. He "immersed himself in the literature on Luther's development that had been pouring out since the discovery of Luther's early commentaries and since the pioneering work of Karl Holl," finding there a continuity of the young Luther with the old and revealing "the misrepresentations perpetrated by later generations."[766] Ten years after his death, he was still being called "one of the most original, prominent, and effective of modern Lutheran theologians."[767] Pelikan regards his *Morphologie des Luthertums* (1931) to be his most important work. At the conclusion of its fourth chapter, "The Church," is a section called simply "Missions."

Unlike Holl who never mentioned Warneck, Elert chides him almost sarcastically by name:

Indeed, as Gustav Warneck pointed out, Luther was not "a man of missions in our sense of the word." The poor man! Instead of founding a missionary society, accompanying Cortez to Mexico, or at least assuring for himself a professorship of missionary science, he devoted himself, of all things, to the reformation of the church![768]

It is as if Warneck requires that Luther's ideas should have to correspond with a nineteenth century definition of mission to qualify. Elert sees both the idea of mission, or "missions" as he calls it, and Luther's approach to it, as much more profound than that.

In the first place mission is not "a theory that has to do with engaging in an undertaking." I take this to mean that it consists not primarily of questions of strategy and logistics—where, when, and how—an effort requiring "special arrangements" or "special call." Neither is mission primarily concerned with "questions of sociology," though some have made it so.[769] It is not dependent upon some longing of the heathen for the Gospel, a thought that Luther himself could not believe in, though he thought that they needed it.[770] Rather, "missions" must be thought of "on the basis of the impact of the Gospel," or "*evangelische Ansatz*,"[771] a term that Engelder of Concordia Seminary translated synonymously with *Rechtfertigungslehre*, the doctrine of justification, though Elert's translator, Walter Hansen has to explain why he chose not to follow him in this.[772] Either way, there is a sense that it needs to be taken much more theologically. For Elert this deeper basis will mean two things: "(1) faith in the omnipotence and the universal teleology of the Gospel and (2) the affirmation of the mission to proclaim the Gospel."[773] That is, the missionary imperative comes from reliance on the power and comprehensive purpose of the message itself, and is not a secondary reflection.

This definition of mission with reference to the heart of the gospel, in the second place, changes the way one speaks of Luther's approach to it. His oft-cited idea that "the Gospel had already fulfilled its mission [to] all nations" doesn't suggest the job is done, but simply flows from his sense of "the universal validity of the Gospel." It means that it is proclaimed "for all," emphasized "to prove that the church of Christ is not bound to a particular locality." The idea that the missionary mandate has ended "would be opposed to the dynamic view of the Gospel and the church." "The course of the Gospel to all nations" is rather "an act in progress . . . ." It passes through the whole world "in the present tense." "It wants to be taught and preached always and always . . . ." It "keeps on going farther . . . ." "The Gospel keeps advancing . . . ."[774] Elert marks Luther's passion for proclamation in all of this, and concludes:

> [T]he eager attention the Gospel pays to its proclamation is independent of the kind of people we have before us. Only from the dynamic of the Gospel itself can the 'idea of missions,' which should be evangelical, get its obligating power, not from reflecting on this or that kind of people.[775]

This gospel-driven obligation "rests upon all Christians." In a place where the gospel is not heard, one speaks no longer of reserving the proclamation to the "duly called," for each Christian has not only "the right and power" but "is under the obligation" to speak. In fact, if he/she doesn't, the believer "runs the risk of losing his soul and of incurring the disfavor of God."[776] Sometimes by chance, as with a prisoner of war, sometimes by direct sending, "the church in motion" comes to new places with its witness.[777]

The history of early Lutheran attempts at mission, despite the energy required to consolidate the reformation, helps show that Lutheranism "never forgot Luther's ideas about the motion of the church and about the boundless dynamic of the Gospel."[778] Elert argues that sixteenth century Lutheran efforts to advance the gospel among southern Slavs, Jews, and Swedish Lapps as well as seventeenth century work in India and Delaware must be considered reflective of Luther's original mission-mindedness, even if, as royal rather than voluntaristic initiatives, they would not meet Warneck's specifications.[779]

Ingemar Öberg

Ingemar Öberg, Swedish-speaking Finnish professor of church history at the School of Mission and Theology at Stavanger, Norway, from 1978 to 1992, has been cited as one of Scandinavia's foremost Luther scholars, remembered for works on Luther's theology of the keys and on his hermeneutics, *Bibelsyn och bibeltolkning hos Martin Luther*. Of primary interest to us is his 1991 Swedish book on mission, *Luther och världsmissionen: Historisk-Systematiska studier med särskild hänsyn till bibelutläggningen*, published in English in 2007 as *Luther and World Mission: A Historical and Systematic Study with Special Reference to Luther's Bible Exposition*.[780] It represents the century-long deepening of the reaction of Luther scholarship to Warneck's challenge and an affirmation of Luther's missional awareness.

There is no question about the context of this book. In the first sentence Öberg names the opposition: "[o]lder historians, as well as some recent writers" who "have painted a remarkably negative picture of Martin Luther's interest in mission." In the second sentence, he names Warneck as his first example, cites five among the many others who followed him up through Latourette, and discusses their position briefly.[781] On page three Öberg states his counterthesis:

> Luther had a mission perspective and directly encouraged mission. . . . Especially important is how the reformer . . . focused mission on the meaning of God's/Christ's church-building work through the Word and the Sacraments, not primarily through organized mission nor the interest of modern mission for mission investments and technique.[782]

Öberg has his own reasons for coming to this view, but in a three page footnote citing the supporting evidence of eighteen other late-century scholars, he confirms that he is not alone.[783]

In an effort to understand the negative view, he sees "an anachronistic blindness" that cannot see "how difficult—not to say impossible—it would have been for Luther and his followers to start a foreign mission." First, as Warneck himself observed, they were surrounded by Roman Catholic and Muslim powers. These "[r]uling authorities were capable of placing many obstacles in the way of mission activity." The reformers had no protection of "Protestant empires."[784] Geographically, foreign mission was an impossibility.

Secondly, Luther "saw as wholly decisive his call and task to reform and to renew the Christian faith in Germany and its borderlands." The work of the Reformation itself was an overwhelming priority for him. This is true even if it is apparent from his exegetical work that he "did not consider world mission to be of secondary importance to reform."[785] Here again, scholarship agreed.

Thirdly, and quite a new consideration, "Luther research is a strenuous enterprise." Since Luther did not develop his material logically, but rather exegetically, as it occurred in the texts, it is not possible easily to access his missional views. With the possible exception of the tract *That Christ Was Born a Jew* (1523) where he expresses evangelical concern for Jews, Luther never wrote extensively on mission as such. Rather his attitude is sprinkled, "dropped here and there," through his lectures and sermons, so that unless one had "penetratingly and objectively" addressed the source material, "Luther's exegesis of the Old and New Testaments, his many writings, and his sermons," it would be perfectly natural to come to a negative assessment. In other words, one can attribute the negative assessments to a relatively superficial grasp of Luther's writings.[786]

Fourthly, Öberg points to a basic difference in the understanding of the task of mission itself. The dominant mission tradition over the past two hundred years, "Pietism, the Baptist movement, and the large folk movements within various denominations," have emphasized "the special office of missionary, the charismatic mission call, fellowship, and mission organization, . . . Second and Third Article concerns, [and] [c]onversion, faith, and life with Jesus." It is true that Luther "considered some of those same themes to be extremely important, but his understanding grew from a different base: creation theology, the inherent power of the Gospel, the doctrine of justification through faith, and that God personally builds his reign throughout the world."[787] That is to say that the dominant ways of thinking and talking about mission during the past two centuries simply had trouble identifying, much less appreciating, the missional in Luther's thought.

The core of Öberg's research is the massive third chapter, "The Mission Perspective in Luther's Commentaries, Lectures, and Sermons on the Bible," which covers almost half the book. In heavily footnoted work Öberg cites evidence of a comprehensive Luther mission motif in his Old Testament commentaries, in his interpretation of the Gospels, and in his interpretation of Acts and the epistles. Here we see attention to theological factors not always linked with conversations about mission: the righteousness of faith, the preached Word, law and gospel, faith and freedom, parenesis, governing authorities, and the like.[788] Treatment of such matters demonstrates the theological depth to which Öberg takes the mission conversation. For example,

> For Luther, Christ and righteousness through faith made the preaching of the Gospel a necessity. That Doctrine, in an almost tiresome manner, became the center for the reformer's ecclesiology and missiology. Without those two pillars, the whole superstructure of Luther's theology would be lost. Luther's writings show that he integrated church and mission, considering the whole apostolic church as being sent and sending.[789]

It's not so much about "organized mission nor the interest of modern mission for mission investments and technique" but rather, once again, about "the meaning of God's/Christ's church-building work through the Word and Sacraments."[790]

The almost-as-massive fourth chapter, "Luther and Mission Praxis," attempts to show that Luther was not just theoretical in his missionary interest, but that he actually acted upon it in his dealings with the only two non-Christian peoples he was aware of: the Jews and the Muslims. In the first part of this chapter, valuable in itself as an extensive review of research on Luther and the Jews, Öberg daringly discerns a mission concern by Luther for Jews even in his later polemical writings.[791] And in the section on Muslims, Luther strategizes towards a hope that "the Turks should once again be visited by the Gospel."[792]

Öberg's extensive work characterizes a growing consensus in Luther studies that Luther was, without himself using a term unknown to his time, missionally oriented, not only theoretically by his theological mindset, but also practically by envisioning concrete steps to see that it might actually happen. Many have argued that his work in large measure prepared his church for the missional tasks that it eventually assumed.[793]

We have now offered a composite sketch of the term "mission" in ways that should be recognizable to scholars in the field today. Though the term, derived from the Latin *missio*, has only recently been used to describe the task of the church as it interfaced with its world, the concept is rooted in the biblical witness itself, in prominent terms like the Hebrew *saleh* and the Greek *apostello*, "to send." Judging the veracity of assertions that Judaism was a missionary religion may depend upon whether intentionality is required or whether simple effect is sufficient. Use of the terms in the New Testament seem, first of all, to point to God's sendings, especially of Jesus, but then also of Jesus' sending his disciples, first to the Jews and only later to the Gentiles. Through Jesus' commissioning Paul understood a sharing of apostolic authority in content of the preaching and the range of its authority.

The task has taken on a number of shapes over the course of church history. Bosch lists six. These include an apocalyptically urgent message creating a single community out of Jews and Gentiles in the primitive church paradigm, a timeless gospel intellectually understood and enfleshed in *theosis*-anticipating lives in the Eastern Church paradigm, a call to penance and the official channels of salvation in the Roman Catholic Church, an assurance of justification by faith "for me" as affirmed by Scriptures in the Reformation churches, an invitation into an expanding church based on concern for the less fortunate in a post-Enlightenment paradigm, and dealing with the post-Enlightenment loss of confidence that characterizes the present era.

Thomas Aquinas first pioneered the use of the term *missio* itself in his *Summa Theologica* to speak of the Father's sending of the Son and of the Holy Spirit. Though linked to the idea of the eternal precessions within the Trinity, he reserved the word *missio* specifically for God's sending into the world. In all his writings there is not the slightest premonition of the future use of the word for human sending. This would come later.

In the twentieth century there occurred a rapid evolution of the term. Yates traces developments that include emphases on geographical expansion, development of a people's church, critical reexamination of missionary practice, exploration of relationship with other world religions, presence and dialogue, liberation, church growth, and addressing pluralism and enlightenment. A final emphasis on accompaniment following Yates' book seems to complete the century. Despite the risks involved, the expansion of the usage of the term term has proceeded apace.

David Bosch's thirteen interrelated elements, and Stephen Bevans and Roger Schroeder's synthesis of three typologies attempt to portray the shape of missiological concerns as it presents itself today. Bosch lists mission as the church with others, *missio Dei*, mediating salvation, a quest for justice, evangelism, contextualization, liberation, inculturation, common witness, ministry by the whole people of God, witness to people of other living faiths, theology, and action in hope, all of these integrated into one motion that we are privileged to participate in. Bevans and Schroeder offer a first typology of mission that focuses on the trinitarian divine nature of mission, a second typology that centers on liberating service as a manifestation of the reign of God, and a third typology that emphasizes mission as proclamation of Jesus Christ as universal Savior. Their own synthesis of the three in "mission as prophetic dialogue" holds together a "bold humility" that respects the other and an over-against-ness that risks bringing a fresh perspective to the other as it tends to six basic components: witness and proclamation; liturgy, prayer and contemplation; justice, peace, and the integrity of creation; interreligious dialogue; inculturation; and reconciliation. It seems that Bosch's inclusive definition emphasizes the diversity implicit in mission and that Bevans and Schroeder's lifts up an attitudinal ideal in the midst of it.

A review of the trajectory of Luther studies on the question of Luther's own missiological awareness offers a slightly different angle on the mission question. At century's beginning Gustav Warneck set the tone with his disheartened, pessimistic verdict: a mission impulse as such was absent in Luther as in all the reformers. Though widely influential and persistent through mid-century, this opinion was challenged, gently by Karl Holl as early as 1924, and sharply by Werner Elert in 1931. The challenge was rooted in two new approaches: a deeper search into the writings of Luther himself, and a questioning of the nineteenth century definition of mission that informed Warneck's analysis. What Holl and Elert began in brief, Ingemar Öberg completed, citing at length examples from Luther's exegetical writing to demonstrate a reformer single-minded about a mission defined, again, by "Christ and righteousness through faith" that "made the preaching of the Gospel a necessity."[794]

CHAPTER 5

Missional Aspects of Forde's Theology

Though no books or articles have been written on the matter, it is this writer's experience that it is not an uncommon idea that Gerhard Forde was unconcerned about mission. In the theological marketplace the Forde name is widely associated with such topics as justification by faith, Martin Luther, law and gospel, and God's saving election, but not with the mission of the church. Over the months of composition of this thesis, the idea of a Forde/mission antipathy occurred again and again in conversations as the thesis title was discussed with friends and colleagues. In fact, this writer once presumed it himself.

One can speculate about source of the idea. In the first place Forde doesn't write any articles specifically about mission. Not only does the word not occur in the titles of any of his articles or books; it does not even occur substantially in the body of any articles or books before 1980. If one happened not to read the right articles, one might never come upon a comment by Forde on mission.

Furthermore, when he finally does bring it up, he can be quite sharply critical of mission as he sees it worked out in the life of the church. For example, he sees the term coopted willy-nilly by the hierarchy of his own church denomination in support of whatever its "program" and its "bureaucratic theology might happen to be at the moment."[795] In his famous critique of the Key 73 campaign, he charged that the aspect of mission he found there, evangelism, was "just form without content," "an empty box," "new technique, bigger and better strategies, grander schemes," "more method than substance, more concern about 'the experience,' 'the decision,' and *how* it is produced than who or what produces it."[796] Such critiques of the church establishment could indeed give the casual reader the impression that Forde was against mission and the evangelism associated with it.

Then again, Forde's reputation with regard to mission may have to do with the impression one sometimes encounters in conversations that Forde was a universalist. The train of reasoning might go like this: if God is the sole actor in our salvation, as Forde fervently insisted, and if the cross is understood to be for all people, then it may be easy to declare, in general, without further thought on the matter, perhaps, that all people are saved, in which case a mission to share the cross with them would be misconceived. To use Forde's own words for the sinner's complaint, "If God elects, what is the use of our preaching? We sit around and pout, perhaps, and say, 'Let God do it then, if He is so pushy!'"[797] As we have seen (p. 251, n505), Forde is clear in "The Work of Christ" and elsewhere about his strong reserve towards a universalist position, but still the opinion persists.

However the idea of a Forde-against-mission came about, this chapter will demonstrate that it is a misconception. We will show that Forde was indeed concerned about an authentic mission of the church, and that his own ministry was a contribution to that mission. We will argue it, first, on the basis of Forde's own writings and, secondly, on the basis of a comparison of Forde with the kinds of definition of mission common in the twentieth century. We will propose three contributions by Forde to the missiological conversation of our age. We will identify three areas of contention between Forde and the missional conversation of our age. And finally, we will discuss in more depth three missiologically related questions raised in our analysis of Forde's theology.

A. Forde's Own Use of "Mission"

A form of the word "mission" occurs at least forty times in no fewer than eleven of Forde's articles and six of his sermons. There are concentrations of ten of these occurrences in a single 1983 article, "The Place of Theology in the Church," twelve of them in a single undated sermon on John 10:22-30 entitled, "My Sheep Hear My Voice," and six in an unpublished proposal to the curriculum revision committee of his seminary, "The Minister as Ambassador."[798] In light of the occasional negative references to mission mentioned above, it must be said that most of the occurrences refer to a positive reality that belongs to the church and to which the church is called: "we never get around to a preaching or a mission which actually 'does' [the justification],[799] or, "I happen to think it is our calling, our mission, to put this [theology of the cross] before the American church and the American public,"[800] or, "precisely words like this, [the assertion of divine power in John 10], confront us most squarely with the question of our mission today."[801] Of course Forde makes other references to what one might associate with mission without using the exact word for it: ministry, for a classic example,[802] but also the concerns of such fields as pastoral theology, proclamation, evangelism, and world mission as well.[803] "Must we not," he asks in an article on church quotas, ". . . operate on the belief that it is our calling to preach that message to all?"[804] Or, in a sermon, "To you dear friends of the class of 74 who are leaving us today I say, 'Go and preach him! Preach until the world wants God. . . . Preach that he who hear[s] might be saved.'"[805] The point is that, first of all, there are just simply many positive affirmations of the idea of mission in Forde's work. In light of the incidence of these references to mission, direct and indirect, the idea of an antithesis between Forde and mission becomes at least problematical, and the question becomes, instead, just what authentic mission might have meant to him.

In a 1980 article that may include his first serious mention of mission, Forde connects the mission of the church to one of his primary themes concerning the proclamation of the gospel:

> We all agree that 'God is love,' but never get around to saying his 'I love you' to anyone. We agree that God justifies sinners by his grace (even Pelagius believed that!), but we never get around to a preaching or a mission which actually *does* it.[806]

Here, mission is a term paralleled with preaching, a speaking of justification of sinners by grace that not only talks about it, as many do, but actually "*does* it." As we saw in chapter three, this is Fordean code language for allowing the dynamic of law-gospel proclamation to bring about the critical eschatological moment of death and new life in the hearer. For Forde to connect mission with this moment is for him to associate it with his highest expectations.[807]

A similar use of the word occurs in the last line of an significant 1990 article, "The Ordained Ministry," in which Forde defines the work of ministry: "making the mystery public":

> The commission that impels ministry in this fallen world is to do the electing authorized by the death and resurrection of Jesus Christ. . . . The entire drive behind ministry is toward making public, bearing witness to, the mystery hidden for ages but now revealed in the church. [808]

This ministry is "service to the divine deed":

> Ministry as obedient service to the divine electing and reconciling deed in Jesus means the announcement of the end of the old and the beginning of the new. Its proclamation, shaped by the theology of the cross, is governed by the distinction between law and gospel.[809]

To that end a public office of ministry is established, and Forde argues for an eschatological understanding of this office and the call and ordination that lead to it. His concluding line makes the connection between healthy ministry and healthy mission: "It is quite possible that renewed understanding of what the office of *ministry* is about could contribute to renewed understanding of what the church and its *mission* is about."[810] Again, the church's mission is identified with the "divine electing and reconciling deed" of a cruciform proclamation.

Apparently, Forde preached his John 10:22-30 sermon at a conference or convention that had as its theme, "Unity in Mission?" It seems that the relation between church unity and church mission was being discussed, perhaps in preparation for the creation of the "new Lutheran church." Forde worries that one of the causes for disunity in the church today might be the diverse theological efforts to make God more manageable. Instead, he proposes that we might find unity in a mission to speak God's word:

> Can the voice [of God] be heard? . . . *Now* we come to the question of our mission, and indeed, the question of unity in that mission. If the voice is to be heard, someone must have the audacity to speak, yes, to speak for the Good Shepherd who said, 'I and the Father are One.' There is our mission and there we will find or lose our unity. It all hinges on whether we can find the courage to speak, not *about* God not merely about the good shepherd, but to speak the word *of* God, *from* God, to speak *in the voice* of the Good Shepherd. To speak the gospel.[811]

This speaking *of* God and *from* God is, again, the very same first order proclamation referred to above. Forde proposes that its exercise is not only our mission as a church, but that in this common mission we will find our unity as a church. "Someone must have the guts to say it. You must say it, I must say it. That is our mission. And if we are driven to say it, then, and only then, I expect, will we find our unity."[812] The church is united in its task of sharing the gospel, Forde's primary understanding of mission.

But there is another. Since, as Forde argues, "theology drives to proclamation," the theology that leads to this missional proclamation may also itself be described as missional. Four years before the formation of "the new Lutheran church," Forde made this connection in his *dialog* article, "The Place of Theology in the Church." There he comments on the popularity of the word mission at the time, and expresses his concern that "in our haste to get at 'mission' we have tended to leave our theology behind, or even to hint that our theology is perhaps responsible for our previous failings in 'mission-mindedness.'" There is an "academic theology" that seems, indeed, to have a "virtual irrelevance" to the church in its intellectual disconnectedness from the message of the pulpit, and there is a "bureaucratic theology," "a curious and deceptive mixture of theological slogans and bureaucratese" designed to make the institution function well, and there is mainstream American theology in its "desperate flight from the orthodoxy of the Calvinist and Puritan founding fathers."[813] In this context Forde argues that "[i]t is simply not responsible just to drift theologically within whatever currents happen along. We must engage in church-wide theological discussion of the many issues affecting the church's *mission*." In particular,

Lutheran theology has a way of dealing with the root problems of American theology which neither surrenders orthodoxy nor succumbs to liberalism and sentimentalization. . . . It is this preeminently to which I refer when I say . . . that the mission of Lutheranism in this country is first and foremost *theological,* and that our primary task is to take stock of and heed our theological calling.[814]

Theology, therefore, is not only to *address* the issues affecting the church's mission—perhaps understood in the proclamatory sense noted above; the defense and advancement of a theology that does this *becomes* itself a mission and a prime responsibility of the church that is capable of it. Forde sees the Lutheran tradition as endowed with such a theology, if it does not neglect it.[815]

There's a practical side to this mission. "If our mission is largely theological we have to tool up to do it."[816] Forde suggested a churchwide "Theological Convocation" of theologians in the new Lutheran church (though this did not win the day) to sort out and discuss theological issues. He suggested that bishops be active teachers and theological overseers to their pastors. And he proposed increased focus in the church's seminary education so that essential doctrinal awareness is retained.[817] As we have seen, he got an opportunity to advance this latter suggestion in a special way through his decisive contribution to the curriculum revision committee at Luther Seminary (see above, pp. 38-39). That the seminary curriculum should be so designed that first-year biblical studies and second-year confession of the faith should lead to third-year study of the church's mission in his proposal suggests, again, the significant part mission plays in the life of the church in Forde's mind.

It is not clear that Forde's own use of the word warrants assigning him a broader understanding of mission than this. In one rare and inconclusive passage, he seems aware of discussions "about whether the church's mission is proclamation *or* development, personal salvation *or* social justice, etc.," but he deems them "silly debates," and thinks that "if somehow [the connection between unconditional gospel and freedom for the world] could be grasped," we could "get on with the business of taking care of this world and the neighbor as lovingly, wisely, and pragmatically as our gifts enable."[818] Rather than connect the care of the world and neighbor firmly with mission, it is almost as if he abandons the term with the unworthy debate and calls the church to get on with its caring task. The point is certainly not that he is against social and ecological concerns. Clearly, he sees an evident connection between the proclamation rightly accomplished and the human freedom that might be able to tend to these concerns. It's just that it he did not connect these various concerns with the term "mission of the church."

That suggests one more observation: Forde seems to use the term "mission" *only* in connection with the mission of the church. It is not used of other agencies at work alongside the church nor of individuals at work on their own. It is always of the church, though certainly not necessarily or maybe even institutionally understood. Neither is it used in the plural, as if particular efforts or areas of work should be called missions. It is reserved for the theological and proclamatory task of the church alone as it prepares to proclaim and actually proclaims the death-and-life word of God.

B. Forde and the Missiological Definitions

Another way to approach the question of the relationship between Forde and mission is to attempt to relate such understandings of twentieth century missiology as we described in chapter four to the work of Forde. There is no sign in the Forde corpus that he has done research in the field as such, so coincidence or divergence cannot be seen as consciously designed by him. This exercise is rather a kind of empirical measure of the incidence of overlap and the possibility of conversation between Forde and the field of missiology today.

With Respect to Yates' Historical Approach

In terms of the nine historical paradigms that Timothy Yates used and we completed for twentieth century mission (see above, pp. 134-140), the strongest correlation is surely with the third paradigm, "mission in critical reexamination." Along with the theologians whom Yates chose as examples of this paradigm, Forde shares a concern that the mission of the church is in danger of going astray, if it has not already done so. Allen critiqued strategic concerns about missionary dependence, Fleming attacked the linkage of mission and imperialism, and the Hocking report proposed a broader definition to include more social attention (pp. 135-136). To these proposals, Forde might say, "no doubt all good and important things," as he wryly liked to affirm penultimate issues.[819] But, in his mind, the things that truly compromise the integrity of the church's mission are much more profound: a synergism that compromises the gospel of God's unconditional election, a use of the law to cover the difference, an understanding of proclamation that replaces actual effect with mere knowledge, and a theology that is not vital towards that end. These are issues much more significant than questions of strategy and definition. Until the church addresses such matters, the missiological conversation will be shallow and ultimately irrelevant, as old Adams and Eves continue to live out their religious lives in the wake of missionary efforts. Forde would certainly see his ministry as a part of this address in what one might call, indeed, "mission in critical reexamination."

Forde was aware of the liberation movement blossoming during his ministry and often voiced concern for the world's poor and oppressed, but he was concerned about the shape of the connection of their political liberation with mission, Yates' sixth paradigm. In his mind, "acts of liberation in the ultimate sense of the word"—liberation from sin, death, and the devil—need to be distinguished from "sundry political liberations, however beneficial they may be to society in this age and however much they may flow from ultimate liberation."[820] The freedom that he saw emerging from the eschatological event in proclamation might well express itself in care towards the world and the neighbor, and the church "cannot but reveal itself except in acts of liberation," but "one does not have to buy in on all the currently popular liberation theology language to maintain this—though such liberation theology is not to be denied either."[821] It is perhaps fair to say that Forde was interested in the liberation theologies and the work with which they were associated, but he was very concerned that they be properly related to the eschatological act. Though he never included them in his understanding of mission, his reflection on them would make strong contributions with this Yates paradigm, "mission as liberation."

Forde's concern for viability of the message in the context of the worldview of the hearers seems to relate to the second Yates paradigm, "the development of a people's church." We have examined in some detail how he wanted the message to have especially theological coherence in terms of worldview for the proclaimer, but also linguistic and cultural viability for the people among whom the proclaimer served. On the other hand, he would resonate with Karl Barth's concern about any compromise of the gospel with natural theology in the process. It's the same concern that, at the 1938 Tambaram IMC meeting, brought Hendrik Kraemer to protest the syncretism he saw threatening the church of his day.

Yates' first paradigm, "mission as expansion," is reflected in the Forde research by only two of the briefest of mentions: one, a completely incidental reference to mission fields in his first article;[822] and a second, that the mission element of the revised seminary curriculum might include, perhaps, world mission, already noted.[823] By themselves these mentions are rather inconclusive. More significant are references like those to the universal force of the great commission,[824] or Forde's excitement over Luther's idea that baptism is a sign of God's covenant with all nations: "Think of that! A covenant with all the heathen!"[825] It does seem that Forde understands a scope for the gospel that is universal and global, if not actually expressed geographically, but that scope as a missional concern is not generally a burden of Forde's message.

For one reason or another, it is problematic to relate Forde to the other paradigms. He was deeply involved in the Lutheran-Roman Catholic dialogues in North America, but one could only imagine how he would have committed himself as deeply to dialogue with people of another religion, Yates' fifth paradigm. Church growth, the seventh paradigm, was virtually an alien concern to him. Sometimes, he expressed confidence in the explosive possibilities of proclaiming the promise truly unconditionally, but he never fretted about how big the resulting church might be. Forde has negative things to say about the dangers of pluralism and the post-enlightenment consensus on truth, the eighth paradigm. It would appear he would warn people away from embracing those phenomena in a missional engagement. And without access to a word by Forde on accompaniment, we can only speculate that he might see it as a bureaucratic approach to an ill-defined togetherness that doesn't get around to proclaiming a vital word.

With respect to Yates' analysis, then, we remark significant affinities between Forde's work and mission in its critical reexamination (point three), but on a level rather theologically more penetrating than usual. We also note serious contributions to a proper understanding of a theology of liberation (point seven), though he never associates it with mission. There are points of contact with the work necessary to make the gospel viable to the worldview of a given people (point two), but with corresponding concern that its vital work not be compromised with the old Adam's syncretistic inclinations as it does so (points two and four). While Forde seems to consider the missional task global, geographical expansion is certainly not a burden of his work (point one).

With Respect to Bosch's Emerging Ecumenical Paradigm

David Bosch's definitive, late-twentieth century portrait of ecumenical missiology as summarized in chapter four included thirteen interrelated elements,[826] and Forde's work relates to a number of them. With Bosch as with Yates, the most striking is undoubtedly the theological aspect. Bosch divided his twelfth element, "mission as theology," into two tasks which Bosch at one point describes as "a missiological agenda for theology" and "a theological agenda for mission."[827] While Forde used none of these slogans as such, one can hear the first in Forde's favored expression, "Theology is for proclamation." Bosch quotes Andersen that "theology ceases to be theology if it loses its missionary character." This is not far from Forde's conviction that theology that does not drive to "deliver the goods" is "a relatively abstract and 'second order' exercise,"[828] that often ends up as "a rather frantic attempt to avoid really encountering God."[829] In other words, Forde would judge the theological enterprise on the basis of its commitment to bring forth a faithful proclamation. The missional praxis needs to flow from sound theological considerations rather than be blown by the fads of the moment, what Forde disdainfully calls "relevance." This translates into a faithfulness to scripture's law-gospel distinction that drives towards the effective killing and life-giving word *extra nos*, as from God's own self. Thus the theological task serves the missional task—"a missiological agenda for theology."

But the second slogan, "a theological agenda for mission," also works for Forde. It suggests that the missional task will have implications on theology, as well. It reminds one of Forde's insistence on viability for the theological formulation, and, we proposed, for the proclamation that that formulation will inform. In other words, it asks for attentiveness to the missional context so that the message and the theology that drives it may be rendered intelligible and vital in the worldview, language, and culture of the hearers. It therefore appears that, in terms of Bosch's twelfth element of missiological definition, both by his missional address to theology and by his theological address to mission, it may be said that Forde was deeply engaged in the theological side of the missiological task.

After describing diverse eschatological errors in mission over the past two centuries Bosch marks as his thirteenth element, the search for "an eschatology for mission which is both future-directed and oriented to the here and now."[830] Forde is certainly not responding to past missiological errors, but a vibrant eschatology is written large across the proclamatory task he calls the church's mission, and we spent almost half the chapter on his theology examining it. Once again, as he writes, "[p]roclamation I take to be the announcement, the declaration in the living present, indeed the opening of the eschatological future or at least the foretaste thereof, that creates faith."[831] Or, citing Ebeling, "The act character of revelation is maintained through the idea that the gospel is the eschatological *event* which brings men freedom from the law in the present. . . . Gospel is the eschatological advent of freedom and life."[832] In Forde, eschatological talk becomes a critical present reality in light of a coming fulfillment, a position poised to make a vigorous contribution to the missiological eschatological conversation.

The expectation of the eschatological is a logical result of the experience of a God who acts in history and will act again, the *extra nos* quality of the message we have examined before in Forde. It could be argued that the twentieth century's rediscovery of the eschatological shape of the gospel is directly connected with the rise of the idea of *missio Dei*, Bosch's second element. While it is not clear that Forde ever uses the phrase in his writings, he has a strong sense that whatever happens at the critical eschatological moment in the proclamation is truly God's own action. It is, in fact, so much God's own action that efforts to describe it otherwise are beside the point. Insofar as the proclamation is associated with mission (see pp. 161-162, above), it is to radicalize the term *missio Dei* at this point around a strong christological focus in such a way as to offer a fresh point of view to the missiological conversation.

On the other hand, the evidence gives no reason to suppose that Forde would follow Hoekendijk in identifying God's political activity in the world with salvation, so that the church's task in affirming the *missio*

Dei might be to discern and support "what God might be up to" out in the world. Luther's concept of a *deus absconditus* whose action apart from Christ the Christian might find quite terrifying, Forde would counsel, ought to keep the church from such audacious talk. Forde's definition of mission was too concise for that, always identifying it with the church and always connecting it with the proclamation that brought about the eschatological moment and with the theology that informed that proclamation.

Evangelism, Bosch's fifth element, is not necessarily Forde's first choice of a word to describe the missional action that leads to the eschatological moment in proclamation. "I am, I believe, as much committed to the evangel as the next person," he writes in his Key 73 critique, "and I do not wish for a moment to discredit the genuine efforts of the church to get that gospel heard." Nevertheless, "[w]henever the evangel becomes an 'ism,' whenever it is caught up in some supposedly 'self-evident' mass movement, we must ask about 'hidden agendas'"[833]—like how to get more influence for the church or how to balance the parish budget, perhaps. In Forde's mind "[e]vangelism is what happens when the church forgets how to preach the gospel." This occurs because "almost from the start Protestant theology has been unable to cope with the idea that in the gospel we have to do with God's gracious decision about us, not our decisions about God." Such theology offers assertions about what God is like and appeals to the hearer to assent or "respond." "Evangelism is the more or less natural outcome of this bankrupt theology."[834]

Forde's theology gives him fresh things to say about what others call evangelism. In his mind the primary task of the church is "to learn how to tell the good news of God's gracious decision about us in Jesus and what that means for our lives." That could be a new definition of the term, evangelism, were it to please him. It is not a strategic program— like techniques on how to do evangelism better. This is a "profoundly theological" program—like the church may not even remember what real evangelism is! "[T]he fact is that we have seldom really dared to preach the gospel and consequently are not very experienced at doing it"![835] Forde's approach to an eschatological act nature of proclamation in law and gospel is his life's proposal to the church to start over. In his mind it's that serious.

Bosch's fourth element is "mission as a quest for justice," and here Forde can be heard in two ways. On the one hand, there is no question that he is concerned about justice. He practically concludes his doctoral dissertation on the subject when he suggests "that in the much neglected concept of the use of the law there are great possibilities for understanding the *positive* relationship of the church to the problems of social justice."[836] It constitutes a potential fruit of his doctoral work. In a sermon that is probably early he challenges his hearers, "Are you concerned only with 'law and order' or with *justice* for all men?"[837] Clearly, he holds out for the latter.

On the other hand, and perhaps more so as he grows older, he seems worried that concern for justice by the church will trump its primary task of proclamation. "[P]erhaps one need only listen to much of the preaching in the church to discover whether proclamation of the gospel is not actually being locked out by concern for what the world calls justice."[838]

> I confess that when "Headquarters" (a euphemism for archa?) sends out its pronouncements or the preacher goes into the peroration in the end—or sometimes in the beginning as well—about social justice and political advocacy and all the latest causes, a deep depression settles over me. And of course I wonder why and even feel a little bit guilty about it because the causes seem generally—though not always—such worthy ones, causes which I myself, indeed, support. But I have come to suspect more and more of late that the cause of my depression rests with the matter of the archa. . . . It seems as though we assume that when we get on to all those grand and pious programs of ours we have gotten to the real business of the church (even if it turns out to be mostly talk). Oh, we can give a little theology a lick and a promise, as in 'The Lutheran,' as long as it isn't more than a page or so or too complicated, but then we can get on with what really matters![839]

It's not that Forde is not interested in justice. He is. But he nowhere shows interest in defining justice in terms of the mission of the church, and he certainly is not interested in justice as the mission of the church if it diminishes the clarity of the church's proclamation, as it appears to him it does.

In his article, "The Viability of Luther Today," he asks, "Does justification by faith alone frustrate the quest for justice and liberation?" He answers that it depends upon one's presuppositions. "Where it is presupposed that justification is to enter into a simple, direct, and positive synthesis with the human quest for justice, justification *by faith alone* will at the very least enervate that quest." Justification by efforts at justice and justification by faith alone enter into competition, and the latter will surely be judged lacking in human eyes. But that is not how it is. "Since justification is by faith alone it does not enter into a positive synthesis with given human quests for justice and liberation." It judges efforts by the old self at justice, efforts which absolutize themselves and lead to tyranny under another name. It exposes the inability of the old nature to do justice at all. "A theology of negation," Forde calls it, is a prerequisite for true caring by the new self for the neighbor in his difficulties.[840]

This is not talk that fits cleanly into missiological conversations about justice as reflected by Bosch's fourth element. It is deeper, somehow, attacking the root of the problem by tending to the necessary prerequisites. It confesses how impulses toward justice actually come to occur rather than calling them forth or debating their relative merit compared to other missional impulses. Again, in all its balkiness and waywardness, we mark another Fordean contribution to a critical missiological element, "the quest for justice."

Bosch's eighth element, "mission as inculturation," takes the conversation farther than our brief connection of Forde's concern for viability with Yates' paradigm of the development of a people's church. The radical refiguring of the message as it penetrates a culture highlights the tension between openness to the contextual shape of the message when it interacts in a given culture and the sense that the message is not innately cultural, but finally from God. In his own culture Forde demonstrated a commitment to do hard work at the *Weltanschauung* level to accomplish vital inculturation, though it was not his particular focus to reflect on the process more generally in the context of other cultures. We saw how his reworking of atonement theory as an accident for the sake of modern sensibilities required reimagining a teaching as basic as the *communicatio idiomatum*. In terms of Bosch's related sixth element, "mission as contextualization," further research might explore how Bosch's interaction of the message with a given situation to produce experience and acting on the message, not mere explaining a textual story, might positively correspond with Forde's act nature of revelation.[841]

These are the most striking of the correlations of Forde with the thirteen Bosch elements. Less needs to be said about the others. For the seventh element, "mission and liberation," we have already noted Forde's measured response to the concept—definitely interested, but, as with justice, not sure that it should be defined as the mission of the church and concerned that it be properly related to the eschatological act. For the ninth element, "mission as common witness," we simply remark Forde's longterm efforts at Lutheran-Roman Catholic dialogue and his discouragement that the drive to unity seemed in his mind to eclipse the search for understanding. In any case, Forde's affirmation that the church gains its unity from the common message it finds it must proclaim (pp. 161-162, above) is reminiscent of the shifts in missionary thinking that brought about the confession of the church as "missionary by its very nature," in Bosch's first element. Forde would simply find less in common with conversations that included a broader definition of salvation (in element three), a diminished role for the ordained (in element ten), and assigning a positive role to the witness of people of other living faiths (element eleven).

To summarize Forde's affinities with the Bosch portrait of an emerging ecumenical missionary paradigm, then, we note Bosch's twelfth element in particular, the strong correlation of the relation between theology and proclamation in Forde and that between theology and mission in Bosch. This proclamation Forde understands in terms of an eschatological event where Bosch's thirteenth element seeks remedial eschatological focus. The *missio Dei* awareness of the twentieth century, Bosch's second, would find both Forde's peculiar kind of affirmation in his active Word *extra nos* and a sharp critique when it was used to identify with the work of the hidden God in the world. Evangelism, Bosch's fifth element, is a damaged word for Forde, but he has fundamental things to say about what he considers to be the almost lost task of proclamation of the gospel that address the conversation directly. The quest for justice, like liberation, Bosch's fourth and seventh, is served by Forde's theology in terms of negation rather than activity in a counterintuitive approach that works against the establishment of a new tyranny. And the inculturation/contextualization conversation, Bosch's eighth and sixth, reminds one of Forde's concern for viability, but also for the act nature of revelation. Other Bosch elements have lesser connections in Forde.

With Respect to Bevans and Schroeder's Missiological Synthesis

In their analysis of mission in *Constants in Context*, as we have seen, Bevans and Schroeder identify three contemporary portraits of mission: mission as participation in the mission of the Triune God (*missio Dei*); mission as liberating service of the reign of God; and mission as proclamation of Jesus Christ as universal Savior. Though an identification of Forde's theology with the latter might seem evident, it is useful to consider his work with respect to each in turn.

In the first of the three Bevans-Schroeder portraits, the missionary church is understood as a reflection of the trinitarian God in its reaching out beyond itself, in its communality with the other, in its mutuality in equality, and in its dialogality in differentness. That is, as is the triune God who created it, so is the church which lives out that creation, and one gains clues to the nature of the church from the doctrine of the Trinity. It must be said that, although Forde refers often enough to the trinitarian character of God, it is hard to see connections between him and this kind of reflection. Instead, it appears that Forde discusses the doctrine of the Trinity in close connection with his understanding of the eschatological moment in the human experience. For instance, where that experience is one of radical discontinuity, death and new life, the triune God of faith offers a different kind of continuity: "the continuity between what was intended and what shall be. The God who created us is one with him who redeems and the Spirit who sanctifies."[842] The continuity is God's, not ours as humanity. Or, for another instance, "God becomes 'other' for us through the cross and resurrection of Jesus. God becomes a God of grace for all. That is what it means to say that God is Triune. The way to salvation leads through negation and death. Only then can there be new life and freedom."[843] Here the awareness of otherness within God arises from God's saving act through death and new life. Forde's understanding tends to be Barthian for the sake of salvation: "God acts to redeem *his* creation. He repeats himself."[844] The point of the Trinity, then, is an understanding of redemption.

There are instances where Forde is critical of efforts to push trinitarian reflection further than that. For instance,

The distinction between God not preached and God preached cannot ultimately be removed by dogmatic or systematic arrangements . . . by seeking to banish that hidden majesty [of God] more or less altogether, seeking to banish eternal abstractions, to concentrate on God in time, collapsing Jesus into God or God into Jesus, the immanent into the economic trinity, sticking strictly to narrative, and so on and so on.[845]

Here Forde rejects using trinitarian and two-nature arguments to make God intelligible apart from the cross event. What he says of atonement seems to work for his approach to the Trinity as well: rather than look at the cross, we look "elsewhere, into the realm behind the scenes somewhere, the realm of ideas and theories . . . looking for the lost pieces of the puzzle which supposedly make 'sense' of this strange event . . . ."[846] One never hears him probing the interior being of God for tropological clues about God or the church. In light of both his critique and his silence, it appears that Forde's work does not easily lend itself to the trinitarian reflection of much contemporary missiology.

The second of the three Bevans-Schroeder portraits emphasizes the wholistic nature of mission as God's reign gradually impacts the many dimensions of human life and culture in continuity with the ministry of Jesus. It is not clear that Forde ever has occasion in his theology to use the word "wholistic," and we have already remarked that his use of the word "mission" is narrower than the full range of helpful human activity that might incidentally witness to one's faith. On the other hand, Forde does identify with many social and political advocacy causes as "worthy."[847] It is just that he is concerned, even alarmed, that church commitment to them seems to overshadow proclamation as the primary task of the church. Attention to God's eschatological act in the present must not be diminished for the church by continual and eclipsing attention to other things. If Forde's theology is to be a contribution to this portrait of the church, it must be in its insistence on the priority of the proclamation in bringing about an eschatological moment, and the freedom of the new person that the eschatological moment creates. Released from nagging defensive cares about doing one's part in the relationship with God, the new self is "hilariously" free to tend to the needs of the neighbor and creation. This is a potent freedom, filled with possibility for the woes of the world, and Forde jealously defends its potency from old Adamly preconditions, lest it be eaten up by new expectations and moral imperatives. Whether its exercise is truly liberating for the neighbor, or whether it serves the reign of God, Forde does not venture to say.

As we have seen, Bevans and Schroeder's third portrait focuses on the uniqueness of Jesus Christ and the urgent need to proclaim his benefits. Again, without using the word, Forde invests considerable effort in articulating what that uniqueness might be, not for uniqueness' sake, but for the sake of the eschatological moment in the experience of the hearer. In his response to the doctrines of the atonement, in the paradigm of an accident, he proposes an understanding that avoids useless speculation about it, but enables the Christ event to impact the hearer in a death- and life-giving way. It's not so much about focusing on Christ's uniqueness as about opening a moment where Christ's unique act may actually happen. It's not so much about proclaiming his benefits as about using the Word to cause a realization of the benefits to occur in the experience of the hearer.

This may indeed be urgent, and occasionally Forde can use expressions that suggest that urgency: "It's a matter of your eternal destiny!"[848] or, "Either we stick in our conditionality and go to that death which is eternal, or we are put to death to be raised to new and eternal life in the one who lives eternally."[849] Nevertheless, Forde never uses the idea to drive mission, probably because it lays a new imperative across the freedom that the new life in Christ brings, if it has not already revived the old Adam's hopes of control with "some little thing to do."[850] Forde would rather look to the *hilaritas* of that new life for all actions that the new self might enter upon for the care of the neighbor and his world. Though he never says so, it would seem this could include the words of care for the neighbor in the gospel as well as the deeds of care for the neighbor in kindness.

All this is to say that just because this Bevans-Schroeder approach shares some vocabulary with Forde, it doesn't mean that Forde fits very cleanly with the evangelical theologians that Bevans and Schroeder identify as often holding this approach. While Forde's contribution might be more coherently made to this portrait of mission than to the others, it would seem that the shape of his contribution would be almost alienatingly radical and fresh.

But it is not Bevans and Schroeder's intent merely to categorize missiology into three broad portraits, among which we might happen to find our favorite theologian in most coherent dialogue with the third. They want to propose a "model of mission" for the beginning of the twenty-first century. This they do through a synthesis of the three broad pictures reviewed above which they call "mission as prophetic dialogue." The dialogue part emphasizes the openness to the other, described in many ways, and the prophetic part emphasizes the over-against-ness of the church in the economic, the social, and the religious settings. This dual shape to mission is then analyzed with respect to each of six "essential components" of mission. It is a complex and, in the minds of the authors, hopefully comprehensive definition.

Consequently, a full analysis of Forde's work in terms of the Bevans Schroeder definition of mission would take more pages than we can offer. Perhaps it is possible to make some useful preliminary comments. First, it would seem that Forde would regard any definition of mission that began with "dialogue" as a weak start. He has much stronger words in mind that go with the alien action of a Word of God: a thunderbolt (of all things!), as we have seen, is a favorite.[851] *Extra nos*, and bondage, and death, and cross are others. It may be a matter of emphasis, for Forde, too, speaks of a concern for viability which implies a listening for worldview and understanding before a coherent speaking can begin. If Forde could be in conversation with Bevans and Schroeder, their encounter might fruitfully begin at such a point. But Forde doesn't dwell there. He moves quickly on to an assertion of the force of the Word of God, and it is unlikely that he would be satisfied with a definition of the task of the church in terms of anything less.

In terms of the six essential components used to flesh out this definition, we have already spoken of the radical shape Forde would give the first, witness and proclamation. Mild phrases that emphasize the gentle invitation and voluntary nature of the response would have to be reworked in light of the actual delivery of the forgiveness that Christ died for. If witness is distinguished from proclamation, there needs to be conversation about what that witness would look like in light of the bondage of the human will. So also, conversation is needed on the role of vulnerability and weakness in light of the "thunderbolt out of heaven." With the second of the components, it is hard to imagine Forde making the claims for prayer and contemplation that the catholics, Bevans and Schroeder, do. With the third, for all his appreciation for these causes, Forde would be sharply critical of giving "justice, peace and the integrity of creation" the same priority as "witnessing to and proclaiming the gospel."[852] With the fourth, Forde simply never enters into a discussion about how the claims of other religions might be understood. There is no sign that he thought an eschatological moment could be experienced in another way but through the word of the cross. It is here that such conversation would have to begin. While he himself might well consider such categories unhelpful, his singlemindedness about the cross mitigates against assigning him a pluralist understanding of religions and his talk of discontinuity would seem to preclude an inclusivism. With the fifth, inculturation, while he held to the broad understanding of law outside the word as is characteristic of many Lutherans, it is not evident that Forde ever entertained any thought of culture as containing "seeds of the word," or "charged with 'immanent transcendence'" in terms of gospel.[853] Once again, while there is room in his theology for whatever careful listening viability might imply, the *extra nos* character of the Word suggests that the impulse of the gospel message itself will not be sought there. And finally, with regard to the sixth component of prophetic dialogue, the research suggests that reconciliation may be a term that Forde uses exclusively of the relationship between God and humankind and not at all among humankind as in Bevans and Schroeder. If human reconciliation is implied in Forde's care of the neighbor, then it is implicit in the eschatological act that makes new life possible, but it is not envisioned as a ministry of the church among people beyond the experience of this act. When Robert Schreiter, cited by Bevans and Schroeder in this context, looks to God as the only one who can accomplish this human reconciliation, it constitutes a strong parallel with Forde's looking to God for the eschatological act that makes the new life possible, but Schreiter's mechanism for this expectation is neither clear nor necessarily connected with Forde's thought.[854]

In summary, it would appear that there are fewer evident connections between Forde's theology and the missiological pictures presented by Bevans and Schroeder. Their portrayal of the trinitarian approach leaves Forde's trinitarianism painfully detached. The liberation portrayal offers a lean immediate connection, but Forde's concept of freedom invites subsequent reflection on how the eschatological event he envisions might impact on situations where liberation is needed. Their proclamation portrayal is defined quite differently than Forde's, which means he has radical new resources to offer those who understand mission in this way. The definition of mission as dialogue, however prophetic, would seem to Forde a weak place to start, but his concern for viability offers handles for conversation about this. An examination of the six components of prophetic dialogue reveal major areas where work would have to be done, with Forde offering sharp critiques at many places.

With Respect to the Field of Luther Studies on Mission

Given the century-long debate over the attitude of Luther towards mission, it is mildly surprising that Forde as a Luther scholar was either not aware of it, or, if he was, he found no cause to mention it in his writing. There is library card evidence, for instance, that in 1978 Forde actually sought out Holl's *Gesammelte Aufsätze,* vol. 1, but a missiological reference to Holl or to any of the other significant Lutheran names that we have examined in this regard—Warneck, Elert, Öberg—is simply absent. It is a reminder once again that, whatever else we may say about Forde and mission, to call him a missiologist would be an unwarranted imposition.

The fact that Forde did not give mission more than a glancing reference until 1980 raises the possibility that he was somehow affected by Warneck's negative assessment of Luther's attitude towards mission that shadowed the first half of the century, so that he therefore avoided the subject. There is no evidence for this. It would not have come through his church, the missionally active Norwegian Evangelical Lutheran Church, heir of the missionally active Norwegian Synod before it, with overseas mission histories in China, Madagascar, and South Africa by the time of his birth. And nothing in his writings suggests the kind of criticism that Warneck levelled against Luther. Forde's criticisms lie elsewhere, in the way church bureaucracy might abuse the term, in the way the Old Adam might preserve itself through it.

More likely was the evangelistic flavor of the modern missional tradition, even in Lutheran circles. Öberg points out that some of the most visible mission tradition over the past two centuries has been dominated by pietistic, Baptistic, and charismatic concerns where the emphasis has been on the missionary as a special office, the inwardness of the missionary call, the fellowship of the redeemed in the missionary task, and a strategizing for future missionary work.[855] Early missiology had been so defined by this conversation that missiologists like Warnack had trouble marking the quite different approach in Luther as recognizably missionary. Most church missionary efforts in the early part of the century were influenced by this perspective, including those of the merged Lutheran church that Forde was a part of. It would likely have been the younger Forde's experience as well. That would explain his early reticence about addressing it as he pursued his studies of Luther and his later careful definition concerning it when he does.

As we have seen, Karl Holl was among the first to challenge the Warneck hypothesis. Holl's Luther was aware of a global scope to the missionary task, all geographical and eschatological considerations notwithstanding, and Holl is impressed with the depth of Luther's insight on mission as God's and Christ's own work. Since Luther was not himself able to participate in mission abroad, he prepared his church for it through such theological concepts as the priesthood of all believers and with missionary advice on matters like language, cultural appreciation, and contact points for the gospel. These are the kind of issues we considered in examining Forde's viability of the message.

We have already remarked Werner Elert's sarcasm towards Warneck's nineteenth century definition: If Luther was not "founding a missionary society, accompanying Cortez to Mexico, or at least assuring for himself a professorship of missionary science" (note the irony in that Warneck himself occupied such a post at Halle), how could he possibly be considered missional![856] For Elert it was not a matter of world geography, cross-cultural strategy, or international logistics, but a theological question, of justification and the impact of the gospel upon a life, of confidence in the universal applicability of the gospel and an affirmation of the mission to proclaim it. Here Elert voices concerns that Forde himself holds. How may the gospel so come upon a hearer that it accomplishes its justifying (read death-and-life giving) work? How may the preliminary theological work be done so that the church is readied effectively to proclaim it? If these are the deeper missional questions, then Forde is at the heart of their asking and answering.

In Öberg's mind and, as he sees it, in the mind of a substantial slice of Luther scholarship, mission for Luther could be defined as "God's/ Christ's church-building work through the Word and the Sacraments." Concerns about how to organize, finance, strategize it, the usual realm of "missions," are quite beside the point.[857] Now, Forde never uses the term "church-building." He is perhaps too reserved about the shape of the church he knows to hope that it should expand on earth, perhaps too serious about discontinuity in this age to make too close a connection between church and the kingdom of God. "Whenever the church begins to claim something more than temporal warrant for its institutions we have trouble. . . . That just spells tyranny."[858] But he does look for an "eschatological community existing in this age" where the new age "breaks in."[859] He does expect the church "to proclaim the gospel in word and deed. Nothing more, nothing less."[860] And he does expect that this word that is "orally preached, and believed, professed, and lived" is not "quiescent," but "truly liberating" and troublemaking! "Wherever there is this kind of trouble you can bet the church is around somewhere!"[861] The church-building of such word-related liberation is not superficially geographic or strategic, but profoundly, if covertly, vital in the community of persons who have experienced it.

The shape of the proclamation by word or by sacramental act that builds this church was the central focus of Forde's career. If this be the defining characteristic of mission as Ölberg's Luther, Öberg himself, and the eighteen Luther scholars whom Öberg cites would maintain, then the heart of Forde's work from this perspective must be seen as unambiguously missional in the deepest theological sense.

C. Forde's Contributions to the Missional Conversation

It can be seen that there is a complex interplay between the concerns of modern missiology and the theological work of Gerhard Forde. It remains in this section to summarize as clearly and succinctly as possible the contributions that Forde's theology might make to the missiological conversation. In the subsequent sections we will consider some of the discontinuities between Forde and missiology as well as missiological questions that arise from the analysis of Forde's theology itself.

Eschatological Act Character of the Proclamation as a Missional Concern

First and most significantly, it appears that Forde's theological understanding of the nature of proclamation finds prominent and recurring connection in the survey of the four missiological approaches. It corresponds (a) with Yates' radical theological reassessment of mission work; (b) with several of Bosch's elements of ecumenical missiology, especially with mission *as* theology (12), an eschatological approach to mission (13), mission as God's own work (2), and what other people call evangelism (5); (c) with the actual realization of Bevans and Schroeder's third portrait of mission and a radical reworking of the first component of their synthesis; and (d) with the central definition of mission to come out of a century of Luther studies as formulated by Elert, Öberg, and others. It is clear from the survey that the scope of missional definition today is so extensive that it is possible to do and say many things that would be considered missional without the slightest reference to Forde's work on proclamation, and Forde would undoubtedly have something to say about that. But it is just as clear that the fresh understanding of proclamation that Forde offers must figure large as a critical contribution to the task of missiology understood through at least these four lenses.

To summarize Forde's contribution, once again, he levels the most radical possible critique of the church's mission: that we may in fact have forgotten how to preach the gospel! This is because we use theological structures to explain away and otherwise stave off the action of a free God who may choose to do as God wills. We create atonement theories to reduce God's action to metaphysical constructs, and we gnosticize the result by making salvation dependent upon our assent to the theories. We preach data about historical events, use our theories to organize the data, and suppose that acceptance of the result is decisive. Forde thinks the result is deadly because it permits the old rebellious self not only to survive, but to participate in its survival by the contribution it can offer. That untrusting self that is bound to do its own saving is thereby permitted its "some little thing" to maintain the control that belongs to God alone. Forde argues that the syncretism that permits this is so pervasive in the ministry of the church of our age that we simply have to start over.

That new start happens, not in a word that brings clearer understanding, but in a word that kills and makes alive. The self cannot be left uninvolved like an observer discerning truth and falsehood. It must be attacked so that it *actually experiences* danger, despair, and a death more real than physical dying. This happens when the realization of our killing role in the "accident" that took Jesus' life comes home to us and when we see God's vindication, not of us, but of the victim, through God's raising him from the dead, so that all our hope in our efforts to be right with God prove wasted. It is accomplished through an active word from without, as from God's own self—a word that actually "does" itself to us. That is, it actually puts an end to the old striving self and actually begins a new existence of trusting God to do what we couldn't. The word that does it is the proclamation that is the accusation of law and the unconditional promise of gospel. The actual proclaiming of such a word in preaching and the sacrament is the point of all theology.

Theology's justification language is affirmed and reinvigorated by this death-and-new-life language. This is talk that the church has persistently used down through the centuries, but almost always compromised. It took a Luther to hear in the unwritten *sola* the fabled "thunderbolt" of the gospel, a word that in the forensic metaphor closed the syncretic gaps of imagined human help and turned every eye to an electing God's cruciform decision. The scandal of such justification is actualized in the death-and-new life experience.

Likewise the response of faith is redefined by such an event. Rather than an intellectual acknowledgment of the facts, or an act of the human will that completes the divine initiative, it becomes something that, like death or birth, happens to one. It is characterized by an end to the attentions paid to the old life and the hope of "being grasped by a new life of love, hope, and care."[862] Not something one can oneself force, it, too, is done to one by the creative word *extra nos*, elicited by the specific unconditional promise of a covenanting God, galvanized by the specific decree of an electing God. We proposed that for Forde faith is the shape of the encounter—grasped, trusting, claimed, joyous—with the will of God through God's word when it kills and makes alive. Its final prayer, "Amen, Amen, so be it[,] Lord," is not the contribution of the believer but the death brought by the preacher's "yes, yes, yes, always yes."[863]

The event of the death and new life may be called an eschatological moment because it comes from God's own self and it is of ultimate significance for the one to whom it comes. Its encounter, when it happens, has the effect of a Last Day or a Final Judgment right now in history.

There is real discontinuity here for the individual with the effect better described by the concept of creation of something new than by rescue of something past. For Forde the hope is in the eschatological newness. His theology which shapes a proclamation towards that end needs to be carefully considered by those who would serve the mission of the church in the world.

Freedom in Christ as a Missional Concern

Secondly, given the significance of concern for justice and liberation in the missiological survey, Forde's interest in these matters and his unorthodox approach to them become missiologically significant, even if it seemed he himself did not consider them so. Repeatedly, we have remarked not a centrality of these concerns in Forde, but a persistence of their appearance throughout his ministry, most notably at conclusions of major works in terms of caring for the world and the neighbor. The location is important. Yates cites his paradigms chronologically and Bosch cites his elements willy-nilly without suggesting any relative significance among them. Bevans and Schoeder take the next step: justice in the world is a missionary matter "equal in importance," no less, to the church's witness.[864] Forde disagrees with them all. Perhaps no less committed to justice and liberation than any of them, he puts the justice and liberation for the other at the end of the conversation. The reason is connected to his understanding of the priority of the eschatological moment, a significant contribution to the discussion.

We have seen that according to Forde, the old self not yet liberated by the unconditional promise does everything in connection with the law, ultimately for the sake of self-preservation before a daunting God. Even efforts ostensibly designed to help the needy neighbor, however outwardly impressive, secretly redound to help the needy self. This is the burden of missional justice and liberation without the eschatological event: true concern for these things is impossible before the perpetual self-assessment. Forde calls this a bondage of the will. We must do our part, not because we have no will, but because we will to. Nothing less than an eschatological event can end this. Forde says everything he has to say about liberation and justice in light of this end. Paradoxically, his contribution is not on the efforts his theology calls forth, but on the negation of those efforts which spring from the self-conscious old Adam and Eve under the law.

The missiological contribution of Forde's theology here is freedom— not only freedom from something old like the law and freedom for something new like service to the neighbor—though these there may be—but undefined and authentic freedom in Christ by which anything might happen. Forde expects that the eschatologically new situation will be so fresh-horizon-creating that the new person in Christ will require outlandish and post-pious paradigms to describe it: *hilaritas*-ly joyful, fun, reckless, spontaneous, wild, dangerous. And he expects, without requiring it as mission, that the unpredictability of the unbound new person in Christ experiencing these things will likely express itself in care for the world and the neighbor.

This is grounding the concern for justice and liberation in quite a different structure of reality, an eschatological reality of possibility and hope rather than a moral reality of duty and responsibility. Once again, it looks for actual fulfillment rather than theoretical proposal or moral obligation. One might say that freedom in Christ through the proclamation in Forde's proposal just might empower and actualize an unprecedented version of the justice and liberation that missiology envisions, though given the radical freedom of this freedom, one can't be sure. This appears to get beyond lists of paradigms or elements or essential components to consider what might actually drive them all. A missiology concerned for justice and liberation might well lend Forde an ear.

Viability of the Message as a Missional Concern

Forde is perhaps less well known for this aspect of his theology, yet missiological correlations with his theology appeared repeatedly in the survey through his attention to viability of the message. We marked it in (a) the coherence of worldview presumed necessary for Yates' development of a people's church, (b) the possible radical refiguring of the message in Bosch's missional inculturation, and (c) the careful listening and understanding that would be required for Bevans-Schroeder's prophetic diaglogue. The concern for the coherence of the message in light of the presuppositions and worldview of the hearer is one that Forde shares with missiologists everywhere, but we find his approach to it not so much by what he says about it as by how he does it in his own culture. Not the center of his attention, the Forde lesson on viability is primarily a hands-on affair!

The laboratory for the Fordean viability experiment was post-Enlightenment America. Some realities for this context were the critical historical and scientific methodology of the age, the avoidance of abstract metaphysical constructs that seemed artificial, and a poignant awareness of the autonomous self dating from the time of Kant. Forde worked with these worldview-related realities as he reflected on the "tradition" so as to avoid unnecessary intellectual offense while serving the intent of the scripture. At the same time he sought *not* to avoid the offense inherent in the message itself, an offense that he saw neutralized by the concept of relevance. The goal was to permit/enable this eschatological offense to do its work on the hearer. The work of the proclaimer as the servant of the message was to bear forward its force in the matrix of the prevailing worldview, culture, and language.

Bosch's inculturation would seem to be fulfilled by Forde's example. The message is so reshaped by the cultural parameters that, from some points of view, it might appear to be a new phenomenon. Unfortunately, Forde's ministry simply didn't give us examples of how he might have done this in another worldview or culture, nor how he might have counselled those who tried. It does give us an example of a theologian who took some risk in a serious attempt on his own culture. It was a risk driven by his concern that the proclaimed message not be compromised by cultural misunderstanding or by metaphysical subtrefuge, but be heard afresh in its killing and life-giving potential. In Forde, missiology finds a stunning example in Western garb of its concern for "worldview-ly" and cultural comprehensibility.

D. Discontinuities between Forde's Theology and Missiology

Sometimes contributions can take the form of critiques and conversation arising out of disagreement. Aware that Forde was not widely recognized in missional circles, we said at the outset that, as we compared the two, we would also be watchful for incongruities between them and consider what might be at stake in the differences. Some of these have already become evident.

The Function of the Doctrine of the Trinity

The fact that Bosch (1991) could devote one single page to the trinitarian aspects of *missio Dei* and not a single mention of it in his index, where Bevans and Schroeder (2006) include it in the title of their *missio Dei* chapter and reference it throughout the last half of their book should probably not be marked up to denominational differences alone. Surely it speaks of the growth of trinitarian talk in missiological circles over the past half century and the striking prominence it has gained there since Bosch wrote. Like the life of the church itself, missional work is relational work, an aspect of life not always addressed by historic dogmatic concerns. If the relational side of the church and its mission is rooted in the relationality within the triune God's own being, it gives weight to the church's missional attention to concerns like community, mutuality, dialogue, and concern for those outside. It means that one is not about the missional task in isolation, but does the task in "participation in the mission of the triune God." It even gives the church a basis for offering a healthy relational model to a wider society preoccupied with hierarchical power structures.

Yet, we have noted that not only does Forde not follow this trend in the use of the doctrine, but he seems on occasion to have reason to criticize it. We noted his own close connection of the doctrine to its role in the eschatological moment where we experience not continuity, but radical discontinuity, with the Trinity. We saw Forde's assertion that God is not "like" us through the theological construction, but "other" for us in the cross. Here the sentiment he voices in his doctoral thesis, and not there for the last time, seems pertinent: "The greatest temptation is for theology itself to take the place of [the event of Jesus Christ]."[865] It would seem that reflection on identity with a triune God by church and society apart from the effect of the cross would mitigate against Forde's idea of a death-and-life eschatological encounter through proclamation. And it would seem that consciousness of participation in the life God as a model for church and society would mitigate against the euphoric freedom in Christ that Forde proposes as a fruit of the eschatological event.

The disjuncture is, as we observed, "painful." This is not the place to solve it, but we may propose some questions for future conversation and research. What might be the relationship between the experience of dying to self and rising to new life in the eschatological moment, on the one hand, and participation in the life of the triune God on the other? Can broadening or narrowing of the definition of either happening to account for the other be authentically attempted? Does a chronological scheme help? Does a psychological scheme help, so that either event becomes unconscious? Can the participation be described eschatologically or the death and rising morally? It would seem unhelpful to label Forde as untrinitarian or participation in God as unevangelical. The incongruity is surely a matter for future reflection and research.

The Universality and Urgency of the Church's Mission

The missiological standard we created made reference several times in different ways to the sense of universal or global scope of the work. Yates mentioned it in terms of geographical expansion and church growth. Bosch referred to it in his lengthiest discussion of an element, evangelism. The third Bevans and Schroeder model of proclamation of Jesus Christ spoke of "obligation" to share and "urgency" of mission.[866] Even Gustav Warneck was aware of Luther's Ascension Day sermon likening the gospel to wavelets in the water reaching the farthest corners,[867] and a subsequent century of Luther scholarship made Luther's commitment to the worldwide character of mission indubitably clear.

We have noted above (p. 165) a kind of guarded response in Forde to the idea of the global scope of the gospel. Only a couple of citations refer to it directly, a fact that is perplexing given the seriousness with which he views the church's task of proclamation, the eschatological import given the death-and-new-life event that God might accomplish by it, and the excitement with which he greets the idea of a divine covenant with *all* nations. There is no evidence that he sees some other way than the proclamation event, and we have demonstrated that he shies away from the idea of universal salvation (see p. 251, n505). The passion that we might expect for a global scope Forde reserves for the shape of the proclamation that his theology describes, a proclamation authorized by Christ himself in his commission and by God in his raising Christ from the dead.

Given Forde's commitment to the proclamation, this disjuncture is not so much painful, as perplexing, and a new set of questions pose themselves. Why did Forde's drive for law-gospel clarity in proclamation not translate explicitly into a sense of urgency to get that proclamation to all people? If it was an eschatological matter of death and new life for one, was it not just as critical for everyone? Did the proclamatory task viewed under these terms begin to look too much like "the little thing" that a religious old Adam or Eve might accomplish? Or did a statement of the urgency of a universal scope detract from the reckless freedom that Forde was sure the new person in Christ experienced, so that urgency might become the shape of the new law? Was it not possible to state the universal scope in terms that take into account Forde's concerns without compromising it?

The Breadth of Missiological Self-Definition

One more significant difference between the missional standard we have created and Forde's approach is so large it would be easy to overlook. It has to do not with this or that aspect, element, or component of mission, but with the definition itself. We have observed in chapter four how the breadth of missiological concerns grew during the course of the century. It began with an interest in the expansion of the gospel, and it ended with such a diversity of ideas and movements that our entire chapter gave no more than a sketch and an outline. Stephen Neill's 1959 warning, "If everything is mission, nothing is mission,"[868] speaks to the broadening, and Ingemar Öberg's definition, "God's/Christ's church-building work through the Word and the Sacraments," seems to react to it. Nevertheless, there is no consensus today on such a precise approach, and the missiological conversation as it currently presents itself seems to ask for a broader description.

By contrast we have observed, above, the restricted definition of mission that Forde offers. After a decade of almost total silence, Forde makes a strong connection between mission and that kind of proclamation of justification of sinners that actually *does* the justifying. This is the driving concern of his career, and it is significant that after waiting so long he makes the connection at this particular point. When one wants to talk of the mission of the church, then, one must talk about the *ministry* of the killing and life-giving word that constitutes this proclamation. Any unity in mission comes from a unity in speaking this word. And for a church that knows such a speaking and unity, mission becomes the defense and advancement of the theology that makes it possible. This "theological witness" *is* that church's mission, "its highest duty and calling—indeed the the best thing it can do for the world."[869] Forde's definition of mission thus includes proclamation and the theology that nourishes it.

Not included is care of the neighbor and care of the world, the very expressions of Forde's new freedom in Christ that emerge from the eschatological event. Over the course of his career Forde evidences plenty of interest in the needs of neighbor and world. He repeatedly preaches and speaks about ecology, marriage, poverty, racism, justice, and other social concerns. Nevertheless he never includes response to them in his definition of mission. There are other aspects of the current missiological conversation like interreligious dialogue that are also absent in Forde's missional definition, but this is not so striking because they don't happen to constitute an important part of his particular ministry. But care of the neighbor and care of the world are significant in Forde's theology, and their exclusion from the definition consequently seems so conscious and purposeful on his part.

Here again, questions are raised in the Forde-missional encounter. Is Forde here, perhaps, after all, reflecting the same Luther study awarenesses that produced the crisp Öberg definition? Does the crispness of such a definition promote clarity for the life of the church, or is there damaging loss in not considering the other things missional? What would be the consequences of identifying mission with ministry of the Word and using some other word, perhaps vocation or civil engagement, to discuss the wider concerns of the church's task? Yet, does not the attention of the church to the wider concerns contribute to the kind of witness usually associated with proclamation?

E. Missional Issues in Forde's Theology

In the course of creating the "summa" in chapter three, we attempted in a preliminary way to be alert for issues that might have further missiological interest. Now, after the survey of missional definitions and an assessment of Forde's contributions, we need to pursue further some of the more striking of these issues.

Hermeneutical Tension: The Role of the Interpreter

Forde holds what is perhaps a higher than usual tension between a strong assertion of the inherent dynamic of a Word of God from without and an insistence that the theology that undergirds that word must be viable today. We marked it again in the difference between the first and the third contributions just noted. On the one hand, the Word demonstrates an eschatological vigor of its own, and the proclaimer *permits* it to do what it intends to do. On the other hand, an understanding of the Word grounded and articulate in the worldview of the age seems necessary for the proclaimer to *enable* it to gain a sufficient engagement with the ears and heart of the hearer to do it. The task of the interpreter thus becomes a complex one, staying out of the way in one sense, yet doing critical *Weltanschauung* and cultural work in another, or perhaps, Forde would rather say, doing that work in order to get out of the way. This is an interesting tension for persons with a high regard for the Word seeking to communicate a message across divisions of worldview and culture.

Incarnational theology has always insisted that God reveals Godself in human form, not incidentally, but intrinsically. In "the tradition," as Forde calls it, the life of Jesus was not merely a vehicle for God's presence; it *was* God's presence. In the actualization of the tradition that Forde proposes, it is not so much the historic *ontological presence* of Jesus, however conceived, that effects the eschatological moment in the hearer as it is the present *action* of Jesus in the proclamation existentially experienced. It would seem, then, that the present action of Jesus in the proclamation is as directly linked to God's presence in the present as his historic person has been linked in the tradition. That action includes the effects of law and gospel that spring from the messsage itself, but its form also takes into account the *Weltanschauung* and cultural shape necessary for that law and gospel to do their present work. The *Weltanschauung* and cultural shape can no more be separated from the action that is God's presence actualizationally conceived than the human body and mind of Jesus could be separated from the person that was God's presence ontologically conceived. In other words, rather than play viability against *extra nos*, an incarnational theology might see them as unified elements of the action of the living Christ in the world today.

In terms of the proclaimer's self-understanding, it may be ventured that the hermeneutical task becomes an element of the incarnation when it leads to the eschatological moment. This is true when the law and gospel which come from God are not merely clothed with, but actually take on the substance of the worldview and culture into which they are addressed. The proclaimer whose work is part of this incarnation of the living Christ in a new place and age must be aware that it is not his/hers to control or force (see above, pp. 116-117). Yet there are proclamatory awarenesses that invite, tempt, or provoke it, and Forde suggests some: a distinction of law from gospel, a seeking after a living worldview and a living expression of it, and an expectation and hope for its happening.

Diversity in Anthropology

Anthropologically, Forde uses a common theological model for the people to whom the Word must come. Starting with St. Paul's discussion of the old Adam and seeming to relate it to the Enlightenment's idea of the autonomous self, he presumes human resistance to God's saving action out of a concern to reserve to itself at least some measure of control. This stands in some tension with the missionary experience of human diversity and especially those who are for one reason or another oppressed by circumstances and for whom control of any kind is simply not on the horizon. We remarked that Forde called the middle class Westerner to the plight of oppressed people, but possibly only once did he formulate an address to these people directly, and then, again, in terms of the desire to retain control. The question of human similarity and diversity within Forde's anthropological system invites further conversation, particularly in light of the interest of the current missiological interest in justice and liberation.

Is it not possible to imagine persons, to use Forde's language, who have been killed but not yet made alive? That is, the law in forms unrelated to proclamation have so pounded some that they have despaired of life itself. Not just the rustling leaf of Luther's analogy, but the guns of war, the brutality of the sweatshop boss, or the rape by the domineering spouse may have so terrorized some that they have no hope left and no will to control, at least for the moment. That is not to say that tomorrow, should their situation improve, the old self could not revive and find itself with the same need to control that others have. But it is to say that proclamation into a moment of despair may need to find ways to talk about the old self differently because its death is already a reality and half the eschatological event seems already to have happened. Such talk would make possible a theological dialogue between Forde and, say, the 1979 bishop's conference at Puebla which coined the phrase, "the preferential option for the poor." If the despairing poor might be said to be already at the pregnant but unfulfilled moment that could be eschatological by Forde's definition, it invites missiological attention.

It is also interesting to consider cultures where the worldview is not post-Enlightenment and the idea of an autonomous self is not dominant. There are societies, for instance, where the group is much more important than the individual, and even in the West there are signs that the medieval individual was more an integrated member of society than a single person.[870] It would seem that the conversation about death and resurrection might have to be approached communally in such situations with an effect no less authentic than in the individualized West.

Common Action in the Civil Use of the Law

The civil use of the law becomes a missiological concern because it is a tool for interaction and cooperation with persons of other religious backgrounds. Forde's strong emphasis on the importance of the eschatological moment in proclamation, it would seem, defines the missional approach towards interreligious conversation, diminishing eschatological expectations of interfaith dialogue. This raises the importance of the law for what might be attempted with persons of other religions. Forde himself says that the faithful have special privileges neither in the use of the law nor in understanding its content, but only in discerning its difference from gospel. Thus, in matters of civil use of the law, one might expect broad opportunities at mutual understanding in interfaith conversations.

However, with Forde's strong emphasis on proclamation, the accusing role of the law seems to struggle with the proper, civil function that, he grants, would actually permit the law to be seen as "friend" to the eyes of faith and would even allow the law to be rewritten, better to serve society—an aspect that suggests a parallel with the hermeneutical tension surrounding the Word, just noted. Might it not be possible, for instance, in consultation with those of other faiths, to design law as a servant of the poor or oppressed, for instance? The idea stands in some tension with law as an incorrigible accuser of the old Adam. As his career developed, it turned out not to be Forde's primary theological task to elaborate further on the care of the neighbor and of creation, and he never wrote extensively on the use of the law on their behalf, but there are reasons to propose the cause was never far from his mind. The missional task would be interested in how the civil function of the law might be further delineated for the sake of justice and ecology, especially in the context of moral deliberation with the non-Christian neighbor.

CHAPTER 6

A Constructive Missional Theology Proposal with Respect to Gerhard Forde's Theology

To conclude with a chapter entitled "Forde's Missiology" or some such thing would seem like a gross imposition. We have seen in chapter five that mission talk was perhaps not Forde's first choice of theological vocabulary, and that missiological treatises were perhaps not Forde's first choice of leisure reading. He did his theology out of other fields of thought—Luther studies and a concern for a dogmatics serviceable to the church, for example. Nevertheless, we have marked a number of areas of convergence between Forde's theology and the concerns of twentieth century missiology. Out of these areas of convergence we have proposed several Fordean contributions to the missional conversation—an awareness of the eschatological act character of the proclamation, a concern for the integrity of the new freedom in Christ, and attention to the viability of the message—contributions that we argued are of potentially transforming value to the missional task. We also marked several areas of divergence, areas full of potential for seminal missiological conversation. And from Forde's own theology we marked several areas for further engagement—a definition of the role of the interpreter, the question of the homogeneity of the anthropology, and uncertainties in the civil use of the law in interfaith conversations—where Forde's work might create interesting challenges by and interaction with missional concerns. Rather than imposing the term missiology on these areas of convergence and divergence, contribution and conversation, it seems better to construct a missiological approach that takes them into account. No doubt this could be attempted in many ways. This chapter constitutes one attempt by one missionary who found Forde's theology helpful to him and who desires to provoke further reflection by other missionally involved leaders on how it might serve them in their contexts as well.

While missiology itself ought not be centered on the autobiographical, nevertheless, all missiology is contextual. The missiological reflections that follow flow from a missionary career that includes nine years in North Dakota, twelve years in Cameroon, and five years in Senegal, West Africa, with special reference to the time of pioneer evangelism in

Senegal. References to these experiences are incidental and not structural, but the reflections are better understood with reference to this story.

A. The Missional Call

It is an audacious act to enter the space of another person or culture with what is considered potentially helpful, or even life transforming, or even killing and life-giving influence, however conceived. Whether or not that act obtains the goals set for it, it will certainly change that person or culture forever. By what right or calling does the missional person or the missional church engage in such disruptive behavior? There has been considerable missional soul-searching in the post-colonial era over just such a question, and, we might say, correspondingly considerable effort to diminish the disruption. Popular emphases today such as walking with the neighbor in her situation, feeding the poor, travelling overseas for better understanding, or cordial dialogue about our faith with a member of another religion would seem to be more innocuous than bold goals like proclaiming the gospel, establishing the church, and creating an educational system, yet even these newer approaches can have ricocheting effects that are hard to predict. By what right do we take the risk of projecting ourselves into another's life with the hope of making a difference?

There are times when awareness of news itself seems to create its own right to share it, as it were (whence expressions like "bursting with the news" or "I just had to tell you"). If one sent from God and put to death by the likes of us happened to be raised by God from the dead, "vindicated" in Forde's thought, then those who saw it might be said to be "authorized" to tell of it in the sense that they find themselves impelled to do so by God's own action.[871] Likewise, with those who have been affected by the event as if they had seen it—maybe even more so if it resulted from Forde's eschatological moment—it is as if God through this event drives its telling in one way or another. There are four accounts in the Gospels where Jesus himself commissions his disciples for this task. These need to be received as the Lord's own authorization to share the forgiving word that constitutes ministry, as Forde suggests.[872] We would understand this authorization to be made vital in the life of believers through the eschatological event so that it becomes incarnate in a human life.

This is quite different from taking the Great Commission or its various versions simply as a command of the Lord to be obeyed. It is not my experience that missionaries are doing what they do because they were ordered to do it, whether by the Lord or anyone else. It is rather more as if they have ingested the task as eschatological witnesses and are driven by what has become their own desire to accomplish it. No doubt missionary motivations are as confused as life itself, but insofar as it reflects the new life in Christ, one usually senses something of Luther/Forde's *hilaritas* about the endeavor. Qualities like spontaneity, risk-taking, not reckoning too seriously the personal consequences, and abandonment to the task better describe the common missional attitude than a consciousness of a command that must be fulfilled or calculating obedience to it. We would argue that the missional call is closely related to the freedom that results from the new life in Christ.

After a vigorous defense of the utter freedom of this life in Christ, as we have seen, Forde risks his vision of how the freedom might express itself: care of the world and care of the neighbor.[873] We commented that Forde's career did not bring him to devote detailed explanation of what this would mean, possibly out of a fear of endangering freedom's freedom, and it seems clear that he himself never connected this freedom with mission. But we suggest now what he apparently did not pursue, that care for the neighbor would surely mean more than simple care for his physical well-being. Care for the neighbor would include a concern for his/her whole life, including, if possible, a life lived in the same freedom that the gospel created for us. That freedom comes by action of the proclaimed word as it brings forth faith. Proclamation of Christ thus becomes an expression of freedom on behalf of freedom. It happens because the *hilaritas* of the gospel has been ingested and seeks expression, and it happens in order that it may be ingested again. We would thus locate the call to mission in Forde's eschatological consequence of proclamation, the freedom of the new person to care for the neighbor, in this case, with explosively good news.

Mission, then, that is understood as a function of eschatological freedom is truly comprehensive, or, to use the popular but threadbare word, "wholistic." This care of the neighbor addresses not only physical well-being, but the life of freedom by faith in Christ as well, and not only the life of faith, but aspects that make for healthy worldly life, too. As expressions of the wider church, it has meant that ELCA missionaries in Senegal found themselves administering a five thousand-member center for mostly Muslim youth on Monday, demonstrating to cattleherders how to vaccinate their cattle on Tuesday, teaching Bible stories in a bush village on Wednesday, receiving eighty women a day at a prenatal clinic on Thursday, preparing a mixture of Christian and civic literature for print on Friday, organizing a baptismal class on Saturday, and presiding over Holy Communion on Sunday. Disruptive is the word! All of these were expressions of concern for the neighbor and his/her world that, we argue, ought to be included in mission. The call to such diverse mission is a *hilaritas*-desire in freedom by persons with a variety of gifts and skills to show such concern. This is a broader definition of mission than Forde proposed, but one that is rooted in Forde's own theological insistence on the *hilaritas*-ly free freedom that comes with the eschatological moment. That is, we would understand mission to result from Forde's freedom of the eschatological moment authorized by the word of Christ rather than from the word of authorization that through proclamation results in that freedom. Mission is not so much doing what Christ authorized us to do, though, in the freedom, it is that, too. Mission is more doing what we are free to do now that we don't have to do anything anymore, a freedom that that authorization obtained for us. Without that freedom, we say, there is no mission and there are no missionaries worth the name because the word of authorization morphs into law and becomes a burden that the old Adam or Eve will either reject entirely or use for his/her own ends.

In this comprehensivity of mission it does seem, however, that proclamation has a certain priority in the life of the church. After all, the church as the people of God shares its life in the world with many other communities, and with these communities, in its freedom, it shares many tasks that they also attempt, but under the law—concern for peoples' health, livelihood, environment, nutrition, peace, and so forth. Individually, corporately, or institutionally, the church finds itself cooperating to these ends with whomever it happens to find aligned with it. On other tasks, like the waging of war or the seeking of financial gain through exploitation of people, the church cannot cooperate but must offer a prophetic critique. But there appears to be one task in which the other communities cannot participate with the church: the witness to the church's faith in such a way that faith may happen afresh in believers and nonbelievers alike. If the church does not tend to this task which belongs to it alone, no one else will do it. And, not being done, it will not create the freedom that enables the doing of the rest. As Forde said even more strongly and in many ways, proclamation has thus a priority among the tasks of the church and cannot be seconded or neglected.

B. Entry

Theoretical

Entry into a missional situation requires more or less time and effort depending on the linguistic, cultural, and worldview challenges involved. If the situation is a parish in one's own country, it may happen over a period of weeks or months. If it is among people of another culture or an elite discipline of some sort, it may take considerably longer. Our first time overseas it took us two years to become what we called marginally functional. That included learning the French and Fulfulde languages, living in the bush long enough to gain a first comfort level in an African lifestyle, and making first friendships and building preliminary trust in the neighborhood. But the ability to debate the price of mangos with a merchant in the market is quite different from the ability to wonder with him about the true meaning of Christmas around the evening fire. Accessible vocabulary needs to be expanded, linguistic skills need to include subtle tonal nuances, and cultural awarenesses must rise to include mere innuendos of gesture and body language. Even more challenging, the metaphysical world of kinship, spirits, magic, evil, shame, and so forth must be appreciated as from within. Years more were required for us before faith sharing could become effective. The miracle is that it happens at all.

Forde had cross-cultural experiences during his student years in Germany and later on sabbatical in France, even preaching in German one Christmas eve,[874] but he never dwelt on the challenges these times raised for him linguistically or culturally. If anything, he found them exhilarating. Rather, it would seem his entry into the philosophical world of studies was more of a cross-cultural experience than his times in Europe, and he complained that its vocabulary never became his "native language."[875] If this is the case, we may say that Forde's cross-cultural experience of "entry" took many years of academic philosophical reflection and included considerable language learning. This is where his repeated concern for viability was focused, on sensitivity to the current philosophical worldview that would make the theology and its subsequent proclamation coherent. The fact that Forde apparently had no occasion to traverse nonwestern *Weltanschauung* barriers does not diminish the force of his concern. We propose a strong correlation between the kind of viability concerns that Forde held with respect to worldview and that he demonstrated with respect to language and culture on the one hand, and the massive effort missionaries make to "enter" a society on the other. If he did not take it as his particular calling to elucidate this process for his students, he was no less committed to its occurrence.

Relational

St. Paul writes, "If I speak in the tongues of mortals and of angels but do not have love, I am a noisy gong or a clanging cymbal" (1 Cor 13:1). All the linguistic, cultural, and metaphysical studies in the world remain mere curios without the relationships upon which communication can be attempted. These relationships need to become durable with enough mutual trust to bear the risk of personal sharing. This is not the place to explore the nature of vibrant relationships, but we do need to mark that they are best accomplished, perhaps even only truly accomplished, from a position of the vulnerability of mutual trust. The tragedy of the colonial era and sometimes even the recent past when the West was often still admired is that the old Adam of the West is tempted to give airs of cultural superiority, and nonwesterners are made to measure themselves by the perceived superiority. The health of resulting relationships and their value for gospel sharing can be much diminished in the event.

It would seem initially that Forde has rather less to say about this relational aspect of the missional task. We have noted (p. 110) that, though he occasionally uses it, the concept of relationship is not Forde's first choice of a word to describe the interaction between God and humankind. One might venture that the force of Forde's portrayal of God is too directional for that—more of a Barthian God *for* us rather than a Bonhoefferian God for and *with* us. It would require further study to confirm a preliminary sense that he does not use relationship to describe human-human interaction. What is clear, however, is that he does not pursue contemporary thought on the doctrine of the Trinity that sees triune relationships as paradigmatic for wholesome human ones. No doubt a prescriptive suggestion for Christian life based on this or any model would seem to him to impinge on the authenticity of eschatological freedom in Christ. At first glance, it does seem to leave this particular aspect of the missional task with something of a dearth of Fordean input.

Assets for relationship can be derived from other of his insights, however. Forde's strong sense of a word that kills and makes alive everybody alike is pertinent in the face of the the superiority complex of the West. Creating solidarity in fallenness and in the need for Christ, it opens the way for a deep sense of mutuality. The cultural debutant can afford to be the clumsy and inadequate member of society that he/she actually is because he/she has nothing to prove. Vulnerability is enabled, the cultural host is given the opportunity to welcome, empathize, and help, and the ensuing relationship has a proper human form. In such a form, God rather than coercive human power structures has a chance to work through the relationship, as Paul testifies of God, "My power is made perfect in weakness" (1 Cor 12:9).

Positively stated, this vulnerability is Forde's spontaneity and recklessness of the new freedom in Christ. One might expect that authenticity before God that surrenders all pretense of self-righteousness might be accompanied by a corresponding authenticity towards other human beings. The freedom from the need to self-justify might then express itself in love and care of the neighbor, and one might understand in it a basis of human relationship defined independently of trinitarian considerations.

C. Conversation and Dialogue

In 2 Timothy 4:2 one reads, "[P]roclaim the message; be persistent whether the time is favorable or unfavorable; convince, rebuke, and encourage, with the utmost patience in teaching." It is apparently possible to read such admonition as license to be insensitively forward about proclamation, as in the case of the fabled missionary preachers on the streetcorners of old. I have never seen this happen, and it is not an approach that crossed our minds as a reasonable course of missional action, even on the off chance that such was the intention of the epistle writer. In the first place, any people with a modicum of civil freedom must give some sort of permission or invitation for one to address them, such as by calling a pastor and coming to church, or even by engaging in conversation and offering friendship. Intrusive address without at least implicit permission creates its own high obstacle of abrasiveness and oppression. But beyond that, God's people are complex creatures! It is not clear that insistent address could in any case make a difference for sheer lack of insight into "where they are at," to use the common slang. Forde's criterion of viability for the message comes to mind here. As we have noted, even after "worldviewly," cultural, and linguistic studies, a coherent address cannot be formed without some relationship with the people that personalizes or socializes all this information.

This happens not in proclamation, but in conversation and its corollary, dialogue. In America we often organize dialogue formally, but in Senegal it usually happens spontaneously in the shade of a grass house over three cups of tea. There is no raised pulpit or lectern that gives priority to the bearer of the message. There is only the equality of mats around the tiny tea oven, and if there's any priority at all, it goes to the preparer of the tea! There are several benefits to this kind of conversaton and dialogue.

Mutual Enrichment

In the growing trust of deepening acquaintance and relationship, talk can range over any subject that interests anyone in the party. For persons open to each other's lives, this is in itself an enriching experience, for missionary as well as host, because human beings of whatever religious or cultural background are remarkable creations of God and bear insights that are provocative and thought-provoking. The missional person might look forward to these times as valuable opportunities to consider his/her own faith and life in a fresh light. There is personal growth in the dialogue, and the authenticity of the conversation is damaged if such growth is not anticipated and appreciated.

Because Forde's focus was elsewhere than on the dialogical, and, perhaps also, because of his awareness of the old Adam's religious self-defenses, it might be possible to miss his expectations and affirmations here. They are, however, evident on at least two occasions. First, in his critique of the Lutheran-Roman Catholic dialogues, he expresses exasperation when the dialogical process was put under distorting pressures that impeded deeper understanding:

> The constant drive for consensus . . . deters understanding by attempting to minimize the differences and thus inhibits

discussion and, finally, genuine understanding. I expect that only a more frank and open discussion of the *differences* will lead to progress on these matters.[876]

Of course, he is speaking of official dialogues concerning justification by faith that are a very special case of the more general dialogical situation we imagine. But we would generalize this desire for a frank and open discussion of differences with the expectation simply of improved understanding as a more prominent and necessary element of the missiological agenda.

Forde's openness and affirmation of dialogue are discernable from a second perspective as well, that of the doctrine of creation. He comments on occasion on the goodness of creation,[877] and on the theological character of the concept of creation as "a perception and existence opened up by faith." That is to say, the moment of faith transforms "nature" so that it becomes "creation," not the mere object of our projects for improvement, but something lacking "nothing by virtue of which it could have been done better."[878] The eschatological moment turns us back to creation to love and care for the neighbor we find there.[879] We suppose that the love and care we have for the world and the neighbor because of the eschatological moment is not only concern for what they have become in their plight, or interest in what they might become in the kingdom, but attention to what they are right now. Put another way,

Because the *futurum* is an absolutely given which negates all humanly contributed futures, precisely because we are judged to be dead in trespasses and sins and nevertheless forgiven, we are turned back absolutely into the world of creation to know ourselves as creatures and to take care. . . . We are restored as creatures, we become historical because we 'have time' for the world and for the other.[880]

We propose this "having time for the world and the other" is not only the action of subject to object, as from caregiver to care receiver, or helper to needy one, though it may include that. It is also the interaction of creature to creature, receiving as well as giving, appreciating as well as being appreciated. It would appear that Forde's eschatological vision of freedom in Christ corresponds with the ability to engage in the truest kind of dialogue, that which is freed of a burdened focus on the self.

Preparation for the Hermeneutical Task

We have argued for the appropriateness of a genuine interest of the host and the missional person in each other. We have even proposed that Forde might see that interest enhanced by the eschatological event that actually opens a person to the world by ending his/her self-centeredness.

The uncalculating shape of resulting engagement is an asset to the dialogue and sign of its authenticity. It is important that the relationship have its own value.

But that does not mean that missional people are undirected. Missionaries have an inclination growing out of the faith event to care for the neighbor, understood spiritually as well as physically. And they have an authorization through Christ's own command to speak the word of forgiveness to them. To say that the engagement is uncalculating is not to say it is purposeless. The relationship may have its own value, but so do the persons with whom the relationship is maintained. Missionaries are impelled by their faith to care for the neighbor. The conversation/dialogue element serves to help them know how this may be done.

We have already discussed Forde's hermeneutical appreciation of viability (pp. 51-59). This requires insight into the worldview, culture, and language of the people among whom the missionary works. Some of this can come by study, but without the conversation and dialogue described above, it remains merely theoretical. Interaction through direct relationships with people is critical for the capability of constructing a theology that is vital. The alert missional person, aware of nuances and perspectives in the conversation and dialogue, is better positioned to address the viability question in theologizing and proclaiming. Conversation and dialogue thus serve the viability of the eventual message.

A Basis for Religious Engagement

Since religion is of wide interest in West Africa and presumably of interest to the missionary as well, it is perfectly natural and proper for the conversation to turn to God, his works, and the worship of him, all participants feeling free to join in with their opinions. The question is sometimes raised whether such dialogue with other faiths about God is even possible, given the radically different understandings that distinguish Christians from other religions—that is, whether Islam's assertions about Allah, for instance, and Christian talk about God even have the same entity in mind. We propose that some cheerful tolerance for ambiguity about antecedents and possible misunderstanding of assertions is simply necessary at the interface of great faiths. Little is gained by denying any correspondence at all—such conversation would be stillborn before it began. More helpful is the assumption that by the use of common vocabulary the two sides are attempting to talk about the same thing, even if they fall short, and refinements can always be made as the conversation continues. Where there is distance in understanding, it is helpful to discover it together and identify it frankly. The respect shown by the participants in the process is more important for the relationship than agreement on understanding itself, and the critical element at this point is the relationship. Consequently the missionary must bravely ("recklessly?!") enter into the dialogue in good faith. Both sides stand to gain from the attempt.

In the give and take of religious conversation both sides have the opportunity to share their point of view on matters of faith, their witness. Such witness offered in a trusted and vulnerable relationship bears its own force. In Senegal it was not uncommon for our hosts to be struck by aspects of our faith much as we were struck by aspects of theirs. For example, the Muslim concern for justice in inheritance seemed a positive contribution to civil life together and their respect before the otherness of God was thought-provoking to secular Westerners with relatively less respect for anything at all. On the other hand, the thought that God might be capable of coming to earth and assuming humanity if God chose, for example, was both scandalous and intriguing to the Muslim partner. The fact that I thought he actually had was absolutely astonishing.

Most participants were satisfied with the conversation, the friendships, and the tea as such, and, when we had finished, bade us farewell to continue their lives as usual. A few, though, were caught up by the relationship and the conversation, even at this pre-proclamatory stage, and wanted to learn more. Thus the conversation and dialogue of life together sometimes blended into the more focussed proclamatory task described below.

Forde would be concerned to note that gospel-related contributions by the missional person to this kind of conversation are second order and without privilege. They constitute human conversation about God, and should not be misunderstood as proclamation, God's address to us. They participate in the acquaintance- and relationship-building process on a deeper level, perhaps opening possibilities for further reflection and maybe even the desire for eventual proclamation, but probably not accomplishing at this point the dynamic role Forde expects of language in proclamation. This is a freeing insight, preserving the missional person from expectations not likely to be fulfilled and from efforts that are oppressive and counterproductive to the ongoing relationship.

D. The Task

In section A we defined the missional call from two perspectives and proposed a connection between them. On the one hand it is witness to the death and resurrection of Christ, commissioned by God through the event itself and laying the basis for the speaking of forgiveness authorized by Christ through his own words. On the other hand it is care for the world and the neighbor that includes both "spiritual" and "physical" aspects and that also witnesses to the event. The connection is a common grounding: both the witness and the care must grow from the spontaneity and *hilaritas* that characterize the eschatological moment or they are mere law-bound semblences of the missional reality.

Early in the analysis of Forde's theology we remarked that the two-sided action of the Word—law and gospel—happens in oral and sacramental proclamation. We wondered at the time if Forde would permit these terms to be stretched in the ambiguous missional situation (see above, p. 243, n168). Here we propose an approach to proclamation using the the word-sacrament paradigm, but stretched to include the kind of borderline situations we faced in Senegal.

By the Sacramental

How does *hilaritas* share its joyful word when it is not yet permitted to speak? How does gospel-driven love and care for the neighbor work when there are restraints on its expression? Life is full of instances where act precedes word: mother's milk before her "I love you," the sweetheart's kiss before the wedding vow, and three cups of tea before the words of friendship and trust. As incarnate beings we are deeply affected by incarnate words, and we often permit the sacramental long before we permit the spoken.

If concern for the neighbor and her world includes the physical, there are enough physical needs in most cultures to permit its abundant expression. In rural Senegal a lack of prenatal care meant fifteen percent of children never made it to the age of five, and many of their mothers never survived childbirth. A cattle culture that depended on herding was not able to vaccinate its herds, was not able to organize to make veterinary care happen. City youth did their schoolwork under streetlights using borrowed books or notes taken in class. The evidence of the need is often apparent, but its shape is defined more carefully in the kind of conversation and dialogue noted above.

In dialogue, too, the viability of the proposed solutions is best discerned communally with respect to prevailing assumptions and mores, and a decision by the church to participate in communal action can be made. In consultation with local people the church invested itself in a prenatal care program of a midwife and eight health huts. Childhood mortality plummeted to six per thousand, and that ELCA midwife was mobbed on her visits by appreciative women as if she were the Messiah. The church sent a veterinarian with community organizing skills and a herders' cooperative learned veterinary science and organized the call of their own veterinarian. In Dakar and Linguere youth centers provided a library, reading room, sewing classes, computer instruction, various sports opportunities, and so forth for thousands of otherwise resourceless young people. Though initially viewed with suspicion by some as a ploy of Christian evangelism, these ministries were eventually accepted for the condition-free improvements of life that they in fact offered—Forde's care of the neighbor. Insofar as these gifts were associated with the church and its message—and they were, though what that meant might not always have been clear—they carry a sacramental character. Though ambiguous, they speak in objects and actions of a grace that could not then be spoken in words but might be someday. If the missional actions were to become unconnected with the word of grace that might one day be spoken, they would lose their sacramental character and become indistinguishable from similar actions by persons acting from other motives. But connected with the word of grace and hope of speaking it, they bear preliminary witness to God's kindness.

By the Oral

What happens, then, if the *hilaritas* is granted the right to speak? If that is the missional hope and desire, then it is right to plan and prepare for its effective accomplishment when it becomes possible. As we converse and dialogue uncalculatingly and with abandon for its own sake, our *hilaritas* drives us to anticipate and strategize towards moments of teaching that prepare the way and moments of preaching that actually do the work.

In a society where Christian proclamation has no role, congenial structures of society can sometimes be made to lend themselves to this work. It is only confusing when the inevitable abrasion that goes with the missional task is wasted on matters of adiaphora and not saved for matters that count, the Word itself. In Senegal there is a category of traditional religious teacher and worship leader known as "*ceerno*" (pronounced <u>tchair</u>-no). A classic image of a *ceerno* at work would have him sitting on mats surrounded by the young as he teaches them the Qur'an. He also leads the faithful in the regular *salat* and also occasional *du'a* prayers. And upon request the *ceerno* also offers blessings of protection and amulets for safety, presence at marriage and burial of the dead. With a congregation of a few Americans and Senegalese looking to me as pastor, I seemed to fit the category of *ceerno* for most people. As a result, despite the overwhelmingly Muslim milieu, it seemed reasonable to most people that this Christian *ceerno* should organize to teach and preach, pray and fast, marry and bury, and they offered him that freedom. The risk in accepting a societal categorization is the potential loss of the possibility for eschatological expectation and newness as people assume they can understand the missionary and his/her message within old structures. In Senegal, for instance, important components of *ceerno*-hood would include instruction in morality, the use of quasi-magical powers, and paternal care of disciples—not the first things Christians associate with the pastoral task. The advantages, however, are also significant. Most importantly, the pre-proclamatory and proclamatory work is granted a kind of safehaven in society from which it might begin its leavening work.

That work takes several shapes: witness, invitation, instruction, and proclamation. We have already considered the fuzzy interface between dialogue and witness. It was not uncommon for respectful witness to one's faith to occur within the relation-building framework of conversation and dialogue, but of course it does not end there. All aspects of life and ministry—from acts of kindness within one's family to projects designed to help the community—are potential confessions of faith, depending on how they are received. The force of witness itself is not enough, usually, to bring about the death-and-new-life experience that Forde describes, but to cause the person who receives it to open to the prospect offered and to seek better understanding.

This happened time and again in Senegal. Several dozen friends and acquaintances became curious enough about Christian faith through relationship and conversation that they wanted to learn more. At that point it became socially possible for a *ceerno* to extend an invitation to study it more carefully in a class situation with the possibility of entering into it in baptism. This required careful planning. Class material had to be translated not only into the language but into the worldview of the community. Class times and places had to be organized in such a way that they would work for migratory herding people without vehicles scattered over hundreds of square miles of the Sahel. Meals and lodging had to be arranged for those who came from a distance. And all this had to happen discreetly for those who were doing this in the face of some social risk. The invitation to pursue a deeper understanding of Christian faith was thus not something lightly given or received. It was a weighty logistical matter of the kingdom on the left for both host and guest.

The instruction itself was primarily a second-order form of discourse that seeks to present and discuss the dogmatic shape of the tradition in terms that make cultural and worldview sense for the hearers. It reminds one again of Forde's viability. Here again, as in the conversation around the teapot, dialogue and witness in Senegal mix as confessions of the faith are both offered and debated. Yet, now in the classroom, the balance of the conversation is tilted since, by common consent, we are gathered to consider specifically *this* religious claim. The possibility of including first order discourse, or the anticipation of first order discourse, is much increased. The question of what this or that individual will come to make of it is still open, but at this point it is *this* claim that has our attention.

There can be no expectation at the outset that the participants will seek baptism when they are finished, since they cannot know their minds, and they are assured of this. Nevertheless, the possibility is raised because it is a part of what Forde called "the tradition." The prospect of God's ending one's old life of sin and struggle and God's beginning a new life of freedom are asserted and discussed. Proclamation as such may enter this conversation in the assertions of forgiveness connected to Christ's work, but for the most part, it remains a consideration of those benefits from afar and an invitation to enter into those benefits through baptism.

Invitation is not a category of theological thought that is prominent in Forde's work. Beyond two early sermons on the wedding feast in Matt 22:1-14 it is not clear he uses the term at all.[881] To the extent that it is connected with the eschatological moment and requires a capability of human response, it would seem quite contrary to Forde's understanding of the bondage of the human will and the freeing power of the law-gospel word. That's not the kind of invitation we propose here. The invitation to attend a catechetical class is a strictly noneschatological human affair, comparable with an invitation to a party or an invitation to church. Like all human events it might (or might not) be used by God to prepare the way for the kind of hearing of law and gospel that might actually do God's eschatological work, but it remains quite distinct from it. Likewise, the invitation to receive baptism bears all the outward marks of an earthly, human event, which one might or might not choose to be part of. This, however, is more risky for the participant because it carries the warning and the promise of an eschatological event out of which life will never be the same.

It is not uncommon for the participants to describe themselves as having *decided* to attend the class, or to be baptized. The word decision when applied to humankind is such a negative word for Forde that it can hardly be used in any sense at all. It suggests the syncretism of the critical "little bit" that the human can add to God's work to make it complete and upon which our salvation then hangs. A classic verdict by Forde is the following: "The hearer is not left to make a decision about God, but has the decision of God announced to her in and by the very fact of the present-tense proclamation in the name of Jesus."[882] When the participants use the word with respect to a catechetical class or even to baptism itself, we understand it, not as the eschatological moment that creates life anew, but as the human willingness to continue exposure to the announcement of God's decision in the word and the sacraments. Through this initiative of God the death-and-life giving action occurs. It is important that this be communicated in the instruction and the subsequent proclamation, lest faith be jeopardized, even though it may not be fully appreciated by the new Christian until later.

More troubling, it is common for Christians later to reflect back and to extrapolate on the catechetical or baptismal decision and report that they had decided to follow Christ or to become a Christian, as if that were in their power. Some of this comes from the customary human way in which we claim responsibility for our actions, but some comes, no doubt, in this interconnected world, from the influence of the Arminian churches that speak and preach this way. It was not as clear to us as it seemed to Forde that this way of speaking is a sign of an old Adamly effort to retain control over the process and thus must be chided and rejected. Often it appeared to be just a habit of speech from the old Adamly "era" that simply hadn't been rethought in light of the new life.

We would propose a pastoral approach to decision language that maintains two elements. On the one hand, it seems that uninformed or even, sometimes, informed use of the idea of human decision to describe a past response to a noneschatological invitation in an eschatological way does not necessarily indicate resistance to the eschatological event. We ought therefore to be forbearing towards those who venture such talk, as with a less articulate brother and sister who may need help formulating their thoughts. On the other hand, as Forde makes clear, the ramifications of such talk when taken seriously are deadly for reflective Christians because it ultimately puts their salvation into their own hands, as it were—never a safe place. It is part of the theological task to help new Christians witness clearly to what happened to them—not psychologically, "I thought it over and decided to come to God," but theologically, "God drew me by his people's witness and declared me his own in his baptism."

By the Means of Grace

As new people approach the means of grace in the missional situation, we are aware of two tasks that need to be done: the old Adam must die, and the new person must be raised to live before God in freedom in Christ. Neither of these are tasks that the bearer of the means of grace may accomplish by his/her own pastoral skill or missionary effort. Certainly they are not tasks that hearers may accomplish for themselves! Forde is particularly helpful at this point in his directionality, in his persistent insistence that God and God alone does what needs to be done for our salvation. God brings down the proud, God lifts up the lowly, God grants life and salvation to all who believe, God by these means even brings about the faith that believes it. Forde's theological incorrigibility as he looks to God's initiative alone for doing what needs to be done is a rare theological gift to the church in mission. It is irritating and not without its problems as the consequences and implications are pondered, to be sure, but it is also full of potential for building the confidence of proclaimer and believer alike as they experience the effects of the Word upon them *extra nos* as from God's own self.

The two tasks are accomplished by words, and words do what they do by the two ways words function in life: conditional statements that threaten and accuse and unconditional statements that offer promise. We call them law and gospel. The concept of law as developed in Luther studies is our missionary experience, too—that broad understanding of law that recognizes its attack as a category of existence long before the arrival of the proclaimer (see pp. 71-72). We thought we discerned a widespread sense in Senegal that God, though generally confessed as merciful, had the right not to be merciful to a given believer and could not be counted upon to be so. A common response to the possibility was a latent fear of God and a kind of helpless casting oneself upon God's will in openness to whatever fate God might have in store for one. "*Insha Alla!*" was a pious phrase that one heard many times an hour in daily life in Senegal. Unable to say for sure what God willed, the Muslim faithful almost reflexively confessed in every situation, "If God wills it," and every waking action was done conscious of the uncertainty. The force of Forde's/Luther's teaching about the hidden God and the importance of the specificity of absolution and the sacraments for each individual seem almost more pertinent in this context than in the West where religious moves are often disguised or suppressed. Sometimes we said that this widespread and public recognition of the law made for a much readier hearing of the gospel than in the United States.

During our consideration of Forde's understanding of the law, we wondered about the uniformity of his anthropology and whether he was not more conscious of those who lived in pride before the law than of those who seemed already beaten down by it (see above, pp. 74-75, 187). However that may be, we propose that there are those for whom the reality of the effects of the law are already palpable through economic, social, or religious oppression. For such persons the problem is not pride but despair, and the address of the proclamation must offer not further death by further accusation, but resurrection from the dead through unconditional promise of God's claim upon them. Of course, as healing occurs and the old Adam revives, it will need to be addressed again and again for the *simul peccator* that it is. It's not that the proclaimer is master of the action of the words, so that he/she can manipulate what is law and what is gospel at will. The law needs to be preached, and will be preached as Christ is preached, but the diverse situations in which humans find themselves do ask for a pastoral effort to attempt to judge and say what needs to be said so that God might bring the eschatological moment in the broken as well as the proud.

The gospel announcement of the unconditional promise through the means of grace is the deepest fulfillment of the eschatological *hilaritas* of the proclaimer. It is realization in the present, this time for others as well as for oneself, of the same inbreaking of God through the action of the word that occurred in the proclaimer's past and has occurred in the church's past since Christ. It is the confession that God has made peace with us, individually, in every nation, through the life, death, and resurrection of a Jewish rabbi named Jesus. It is the sheer gift of God, given at the cross. People to whom it is given, who live in this gift rather than under the law, will find themselves experiencing what we have followed Forde in calling the eschatological event and the fundamentally new existence that flows from it. Nothing is more of a delight to the missional person than to be part of the beginning of this new life by new people.

Here is a temptation for the missionary. Hidden in this *hilaritas* of sharing the news is the old Adamly urge to take charge of it from the proclaimer's side and to believe one can make it happen. Forde says of justification, "I must say it [the absolution] one more time since it is a matter of your eternal destiny, and it is so much fun to say."[883] It can and often does happen that the missionary "fun" of participating in the eschatological moment for new people moves beyond the speaking of absolution, and the proclaimer winds up preaching faith as such, prescribing what must be done for there to be true belief (see above, p. 115). It won't work, Forde warns. "Preaching faith is like trying to make flowers grow by pulling on them. The very thing one wants to promise is killed."[884] The eschatological event cannot be humanly compelled or contrived, added to or arbitrated. If it happens, it happens by God's work, and if it doesn't happen, it just doesn't happen. Moves on the part of the proclaimer to take charge of or force the promise conditionalize it and render it unsure. Forde's incorrigible (once again!) resistance to those moves helps keep the missionary in line. He calls upon all missional persons to leave it in God's hands and look to him to do his endtime work in the present. Forde helps us speak the words, then leave them alone, trust God, and so, finally, let the gospel be gospel.

This does not mean that the proclaimer can be thoughtless or lazy in preparation because God is doing the work! Even within one's own culture, good proclamation requires good listening and thoughtful reflection to permit its expression in the language, culture, and thoughtforms of the listener. The challenge is only multiplied in another. Though Forde has rather less counsel to offer missional people facing this challenge, we have seen in his example a rather radical commitment to its address from within his own culture and his repeated concern that it not be neglected (see above, pp. 51-59 and 181-182). We have remarked the tension between looking to the proclamation as a divine action and this vigorous human effort in its service (see pp. 185-186). We have wondered whether that human effort should read "permit" or "enable." Does the proclaimer permit the word to do its killing and life-giving work, or does he/she enable it? Or perhaps it helps to say that, after all, he/she simply delivers it. The paradox is that the very Word which is God's own eschatological vehicle is the frail fruit of the human proclaimer's hermeneutical efforts. It is a healthy confession for both speaker and hearer when it heightens the anticipation of the law-gospel encounter with God.

There is not a great need to distinguish between preaching and sacraments at this point. They are united in their directionality, in their "present-tense-doing" of the text to the hearers (see pp. 115-116). As new people expose themselves to these means of grace, they risk the *extra nos* action that is common to both that creates faith when and where God pleases.

E. The Consequences

The Eschatological Event

In mission everything ultimately depends upon the actual occurrence of the eschatological event—the realization of the death of Jesus at our hands in such a way that all hope fails and we are hopeless until we understand his living embrace and hope again. It is the climax of the approach of a new person to Christian faith as he/she makes a friend with a Christian, dialogues about faith matters, is struck by the friend's witness, accepts an invitation to pursue more information, and decides to risk further exposure to the means of grace in baptism and the Holy Communion and the preached word. And it is the source of all the kinds of elements of mission that Bosch, for instance, describes. Every missionary can tell stories of persons who apparently faked, forced, or otherwise fabricated the event for the best or the worst of reasons. Nothing but God's own event will do.

That event is well described by Forde and we spent a considerable part of chapter three exploring it. We found he characterized it in at least three ways. First, the concept of justification by faith alone brings clarity through the forensic metaphor of "an absolutely unconditional affirmation and promise" without any contribution of moral or personal goodness whatsoever. The judgment is made by an omnipotent and electing God upon a humanity bound in sin and unable to participate in any way.[885] Secondly, the concept of death and new life provides the "missing metaphor" that renders the justification language potent in the present. It corrects the impression of the continuity that might be possible under justification where someone is declared just and permitted to go free. Here the radical discontinuity is made apparent by the image of a death to an old way that is a more real death than physical death and a new calculation- and scheme-free life that is so different from the old way that descriptions like conversion and transformation have to be coined afresh and words like progress and growth virtually abandoned (see above, pp. 101-107). And thirdly, the concept of faith must be more than the mere act of recognition of the facts of the tradition. It is rather the experience of the eschatological event—the state of knowing the end of the old attentions to one's efforts, progress, and personal goals and the beginning of "a new life of love, hope, and care."[886] It is the experience of the force of the creative Word that formed it, the trust that that word engenders, "the state of being grasped and captivated in the Spirit by the proclamation of what God has done in Jesus."[887] We proposed that faith is the shape of the living encounter with the will of God through God's word when it kills and makes alive (pp. 107-110). These descriptions characterize our missiological expectation of that actual event when God impinges upon a human life in grace.

Freedom

Old patterns die hard. A new Christian whose habit for forty years has been an attempt to follow Islamic law may take some time to transition into another mode of thought and action. What should he do? How should he live? A new set of rules are called for, no doubt, and missionaries badly compromise their message when they tumble over one another to provide it: come to church rather than observe the Muslim prayer times, have only one wife instead of three, memorize scripture rather than the Qur'an, give a tenth of your calf crop to the church rather than a fiftieth of all sales to the poor.

Forde calls for some restraint, here, since the consequence of the eschatological event is freedom. And, lest some enthusiastic missional type agree with him and jump in to shape the freedom, Forde calls for restraint again. It's not just freedom from this and freedom for that; it's freedom that is truly free: freedom *in* Christ. Outside of Christ the law still works its accusing work, there are rules aplenty, and the sinner stands judged. But *in* Christ, *under* the word of forgiveness, the new Christian is *free*.

Rather than define and destroy that freedom, Forde, in effect, calls upon missionaries to discuss and digest with new Christians just what has happened to us and where that leaves us. Nothing further is required for our salvation. What stands before us as Christians is better defined as new possibility than restraint. Forde's descriptions of *hilaritas*, spontaneity, recklessness, genuineness, and joy invite a new way of thinking about an open and exciting future. Caring for the world and the neighbor occur as expressions of this freedom, but Forde's approach rather invites the new Christian to discover these. We propose that it is part of the missional task to "acccompany" the new Christian into this discovery (see above, pp. 139-140), not directing, but helping fully to notice and to reflect on freedom's freedom.

The Community of Faith

Post-eschatological-moment people have a common experience of which to speak. It includes a common baptism in the triune Name, a closing down of old striving, a new hope in daily life, and a witness to our experience by a meal and a word among insiders and outsiders alike.

It invites a life together and a common mission, but our work in Senegal suggests that inexperience stands in the way of its effective accomplishment. Although Christ's resurrection from the dead is a fact of life, it may not occur to a new Christian to celebrate a specific day for it in a culture that marks many other festivals. Although it may feel good to get together with other Christians, it is not clear what to do with them when there is no tradition of hymnody and no pattern of sharing scripture. Although there may be a desire to do good to neighbors in the name of the new Lord, it is not clear just how a Christian body should go about that in a Muslim world in such a way that it is good news. In other words, inexperience in being the church offers challenges and possibilities unknown to more established congregations.

Just as it is part of the missional task to accompany new Christians into an individual life of faith, we propose that it is part of the task to accompany them into a corporate life of faith. New Christians appreciate the insights and interaction of respectful missional friends in their new walk together. The danger, just as with their personal lives, is that those friends will impose a pattern of parish life upon them that is neither culturally "viable" nor evangelically helpful. Forde's call for viability reminds missional people of this danger.

In Senegal this meant meeting again and again with the new community of feisty and independent cattlepeople to try to imagine what their life together might look like. It meant being broken as a missional person as the will of the community in its culture clashed with ideas brought from the missionary's heritage and culture. It meant painful mediation as the missional person attempted to connect ideas and resources between the new community's world and the wider missionary and ecumenical world. A worship order was constructed. A pattern of meeting together was proposed, failed, and proposed again. A hymnal was assembled. A call for baptismal classes was responded to. International contacts with other Christians were arranged. Aspirations to community service were reviewed and attempts made to make it possible. All the hermeneutical complexity implicit in Forde's call for viability was lived out in the flesh by the missional community during this time. Among *simul peccator* people still new to the faith this can be an excruciating and thankless task for the missional person, unintelligible even, except through an awareness of the topsy-turvy freedom of post-eschatological-event that seeks expression in care for the world and the neighbor.

Precisely in the midst of failure, God seems to build God's church. In Senegal leadership was called away from the fray by medical crisis, other leadership apostisized under stresses that would break many a more seasoned Christian, splintered and lonely believers hid their faith or bravely confessed it under challenge. The missional person should not be surprised that the result of the struggle often looks entirely different from the missional vision, but we always are. Forde, I think, would not have been surprised. He had enough reservations about corporate church efforts that the shattering would make perfect sense to him.

Yet, today a church meets in Linguere where once it was considered inconceiveable that there could be a church. Missional people continue to accompany a naissant community. Whole families gather for worship where once there were only men. Former Christians regret their loss and ask their brethren to pray for them. It's an example of missional people attempting their finest effort and then seeing God use what he chooses in their effort almost despite their work. Forde would understand.

This is not the place to write a full-blown missiology. There are aspects of the missional task that have not even been touched upon in this summary—for instance, missional concern for justice, joint efforts with persons of other faiths in civil affairs, ecumenical cooperation. Other aspects that have been mentioned here have been barely introduced: the ethical implications of the missional intent, deeper questions of interfaith dialogue, the culture of worship and hymnody, and the like. But perhaps enough has been said to demonstrate the vibrant sort of conversation that one missionary had with his theology professor over twenty years of overseas service. Perhaps enough has been said to show the lively linkage between theology and mission, and, in particular, between the theology of Gerhard Forde and the modern ecumenical missionary task.

We propose, therefore, that, though he never considered himself a missiologist, Gerhard Forde spoke and wrote a theology that had powerful implications for the very center of the modern ecumenical missiological enterprise. His high expectation of the eschatological act character of the proclamation, his insistence on the authenticity of the freedom in Christ, and his appeal for and his modelling of a viability of the message all offer strong contributions to the missional conversation, as we have seen. At the same time disjunctures between Forde's theology and missional thought provoke useful questions with their own potential contribution: his apparent reserve about the function of trinitarian reflection, his restraint in assertion of the universality of the missional task, and his narrower missiological self-definition. And finally questions raised by Forde's thought itself seem to offer interesting contributions to conversations important to missiology, for instance, those surrounding his strong hermeneutical tension concerning the role of the interpreter, the uniform anthropology apparently so central to his system, and the tension between the accusing function of the law and a legitimate first use of the law in making common action with those of other faiths for a better world. These are not insignificant contributions and conversations. Surely they deserve every careful attention of the missiological endeavor.

Chronological List of Forde's Published Works

A list of Forde's entire published literary corpus available to date, cited chronologically by year and alphabetically within each year, then numbered:

1962 1. Review of *Dogmatics* by Herman Diem. *dialog* 1/2 (Spr 1962) 69-70.

    2. Review of "Creation and Law" by Gustav Wingren. *dialog* 1/4 (Aug 1962) 78-79.

1963 3. Review of *The Place of Bonhoeffer* by Peter Berger *et al. dialog* 2/4 (Aut 1963) 334-335.

1964 4. "Law and Gospel as the Methodological Principle of Theology." In *Theological Perspectives: A Discussion of Contemporary Issues in Lutheran Theology* by Luther College (Decorah, Iowa) Department of Religion, 50-69. Decorah, Iowa: Luther College Press, 1964.

    5. Review of *The Structure of Lutheranism* by Werner Elert. *dialog* 3/1 (Wint 1964) 77-78.

1965 6. Review of *Word and the Spirit* by Regin Prenter. *dialog* 4/4 (Aut 1965) 304-306.

1966 7. Review of *Gospel and Church* by Gustaf Wingren and *Theology and Preaching* by Heinrich Ott. *dialog* 5/2 (Spr 1966) 150-153.

    8. Review of *Revolt against Heaven: An Enquiry into Anti-Supernaturalis* by Kenneth Hamilton. *dialog* 5/4 (Aut 1966) 312-314.

1967 9. Review of *Faith and the Vitalities of History: A Theological Study Based on the Work of Albrecht Ritschl* by Philip Hefner. *Interpretation* 21/4 (O 1967) 486-489.

   10. Review of *Formation of Historical Theology* by Peter C. Hodgson. *Una Sancta* 24/3 (Trinity 1967) 69-72.

   11. "The Newness of the Gospel." *dialog* 6/2 (Spr 1967) 87-94.

   12. Review of *Theology and Proclamation: Dialogue with Bultmann* by Gerhard Ebeling. *dialog* 6/4 (Aut 1967) 299-302.

1969 13. Review of *Christianity and Humanism: Studies in the History of Ideas* by Quirinus Breen. *Lutheran World* 16/2 (1969) 193-194.

   14. *The Law-Gospel Debate: An Interpretation of its Historical Development.* Minneapolis: Augsburg, 1969.

1970   15. *"lex semper accusat?* Nineteenth Century Roots of Our Current Dilemma." *dialog* 9/4 (Aut 1970) 265-274.

16. "The Revolt and the Wedding: An Essay on Social Ethics in the Perspective of Luther's Theology." In *The Reformation and the Revolution: A Series of Lectures Celebrating the Protestant Reformation and Commemorating the Bolshevik Revolution,* 79-88. Sioux Falls, South Dakota: The Augustana College Press, 1970.

1971   17. "The Problem of Law and Gospel Today." *Luther Seminary Cassette Service* (S 1971). St. Paul.

18. "Sense and Nonsense about Luther [reply to H. Bauman]," *dialog* 10/1 (Wint 1971) 65-67.

1972   19. "Luther Seminary Chapel Talks: The Theology of Martin Luther." *Luther Seminary Cassette Service* (Fe 1972). St. Paul.

20. *Where God Meets Man: Luther's Down-to-Earth Approach to the Gospel.* Minneapolis: Augsburg, 1972.

1973   21. "The Distinction between Law and Gospel for the Preaching of the Church." *Resource Cassette Tapes* (Aug 1973). Minneapolis: Augsburg Publishing House.

22. "Once More Into the Breach? Some Questions about Key 73." *dialog* 12/1 (Win 1973) 7-14.

23. Review of *The Reality of the Devil: Evil in Man* by Ruth Nanda Anshen. *dialog* 12/2 (Spr 1973) 156-158.

1974   24. Review of *Critical Issues in Modern Religion* by Roger A. Johnson and Ernest Wallwork *et al. dialog* 13/3 (Sum 1974) 232-233.

1975   25. *Free to Be: A Handbook to Luther's Small Catechism.* coauthored with James Nestingen. Minneapolis: Augsburg, 1975, revised 1993.

26. "How to Preach the Law" (S 1975) *Resource Cassette Tapes,* Augsburg Publishing House.

1976   27. "Bound to Be Free." In *Encounters with Luther,* 2:67-80, ed. Eric Gritsch. Gettysburg, PA: Lutheran Theological Seminary at Gettysburg, 1976.

28. "The Formula of Concord Article V: End or New Beginning?" *dialog* 15/3 (Sum 1976) 184-191.

1977   29. "The 'Old Synod:' A Search for Objectivity." In *Striving for Ministry: Centennial Essays Interpreting the Heritage of Luther Theological Seminary,* ed. Warren A. Quanbeck, Eugene L., Fevold, Gerhard E. Frost, and Paul G. Sonnack, 67-80. Minneapolis: Augsburg, 1977.

1978   30. "Bultmann: Where Did He Take Us?" *dialog* 17/1 (Wint 1978) 27-30.

31. "The Eucharistic Prayer in the LBW: Two Perspectives: 1. The LBW Goes Too Far." *Resource Cassette Service* (O 1978). Minneapolis: Augsburg Publishing House.

32. "Infallibility Language and the Early Lutheran Tradition." In *Teaching Authority and Infallibility in the Church: Lutherans and Catholics in Dialogue VI,* ed. Paul C. Empie, T. Austin Murphy, and Joseph A. Burgess, 120-137. Minneapolis: Augsburg, 1978, 1980.

33. "Luther and the Jews." *Resource Cassete Service* (Jul 1978). Minneapolis: Augsburg Publishing House.

1979   34. "Outside the Gate: Atonement as Actual Event." *dialog* 18/4 (Aut 1979) 247-254.

1980   35. "The Exodus from Virtue to Grace: Justification by Faith Today."
        Interpretation 34/1 (Jan. 1980) 32-44.

1981   36 "A Matter of Death and Life: Appropriating the Confessions for Today."
        3 vol., Knubel-Miller-Greever Foundation Lectures. Audiocassette.
        Trinity Lutheran Seminary, January 20-21, 1981.

        37. "The Augsburg Confession, Article 4." *Resource Cassette Service* (Jn
        1981) Minneapolis: Augsburg Publishing House.

        38. "A Short Word." *dialog* 20/2 (Spr 1981) 88-92.

        39. "Unity without Concord?" *dialog* 20/2 (Spr 1981) 166-173.

        40. "Declaring our Faith Today." In "Papers Requested by the Committee on
        Lutheran Unity," edited by Commission for a New Lutheran Church,
        edited by Faith Burgess, 1981.

1982   41. *Justification by Faith: A Matter of Death and Life.* Philadelphia: Fortress
        Press, 1982.

        42. Review of *Luther and Staupitz: An Essay in the Intellectual Origins of the
        Protestant Reformation* by David C. Steinmetz. *Interpretation* 36/2 (Ap
        1982) 196-199.

        43. "Theology as *Modus Operandi*." *dialog* 21/3 (Sum 1982) 175-179.

1983   44. "Caught in the Act: Reflections on the Work of Christ." *Word & World* 3/
        1 (Wint 1983) 22-31.

        45. "Fake Theology: Reflections on Antinomianism Past and Present." *dialog*
        22/4 (Fall 1983) 246-251.

        46. "Law and Gospel in Luther's Hermeneutic." *Interpretation* 37/3 (Jul
        1983) 240-252.

        47. "The Place of Theology in the Church." *dialog* 22/2 (Spr 1983) 121-
        130.

1984   48. "The Christian Life." In *Christian Dogmatics*, edited by Carl E. Braaten
        and Robert W. Jenson, 2:391-469. Philadelphia: Fortress, 1984.

        49. Review of *God as Mystery of the World* by Eberhard Juengel. *Word &
        World* 4 (Fall 1984) 458-461.

        50. "The Power of Negative Thinking: On the Principle of Negation in
        Luther and Hegelianism." *dialog* 23/4 (Aut 1984) 250-256.

        51. "Preaching the Sacraments." *Lutheran Theological Seminary Bulletin*
        64/4 (Fall 1984) 3-27.

        52. "Romans 8:18-27." *Interpretation* 38/3 (Jul 1984) 281-285.

        53. "When the Old Gods Fail: Martin Luther's Critique of Mysticism." In
        *Piety, Politics, and Ethics: Reformation Studies in Honor of George
        Wolfgang Forell*, edited by Carl Lindberg. Kirksville, MO: The Sixteenth
        Century Journal Publishers, Inc., 1984.

        54. "The Word of God." Videorecording. Columbus, OH: SELECT, 1984.

        55. "The Work of Christ." In *Christian Dogmatics*, edited by Carl E. Braaten
        and Robert W. Jenson, 2:1-99. Philadelphia: Fortress Press, 1984.

1985   56. "Dogmatics." *dialog* 24/4 (Aut 1985) 297-299.

        57. "Forensic Justification and Law in Lutheran Theology." In *Justification
        by Faith: Lutherans and Catholics in Dialogue VII*, edited by H. George
        Anderson, T. Austin Murphy, and Joseph A. Burgess, 278-303. Minne-
        apolis: Augsburg, 1985.

58. Review of *Luther in Mid-Career 1521-1530* by Heinrich Bornkamm. *Interpretation* 39/4 (O 1985) 436.

59. "Some Remarks on [Ted] Peters' Review of *Christian Dogmatics*." *dialog* 24/4 (Fall 1985) 297-299.

1986   60. "Karl Barth, 1886-1986." Videorecording. Philadelphia: Luther Theological Seminary, 1986.

1987   61. "Radical Lutheranism: Lutheran Identity in America." *Lutheran Quarterly* 1/1 (Spr 1987) 5-18.

62. "The Viability of Luther Today: A North American Perspective." *Word & World* 7/1 (Wint 1987) 22-31.

1988   63. Review of *Eberhard Jüngel: An Introduction to His Theology* by J. B. Webster. *Lutheran Quarterly* 2/4 (Wint 1988) 531-533.

64. "Justification by Faith Alone: The Article by Which the Church Stands or Falls?" *dialog* 27/4 (Fall 1988) 260-267.

65. "The Lutheran View." In *Christian Spirituality: Five Views of Sanctification*, edited by Donald L. Alexander, 13-32. Also brief responses to other denominational positions, 77-82, 119-122, 155-157, 190-192. Downers Grove, IL: Intervarsity, 1988.

1989   66. "The Catholic Impasse: Reflections on Lutheran-Catholic Dialogue Today." In *Promoting Unity: Themes in Lutheran-Catholic Dialogue*, edited by H. George Anderson and James R. Crumley Jr., 67-77. Minneapolis: Augsburg, 1989.

67. "Full Communion?" *dialog* 28/2 (Spr 1989) 85-86.

68. "What's in a Name? Eucharist or Lord's Supper." *Word & World* 9/1 (Wint 1989) 52-55.

1990   69. "Karl Barth on the Consequences of Lutheran Christology." In *The Consequences of Christology: Papers Presented at a Conference at Luther Northwestern Theology,* part 5. Videorecording. St. Paul: Luther Northwestern Theological Seminary, 1990.

70. "The Ordained Ministry." In *Called & Ordained: Lutheran Perspectives on the Office of the Ministry*, edited by Todd Nichol and Marc Kolden, 117-136. Minneapolis: Fortress Press, 1990.

71. "Proclamation: The Present Tense of the Gospel." *dialog* 29/3 (Sum 1990) 167-173.

72. Coproduced with Lazareth, William. "The Special Ministry." In *Papers Read at the Call to Faithfulness Conference (1990, Northfield)*, cassette 2. Videorecording. Northfield, Minnesota: St. Olaf College, 1990.

73. "The Systematics of Proclamation." In *The Small Church: Closed Community or Caring Cell?* Audiocassette. Aug. 1990.

74. *Theology is for Proclamation*. Minneapolis: Fortress Press, 1990.

1991   75. "Confessional Subscription: What Does It Mean for Lutherans Today?" *Word & World* 11/3 (Sum 1991) 316-320.

76. "Justification by Faith Alone." In *Search of Christian Unity: Basic Consensus/Basic Differences*, edited by Joseph A. Burgess, 64-76. Minneapolis: Fortress Press, 1991.

77. "A Movement without a Move?" *dialog* 30/2 (Spr 1991) 83-84.

78. "Public Ministry and Its Limits." *dialog* 30/2 (Spr 1991) 102-110.

1992   79   "The Christian Apprehension of God the Father." In *Speaking of the Christian God: The Holy Trinity and the Challenge of Feminism*, edited by Alvin Kimel. Grand Rapids, MI: Eerdmans, 1992.

80.   "Futurum Resurrectionis: Barth's Romans revisited." In *Christian Hope and the Human Future*, cassette 2. Videorecording. St. Paul: Luther Northwestern Theological Seminary, 1992.

81.   "Is Invocation of Saints an Adiaphoron?" In *The One Mediator, The Saints, and Mary: Lutherans and Catholics in Dialogue VIII*, edited by H. George Anderson, J. Francis Stafford, and Joseph A. Burgess, 327-338. Minneapolis: Augsburg, 1992.

82.   "Justification." In *A New Handbook of Christian Theology*, ed. Donald W. Musser and Joseph L. Price, 271-273. Nashville, TN: Abingdon, 1992.

83.   "The Meaning of *Satis Est.*" *Lutheran Forum* 26/4 (Nov 1992) 14-18.

84.   "Naming the One Who is Above Us." In *Speaking the Christian God: The Holy Trinity and the Challenge of Feminism*, edited by Alvin F. Kimel, Jr., 110-119. Grand Rapids: Eerdmans, 1992.

85.   "The Newness of the New Testament." In *All Things New: Essays in Honor of Roy A. Harrisville*, edited by Arland J. Hultgren, Donald H. Juel, and Jack D. Kingsbury, 175-180. St. Paul, MN: Luther Theological Seminary *Word & World* supplement, 1992.

86.   "Response to James Nestingen's Article." *dialog* 31/1 (Wint 1992) 34-35.

87.   "The Word on Quotas." *Lutheran Quarterly* 6/2 (Sum 1992) 119-126.

1993   88.   "Called to Freedom." In *Befreiung und Freiheit: Martin Luthers Beitrag: Eighth International Congress for Luther Research*, tape 1. Videorecording. St. Paul: Luther Northwestern Theological Seminary, 1993.

89.   Review of "Göttingen Dogmatics: Instruction in the Christian Religion." *Pro Ecclesia* 2/2 (Spr 1993) 240-242.

90.   "Luther and the *Usus Pauli.*" *dialog* 32/4 (Fall 1993) 275-282.

91.   "Lutheranism." In *The Blackwell Encyclopedia of Modern Christian Thought*, edited by Alister McGrath, 354-358. Cambridge, MA: Blackwell, 1993.

92.   "Something to Believe: A Theological Perspective on Infant Baptism." *Interpretation* 47/2 (Apr 1993) 229-241.

1994   93.   "Does the Gospel Have a Future? Barth's Romans Revisited." *Word & World* 14/1 (Wint 1994) 67-77.

94.   "God's Freedom for Us. Our Freedom for God." In *God's Freedom and Ours: Soteriology, Ethics, and the Mission of the Church Today*, lectures 1 and 2. St. Paul: Luther Northwestern Theological Seminary, 1994.

95.   "The Normative Character of Scripture for Matters of Faith and Life: Human Sexuality in Light of Romans 1:16-32," *Word & World* 14/3 (Sum 1994) 305-314.

1995   96.   "Law and Sexual Behavior." *Lutheran Quarterly* 9/1 (Spr 1995) 3-22.

1996   97.   "The Apocalyptic 'No!' and the Eschatological 'Yes!'" In *The Necessary "No!" and the Indispensable "Yes!": Theological Controversy, Christology and the Mission of the Church Today*. [videorecording], Cassette 2. St. Paul, Minnesota: Luther Seminary, [1996].

98. "Is Forgiveness Enough? Reflections on an Odd Question." *Word & World* 16/3 (Sum 1996) 302-308.

99. "Martens on the Condemnations." *Lutheran Quarterly* 10/1 (Spr 1996) 67-69.

1997 100. Cosigned with others. "A Call for Discussion of the 'Joint Declaration on the Doctrine of Justification.'" *dialog* 36/3 (Sum 1997) 224-229.

101. "The End of Theology." In *Mid-Winter Convocation: What Are We Up To? Systematic Theologians at Work*, casssette 8. Videorecording. St. Paul: Luther Seminary, 1997.

102. "The Lord's Supper as the Testament of Jesus," *Word & World* 17/1 (Wint 1997) 5-9.

103. "On Being a Theologian of the Cross," *Christian Century* 114/29 (Oct. 22, 1997) 947-949.

104. *On Being a Theologian of the Cross: Reflections on Luther's Heidelberg Disputation, 1518.* Grand Rapids: Eerdmans, 1997.

105. "The One Acted Upon [Theological Autobiography]," *dialog* 36/1 (Wint 1997) 54-61.

106. "What Finally to Do about the (Counter-) Reformation Condemnations," *Lutheran Quarterly* 11/1 (Spr 1997) 3-16.

1998 107. "What Next?" *dialog* 37/3 (Sum 1998) 163.

1999 108. Cosigned with others. "The Critical Response of German Theological Professors to the Joint Declaration on the Doctrine of Justification," *dialog* 38:1 (Wint 1999) 71-72.

109. "The Word That Kills and Makes Alive." In *Marks of the Body of Christ*, edited by Carl E. Braaten and Robert W. Jenson, 1-12. Grand Rapids: Eerdmans, 1999.

2000 110. "Robert Jenson's Soteriology." In *Trinity, Time, and Church: A Response to the Theology of Robert W. Jenson*, edited by Colin Gunton, 126-138. Grand Rapids: Eerdmans, 2000.

2003 111. "Lutheran Ecumenism: With Whom and How Much?" *Lutheran Quarterly* 17/4 (Wint 2003) 436-455.

2004 112. *A More Radical Gospel: Essays on Eschatology, Authority, Atonement and Ecumenism.* In Lutheran Quarterly Book Series, edited by Mark C. Mattes and Steven D. Paulson. Grand Rapids: Eerdmans, 2004.

2005 113. *The Captivation of the Will: Luther vs. Erasmus on Freedom and Bondage*, edited by Steven D. Paulson. Grand Rapids: Eerdmans, 2005.

2007 114. *The Preached God: Proclamation in Word and Sacrament*, edited by Mark C. Mattes and Steven D. Paulson. Grand Rapids: Eerdmans, 2007.

The Sermons and Manuscripts of Gerhard Forde

Listed here are the one hundred forty-three extant sermon manuscripts of Gerhard Forde known at this time. It includes the one hundred forty sermon manuscripts that Marianna Forde identified among her husband's letters and papers in the third year after his death. Presented without apparent order, many of them both undated and untitled, they were tentatively organized according to scriptural text where that was possible. Brief descriptions of the manuscripts themselves offer clues in dating. Where a title was lacking, the first words of the manuscript help further identify the sermon. At this writing, Marianna Forde retains the original collection, and the author has a copy.

Thirty-one of the sermons have been published in recent *Lutheran Quarterly* editions of Forde's works edited by Mark Mattes and Steven Paulson, including three not present in Marianna Forde's collection. These are indicated.

Gen 2:15-17; 3:1-13: "On Sin"
  5 pages. Invocavit. A carbon copy perhaps, typed on plain, yellowing paper.
Gen 3:1-5; Col 3:3: "You Will Not Die"
  3 pages. Chapel, May 12, 1998. Computer printed on folded, slightly wrinkled white paper.
Gen 11:1-9: "Explosions and the Christian Faith"
  4 pages. Handwritten on slightly smaller-sized Mansfield College Oxford stationery.
Ex 4:21-26: "At a lodging place on the way the Lord met Moses. . . "
  5 pages. Baccalaureate, May 23, 1998. Computer printed on white paper. Ink stain bottom center. Published in *The Preached God*, 286-287 as "Moses' Baccalaureate."

2 Sam 24:1-5, 10-14: "A Gracious Neighbor or a Gracious God?"
  4 pages. Typed on plain, slightly yellowing paper. Published in *The Preached God*, 311-315.
Ps 13: "He Who Is to Come"
  2 pages. Handwritten on Forde's own LTS stationery.
Ps 13: "One of the anxieties we have as human beings..."
  2 pages. Chapel, Nov 8, 9. Typed on thin, yellowing plain paper, folded in quarters.
Ps 25:4-5: "Make Me to Know Thy Ways O Lord"
  2 pages. Typed on thin, yellowing plain paper, folded in quarters.
Ps 51:15: "Breaking the Conspiracy of Silence"
  Published in *The Preached God*, 291-297. Not in Marianna Forde's collection.

Ps 51:15: "O Lord, Open Thou My Lips"
2 pages. Handwritten on thin, yellowing plain paper, folded in quarters. Published in *The Preached God*, 291-297.

Ps 51:15: We are gathered here in this ancient place..."
2 pages. Computer printed on white paper. "?" penned in the upper right corner.

Ps 65:5: "Loose Ends?
2 pages. Chapel: 10/22/92. Computer printed on slightly yellowing paper, folded in quarters.

Ps 74:22-23: "Exsurge Domine! Judica Causam Tuam!"
4 pages. Typed on very slightly yellowed paper, stain along top edge, stapled, used appearance. Published in *A More Radical Gospel*, 206-210.

Ps 106:1: "O Give Thanks to the Lord, for He is Good"
2 pages. Typed on thin, yellowing, folded paper.

Ps 107:1-3: "Indherred 125th Anniversary
4 pages. June 25, 1995. Computer printed on white, faintly wrinkled, stapled pages.

Is 11:1-5: "Das Helle Licht der Weihnacht Bricht Wieder"
11 pages. Christmas, 1958. Handwritten on 15 cm x 21cm, punched, binder pages.

Is 40:6-10: "A Voice Says, 'Cry!' and I Said, 'What Shall I Cry?'"
2 pages. Typed on yellowing, folded plain pages.

Is 53:2-3: "Loser Takes All: The Victory of Christ"
3 pages. Typed on Forde's own LTS stationery.

Jer 23:23-32: "A Word from Without"
2 pages. Chapel, Oct 27. Computer printed in two copies on white paper, the uncorrected one stapled. Published in *The Captivation of the Will*, 91-93.

Lam 1:12: "Behold and See!"
3-page draft handwritten on scratch paper dated 3/17/75, 5-page revision dated Good Friday, Northfield 1975, typed on LTS stationery.

Ezek 3:4-15: "The Discipline of Silence"
3 pages. Typed on yellowing plain paper, folded.

Mic 4:5: "For All Peoples Walk Each in the Name of Its God"
3-page handwritten draft and 3-page typed version on folded, yellowing paper.

Mic 4:5: "The Grace of a Name"
4 pages. Typed on yellowing paper folded into quarters.

Matt 2:9-11: "And Lo, the Star Which They Had Seen in the East"
3 pages. Typed on yellowing paper folded into quarters.

Matt 2:13-15, 19-23: "The Other Side of Christmas"
3 pages draft handwritten on Forde's LTS stationery, then 3 pages typed on the same, folded.

Matt 3:1-10: "On New Ideas and Old Traditions"
2 pages. Typed on yellowing paper, folded in quarters.

Matt 3:1-10" "The Season of Lent"
1 page. Handwritten on a Bible 102 exam folded in half.

Matt 5:13: "You Are the Salt of the Earth"
2 pages. Typed on yellowing paper folded in quarters.

Matt 6:1-6, 16-21: "The End of Religion"
5 pages. Ash Wednesday. Typed on yellowing paper, folded.

Matt 8:1-13: "Our text for today, the account of the healing..."
5 pages. Typed on yellowing pages folded and folded again kitty-corner along the left side.

Matt 8:28-34: "Go Away Jesus!"
3 pages. Computer printed on white pages and stapled. Published in *The Captivation of the Will*, 102-104.

Matt 9:1-8: "Take Heart, My Son, Your Sins Are Forgiven"
2 pages. Handwritten, the first page on a presidency questionnaire on LTS stationery, the second page on lined paper.

Matt 9:1-8: "Something for Nothing"
2 pages. Typed on LTS stationery.

Matt 9:10-13: "Not the Well, But the Sick"

1 page. Typed on a plain, yellowing page and folded in quarters. Published in *A More Radical Gospel*, 223.

Matt 11:2-5 and Mark 14:3-9: "On Preaching Good News to the Poor"

The 3-page version typed, the 2-page version inkjet printed, both on folded yellowing paper. Published in *The Preached God*, 303-305.

Matt 11:2-11: "He Who Is to Come"

3 pages. Typed on Forde's LTS stationery, folded in quarters.

Matt 11:25-30: "The Easy Yoke"

3 pages. Computer printed on white paper. Published in *The Captivation of the Will*, 83-85.

Matt 13:44: "Hidden Treasure"

3-page version typed on particularly worn and folded paper, 4-page version computer printed. Published in *A More Radical Gospel*, 211-214.

Matt 17:21-27 and Matt 26:47-56: "On Death to Self"

5 pages. Computer printed on white paper. Published in *Captivation of the Will*, 108-111.

Matt 18:21-35: "Immanuel: An Outpost of Forgiveness"

5 pages. Two nearly identical versions, inkjet printed.

Matt 20:1-16: "God's Rights"

2 pages. Typed on yellowing paper, folded in quarters. Published in *A More Radical Gospel*, 203-205.

Matt 20:1-16: "They All Got the Same!"

2 pages. Typed on yellowing onionskin paper folded in half. Published in *The Preached God*, 316-318.

Matt 22:1-14: "Our text today compares the Kingdom of Heaven..."

2 pages. Chapel, Sept. 26, '66. Typed on yellowing paper, folded in quarters.

Matt 22:1-14: "The Wedding Feast"

2 pages. Handwritten on a memorandum from Paul Sponheim dated 9/3/75.

Matt 22:1-14: "A God Who Acts"

4 pages. Typed on yellowing paper, folded.

Matt 23:37: "O Jerusalem, Jerusalem, Killing the Prophets"

6-page draft on yellow, blue-lined notepaper, then 5-page typed version on plain, yellowing paper.

Matt 25:1-13: "Meditation on All-Fools Day"

2 pages. April 1, 1968. Typed on folded yellowing paper. The second sheet has an extension.

Matt 25:1-13: "There Were Ten Maidens"

4 pages. Typed on plain yellowing paper, folded.

Matt 26:29: "I Tell You I Shall Not Drink Again of this Fruit"

1 page. Computer printed on white paper.

Matt 27:46: "The Cross as Sign of Faith"

5 pages. Typed on Forde's own LTS stationery, folded in half.

Matt 27:46: "'My God, My God...' I Could Wish..."

3-page handwritten draft, then 3-page typewritten on Forde's own LTS stationery.

Matt 27:46: "'My God, My God...' Surely These Words.."

3 pages. Handwritten on yellow, blue-lined notepaper. Wrinkled lower left corner.

Matt 27:46: "'My God, My God...' Today, on Good Friday..."

3 pages. Typed on plain, faintly yellowing paper, folded.

Matt 28:6: "Thought for Easter Sermon"

4 pages. Two folded yellowing sheets, one inside the other to form a small booklet.

Mark 1:21-28: "A Voice from the Darkness"

4 pages. Handwritten draft on yellow, blue-lined notepaper, then typed on LNTS stationery. Published in *The Preached God*, 306-310.

Mark 8:35 and Col 3:3: "On Losing One's Life"

2 pages. Two computer printed versions on yellowing paper, folded, one front-to-back.

Mark 10:17ff and Luke 10:25: "What Shall I Do to Get Saved?"

1 page. Handwritten on a heavily yellowed, folded page.

Mark 14:25: "Truly I Say to You, I Shall Not Drink Again"

2-page version handwritten on yellow, blue-lined notepaper, 1-page version typed on yellowing, folded LNTS stationery. Published in *The Preached God*, 280-281, under the title "Abstractions Aside."

Mark 14:25: "The Interrupted Party"

1 page. Computer printed on a plain yellowing paper cut off at the top to leave an 8" length. Published in *The Preached God*, 278-279.

Mark 14:25: "Celebrating the Future"

Published in *The Preached God*, 282-283. Not in Marianna Forde's collection.

Mark 16:6: "He Has Risen, He Is Not Here"

2 pages. Typed on Forde's own LTS stationery.

Luke 2:10-11: "And the Angel Said unto Them, Fear Not"

1-page, densely handwritten draft in pencil on a thin, worn, folded paper, 2-page version typed and folded.

Luke 2:22-40 and Heb 2:14-18: "The Presentation of our Lord"

2 pages. Published in the Luther-Northwestern "Semogram," March 1977.

Luke 3:1-14: "He Who Comes"

2 pages. Dec 12, 1967. Typed on slightly yellowed, folded paper.

Luke 7:31ff: "To What Then Shall I Compare the Men"

2 pages. Typed on thin, folded yellowing paper.

Luke 9:24: "For Whoever Would Save His Life Will Lose It"

2 pages. Feb. 22, 1965. Typed on brittle, yellowing paper, folded in quarters.

Luke 10:25-37: "A Certain Man Was Going Down One Day"

3 pages. Typed, perhaps by a secretary on an office machine. Ten copies are saved.

Luke 11:24-26: "My talk this morning..."

2 pages. Chapel, Luther Seminary, Jan 17, 1967. Typed on yellowing plain paper.

Luke 11:24-26: "Seven More Demons!"

3 pages. Typed on St. Olaf College Dept. of Religion stationery, tarnished seam on the fold.

Luke 11:24-26: "When the Unclean Spirit Has Gone Out of a Man"

3 pages. Typed on yellowing, twice-folded paper, a close modification of the previously listed sermon.

Luke 14:1-11: "Christ and the Teachers"

5-page handwritten version on Forde's LTS stationery, then a 6-page typed version, both folded once.

Luke 15:1-7: "The Perilous Journey" with fragment attached

3 pages. Drafted on the back of a bibliography, then typed, folded.

Luke 15:1-7: "The Perilous Journey" in four pages

4 pages. Computer printed on plain yellowing folded paper.

Luke 15:1-7: "The Perilous Journey" in two pages

2 pages. Computer printed, unfolded, stapled. Published in *Captivation of the Will*, 99-103.

Luke 16:10-13: "On Serving God and Mammon"

3 pages. Typed on brittle, slightly yellowing paper.

Luke 17:11-19: "Possible Sermon? Where Are the Nine?"

1 page. Musings on yellow, blue-lined notepaper, folded and kitty-corner folded.

Luke 18:35-43: "A Refuge for Beggars"

5 pages. Typed on heavily yellowed, paper, folded.

Luke 23:32-38: "'Father, Forgive Them.' Well, He Is at It Again!"

2 pages. Handwritten on yellow blue-lined notepaper. An eyewitness dates it to about 2001.

Luke 23:32-38: "Father, forgive them, for they know not..."

2 pages. A computer printed draft with two computer versions, one on brittle paper, folded.

Luke 24:44-49: "You Are Witnesses"

3 pages. Typed on Forde's LTS stationery. Published in *The Preached God*, 298-302.

John 1:6-8, 19-28: "On Getting Out of the Way for Jesus"

2-page version without an ending, folded, and a 6-page version on very white paper, both computer printed. Published in *Captivation of the Will*, 94-98.

John 1:18 and John 5:19: "No One Has Ever Seen God..."

2 pages. Handwritten on yellowing, folded paper. Published in *The Preached God* under the title "The Doing of God."

John 1:43-51: "On God's Godness"

2 pages. Handwritten on yellowing, folded paper.

John 3:16: "For God So Loved the World"

2 pages. Typed on smooth, yellowing, folded paper.

John 6:53-60: "Food and Drink Indeed!"

2 pages. Computer printed on both sides of slightly yellowed paper, folded and slightly bent.

John 10:1-15: "The Good Shepherd"

2 pages. Typed on folded LTS stationery, computer printed on unfolded onionskin.

John 10:17-19? 21?: "On the Ending and Goal of Life"

3 pages. Handwritten on yellowing scratch paper dated 4/30/74.

John 10:22-30: "My Sheep Hear My Voice"

4 pages. Typed on yellowing, plain paper, folded.

John 15:9-17: "I Chose You"

3 pages. Typed on yellowing paper with note attached. Computer printed on white paper. Published in *The Captivation of the Will*, 105-107.

John 19:28-30: "'It Is Finished!' I suppose it might seem strange..."

4-page handwritten draft and 3-page typed revision, both on yellowing paper, the latter folded.

John 19:28-30: "'It Is Finished' In a world like ours..."

5 pages. Handwritten on yellowing plain paper.

John 19:28-30: "'It Is Finished!' In this half-done world..."

Two versions, each 2 pages, both computer printed, but with alternate endings, both folded.

John 19:29: "'It Is Finished!' It is finished, completed . . ."

2 pages. Typed on yellowing paper, unusually folded, three folds straight across.

John 19:28-30: "'It Is Finished!' It is over and at the same time..."

2 pages. Computer printed on slightly yellowed paper, folded in quarters.

John 19:30: "'It Is Finished.' Over. But not just ended."

2 pages. Jan. 31, 2000, Arden Hills. Computer printed for a preaching seminar.

John 19:28-30: "'It Is Finished!' What does mean? The word has..."

2 pages. Typed on yellowing paper, folded once.

John 20:19-29: "Faith and Doubt"

4 pages. Typed on onionskin paper, folded once.

John 20:19-23: "On the evening of that day, the first day of the week..."

7 pages. Typed on LTS stationery, with 6th page handwritten, coming from four documents.

Acts 1:6-9: "Later"

1 page. Chapel Homily for Ascension. Computer printed. Published in *The Preached God*, 284-285.

Acts 1:8: "But You Shall Receive Power"

2 pages. Typed on plain, yellowed paper, folded.

Acts 4:5-12: "No other name!"

3 pages. Typed on plain, yellowed paper, folded.

Rom 1:16: "I Am Not Ashamed of the Gospel"

3 pages. Typed on heavy, plain, slightly yellowed paper.

Rom 3:19-28: "'Justification by Faith Alone.' I declare unto you...."

4 pages. Reformation Sunday, 1990/2. Typed on plain yellowing paper.

Rom 3:28: "'Justification by Faith Alone.' That is the word that..."

Three versions: 4-page computer printed, 7-page large computer printed, and 5-page new computer printed on white paper. Reformation. 1992. Published in *The Captivation of the Will*, 86-90.

Rom 3:28: Two titles: "Sola" and "Justification by Faith Alone. Those words touched..."

5-page handwritten version, and a 4-page typed version, both dated 10/16/86 and written on yellowing paper, folded.

Rom 5:1-5: "Rejoice in your Sufferings"

2 pages. Typewritten on unfolded yellowing plain paper.

Rom 6:1-11: "Are We to Continue in Sin"

2 pages. Typed on Forde's own LTS stationery, folded in quarters.

Rom 6:12-14: "Sin Will Have No Dominion"

2 pages. Typed on Forde's own LTS stationery, folded unusually, three times across.

Rom 12:1-3: "We Are Being Transformed"

1-page version, typed on LNTS stationery, and 4-page, new computer printed on white paper.

1 Cor 2:1-2 and 2 Cor 4:5-6: "Testimony!"

Two independent 2-page versions, computer printed, back on front.

1 Cor 3:18ff: "Let no one deceive himself. If any one..."

2 pages. Typewritten on unfolded onionskin.

1 Cor 9:16-18: "If I preach the Gospel, that gives me no ground..."

2 pages. Handwritten on yellowing pages, folded.

1 Cor 11:23-26: "The Bread of Life"

1 page. Handwritten densely on a yellowing, folded sheet, wrinkled at the bottom.

1 Cor 11:23-26: "The Lord's Supper"

4 pages. Typed on yellowing paper, folded in quarters.

1 Cor 11:26: "It wasn't fair, you know, to go away and leave us . . ."

1 page. Computer printed. Published in *The Preached God*, 276-277.

1 Cor 13:1: "Though I Speak in the Tongues of Mortals and of Angels"

2 pages. Typed on yellowing paper, folded.

1 Cor 14:20: "Brethren, do not be children in your thinking..."

1 page. Handwritten on heavily yellowed paper, folded into quarters.

1 Cor 15:25: "He must reign until he has put all his enemies..."

2 pages. Handwritten on yellow, blue-lined notepaper.

2 Cor 1:17b-22: "Yes! How would you like to take a bite . . ."

2 pages. Computer printed on fairly unyellowed plain paper. Published in *The Preached God*, 319-321.

2 Cor 3:1-6, 12-18: "Where the Spirit of the Lord Is"

4 pages. Typed on Mansfield College Oxford stationery. The copy used is folded.

2 Cor 12:9: "The Paradoxes of Faith: Poison or Promise"

2 pages. Typed on yellowing paper, folded into quarters.

Gal 2:15-16: "'Justification By Faith.' On this festival . . ."

3 pages. A Reformation sermon, typed on a professor roster, yellowing, not folded.

Gal 6:14-16: "What Matters"

3 pages. New computer printed on white paper and not folded. Published in *The Captivation of the Will*, 116-118.

Eph 4:1-16: "The Priesthood of Believers"

5 pages. Typed on lighter yellowing paper, folded.

Phil 1:21: "For Me to Live Is Christ and to Die Is Gain."

2 pages. Chapel Sept 27, 1962, typed on onionskin, folded.

Col 2:8: "Christian Education"

3 pages. Perhaps a lecture, handwritten on heavily yellowed paper, folded.

Col 2:8-3:4: "Christ and Man"

7 pages. Carefully typed, perhaps a carbon copy on smaller 8"x10" yellowed paper.

Col 2:8-15: "A Real Person"

2 pages. Oct 1, '64 written on back of a page. Typed on yellowing paper, folded.

Col 2:20-3:4: "You Have Died"

2 pages. Handwritten on yellow, blue-lined notepaper. Published in *A More Radical Gospel*, 215-217.

2 Tim 1:7: "Faith or Fear?"

3 pages. Typed on yellowed, plain paper, folded, with notes on back, arranged in unusual booklet form.

Heb 10:11-2: "The Priest"

5 pages. Typed on Forde's own LTS stationery.

James 3:13ff: "Religion can do one of two things for a person."

1 page. Handwritten on yellowed page, sharply folded.

2 Peter 3:8-14: "The Day of the Lord"

Two 1-page computer-printed versions, one longer than the other. Published in *A More Radical Gospel*, 218-219.

1 John 3:1-3: "Patience & Hope – Purification – Protest"

6 pages. Handwritten, extraordinarily, on brown blue-lined writing pages, folded at the bottom.

Rev 7:1-10: "The Other Worldly Vision"

1-page version typed on Mansfield College Oxford stationery, a 3-page version typed on LTS stationery, and a 4-page version, mimeographed with many copies.

Rev 21:5-6: "Remembering Ralph"

5 pages. Funeral sermon for Ralph Samuel Forde. Fairly white, folded paper.

"Wedding Sermon"

2 pages with no apparent textual basis. Marriage of "Barbara" and "Daniel." Handwritten on brittle paper.

"Jesus Died for You"

Published in *A More Radical Gospel*, 220-222. Not in Marianna Forde's collection.

Non-Text-Specific Sermons and Addresses (alphabetically by title)

"The Freedom to Reform"

7 pages, based on Luther's "Freedom of a Christian." A 7-page draft typed, a 12 page version on lighter, smaller-sized paper. Perhaps an evening lecture.

"It Happened!"

2 pages with no apparent basis. Typed on yellowing onion-skin paper, folded.

"A Place That Knows Me"

5 pages, based on Psalm 103:15-16, Matt 8:18-20, and John 14:1-3. New computer printed neatly on fairly unyellowed paper.

"Some Images of Manhood in Today's World"

3 pages. Densely handwritten on quite yellowed paper, folded.

"Starbuck High Forever?"

4 pages, based on 1 Kings 8:22-26, 1 Peter 2:4-9, and Matt 28:16-20. Starbuck All School Reunion worship service, 6/30/1991. Flawlessly computer printed on fairly unyellowed paper.

APPENDIX C

An Overview of Gerhard Forde's Life

1927 Sept. 10   Born in Starbuck, Minnesota
                 Father: Gerhard Forde, Sr. (1884-1964)
                 Mother: Hanna Halvorson Forde (1877-1928)
                 Stepmother: Astrid Oliva Flack Forde (1908-2009)
                 Grandfather: Rev. Nils Førde (1849-1917)
                 Grandmother: Nora Otilia Erickson
1927   "Same year" Baptized at Indherred Lutheran Church near Starbuck
1928   "Six months old" Mother killed in a car-train accident; cared for
                 by an aunt
1933-1941   Grammar school at District No. 3
                 Parochial school on Wednesdays through 1941?
                 VBS summers through 1945?
1939   His father remarried Astrid Flack
1939-1941   Confirmation instruction at Indherred Lutheran Church
1943 Winter   Skiing accident at 16 that would cause later difficulty
1945 May   Graduation from Starbuck High School, Starbuck, Minnesota
1945 Fall   Began studies, Luther College, Decorah, Iowa
1946? Jan?   Enlisted in the U. S. Army
                     Served the Army Medical Corps
                 Stationed at various hospitals and camps in the United States
1947 July   Discharged from military service
1947 Fall   Continued studies, Luther College, Decorah, Iowa
1950 June   Graduation from Luther College with B.A.
                 Major: chemistry. Minors: mathematics and German
1950-1951   Attended University of Wisconsin, Madison, Wisconsin
                 Field: organic chemistry
                 Research: synthesis of cholesterol
1951?   Began studies, Luther Theological Seminary, St. Paul, Minnesota
1955   Graduation from Luther Theological Seminary with a BTh

1955-1956	Teaching at St. Olaf College, Northfield, MN: instructor in religion
	Courses: Introduction to the Bible and Survey Course
1956-1958	Harvard Divinity School
1958-1959	Tübingen University, Germany: research
1959 Mar.	In midst of a two month semester break at Tübingen
	Broke ankle in a week's skiing trip
	Toured Italy: Verona, Pisa, Florence, Rome, Sorrento, Pompei, Palstrum, Assissi, Ravenna, and Venice. Saw ruins, art galleries, etc.
	LWF tour of the church of the Rhineland
1959 July 31	Semester ends at Tübingen, Germany
Aug. 31	Sails from Oslo for the States
Sept. 10 or 12	Arrival in Minnesota
1959-1961	Teaching, Luther Theological Seminary: History of Christian Thought—a one-year assignment, renewed
	Shuttling between Luther and Harvard for work on his thesis
1961-1963	Teaching, Luther College, Decorah, Iowa: assistant professor of religion
1963-1964	Harvard Divinity School leave, finishing his dessertation
1964	Marriage to Marianna Carlson—she, a NJ-born, Yale PhD, French teacher at Wellesley College
1964-1966	Returned to Luther Seminary as instructor
1966-1968	Named Assistant Professor at Luther Seminary
1967	Graduation, ThD from Harvard Divinity School
1968	Ordained in The American Lutheran Church
1968	Named Associate Professor of Church History, Luther Seminary
1968-1970	Oxford University, M.A., 1968
	Mansfield College, Lutheran Tutor and Chaplain to Lutherans
1969-1998	Teaching, Luther Seminary, St. Paul, Minnesota
1971	Named Associate Professor at Luther.
1972-1973	Sabbatical: Harvard Divinity School
1974?	Associate Professor of Systematic Theology
1974-2000+	Member, Lutheran-Roman Catholic Dialogue
1979-1980	Sabbatical: Strasbourg University
1982-1988	Member, Commission for the New Lutheran Church, the ELCA

1988	Sabbatical: St. John's University, Collegeville, Minnesota
	Institute for Ecumenical and Cultural Research
1998	Retirement
	Long illness
2005 Aug. 9	Death
	Buried at Indherred Lutheran Cemetery

Memberships: American Academy of Religion
dialog board
Journal of Theology
The Lutheran-Roman Catholic dialogue
Commission for the New Lutheran Church
Lutheran Quarterly board
International Congress for Luther Research

Children: Timothy
Geoffrey
Sarah (Mrs. Joe) Monn

Bibliography

A. Works by Forde

Forde, Gerhard O. "The Apocalyptic 'No!' and the Eschatological 'Yes!'" In *The Necessary "No!" and the Indispensable "Yes!": Theological Controversy, Christology and the Mission of the Church Today,* cassette 2. Videorecording. St. Paul, Minnesota: Luther Seminary, [1996].

————. "The Augsburg Confession, Article 4." *Resource Cassette Service* (Jn 1981). Minneapolis: Augsburg Publishing House.

————. "Bound to Be Free." In *Encounters with Luther,* edited by Eric Gritsch, 2:67-80. Gettysburg, PA: Lutheran Theological Seminary at Gettysburg, 1976.

————. "Bultmann: Where Did He Take Us?" *dialog* 17/1 (Wint 1978) 27-30.

————, *et al.* "A Call for Discussion of the 'Joint Declaration on the Doctrine of Justification.'" *dialog* 36/3 (Sum 1997) 224-229.

————. "Called to Freedom." In *Befreiung und Freiheit: Martin Luthers Beitrag: Eighth International Congress for Luther Research,* tape 1. Videorecording. St. Paul: Luther Northwestern Theological Seminary, 1993.

————. *The Captivation of the Will: Luther vs. Erasmus on Freedom and Bondage.* Edited by Steven D. Paulson. Grand Rapids: Eerdmans, 2005.

————. "The Catholic Impasse: Reflections on Lutheran-Catholic Dialogue Today." In *Promoting Unity: Themes in Lutheran-Catholic Dialogue,* edited by H. George Anderson and James R. Crumley, Jr., 67-77. Minneapolis: Augsburg, 1989.

————. "Caught in the Act: Reflections on the Work of Christ." *Word & World* 3/1 (Wint 1983) 22-31.

————. "The Christian Life." In *Christian Dogmatics,* edited by Carl E. Braaten and Robert W. Jenson, 2:391-469. Philadelphia: Fortress, 1984.

————. "Confessional Subscription: What Does It Mean for Lutherans Today?" *Word & World* 11/3 (Sum 1991) 316-320.

————, *et al.* "The Critical Response of German Theological Professors to the Joint Declaration on the Doctrine of Justification." *dialog* 38:1 (Wint 1999) 71-72.

————, and Gritsch, Eric. "Discussion." In *Encounters with Luther,* edited by Eric Gritsch, 2:81-83. Gettysburg, PA: Lutheran Theological Seminary at Gettysburg, 1976.

————. "The Distinction between Law and Gospel for the Preaching of the Church." *Resource Cassette Tapes* (Aug 1973). Minneapolis: Augsburg Publishing House.

————. "Does the Gospel Have a Future? Barth's Romans Revisited." *Word and World* 14/1 (Wint 1994) 67-77.

————. "The End of Theology." In *Mid-Winter Convocation: What Are We Up To? Systematic Theologians at Work,* cassette 8. Sound recording. St. Paul: Luther Seminary, 1997.

————. "The Eucharistic Prayer in the LBW: Two Perspectives: 1. The LBW Goes Too Far." *Resource Cassette Service* (O 1978). Minneapolis: Augsburg Publishing House.

———. "The Exodus from Virtue to Grace: Justification by Faith Today." *Interpretation* 34/1 (Jan 1980) 32-44.

———. "Fake Theology: Reflections on Antinomianism Past and Present." *dialog* 22/4 (Fall 1983) 246-251.

———. "Forensic Justification and Law in Lutheran Theology." In *Justification by Faith: Lutherans and Catholics in Dialogue VII*, edited by H. George Anderson, T. Austin Murphy, and Joseph A. Burgess, 278-303. Minneapolis: Augsburg, 1985.

———. "The Formula of Concord Article V: End or New Beginning?" *dialog* 15/3 (Sum 1976) 184-191.

———, and James Nestingen. *Free to Be: A Handbook to Luther's Small Catechism.* Minneapolis: Augsburg, 1975, revised 1993.

———. "Full Communion?" *dialog* 28/2 (Spr 1989) 85-86.

———. "Futurum Resurrectionis: Barth's Romans revisited." In *Christian Hope and the Human Future*, cassette 2. Videorecording. St. Paul: Luther Northwestern Theological Seminary, 1992.

———. "God's Freedom for Us. Our Freedom for God." In *God's Freedom and Ours: Soteriology, Ethics, and the Mission of the Church Today*, lectures 1 and 2. Videorecording. St. Paul: Luther Northwestern Theological Seminary, 1994.

———. "Göttingen Dogmatics: Instruction in the Christian Religion. *Pro Ecclesia* 2/2 (Spr 1993) 240-242.

———. "How to Preach the Law." *Resource Cassette Tapes* (S 1975). Minneapolis: Augsburg Publishing House.

———. "Infallibility Language and the Early Lutheran Tradition." In *Teaching Authority and Infallibility in the Church: Lutherans and Catholics in Dialogue VI*, edited by Paul C. Empie, T. Austin Murphy, and Joseph A. Burgess, 120-137. Minneapolis: Augsburg, 1978, 1980.

———. "Is Forgiveness Enough? Reflections on an Odd Question." *Word and World* 16:3 (Sum 1996) 302-308.

———. "Is Invocation of Saints an Adiaphoron?" In *The One Mediator, The Saints, and Mary: Lutherans and Catholics in Dialogue VIII*, edited by H. George Anderson, J. Francis Stafford, and Joseph A. Burgess. Minneapolis: Augsburg, 1992.

———. "Justification." In *A New Handbook of Christian Theology*, edited by Donald W. Musser and Joseph L. Price, 271-273. Nashville, TN: Abingdon, 1992.

———. *Justification by Faith: A Matter of Death and Life.* Philadelphia: Fortress Press, 1982.

———. "Justification by Faith Alone." In *Search of Christian Unity: Basic Consensus/Basic Differences*, edited by Joseph A. Burgess, 64-76. Minneapolis: Fortress Press, 1991.

———. "Justification by Faith Alone: The Article by Which the Church Stands or Falls?" *dialog* 27/4 (Fall 1988) 260-267.

———. "Karl Barth on the Consequences of Lutheran Christology." In *The Consequences of Christology*, part 5. Videorecording. St. Paul: Luther Northwestern Theological Seminary, 1990.

———. "Law and Gospel as the Methodological Principle of Theology." In *Theological Perspectives: A Discussion of Contemporary Issues in Lutheran Theology*, 50-69. Decorah, Iowa: Luther College Press, 1964.

————. "Law and Gospel in Luther's Hermeneutic." *Interpretation* 37/3 (Jul 1983) 240-252.

————. "Law and Sexual Behavior." *Lutheran Quarterly* 9/1 (Spr 1995) 3-22.

————. *The Law-Gospel Debate: An Interpretation of its Historical Development.* Minneapolis: Augsburg, 1969.

————. "*lex semper accusat?* Nineteenth Century Roots of Our Current Dilemma." *dialog* 9/4 (Aut 1970) 265-274.

————. "The Lord's Supper as the Testament of Jesus," *Word & World* 17/1 (Wint 1997) 5-9.

————. "Luther and the Jews," *Resource Cassete Service* (Jul 1978). Minneapolis: Augsburg Publishing House.

————. "Luther and the *Usus Pauli*." *dialog* 32/4 (Fall 1993) 275-282.

————. "Luther Seminary Chapel Talks." *Luther Seminary Cassette Service* (Feb 1972).

————. "Lutheran Ecumenism: With Whom and How Much?" *Lutheran Quarterly* 17/4 (Wint 2003) 436-455.

————. "A Lutheran Response [to the Contemplative View]." In *Christian Spirituality: Five Views of Sanctification*, edited by Donald L. Alexander, 190-192. Downers Grove, IL: Intervarsity, 1988.

————. "The Lutheran Response [to the Pentecostal View]." In *Christian Spirituality: Five Views of Sanctification*, edited by Donald L. Alexander, 155-157. Downers Grove, IL: Intervarsity, 1988.

————. "The Lutheran Response [to the Reformed View]. In *Christian Spirituality: Five Views of Sanctification*, edited by Donald L. Alexander, 77-82. Downers Grove, IL: Intervarsity, 1988.

————. "A Lutheran Response [to the Wesleyan View]." In *Christian Spirituality: Five Views of Sanctification*, edited by Donald L. Alexander, 119-122. Downers Grove, IL: Intervarsity, 1988.

————. "The Lutheran View." In *Christian Spirituality: Five Views of Sanctification*, edited by Donald L. Alexander, 13-32. Downers Grove, IL: Intervarsity, 1988.

————. "Lutheranism." In *The Blackwell Encyclopedia of Modern Christian Thought*, edited by Alister McGrath, 354-358. Cambridge, MA: Blackwell, 1993.

————. "Martens on the Condemnations." *Lutheran Quarterly* 10/1 (Spr 1996) 67-69.

————. "The Meaning of *Satis Est*." *Lutheran Forum* 26/4 (Nov 1992) 14-18.

————. *A More Radical Gospel: Essays on Eschatology, Authority, Atonement and Ecumenism.* Edited by Mark C. Mattes and Steven D. Paulson. Grand Rapids: Eerdmans, 2004.

————. "A Movement without a Move?" *dialog* 30/2 (Spr 1991) 83.

————. "Naming the One Who is Above Us." In *Speaking the Christian God: The Holy Trinity and the Challenge of Feminism*, edited by Alvin F. Kimel, Jr., 110-119. Grand Rapids: Eerdmans, 1992.

————. "The Newness of the Gospel." *dialog* 6/2 (Spr 1967) 87-94.

————. "The Newness of the New Testament." In *All Things New: Essays in Honor of Roy A. Harrisville*, edited by Arland J. Hultgren, Donald H. Juel, and Jack D. Kingsbury, 175-180. St. Paul, MN: Luther Theological Seminary *Word & World* supplement, 1992.

———. "The Normative Character of Scripture for Matters of Faith and Life: Human Sexuality in Light of Romans 1:16-32." *Word & World* 14/3 (Sum 1994) 305-314.

———. "The 'Old Synod:' A Search for Objectivity." In *Striving for Ministry: Centennial Essays Interpreting the Heritage of Luther Theological Seminary*, edited by Warren A. Quanbeck, Eugene L., Fevold, Gerhard E. Frost, and Paul G. Sonnack, 67-80. Minneapolis: Augsburg, 1977.

———. "On Being a Theologian of the Cross." *Christian Century* 114/29 (Oct. 22, 1997) 947-949.

———. *On Being a Theologian of the Cross: Reflections on Luther's Heidelberg Disputation, 1518*. Grand Rapids: Eerdmans, 1997.

———. "Once More Into the Breach? Some Questions about Key 73." *dialog* 12/1 (Win 1973) 7-14.

———. "The One Acted Upon [Theological Autobiography]." *dialog* 36/1 (Wint 1997) 54-61.

———. "The Ordained Ministry." In *Called & Ordained: Lutheran Perspectives on the Office of the Ministry*, edited by Todd Nichol and Marc Kolden, 117-136. Minneapolis: Fortress Press, 1990.

———. "Outside the Gate: Atonement as Actual Event." *dialog* 18/4 (Aut 1979) 247-254.

———. "The Place of Theology in the Church." *dialog* 22/2 (Spr 1983) 121-130.

———. "The Power of Negative Thinking: On the Principle of Negation in Luther and Hegelianism." *dialog* 23/4 (Aut 1984) 250-256.

———. *The Preached God: Proclamation in Word and Sacrament*. Edited by Mark C. Mattes and Steven D. Paulson. Grand Rapids: Eerdmans, 2007.

———. "Preaching the Sacraments." *Lutheran Theological Seminary Bulletin* 64/4 (Fall 1984) 3-27.

———. "The Problem of Law and Gospel Today." *Luther Seminary Cassette Service* (S 1971).

———. "Proclamation: The Present Tense of the Gospel." *dialog* 29/3 (Sum 1990) 167-173.

———. "Public Ministry and Its Limits." *dialog* 30/2 (Spr 1991) 102-110.

———. "Radical Lutheranism: Lutheran Identity in America." *Lutheran Quarterly* 1/1 (Spr 1987) 5-18.

———. "Response to James Nestingen's Article." *dialog* 31/1 (Wint 1992) 34-35.

———. Review of *Christianity and Humanism: Studies in the History of Ideas* by Quirinus Breen. *Lutheran World* 16/2 (1969) 193-194.

———. Review of *Creation and Law* by Gustav Wingren. *dialog* 1/4 (Aug 1962) 78-79.

———. Review of *Critical Issues in Modern Religion* by Rover A. Johnson and Ernest Wallwork *et al. dialog* 13/3 (Sum 1974) 232-233.

———. Review of *Dogmatics* by Herman Diem. *dialog* 1/2 (Spr 1962) 69-70.

———. Review of *Eberhard Jüngel: An Introduction to His Theology* by J. B. Webster. *Lutheran Quarterly* 2/4 (Wint 1988) 531-533.

———. Review of *Faith and the Vitalities of History* by Philip Hefner. *Interpretation* 21/4 (O 1967) 486-489.

———. Review of *Formation of Historical Theology* by Peter C. Hodgson. *Una Sancta* 24/3 (Trinity 1967) 69-72.

———. Review of *God as Mystery of the World* by Eberhard Juengel. *Word & World* 4 (Fall 1984) 458-461.

———. Review of *Gospel and Church* by Gustaf Wingren and *Theology and Preaching* by Heinrich Ott. *dialog* 5/2 (Spr 1966) 150-153.

———. Review of *Luther and Staupitz: An Essay in the Intellectual Origins of the Protestant Reformation* by David C. Steinmetz. *Interpretation* 36/2 (Ap 1982) 196-199.

———. Review of *Luther in Mid-Career, 1521-1530* by Heinrich Bornkamm. *Interpretation* 39/4 (O 1985) 436.

———. Review of *The Place of Bonhoeffer* by Peter Berger *et al. dialog* 2/4 (aut 1963).

———. Review of *The Reality of the Devil: Evil in Man* by Ruth Nanda Anshen. *dialog* 12/2 (Spr 1973) 156-158.

———. Review of *Revolt against Heaven: An Enquiry into Anti-Supernaturalism* by Kenneth Hamilton. *dialog* 5/4 (aut 1966).

———. Review of *The Structure of Lutheranism* by Werner Elert. *dialog* 3/1 (Wint 1964) 77-78.

———. Review of *Theology and Proclamation: Dialogue with Bultmann* by Gerhard Ebeling. *dialog* 6/4 (Aut 1967) 299-302.

———. Review of *Word and the Spirit* by Regin Prenter. *dialog* 4/4 (Aut 1965) 304-306.

———. "The Revolt and the Wedding: An Essay on Social Ethics in the Perspective of Luther's Theology." In *The Reformation and the Revolution: A Series of Lectures Celebrating the Protestant Reformation and Commemorating the Bolshevik Revolution*, 79-88. Sioux Falls, SD: The Augustana College Press, 1970.

———. "Robert Jenson's Soteriology." In *Trinity, Time, and Church: A Response to the Theology of Robert W. Jenson*, edited by Colin Gunton, 126-138. Grand Rapids: Eerdmans, 2000.

———. "Romans 8:18-27." *Interpretation* 38/3 (Jul 1984) 281-285.

———. "Sense and Nonsense about Luther [reply to H. Bauman]." *dialog* 10/1 (Win 1971) 65-67.

———. "A Short Word [language use in the church]." *dialog* 20/2 (Spr 1981) 88-92.

———. "Some Remarks on [Ted] Peters' Review of *Christian Dogmatics*." *dialog* 24/4 (Fall 1985) 297-299.

———. "Something to Believe: A Theological Perspective on Infant Baptism." *Interpretation* 47/2 (Apr 1993) 229-241.

———, and William Lazareth. "The Special Ministry." In *Papers Read at the Call to Faithfulness Conference,* part 2. Audiocassette. Northfield, MN: St. Olaf College, 1990.

———. "Theology as *Modus Operandi*." *dialog* 21/3 (Sum 1982) 175-179.

———. *Theology Is for Proclamation*. Minneapolis: Fortress Press, 1990.

———. "Unity without Concord?" *dialog* 20/2 (Spr 1981) 166-173.

———. "The Viability of Luther Today: A North American Perspective." *Word & World* 7/1 (Wint 1987) 22-31.

————. "What Finally to Do about the (Counter-) Reformation Condemnations." *Lutheran Quarterly* 11/1 (Spr 1997) 3-16.

————. "What Next?" *dialog* 37/3 (Sum 1998) 163.

————. "What's in a Name? Eucharist or Lord's Supper," *Word & World* 9/1 (Wint 1989) 52-55.

————. *Where God Meets Man: Luther's Down-to-Earth Approach to the Gospel.* Minneapolis: Augsburg, 1972.

————. "The Word on Quotas." *Lutheran Quarterly* 6/2 (Sum 1992) 119-126.

————. "The Word That Kills and Makes Alive." In *Marks of the Body of Christ*, edited by Carl E. Braaten and Robert W. Jenson, 1-12. Grand Rapids: Eerdmans, 1999.

————. "The Work of Christ." In *Christian Dogmatics*, edited by Carl E. Braaten and Robert W. Jenson, 2:1-99. Philadelphia: Fortress Press, 1984.

B. Works associated with Forde's Theology and Life

Barth, Karl. *Church Dogmatics*, edited by G. W. Bromiley and T. F. Torrance, translated by G. T. Thompson and H. Knight. New York: Scribners, 1956.

Bonhoeffer, Dietrich. *Christ the Center*, translated by Edwin H. Robertson. San Francisco: Harper & Row, 1987.

Book of Concord: The Confessions of the Evangelical Lutheran Church, edited by Robert Kolb and Timothy J. Wengert, translated by Charles Arand *et al.* Minneapolis: Fortress Press, 2000.

Burgess, Joseph A., and Marc Kolden. "Introduction: Gerhard O. Forde and the Doctrine of Justification. In *By Faith Alone: Essays on Justification in Honor of Gerhard O. Forde*, edited by Joseph A. Burgess and Marc Kolden. Grand Rapids, MI: Eerdmans, 2004.

Ebeling, Gerhard. *Word and Faith*, translated by James W. Leitch. Philadelphia: Fortress Press, 1963.

Empie, Paul C. *Lutherans and Catholics in Dialogue: Personal Notes for a Study.* Philadelphia: Fortress Press, 1981.

————_ and William W. Baum. "Foreword." In *The Status of the Nicene Creed as Dogma of the Church*. Washington, D.C.: National Catholic Welfare Conference, 1965.

Fevold, Eugene Lysne. "The History of Norwegian-American Lutheranism, 1870-90." Ph.D. diss., University of Chicago, 1951.

Forde, Gerhard O. Papers. Evangelical Lutheran Chruch in America Region 3 Archives, St. Paul, MN.

Haikola, Lauri. "A Comparison of Melanchthon's and Luther's Doctrine of Justification." *dialog* 2/1 (1963) 32-39.

————. *Gesetz und Evangelium bei M. Flacius.* Lund: C. W. K. Gleerup, 1952.

————. *Studien zu Luther und zum Luthertum.* Uppsala: A. B. Lundquistika Bokhandeln, 1958.

————. *Usus Legis.* Uppsala: A.-B. Lundquistika Bokhandeln, 1958.

Harrisville, Roy A. "Luther Theological Seminary, 1876-1976." In *Thanksgiving and Hope: A Collection of Essays Chronicling 125 Years of the People, Events and*

Movements in the Antecedent Schools That Have Formed Luther Seminary. Northfield, MN: Northfield Printing, Inc., 1998.

Iwand, Hans Joachim. *Nachgelassene Werke*, edited by J. Haar. Munich: Chr. Kaiser, 1974.

———. *Um den Rechten Glauben.* München: Chr. Kaiser Verlag, 1959.

———. "Wider den Missbrauch des pro me als methodisches Princip in der Theologie." *Theologische Literaturzeitung*, 7/8 (1954) 454-458.

Johnson, Kent. "An Era of Transitions, 1976-1996." In *Thanksgiving and Hope: A Collection of Essays Chronicling 125 Years of the People, Events and Movements in the Antecedent Schools That Have Formed Luther Seminary.* Northfield, MN: Northfield Printing, Inc., 1998.

Luther, Martin. *D. Martin Luthers Werke.* Kritische Gesamtausgabe. Weimar: Herman Böhlaus Nachfolger, 1883-.

Menacher, Mark David. "A Gracious God Today? The Metaphor of Language in Gerhard Ebeling's Theological Method." Ph.D. diss., University of Manchester, 1998.

Moltmann, Jurgen. *The Crucified God.* New York: Harper & Row, 1974.

Nelson, E. Clifford. "The Union Movement among Norwegian-American Lutherans from 1880 to 1917." Ph.D. diss., Yale University, 1952.

———, and Fevold, Eugene. *The Lutheran Church Among Norwegian Americans.* Minneapolis: Augsburg Publishing House, 1960.

Nestingen, James Arne. "Examining Sources: Influences on Gerhard Forde's Theology." In *By Faith Alone: Essays on Justification in Honor of Gerhard O Forde*, edited by Joseph A Burgess and Marc Kolden. Grand Rapids, MI: Eerdmans, 2004.

Olsen, Arthur L. "After Ten Years: *Dialog*'s Self-Dialogue about Its Future." *dialog* 11/1 (Wint 1972).

Pontoppidan, Erik. *Sandhed til Gudfrygtighed.* Norway, IL: O. Andrewson, 1886.

Quanbeck, Warren A. *Search for Understanding: Lutheran Conversations with Reformed, Anglican, and Roman Catholic Churches.* Minneapolis: Augsburg Publishing House, 1972.

Ritschl, Albrecht. *Jahrbücher für deutsche Theologie*, vol. II. no. 4. Stuttgart: R. Besser, 1857.

Schueler, Timothy J. "Hans Joachim Iwand's Interpretation of the Lutheran Understanding of the Law and its Relevance for Preaching." MTh thesis, Luther Seminary, 1989.

Seeberg, Reinhold. *Die Kirche Deutschlands im 19. Jahrhundert*, 2nd edition. Leipzig: A. Deichert, 1904.

C. Works associated with Missiology

Ad Gentes. http://www.vatican.va/archive/hist_councils/ii_vatican_council/documents/vat-ii_decree_19651207_ad-gentes_en.html (accessed March 12, 2009).

Aquinas, Thomas. *Summa Theologiae*, translated by T. C. O'Brien. New York: Blackfriars, 1976.

Bamberger, Bernard J. "Proselytes." In *The Universal Jewish Encyclopedia*, edited by Simon Cohen and Isaac Landman, 9:1-3. New York: Universal Jewish Encyclopedia Co., Inc, 1943.

Barrett, David B. *Evangelize! A Historical Survey of the Concept*. Birmingham, AL: New Hope, 1987.

Barth, Karl. "Die Theologie und die Mission in der Gegenwart." In Karl Barth, *Theologische Fragen und Antworten*. Zollikon-Qürich: Evangelischer Verlag, 1932, 1957.

Bedell, Clifford. "Mission in Intertestamental Judaism," in *Mission in the New Testament: An Evangelical Approach*, edited by William J. Larkin, Jr., and Joel F. Williams, 21-29. Maryknoll, NY: Orbis, 2003.

Bevans, Stephen B., and Schroeder, Roger P. *Constants in Context: A Theology of Mission for Today*. Maryknoll, NY: Orbis, 2004.

Bosch, David J. *Transforming Mission: Paradigm Shifts in Theology of Mission*. Maryknoll, NY: Orbis, 1991.

Braaten, Carl. *The Flaming Center*. Philadelphia: Fortress, 1977.

Dulles, Avery. *Models of the Church*. Garden City, NY: Doubleday, 1974.

Elert, Werner. *The Structure of Lutheranism*, translated by Walter A. Hansen. St. Louis: Concordia, 1962.

Evangelii Nuntiandi. http://www.vatican.va/holy_father/paul_vi/apost_exhortations/documents/hf_p-vi_exh_19751208_evangelii-nuntiandi_en.html (accessed March 13, 2009).

Gaudium et Spes. http://www.vatican.va/archive/hist_councils/ii_vatican_council/documents/vat-ii_cons_19651207_gaudium-et-spes_en.html (accessed March 13, 2009).

Glazik, Josef. "Missiology." In *Concise Dictionary of the Christian World Mission*, edited by Stephen Neill, Gerald Anderson and John Goodwin, 387-389. New York: Abingdon, 1971.

"Global Mission in the Twenty-First Century: A Vision of Evangelical Faithfulness in God's Mission," http://archive.elca.org/globalmission/policy/gm21full.pdf (accessed July 10, 2008).

"Go Forth in Peace: Orthodox Perspectives on Mission." In *New Directions in Mission and Evangeliztion 1: Basic Statements 1974-1991*, edited by James A Scherer and Stephen B. Bevans. Maryknoll, NY: Orbis Books, 1992.

Harvey, John D. "Mission in Jesus' Teaching." In *Mission in the New Testament: An Evangelical Approach*, edited by William J. Larkin, Jr., and Joel F. Williams, 30-49. Maryknoll, NY: Orbis, 2003.

Heim, S. Mark. *The Depth of the Riches: A Trinitarian Theology of Religious Ends*. Grand Rapids, MI: Eerdmans, 2001.

Hengel, Martin. *Between Jesus and Paul: Studies in the Earliest History of Christianity*, translated by John Bowden. Philadelphia: Fortress, 1983.

Hoekendijk, Johannes C. *Kirche und Volk in der deutscher Missionswissenschaft*. Munich: Kaiser, 1967.

Holl, Paul. *Gesammelte Aufsätze zur Kirchengeschichte*. Tübingen: Verlag von J. C. B. Mohr (Paul Siebeck), 1932.

Howell, Don N. "Mission in Paul's Epistles: Genesis, Pattern, and Dynamics." In *Mission in the New Testament: An Evangelical Approach,* edited by William J. Larkin, Jr., and Joel F. Williams. Maryknoll, 63-91. NY: Orbis Books, 1998, 2003.

Jeremias, Joachim. *Jesus' Promise to the Nations,* translated by S. H. Hooke. Naperville, IL: Alec R. Allenson, Inc., 1958.

Johnson, Elizabeth. *She Who Is: The Mystery of God in Feminist Discourse.* New York: Crossroad, 1992.

Kraemer, Hendrik. *The Christian Message in a Non-Christian World.* Grand Rapids, MI: Kregel Publications, 1938, 1956.

Küng, Hans. "Paradigm Change in Theology." In Hans Küng and David Tracy, *Paradigm Change in Theology,* 3-33. New York: Crossroad, 1989.

Löhe, Wilhelm. *Three Books about the Church,* translated and edited by James L. Schaaf. Philadelphia: Fortress, 1969.

Lumen Gentium. http://www.vatican.va/archive/hist_councils/ii_vatican_council/documents/vat-ii_const_19641121_lumen-gentium_en.html (accessed March 15, 2009).

Luther, Martin. *D. Martin Luthers Werke.* Kritische Gesamtausgabe. Weimar: Herman Böhlaus Nachfolger, 1883-.

———. *Sermons of Martin Luther,* edited and translated by John Nicholas Lenker. Grand Rapids, MI: Baker Books, 1907, 1983, 1995.

———. *Small Catechism.* In *The Book of Concord,* edited by Robert Kolb and Timothy J. Wengert, 345-376. Minneapolis: Fortress Press, 2000.

McDaniel, Farris L. "Mission in the Old Testament." In *Mission in the New Testament: An Evangelical Approach,* edited by William J. Larkin, Jr., and Joel F. Williams, 11-20. Maryknoll, NY: Orbis, 2003.

McKnight, Scot. *A Light among the Gentiles: Jewish Missionary Activity in the Second Temple Period.* Minneapolis: Fortress Press, 1991.

Moreau, A. Scott. "Mission and Missions." In *Evangelical Dictionary of World Mission,* edited by A. Scott Moreau, 636-638. Grand Rapids, MI: Baker, 2000.

Neill, Stephen. *Creative Tension.* London: Edinburg House Press, 1959.

Nemer, Lawrence. "Mission and Missions." In *New Catholic Encyclopedia,* 2nd ed., 683-639. New York: Thompson Gale, 2003.

Nostra Aetate. http://www.vatican.va/archive/hist_councils/ii_vatican_council/documents/vat-ii_decl_19651028_nostra-aetate_en.html (accessed March 15, 2009).

Nygard, Mark. "Preaching in Rey Bouba: An Analysis of its Call to Faith in Light of Luther's Church Postil." MTh thesis, Luther Seminary, St. Paul, 1988.

Öberg, Ingemar. *Luther and World Mission: A Historical and Systematic Study with Special Reference to Luther's Bible Exposition,* translated by Deal Apel. St. Louis: Concordia Publishing House, 2007.

Plitt, Gustav Leopold. *Kurze Geschichte der lutherischen Mission in Vorträgen.* Erlangen: A. Deichert, 1871.

Redemptoris Missio. http://www.vatican.va/holy_father/john_paul_ii/encyclicals/documents/hf_jp-ii_enc_07121990_redemptoris-missio_en.html (accessed March 13, 2009).

Schreiter, Robert, J. *The Ministry of Reconciliation: Spirituality and Strategies.* Maryknoll, NY: Orbis, 1998.

———. "Mission for the Twenty-First Century: A Catholic Perspective." In *Mission for the Twenty-First Century,* edited by Steven Bevans and Roger Schroeder, 30-40. Chicago: CCGM Publications, 2001.

Stott, John. *Christian Mission in the Modern World.* Downers Grove, IL: InverVarsity Press, 1979.

Teasdale, Wayne. *A Monk in the World: Cultivating a Spiritual Life.* Novato, CA: New World Library, 2002.

Vandervelde, George. "Introduction." *Evangelical Review of Theology* 23/1 (January 1999) 6-10.

Walls, Andrew. *The Missionary Movement in Christian History: Studies in the Transmission of Faith.* Maryknoll, NY: Orbis, 2005.

Warneck, Gustav. *Outline of a History of Protestant Missions from the Reformation to the Present Time,* edited by George Robson. New York: Fleming H. Revell Company, 1901.

Warren, M. A. C. "General Introduction." In A. K. Cragg, *Sandals at the Mosque: Christian Presence amid Islam,* 5-11. London: Oxford, 1959.

Wetter, Paul. *Der Missionsgedanke bei Martin Luther.* Bonn: Verlag für Klutur und Wissenschaft, 1999.

"Witnessing in a Divided World." In *New Directions in Mission and Evangelization 1: Basic Statements 1974-1991,* edited by James A Scherer and Stephen B. Bevans. Maryknoll, NY: Orbis, 1992.

Wolanin, Adam. "Trinitarian Foundation of Mission." In *Following Christ in Mission: A Foundational Course in Missiology,* edited by Sebastian Karotremprel *et al.* Boston: Pauline Books and Media, 1996.

Yates, Timothy. *Christian Mission in the Twentieth Century.* Cambridge: Cambridge University Press, 1994.

D. Other Works Cited

Anderson, Anderson. *Theological Anthropology and Christian Ethics: The Imago Dei as Relational Ontology in the Political Thought of Brunner and Hall.* Ph.D. diss., Luther Seminary, 1997.

The New Oxford Annotated Bible: New Revised Standard Version. New York: Oxford University Press, 1991.

Cooperrider, D. L., and S. Svivastva. "Appreciative Inquiry in Organizational Life." In *Research in Organizational Change and Development,* edited by R. Woodman and W. Pasmore. Greenwich, CT: JAI Press, 1987.

Greenburg, Robert. *How to Listen to and Understand Great Music.* Chantilly, VA: The Teaching Company Limited Partnership.

The Random House Dictionary of the English Language, second edition. New York: Random House, 1987.

Acknowledgments

I did not set out in life to write a doctoral thesis; it rather came upon me through forces and influences more or less beyond my control. I am grateful to the Lord for putting these influences in my way, and to faithful people in His Church for their witness, encouragement, and help. In particular, I need to express appreciation:

• For my father, Lloyd, and my mother, Martha, whose authentic lives nurtured me in the faith delivered to the saints.

• For many seminary professors over the years and, in particular, Gerhard Forde, whose insistent clarity about the gospel has echoed through my ministry.

• For friends, colleagues, and parishioners in North Dakota, Cameroon, and Senegal, whose shared life with me set the arena for my own proclamation.

• To Luther Seminary's graduate studies dean, Paul Lokken, who turned a stray exploratory visit into a compelling welcome to doctoral work.

• To a supporter of the seminary, Dagmar (Mrs. Warren) Quanbeck, recently deceased, for the full tuition scholarship that she offered my study.

• To my doctoral advisor, Gary Simpson, whose electric response to this particular project proposal gave it life, definition, and direction.

• To Marianna Forde, Gerhard's wife of 42 years, who lent me access to her husband's surviving sermon manuscripts and time for repeated interviews.

• To a pivotal influence on my own theological journey, Marc Kolden, whose painstaking reading of the manuscript offered many improvements.

• To a missional seminary president, Rick Bliese, who took time to give valuable guidance at a critical juncture and an appreciative reading of the manuscript.

• To grad studies secretary, Katie Dahl, for her several critical readings and her patience over missed deadlines.

• To my children, Pauline, Matthew, and John, and their families, who in their amazingly unique ways stood behind their dad in his eccentric quest.

• And to my dear wife, Linda, who cheerfully modified her lifestyle to permit this study, let me talk Forde with her in the middle of the night, scoured the text for errors prior to printing, and now gracefully walks with me into a new phase of ministry based on this work.

Clearly, we are blessed to be heirs of a great tradition, with diverse and vibrant voices speaking again and again of Jesus. May this work serve to lift up the gifts of one of them for that speaking, that that tradition may carry its blessing to another generation.

Endnotes

[1] Joseph A. Burgess and Marc Kolden, "Introduction: Gerhard O. Forde and the Doctrine of Justification," in *By Faith Alone: Essays on Justification in Honor of Gerhard O. Forde*, ed., Joseph A. Burgess and Marc Kolden (Grand Rapids: Eerdmans, 2004) 4.

[2] D. L. Cooperrider, and S. Svivastva, "Appreciative Inquiry in Organizational Life," in *Research in Organizational Change and Development*, ed. R. Woodman and W. Pasmore (Greenwich, CT: JAI Press, 1987) I:129-169.

[3] For example, Carlton Anderson referenced no fewer than 850 books and articles by Emil Brunner and was obliged to establish a narrower field of inquiry for his doctoral thesis, "Theological Anthropology and Christian Ethics: The Imago Dei as Relational Ontology in the Political Thought of Brunner and Hall" (Ph.D. diss., Luther Seminary, 1997). For another example, one single title from Karl Barth's career, *Church Dogmatics*, covers more than 8,500 pages, not counting his other books and articles — a daunting task for the Barth scholar.

[4] It might helpful for the reader to imagine this data bank if some of these categories were named. Examples include such diverse subjects as absolution, antinomianism, care, christology, church polity, contemporary, discontinuity, Gerhard Ebeling, election, eschatological limits, evangelism, Forde-isms, God from without, good works, Lauri Haikola, human inability, human questions, human schemes, humanness positively viewed, Jesus as law, the law's changeability, Melanchthon, movement, neighborly concern, t he poor, pride, proclamation as an act, quotes cited by Forde, reason, reckless, reconciliation, repentance, sacramental elements, *satis est*, scripture, sexuality, social concern, theology's task, universalism, virtue, and witness.

[5] Marianna Forde, a brief family tree prepared in consultation with the family and given to me and to Evangelical Lutheran Church in America Region 3 Archives, St. Paul, MN, December 5, 2008.

[6] Gerhard Forde, "The One Acted Upon [Theological Autobiography]," *dialog* 36/1 (Wint 1997) 54. Exact lengths of service come from Marianna Forde, interview by author, St. Paul, MN, November 18, 2008.

[7] Ibid.," 54.

[8] Marianna Forde, interview by author, St. Paul, MN, November 18, 2008.

[9] Registration Card, Luther Theological Seminary, Gerhard Forde papers, Evangelical Lutheran Church in America Region 3 Archives, St. Paul, MN.

[10] Marianna Forde, interview by author, St. Paul, MN, November 18, 2008.

[11] Forde, "The One Acted Upon," 55.

[12] Marianna Forde, interview by author, St. Paul, MN, November 18, 2008. Apparently he was twice injured in skiing accidents. See Gerhard Forde, "The Lutheran View," in *Christian Spirituality: Five Views of Sanctification*, ed. Donald L. Alexander (Downers Grove, IL: Intervarsity, 1988) 32; Gerhard Forde to Al Rogness, March 31, 1959, Gerhard Forde papers, Evangelical Lutheran Chruch in America Region 3 Archives, St. Paul, MN.

[13] Forde, "The One Acted Upon," 55.

[14] Gerhard Forde, "Autobiographical Sketch." Gerhard Forde papers, Evangelical Lutheran Chruch in America Region 3 Archives, St. Paul, MN.

[15] "Forde, "The One Acted Upon," 54-55.

[16] Ibid., 56.

[17] Ibid., 56-57.

[18] Ibid 57. Also, Marianna Forde, interview by author, St. Paul, MN, November 18, 2008.

[19] Ibid., 55, 57.

[20] Ibid., 58; Gerhard Forde to Al Rogness, March 31, 1959; Gerhard Forde to Al Rogness, March 25, [1964]; Marianna Forde, interviews by author, St. Paul, MN, November 18, 2008, December 19, 2008; "Class of 1955 Survey: Augsburg, Luther and Northwestern Seminary Basis for Memory Book —45th Class Reunion," Gerhard Forde papers, Evangelical Lutheran Chruch in America Region 3 Archives, St. Paul, MN.

[21] Forde, "The One Acted Upon," 61.

[22] Lloyd Svendsby to Patrick Henry, December 31, 1986.

[23] Forde, "The One Acted Upon," 60.

[24] For a sketch of first form and second form positions, see pp. 26-27 and 37.

[25] Forde, "The One Acted Upon," 59.

[26] Joseph A. Burgess and Marc Kolden, "Introduction: Gerhard O. Forde and the Doctrine of Justification," 6; Marianna Forde, interview by author, St. Paul, MN, December 4, 2008.

[27] Gerhard Forde, "Once More Into the Breach? Some Questions about Key 73," *dialog* 12/1 (Wint 1973) 14; Gerhard Forde, "Theology as *Modus Operandi*," *dialog* 21/3 (Sum 1982) 176.

[28] Lloyd Svendsbye to Patrick Henry, December 31, 1986.

[29] Forde, "The One Acted Upon," 58-60.

[30] E. Clifford Nelson, "The Union Movement among Norwegian-American Lutherans from 1880 to 1917" (Ph.D. diss., Yale University, 1952) 127.

[31] Gerhard Forde, "The 'Old Synod:' A Search for Objectivity," in *Striving for Ministry: Centennial Essays Interpreting the Heritage of Luther Theological Seminary*, ed. Warren A. Quanbeck, Eugene L. Fevold, Gerhard E. Frost, and Paul G. Sonnack (Minneapolis: Augsburg, 1977) 68.

[32] E. Clifford Nelson and Eugene Fevold, *The Lutheran Church Among Norwegian Americans* (Minneapolis: Augsburg Pulbishing House, 1960) I:189-190, as quoted in Forde, "The 'Old Synod,'" 73.

[33] Forde, "The 'Old Synod,'" 76.

[34] Eugene Lysne Fevold, "The History of Norwegian-American Lutheranism, 1870-90" (Ph.D. diss., University of Chicago, 1951) 61.

[35] Ibid., 60-61.

[36] Ibid., 61-62.

[37] Forde, "The 'Old Synod,'" 74.

[38] Fevold, "The History of Norwegian-American Lutheranism," 307-313.

[39] Erik Pontoppidan, *Sandhed til Gudfrygtighed* (Norway, IL: Trykt hos O. Andrewson, 1886) 88, as quoted by E. Clifford Nelson, "The Union Movement," 126-127.

[40] Formula of Concord, Solid Declaration, Article XI, "Election," *The Book of Concord: The Confessions of the Evangelical Lutheran Church*, ed. Robert Kolb and Timothy J. Wengert, trans. Charles Arand *et al*. (Minneapolis: Fortress Press, 2000) 654. See also Formula of Concord, Epitome, Article XI, "Concerning the Eternal Predestination and Election of God," 519.

[41] Fevold, "The History of Norwegian-American Lutheranism," 329.

[42] Ibid., 333.

[43] Ibid., 336.

[44] Ibid., 371.

[45] Ibid., 374.

[46] Forde, "The One Acted Upon," 54-55.

[47] Forde, "The 'Old Synod,'" 78.

[48] "I know what accepting Jesus as my personal savior has meant to me, and that if I could be instrumental in showing others the way, then and only then would I feel that I had fulfilled my obligations to Him." Forde, "Autobiographical Sketch."

[49] E. Clifford Nelson, *The Union Movement*, 407.

[50] Ibid., 409-425, where Nelson summarizes the direction of these meetings.

[51] Ibid., 436-437.

[52] Ibid., 512-513.

[53] Ibid., 511.

[54] Forde, "The One Acted Upon," 60.

[55] Gerhard Forde, "Does the Gospel Have a Future? Barth's Romans Revisited," *Word & World* 14/1 (Wint 1994) 67.

[56] Gerhard Forde, *The Law-Gospel Debate: An Interpretation of its Historical Development* (Minneapolis: Augsburg, 1969) 149.

[57] Ibid., 140.

[58] Ibid., 144-145.

[59] Gerhard Forde, "Karl Barth on the Consequences of Lutheran Christology," in *The Preached God: Proclamation in Word and Sacrament*, ed. Mark C. Mattes and Steven D. Paulson (Grand Rapids, MI: Eerdmans, 2007) 71-73.

[60] Ibid., 78, 80.

[61] Ibid., 80-81.

[62] Forde, "The One Acted Upon," 59. Gerhard Forde, "The Exodus from Virtue to Grace: Justification by Faith Today," *Interpretation* 34/1 (Jan 1980) 32.

[63] James Arne Nestingen, "Examining Sources: Influences on Gerhard Forde's Theology," in *By Faith Alone: Essays on Justification in Honor of Gerhard O Forde*, ed. Joseph A Burgess and Marc Kolden (Grand Rapids, MI, Eerdmans, 2004) 19. There are in fact more citations of Hans Kessler, P. T. Forsyth, and Gustav Aulèn, but these are clumped around specific discussions and are indeed not so pervasive as Iwand's.

[64] In *The Law-Gospel Debate* Forde cited only Iwand's *Um den Rechten Glauben* (München: Chr. Kaiser Verlag, 1959), but in his *Christian Dogmatics* articles, "The Work of Christ" and "Christian Life," *Christian Dogmatics*, ed. Carl E. Braaten and Robert W. Jenson (Philadelphia: Fortress Press, 1984), he also referred to Iwand's volume on *Luthers Theologie* in *Nachgelassene Werke*, ed. J. Haar (Munich: Chr. Kaiser, 1974) and to other articles, published and unpublished.

[65] Timothy J. Schueler, "Hans Joachim Iwand's Interpretation of the Lutheran Understanding of the Law and its Relevance for Preaching" (MTh thesis, Luther Seminary, 1989) 3. James Nestingen calls Schueler's thesis "the best English language introduction to Iwand" ("Examining Sources," 15).

[66] Ibid., 20-21, 45-47, 53, 76-84.

[67] Forde, "The One Acted Upon," 59. Emphases Forde's.

[68] Ibid., 59. All emphases Forde's.

[69] Gerhard Forde, "The Formula of Concord Article V: End or New Beginning?" *dialog* 15/2 (1976) 190; Forde, "The Work of Christ," 43, and "Christian Life," 423, 442.

[70] James Arne Nestingen, "Examining Sources," 17.

[71] Forde, "The One Acted Upon," 60.

[72] Lauri Haikola, *Gesetz und Evangelium bei M. Flacius* (Lund: C. W. K. Gleerup, 1952); *Studien zu Luther und zum Luthertum* (Uppsala: A. B. Lundquistika Bokhandeln, 1958); *Usus Legis* (Uppsala: A.-B. Lundquistika Bokhandeln, 1958); and "A Comparison of Melanchthon's and Luther's Doctrine of Justification," trans. Robert Schultz, *dialog* 2/1 (1963) 32-39.

[73] Gerhard Forde, "The Formula of Concord Article V," 190.

[74] Forde, *The Law-Gospel Debate*, 189-190.

[75] Forde, "The One Acted Upon," 60.

[76] Nestingen, "Examining Sources," 11.

[77] Gerhard Ebeling, *Wort und Glaube* [Tübingen: J. C. B. Mohr (Paul Siebeck), 1960], translated by James W. Leitch as *Word and Faith*, (Philadelphia: Fortress Press, 1963).

[78] Forde, *The Law-Gospel Debate*, 170-171.

[79] Ibid., 174, 177, 180, 192; "The Christian Life," 419.

[80] Ibid., 184.

[81] Ibid., 183, 192.

[82] Ibid., 199.

[83] Ibid., 206, 226.

[84] Gerhard Forde, review of *Theology and Proclamation: Dialogue with Bultmann*, by Gerhard Ebeling, trans. John Riches, *dialog* 6/4 (Aut 1967) 302.

[85] Ibid.

[86] Forde, "The One Acted Upon," 60.

[87] Nestingen, "Examining Sources," 11.

[88] Forde, *The Law-Gospel Debate*, 159-160.

[89] Ibid., 160.

[90] Ibid., 160-161.

[91] For examples, see Forde "The Exodus from Virtue to Grace," 33; and Gerhard Forde, "Something to Believe: A Theological Perspective on Infant Baptism," *Interpretation* 47/2 (Apr 1993) 234.

[92] Gerhard Forde, "Preaching the Sacraments," *Lutheran Theological Seminary Bulletin* 64/4 (Fall 1984) 21.

[93] Gerhard Forde, review of *The Place of Bonhoeffer*, by Peter Berger *et al .*, *dialog* 2/4 (aut 1963) 335.

[94] Ibid.

[95] Gerhard Forde, review of *Revolt against Heaven: An Enquiry into Anti-Supernaturalism*, by Kenneth Hamilton, *dialog* 5/4 (Aut 1966) 313.

[96] Ibid.

[97] Forde, "The Work of Christ," 95.

[98] Gerhard Forde, *Theology is for Proclamation* (Minneapolis: Fortress Press, 1990) 60, 121, quoting Dietrich Bonhoeffer, *Christ the Center*, trans. Edwin H. Robertson (San Francisco: Harper & Row, 1987) 35.

[99] Forde, *The Law-Gospel Debate*, 222-224, 231-232.

[100] Roy A. Harrisville, "Luther Theological Seminary, 1876-1976," in *Thanksgiving and Hope: A Collection of Essays Chronicling 125 Years of the People, Events and Movements in the Antecedent Schools That Have Formed Luther Seminary* (Northfield, MN: Northfield Printing, Inc., 1998) 46.

[101] Ibid., 47.

[102] Kent Johnson, "An Era of Transitions, 1976-1996," in *Thanksgiving and Hope: A Collection of Essays Chronicling 125 Years of the People, Events and Movements in the Antecedent Schools That Have Formed Luther Seminary* (Northfield, MN: Northfield Printing, Inc., 1998) 93.

[103] Roland Martinson, interview by author, St. Paul, MN, January 4, 2008.

[104] Gerhard Forde, "The Minister as Ambassador: Reflections for a Revised Curriculum at LNTS" [paper presented before the Curriculum Revision Committee, August, 1990]. Papers of James Boyce, curriculum revision committee member, April 4, 2008.

[105] Gerhard Forde, "Some Thoughts on the Current Draft of the Curriculum proposal," March 11, 1992. Papers of James Boyce, curriculum revision committee member, April 4, 2008.

[106] *dialog*, 1/1 (Wint 1962) 2.

[107] Arthur L. Olsen, "After Ten Years: *Dialog* 's Self-Dialogue about Its Future," *dialog* 11/1 (Wint 1972) 16.

[108] The Editors, [Introduction to the new journal], *dialog* 1/1 (Wint 1962), 5-6, 8.

[109] Olsen, "After Ten Years," 17.

[110] Jack Eichhorst, interview by author, Washburn, ND, November 18, 2008.

[111] Warren A. Quanbeck, *Search for Understanding: Lutheran Conversations with Reformed, Anglican, and Roman Catholic Churches* (Minneapolis: Augsburg Publishing House, 1972) 20-22.

[112] Paul C. Empie, *Lutherans and Catholics in Dialogue: Personal Notes for a Study* (Philadelphia: Fortress Press, 1981) 4.

[113] Quanbeck, *Search for Understanding*, 88-90.

[114] Empie, *Lutherans and Catholics in Dialogue*, 4-5.

[115] Paul C. Empie and William H. Baum, "Foreword," in *The Status of the Nicene Creed as Dogma of the Church*, published jointly by representatives of the U.S.A. National Copmmittee of the Lutheran World Federation and the Bishop's Commission for Ecumenical Affairs, 1965. See also http://en.wikipedia.org/wiki/Lutheran-Roman_Catholic_Dialogue (accessed December 18, 2008).

116 Gerhard Forde, "Theology as *Modus Operandi*," *dialog* 21/3 (Sum 1982) 176.

117 Gerhard Forde, "Justification by Faith Alone: The Article by Which the Church Stands or Falls?" *dialog* 27/4 (Fall 1988) 261.

118 Ibid., 265.

119 Gerhard Forde, "Lutheran Ecumenism: With Whom and How Much?" *Lutheran Quarterly* 17/4 (Wint 2003) 453. Emphasis added.

120 Marianna Forde, interview by author, St. Paul, MN, November 18 and December 19, 2008.

121 Gerhard Forde, "God's Rights" [sermon on Matt 20:1-16], in *A More Radical Gospel: Essays on Eschatology, Authority, Atonement and Ecumenism*, ed. Mark C. Mattes and Steven D. Paulson (Grand Rapids: Eerdmans, 2004) 205. Thirty-one of Forde's sermons have been published, and where this is the case they will be cited as published articles.

122 Gerhard Forde, "The Wedding Feast" [sermon on Matt 22:1-14], 1, in the collection of sermon manuscripts held by Marianna Forde with copies held by the author. Approximately one hundred twelve of Forde's sermons have not been published. When sermons are cited in this thesis without reference to published source, it can be assumed that they come from this manuscript collection. The contents of this collection are listed in Appendix B as "Register of the Sermon Manuscripts of Gerhard Forde," ed. Mark Nygard, 2008. It includes the one hundred forty complete sermon manuscripts that Marianna Forde identified among her husband's letters and papers in the third year after his death. Without apparent order and many of them undated, they were tentatively organized by the author according to scriptural text where that was possible. Thirty-one semons, including twenty-eight from Mrs. Forde's collection, have been published in recent *Lutheran Quarterly* editions of Forde's works edited by Mark Mattes and Steven Paulson.

123 Gerhard Forde, "The Work of Christ," in *Christian Dogmatics*, II:9.

124 Gerhard Forde, "The One Acted Upon," 58.

125 Gerhard Forde, "The Normative Character of Scripture for Matters of Faith and Life: Human Sexuality in Light of Romans 1:16-32," *Word & World* 14/3 (Sum 1994) 310.

126 Gerhard Forde, " *Scriptura Sacra sui ipsius interpres*: Reflections on the Question of Scripture and Tradition," in *A More Radical Gospel: Essays on Eschatology, Authority, Atonement and Ecumenism*, ed. Mark C. Mattes and Steven D. Paulson (Grand Rapids: Eerdmans, 2004) 73.

127 Ibid.

128 For parallel concerns on the role of theology, see Gerhard Forde, "Karl Barth on the Consequences of Lutheran Christology,"in *The Preached God*, 77: "How can dogmatic Christology secure the field against the twin problems of abstraction and subjectivism? It cannot — at least not in and of itself. Because dogmatics *is* abstraction and *abstraction is always the subject's activity* — or even its way of salvation if one is not careful!" Second emphasis added. See also articles by Gerhard Forde, "Naming the One Who is Above Us," in *Speaking the Christian God: The Holy Trinity and the Challenge of Feminism*, ed. Alvin F. Kimel, Jr. (Grand Rapids: Eerdmans, 1992) 112; and "Response to James Nestingen's Article," *dialog* 31/ 1 (Wint 1992) 34.

129 Forde, " *Scriptura Sacra sui ipsius interpres*, " 74.

130 Gerhard Forde, "Luther and the *Usus Pauli*," *dialog* 32/4 (Fall 1993) 276.

131 Gerhard Forde, "Proclamation: The Present Tense of the Gospel," *dialog* 29/3 (Sum 1990) 169.

132 Forde, "The Normative Character of Scripture for Matters of Faith and Life," 309.

133 Ibid.

134 Gerhard Forde, "A Word from Without" [sermon on Jer 23:23-32], in *The Captivation of the Will: Luther vs. Erasmus on Freedom and Bondage*, ed. Steven D. Paulson (Grand Rapids: Eerdmans, 2005) 92; and Gerhard Forde, "A Lutheran Response [to the Contemplative View]," in *Christian Spirituality: Five Views of Sanctification*, ed. Donald L. Alexander (Downers Grove, IL: Intervarsity, 1988) 192.

135 For use of the word, see Gerhard Forde, "Infallibility Language and the Early Lutheran Tradition," in *Teaching Authority and Infallibility in the Church: Lutherans and Catholics in Dialogue VI*, ed. Paul C. Empie, T. Austin Murphy, and Joseph A. Burgess (Minneapolis: Augsburg, 1978, 1980) 133; and "The Normative Character of Scripture for Matters of Faith and Life," 309-310.

136 Gerhard Forde, "Law and Gospel as the Methodological Principle of Theology," in *Theological Perspectives: A Discussion of Contemporary Issues in Lutheran Theology* (Decorah, IA: Luther College Press, 1964) 59. Actually, the idea of an infallible scripture has proven to be a quite compelling argument for many preliterate people, as evidenced by the widespread appeal of both the Bible and the Qur'an as divinely-given and inerrant books to their respective faithful. See my research in "Preaching in Rey Bouba: An Analysis of It's Call to Faith in Light of Luther's Church Postil" (MTh thesis, Luther Seminary, 1988) 37.

137 Forde, "The One Acted Upon," 57. The offensiveness surely signals the post-Enlightenment, critical worldview of which Forde was a part.

138 Gerhard Forde, "The Catholic Impasse: Reflections on Lutheran-Catholic Dialogue Today," in *Promoting Unity: Themes in Lutheran-Catholic Dialogue*, ed. H. George Anderson and James R. Crumley, Jr. (Minneapolis: Augsburg, 1989) 72.

139 Forde, sermon on Luke 9:24, 1.

140 Gerhard Forde, "Radical Lutheranism: Lutheran Identity in America," *Lutheran Quarterly* 1/1 (Spr 1987) 13.

141 Forde, "The One Acted Upon," 59.

142 Forde, "Proclamation: The Present Tense of the Gospel," 171.

143 Forde, "Infallibility Language and the Early Lutheran Tradition," 129.

144 Forde, " *Scriptura Sacra sui ipsius interpres*," 69.

145 Forde, "Law and Gospel as the Methodological Principle of Theology," 61.

[146] Ibid., 62

[147] Gerhard Forde, "A Short Word [language use in the church]," *dialog* 20/2 (Spr 1981) 90.

[148] Forde, "Law and Gospel as the Methodological Principle of Theology," 60-61. Emphases Forde's.

[149] Forde, " *Scriptura Sacra sui ipsius interpres*," 72, citing Walter Mostert, " *Scriptura Sacra sui ipsius interpres*," in *Lutherjahrbuch* 46, ed. Helmar Junghans (Göttingen: Vandenhoeck & Ruprecht, 1979), 70.

[150] Gerhard Forde, "Forensic Justification and Law in Lutheran Theology" in *Justification by Faith: Lutherans and Catholics in Dialogue VII*, ed. H. George Anderson, T. Austin Murphy, and Joseph A. Burgess (Minneapolis: Augsburg, 1985) 294. This distinction between the content and the action of the proclaimed word with rather more investment in the action recurs with consistency in the course of Forde's work. It appears to raise a theoretical question about the relative importance of the content of the gospel.

[151] For instance, see Forde "A Short Word," 90; "Theology as *Modus Operandi*," 175; and "Karl Barth on the Consequences of Lutheran Christology," in *The Preached God*, 83. The classic statement is the title of Forde's fifth book, *Theology Is for Proclamation* (Minneapolis: Fortress Press, 1990).

[152] All biblical citations are from New Revised Standard Version.

[153] Gerhard Forde, "The Word That Kills and Makes Alive," in *Marks of the Body of Christ*, ed. Carl E. Braaten and Robert W. Jenson (Grand Rapids: Eerdmans, 1999) 7-8.

[154] Forde, "Forensic Justification and Law in Lutheran Theology," 300. Forde seems to maintain this accusing function even when he talks of the civil use of the law. See pp. 112-113.

[155] Forde, "Law and Sexual Behavior," *Lutheran Quarterly* 9/1 (Spr 1995) 17.

[156] Ibid., 5.

[157] Ibid., 18. Emphasis Forde's.

[158] See Gerhard Forde, "The Lutheran View," 18. Though he uses unconditional promise language intensely in this piece (twelve times over five pages), it seems that promise as such is not generally quite as central a word in the work of this law-gospel theologian as one might expect (at least fifteen other times over seven other articles and four sermons) and the force of its use here seems to be more on "unconditional" than on "promise." In fact, as the piece develops, he gradually replaces "promise" with other words: "unconditional fact," "sheer and unconditional announcement," "unconditional justification," "unconditional grace" (pp. 21-22), or, elsewhere, "unconditional claim and promise" in *Justification by Faith*, 22, or "unconditional affirmation and promise" in "The Exodus from Virtue to Grace," 42. The surprisingly light sprinkling of promise talk through Forde's works raises the possibility that he, indeed, prefers other terms. This stands in striking contrast with work by his classmate, Robert Jenson, who spends an entire book dwelling precisely on promise and its ramifications [see Robert W. Jenson, *Story and Promise* (Ramsey, NJ: Sigler Press, 1989)]. Granting the evident overlap of their positions at this point, it might be ventured that Forde's preferred "announcement" emphasizes the present reality of the eschatological moment in the life of the hearer in confidence of a future fulfillment, while Jenson's preferred "promise" emphasizes the future fulfillment for which the present reality includes sometimes painful waiting. Perhaps it may be said that Forde's gospel frees one particularly for the present, while Jen son's frees particularly for the future.

[159] Ibid., 21-22.

[160] Gerhard Forde, "The Newness of the Gospel," *dialog* 6/2 (Spr 1967) 88.

[161] On the definition of first and second order discourse, see pp. 50-51, below. For the distinction between proclamation and dogma, see "Proclamation as the Vehicle of the Event," pp. 110ff, below.

[162] Forde, "Hidden Treasure" [sermon on Matt 13:44], in *A More Radical Gospel: Essays on Eschatology, Authority, Atonement and Ecumenism*, ed. Mark C. Mattes and Steven D. Paulson, 214, but quoted from original manuscript.

[163] Forde, "God's Rights" [sermon on Matt 20:1-16], in *A More Radical Gospel*, 204-205.

[164] Forde, sermon on Matt 22:1-14 beginning, "Our text today compares the Kingdom of Heaven . . .," 2.

[165] Gerhard Forde, "Preaching the Sacraments," *Lutheran Theological Seminary Bulletin* 64/4 (Fall 1984) 5.

[166] Forde, "Infallibility Language and the Early Lutheran Tradition," 135. Forde marks again, here, his appreciation for the kind of functional approach to the language that Ebeling espouses. See Mark David Menacher, "A Gracious God Today? The Metaphor of Language in Gerhard Ebeling's Theological Method" (Ph.D. diss., University of Manchester, 1998). The missional question arises at this point just who the listener might be and how the word might have to do its own business on that listener. The fact that listeners in West Africa and North America, for instance, may have critical theological characteristics in common, like createdness in God's image or Old Adam-ness, does not undo the fact that such listeners operate out of considerably different theological worldviews and religious paradigms. Forde is focusing on the effect of the words on the listeners at this point rather than any effect the diversity of listeners might need to have on the words. The question of interpretation is raised onc e again by the prospect of radically different hearing of the same words by different people, even in the same culture.

[167] Ibid., 136.

[168] In the missional context the question of the breadth of meaning of "oral or sacramental proclamation" arises. Forde surely has pulpit and altar in mind here. Where the missionary has not been accorded pulpit and altar by the hearer, would Forde call witness to a friend on a dusty road oral proclamation, or an act of kindness associated with the witness sacramental proclamation? These, too, can seem first order. The uneven edges of proclamation will be considered further in chapter six.

[169] Gerhard Forde, "Law and Gospel in Luther's Hermeneutic," *Interpretation* 37/3 (Jul 1983) 242, 247. Forde here himself calls interpretation a problem — how it might be done in such a way as to avoid

objectivizing and taming the word — and he offers his solution: proclamation as God's own speech addressing the listener. Once again the question arises whether the diversity of listeners does not require some attention, all common characteristics of fallen humanity notwithstanding.

[170] Forde, "Theology as *Modus Operandi*," 176. See also Gerhard Forde, "Whatever Happened to God? God Not Preached," in Gerhard Forde, *The Preached God: Proclamation in Word and Sacrament*, ed. Mark C. Mattes and Steven D. Paulson (Grand Rapids, MI: Eerdmans, 2007), 44-48.

[171] Gerhard Forde, "Once More Into the Breach?" 14.

[172] See Forde, "Proclamation: The Present Tense of the Gospel," 169.

[173] *The Random House Dictionary of the English Language*, 2nd ed. (New York: Random House, 1987), 2118.

[174] Gerhard Forde, "On Sin" [sermon on Gen 2:15-16; 3:1-13], 2.

[175] Gerhard Forde, "The Revolt and the Wedding: An Essay on Social Ethics in the Perspective of Luther's Theology" in *The Reformation and the Revolution: A Series of Lectures Celebrating the Protestant Reformation and Commemorating the Bolshevik Revolution* (Sioux Falls, SD: The Augustana College Press, 1970) 83.

[176] Gerhard Forde, "On New Ideas and Old Traditions" [sermon on Matt 3:1-10], 1-2.

[177] Ibid., 2.

[178] Forde, "The One Acted Upon," 58.

[179] Perhaps the only exception is in Gerhard Forde, "Preaching the Sacraments," 5: "The overwhelming, well-nigh incurable tendency we have is to run to some sort of translation, to try to make the text relevant by translating it into more viable terms, either of a more 'timeless' metaphysical sort . . . or . . . into more contemporary terms and stories." This is a phenomenon he usually reserves for the term, "relevance." See pp. 57-58, below.

[180] Forde, "Once More into the Breach?" 10.

[181] Ibid., 14, and "The 'Old Synod': A Search for Objectivity," 75.

[182] Gerhard Forde, "Confessional Subscription: What Does It Mean for Lutherans Today?" *Word & World* 11/3 (Sum 1991) 320.

[183] Forde, "Preaching the Sacraments," 7.

[184] Forde, "The Law-Gospel Debate," 218.

[185] Ibid., 197.

[186] Forde, "The Newness of the Gospel," 89.

[187] Gerhard Forde, "The Viability of Luther Today: A North American Perspective," *Word & World* 7/1 (Wint 1987) 22.

[188] Forde, "The Work of Christ," 9.

[189] This is a common and significant expression, but, for an example, see Gerhard Forde, "Speaking the Gospel Today," in Gerhard Forde, *The Preached God: Proclamation in Word and Sacrament*, ed. Mark C. Mattes and Steven D. Paulson (Grand Rapids, MI: Eerdmans, 2007) 193.

[190] Most prominently, perhaps, enshrined in the title of his book, *Theology Is for Proclamation* . But see also Gerhard Forde, "Karl Barth on the Consequences of Lutheran Christology," in *The Preached God*, 77; "Proclamation: The Present Tense of the Gospel," 171; and "Martens on the Condemnations," *Lutheran Quarterly* 10/1 (Spr 1996) 67.

[191] Forde, "The One Acted Upon," 57-58.

[192] Gerhard Forde, "Confessional Subscription," 320.

[193] Forde, "Law and Gospel as the Methodological Principle of Theology," 68.

[194] Gerhard Forde, "On New Ideas and Old Traditions" [sermon on Matt. 3:1-10], 1-2.

[195] Gerhard Forde, review of *Gospel and Church*, by Gustaf Wingren, trans. Ross Mackenzie, and of *Theology and Preaching*, by Heinrich Ott, trans. Harold Knight, *dialog* 5/2 (Spr 1966) 153.

[196] Forde, "The Work of Christ," 90.

[197] Forde. "Law and Gospel as the Methodological Principle of Theology," 66.

[198] Forde, Ibid., 56.

[199] Gerhard Forde, sermon on Isaiah 40:6-10, 2; and "Behold and See!" [sermon on Lam 1:12], 2-3.

[200] Gerhard Forde, "Outside the Gate: Atonement as Actual Event," *dialog* 18/4 (Aut 1979) 249.

[201] Forde, "The Work of Christ," 61.

[202] Forde, "Bound to Be Free," 75.

[203] Forde, "The Work of Christ," 51.

[204] Ibid., 53.

[205] Forde, "Preaching the Sacraments," 14.

[206] Forde, "Called to Freedom," in *The Preached God: Proclamation in Word and Sacrament*, ed. Mark C. Mattes and Steven D. Paulson (Grand Rapids: Eerdmans, 2007) 268.

[207] Gerhard Forde, "The Power of Negative Thinking: On the Principle of Negation in Luther and Hegelianism," *dialog* 23/4 (Aut 1984) 252-256.

[208] Ibid., 251.

[209] If human aspirations to autonomous selfhood have these connections in Forde, it may fairly be asked in Feuerbachian manner how the selfhood of God with which they compete may be related to nineteenth century thought in Forde's theology. May it be said that Forde also draws his understanding of the selfhood of God, perhaps unconsciously, from the Kantian understanding of the autonomous self? Rebekah L. Miles and a number of feminist theologians might say so. They see Reinhold Neibuhr's "individualist" an d non-relational model of the self applied to God in such a way that God is

transcendent and separate rather than imminent and relational. See Rebekah L. Miles, *The Bonds of Freedom: Feminist Theology and Christian Realisim* (Oxford: Oxford University Press, 2001) 29-34. The question of how Forde might relate to such a question, or even whether Forde addressed this issue directly, would require further research.

[210] For example, Forde, "The Normative Character of Scripture for Matters of Faith and Life," 308.

[211] Forde, "Absolution: Systematic Considerations," in Gerhard O. Forde, *The Preached God: Proclamation in Word and Sacrament,* (Grand Rapids: Eerdmans, 2007) 160.

[212] Forde, "Law and Gospel as the Methodological Principle of Theology," 128.

[213] Forde, "The Exodus from Virtue to Grace," 40.

[214] Gerhard Forde, "Speaking the Gospel Today," in Forde, *The Preached God*, 160.

[215] See, for example, Gerhard Forde, sermon on John 19:28-30 beginning "It is Finished! In this half-done world . . .," 2.

[216] Gerhard Forde, "He is not here; He is risen" [sermon on Mark 16:6], 2.

[217] Forde, "God's Rights [sermon on Matt 20:1-16], in *A More Radical Gospel*, 204-205.

[218] Forde, sermon on John 19:29-30 beginning with "'It is Finished!' I suppose it might seem strange . . .," 3.

[219] Gerhard Forde, *Justification by Faith: A Matter of Death and Life* (Philadelphia: Fortress Press, 1982) 4.

[220] Forde, "A Short Word," 91.

[221] Forde, "The Cross as Sign of Faith" [sermon on Matt 27:46], 2.

[222] Forde, "The One Acted Upon," 55.

[223] Gerhard Forde, "The Irrelevance of the Modern World for Luther," in *A More Radical Gospel* (Grand Rapids: Eerdmans, 2004) 75. This would be the positive sense of the word in fourth chapter of Locus XI, "Christian Life," 466, where this more universal understanding relevance actually places it in the subheadings and therefore includes "the kind of vision, the basic hope in life, that it inspires."

[224] Forde, "Preaching the Sacraments," 6.

[225] Forde, "On Being a Theologian of the Cross," *Christian Century* 114/29 (Oct. 22, 1997) 949.

[226] Gerhard Forde, *The Law-Gospel Debate*, 3-6.

[227] Ibid., 5.

[228] Ibid., 6.

[229] Ibid., 9

[230] Ibid., 9-11.

[231] Ibid., 11.

[232] Ibid., 17.

[233] Ibid., 16.

[234] Ibid., 20-22.

[235] Ibid., 23.

[236] Ibid., 23-24

[237] Ibid., 28.

[238] Ibid. Original German words cited by Forde in his translation are omitted.

[239] Ibid., 29.

[240] Ibid., 30.

[241] Ibid., 31.

[242] Ibid., 32.

[243] Ibid., 81. This is not the place for it, but given Forde's own use of experience in the discernment of scripture's divine work (pp. 47-48) and his insistence that actual existential death and life characterize the faith of the Christian (pp. 101-107), and his understanding of the eschatological event (pp. 96ff), it would be interesting to consider further to what extent Hofmann's unfolding the content of the experience from within the experience could describe Forde's epistemology. If the perception of "from-within-ness" corresponds to an experiential phenomenon, what would they say to each other? This would require further research.

[244] Ibid., 93.

[245] Ibid., 84-86.

[246] Ibid., 93-94.

[247] Ibid., 87.

[248] Ibid., 88, 93.

[249] Reinhold Seeberg, *Die Kirche Deutschlands im 19. Jahrhundert*, 2nd ed. (Leipzig: A. Deichert, 1904) 259, quoted in Forde, *The Law-Gospel Debate*, 96.

[250] Forde, *The Law Gospel Debate*, 100.

[251] Ibid.

[252] Ibid., 101.

[253] Albrecht Ritschl, *Jahrbücher für deutsche Theologie*, Vol. II, no. 4 (Stuttgart: 1857) 828, quoted in Forde, *The Law-Gospel Debate*, 105.

[254] Forde, *The Law-Gospel Debate*, 105.

[255] Ibid., 106, 117. Forde later remarks how this point makes Ritschl's position vulnerable to "quest of the historical Jesus" research. If community creation were to be demonstrated not to be Jesus' vocation, Ritschl's system would lose credibility.

[256] Ibid., 107-108.

[257] Ibid., 110-111.
[258] Ibid., 113.
[259] Ibid., 114.
[260] Ibid., 139.
[261] Ibid., 140.
[262] Ibid., 141.
[263] Ibid., 142.
[264] Ibid., 143-144.
[265] Ibid., 144.
[266] Ibid.
[267] Ibid.
[268] Karl Barth, *Church Dogmatics*, ed. G. W. Bromiley and T. F. Torrance, trans. G. T. Thompson and H. Knight (New York: Scribners, 1956) II:584-585, quoted in Forde *The Law-Gospel Debate*, 145.
[269] Forde, *The Law-Gospel Debate*, 146.
[270] Ibid., 147. The biblical reference is Romans 8:2.
[271] Ibid., 147.
[272] Ibid., 141.
[273] Karl Barth, *Church Dogmatics*, II:584-585, quoted in Forde, *The Law-Gospel Debate*, 147.
[274] Forde, *The Law-Gospel Debate*, 149.
[275] Ibid., 175.
[276] Ibid., 176.
[277] Ibid., 177.
[278] Ibid., 178-179.
[279] Martin Luther, "Die zweite Disputation gegen die Antinomer" [1538], in WA 39/1:455, quoted in Forde, *The Law-Gospel Debate*, 179. In this broad Lutheran understanding of law, all humankind across cultural differences is addressed in common. Missiologically, it asks for a basic singularity of theological address, though culturally it will surely appear diverse forms. See fn 166, p. 243.
[280] Ibid., 183.
[281] Ibid., 185.
[282] Ibid., 186.
[283] Ibid., 187.
[284] Ibid.
[285] Ibid., 187-188.
[286] Ibid., 189-190.
[287] Ibid., 195-197.
[288] Ibid., 194.
[289] Ibid., 199.
[290] Forde, "The Newness of the Gospel," 90.
[291] Forde, "Christian Life," 400.
[292] Forde, "The Law-Gospel Debate," 178.
[293] Ibid., 211.
[294] Forde, "Forensic Justification and the Law in Lutheran Theology," 295.
[295] Gerhard Forde, "Fake Theology: Reflections on Antinomianism Past and Present," *dialog* 22/4 (Fall 1983) 250.
[296] Forde, "The Law-Gospel Debate," 179.
[297] Forde, "Law and Sexual Behavior," 17.
[298] Forde, "The Work of Christ," 418.
[299] Forde, "Forensic Justification and the Law in Lutheran Theology," 300.
[300] Ibid., 300.
[301] Forde, "Law and Sexual Behavior," 6.
[302] Gerhard Forde, "Authority in the Church: The Lutheran Reformation," in Gerhard Forde, *A More Radical Gospel: Essays on Eschatology, Authority, Atonement, and Ecumenism*, ed. Mark C. Mattes and Steven D. Paulson (Grand Rapids, MI: Eerdmans) 59.
[303] Forde, "Law and Sexual Behavior," 6-7.
[304] Forde, *The Law-Gospel Debate*, 212.
[305] Forde, "Law and Sexual Behavior," 7. There are oblique references to the uses of the law in chapter three of "Christian Life:" on 448: "[J]ustification exposes sin [second use?] and upholds the law against sin [first use?] at the same time . . ."; on 449: "The question is whether one can or should speak of a 'third ' use of the law in addition to the political use (to restrain evil) and the theological use (to convict of sin); and on 450: "[T]hat is not to say that one sees a 'third' use. What one sees is precisely the difference between law and gospel, so that law can be established in its *first* two uses this side of the eschaton" [emphasis Forde's]. This entire discussion is, however, couched in a refutation of both antinomianism and a third use of the law. It is like Forde would never have brought it up if it were not connected to these wayward tendencies. It would require further research to verify the preliminary impression that Forde simply never uses the expressions "first use of the law" and "second use of the law" in the entire corpus.

[306] Gerhard Forde, " *lex semper accusat* ? Nineteenth Century Roots of Our Current Dilemma," *dialog* 9/4 (Aut 1970) 274; and Forde, *The Law-Gospel Debate*, 211;

[307] Ibid., 7-9.

[308] Ibid., 20, n9. For an exception, see "Christian Life," 452, and below n312.

[309] Forde, "Viability of Luther Today," 28.

[310] Gerhard Forde, "Speaking the Gospel Today," in *The Preached God*, 184.

[311] Forde, "Viability of Luther Today," 28-29.

[312] These lines are written in the face of Forde's possibly unique appelation of the law as friend in his Locus XI, "Christian Life," 452. There he is describing the life of "the new being" in Christ which knows the eschatological end of the law. In that context he can propose "the law of God is ultimately not an enemy or an emasculated guide but a true and loved friend." But even then, Forde understands the law as doing its "friendly" work by unfriendly means, menace and threat. Again, there seems to be relatively little explication of the civil use of the law in Forde, that use that promotes the good and prevents evil.

[313] Gerhard Forde, "He who comes" [sermon on Luke 3:1-14], 2. Emphasis Forde's.

[314] Gerhard Forde, *Where God Meets Man: Luther's Down-to-Earth Approach to the Gospel* (Minneapolis: Augsburg, 1972) 7.

[315] Forde, sermon on John 19:28-30 beginning "'It is Finished.' In a world like ours...," 2. See also Forde, "Christ and the teachers" [sermon on Luke 14:1-11], 5.

[316] Forde, "The Lutheran View," 19. For other examples see Forde, "A God Who Acts" [sermon on Matt 22:1-14] 2-3; "A Voice from the Darkness" [sermon on Mark 1:21-28], in *The Preached God: Proclamation in Word and Sacrament*, (Grand Rapids: Eerdmans, 2007) 319; and "My Sheep Hear My Voice" [sermon on John 10:22-30], 4.

[317] Ibid., 22.

[318] Forde, "The Word That Kills and Makes Alive," 2. Forde proposes that these are questions by the old Being designed to trap the witness, and that their best reply is another question that might expose the questioner. For instance, the protest, "Why not, then, just a mass baptism; hose 'em down," Forde suggests answering with "Would that not be fun. Would it not be marvelous if we were in a position to do that? . . . Most of us, after all, would probably not be Christian today if it were not for some such wild event far back in our history" (Forde, "Something to Believe," 238). Forde's persistent theological offensive at this point renders further missiological conversation about the diversity of cultural interactions with the law problematic.

[319] Forde, "The Newness of the Gospel," 92.

[320] Gerhard Forde, "Bound to Be Free," in *Encounters with Luther*, ed. Eric Gritsch (Gettysburg, PA: Lutheran Theological Seminary at Gettysburg, 1976) 2:76.

[321] Gerhard Forde, "Caught in the Act: Reflections on the Work of Christ," *Word & World* 3/1 (Wint 1983) 28.

[322] Forde, "The Power of Negative Thinking" 251.

[323] Ibid., 252.

[324] Forde, *The Law-Gospel Debate*, 120.

[325] Forde, "Once More into the Breach," 13.

[326] Forde, "Bound to Be Free," 75. There are parallels from diverse cultures, ancient and modern, Western and traditional, where interference by the gods or God was an unwanted possibility because it was unpredictable, and measures had to be taken to hold them off. The author recalls a particular feeding station outside the door of a home in Cameroon where token food was offered to the ancestor-spirits.

[327] For examples see Forde, "Bound to Be Free," 77; "Theology as *Modus Operandi*, " 178; "Caught in the Act," 22; "Fake Theology," 249; "Law and Gospel in Luther's Hermeneutic," 251; "The Lutheran View," 17; "Karl Barth on the Consequences of Lutheran Christology," in *The Preached God*, 78; sermon on Luke 10:25-37, 3; and "Naming the One Who Is Above Us," 116.

[328] Gerhard Forde, "The Easy Yoke" [sermon on Matt 11:25-30], in Forde, *The Captivation of the Will: Luther vs. Erasmus on Freedom and Bondage*, ed. Steven D. Paulson (Grand Rapids: Eerdmans, 2005) 85. Emphasis Forde's.

[329] Forde, "Fake Theology," 246.

[330] Ibid., 249-250.

[331] Ibid., 249.

[332] Ibid.

[333] Forde, *The Law-Gospel Debate*, 226-227.

[334] Ibid., 228. There is a kindred solidarity in Forde, "Christian Life," in *Christian Dogmatics*, II:464, where Becker's quote from Otto Rank is cited approvingly, "Every human being is . . . equally unfree, that is *we . . . create* out of freedom, a prison." Not unrelated to the law, this prison solidarity comes from a common fear of death that takes away the possibility of authentic living.

[335] Forde, "The Normative Character of Scripture," 309.

[336] Gerhard Forde, "Is Forgiveness Enough? Reflections on an Odd Question," *Word and World* 16/3 (Sum 1996) 305.

[337] Forde, "The Normative Character of Scripture for Matters of Faith and Life," 309.

[338] Ibid., 305. Emphasis Forde's.

[339] Forde, review of *Gospel and Church*, by Gustaf Wingren, 151. Emphasis Forde's.

[340] Gerhard Forde, "The Formula of Concord Article V," 188. Emphasis Forde's.

[341] Forde, " *lex semper accusat?* " 274. Emphasis Forde's.

[342] Forde, *The Law-Gospel Debate*, 210-211.

[343] Forde, "The Viability of Luther Today," 27.

[344] Forde, "Law and Sexual Behavior," 9.

[345] Forde, " *lex semper accusat?* " 274.

[346] Ibid.

[347] Forde, "Fake Theology," 249; and "Law and Sexual Behavior," 8.

[348] Forde, "Law and Sexual Behavior," 8. There's considerable tension between the the alien nature of an uncompromisingly accusatory law that God uses and stewardable nature of a justice-fostering law that must actually be humanly tailored to care for the world (pp. 73-75). The diversity of human situations calls for the latter and Forde affirms this, yet he would not have us in this age forgo the former. Moreover, stewardship suggests the same interpretive cultural and societal investment in the proclama tion that we highlighted before.

[349] Forde, "Forensic Justification and Law," 301.

[350] Forde, "The Viability of Luther Today," 24.

[351] Forde, *The Law-Gospel Debate*, 232.

[352] Forde, "The Meaning of *Satis Est*," *Lutheran Forum* 26/4 (Nov 1992) 18; and "The Word That Kills and Makes Alive," 2; and "Lutheran Ecumenism," 446.

[353] Forde, "Authority in the Church," 60. For other examples of Forde's use of "tyranny," see his sermon on Ps 25:4-5 beginning "Make me to know thy ways O Lord...," 1; "Once More Into the Breach?" 14; "Unity without Concord?" *dialog* 20/2 (Spr 1981) 171; "The Viability of Luther Today," 27, 30; "A Lutheran Response [to the Wesleyan View]," in *Christian Spirituality: Five Views of Sanctification*, ed. Donald L. Alexander (Downers Grove, IL: Intervarsity, 1988) 120; and "Called to Freedom," in *The Preached God*, 268. It is not clear how Forde's message to the tyrannized and sacrificed will be different from the one he offers to Old Adams and Eves the world over. In fact, the shape of his career was such that he may never addressed them as a social class directly, though he often lifts up their plight indirectly before those who might help them. In maintaining a consistent anthropology for all humankind, even those faced by oppressive forces, he begs the missiological question what if anything would need to be different in a direct address by Forde to such people.

[354] Forde, *The Law-Gospel Debate*, 232.

[355] Ibid. Emphasis Forde's.

[356] Forde often concluded his longer works with a reference to the social justice and care of the earth that followed from a proper understanding of law and gospel. For instance, *The Law-Gospel Debate*, 233 (last page); *Where God Meets Man*, 128 (last page); "Christian Life" in *Christian Dogmatics*, II:457-460 (last three pages); *Theology is for Proclamation*, 190 (last page); and *On Being a Theologian of the Cross*, 114-115 (last pages).

[357] Forde, "The Work of Christ," 11-12.

[358] Ibid., 12-13.

[359] Ibid., 13-14.

[360] Ibid., 14-15.

[361] Ibid., 16.

[362] Ibid., 17-18.

[363] Ibid., 18.

[364] Ibid., 18-19.

[365] Ibid., 20.

[366] Ibid.

[367] Ibid., 21.

[368] Ibid., 21-22.

[369] Ibid., 22.

[370] Ibid., 23.

[371] Ibid., 24-25.

[372] Ibid., 25.

[373] Ibid., 23.

[374] Ibid., 23-24.

[375] Ibid., 24.

[376] Ibid., 26.

[377] Ibid., 27.

[378] Ibid., 27-28.

[379] Ibid., 28.

[380] Ibid., 31, citing H. J. Iwand, "Wider den Missbrauch des pro me als methodisches Princip in der Theologie," *Theologische Literaturzeitung* 7/8 (1954) 454-458. Emphasis added.

[381] Forde, "The Work of Christ," 31.

[382] Ibid., 32-33.

[383] Ibid., 33.

[384] Ibid., 35-36.

[385] Ibid., 36-37.

[386] Ibid., 40.

[387] Ibid., 38-39.

[388] Forde, "Outside the Gate," 249.

[389] Ibid.

[390] Ibid., 41. For this idea Forde cites J. W. C. Wand, *The Atonement* (London: SPCK, 1963) 1, in "Outside the Gate," 249.

[391] Forde likes the phrase "roses on the cross" to describe the domestication of the scandal, and uses it repeatedly in his discussion of atonement theory in "The Work of Christ," 9, 30, 40, 41, 52, 60, 71, 80, and its precursor article, "Outside the Gate," 252. In both works the phrase appears to enter the conversation through two references to an unpublished article by H. J. Iwand, *Christologievorlesung*, 288 and 289, as quoted in Jurgen Moltmann, *The Crucified God*, trans. R. A. Wilson and John Bowden (New York: Harper & Row, 1974) 36 [misprinted as 63 in "Outside the Gate"] and 41. Moltmann further traces the phrase to its use by Hegel and Goethe as described in detail by Karl Löwith, *From Hegel to Nietzsche: The Revolution in Nineteenth-Century Thought*, trans. David E. Green (New York: Holt, Rinehart and Winston, 1964) 14-29, in a subsection entitled "Rose and Cross." Hegel introduced the term in his 1822 *Rechtsphilosophie*, using a "rose within the cross of the present" to propose an interaction of reason and theology of the cross in a unifying synthesis. By itself the cross was too harsh and abrasive for public use; it needed some humanization to serve Hegel's purpose, the illustration of philosophical concepts. For him it was a "rational cross." In 1830 Hegel's students presented their teacher with a medal inscribed with an owl (philosophy) and a cross (religion). A copy of this medal presented to Hegel's friend Goethe upon Hegel's death in 1831 occasioned a poem, "Die Geheimnisse." Here we find Goethe's own version of a poetic humanization of the cross that, like Hegel, mitigated its "theological rigor," but, unlike Hegel, rejected its association with philosophy. His was a "humanistic cross" (Löwith, 18). A new generation of philosophers could not abide the roses, and rejected the cross altogether. Nietzsche, for example, in *The Antichrist* saw the Christianity of a crucified messiah as a "religion of decadence" with its rejection of much that Nietzsche understood as good in humanity: pride, freedom, sensual joy, and resistance of the lowly to oppressors. The unadorned cross was "morality for slaves." Marx, likewise seeing through the flowers, called on people to break with its morality. Moltmann summarizes, "Modern, post-Christian humanism has done a great service by bringing to the fore once again this original and natural dislike of the cross. In this way it has reminded Christianity, which has made itself so much at home in European civilization, of its original and fundamental alienation" (p. 34). Forde appreciates this service and resists the fresh roses offered by his own era. As he summarizes his atonement position, "A cross without roses brings something new: it puts to death and it raises up," *Christian Dogmatics*, 60.

[392] Forde, "Outside the Gate," 253. See also "The Work of Christ," 88-98.

[393] Ibid., 251.

[394] Ibid.

[395] Ibid.

[396] Examples cited include Matt 27:25, John 19:15-16, and Luke 23:28.

[397] Forde, "Outside the Gate," 251-252.

[398] Ibid., 252.

[399] Ibid.

[400] Forde, "He is risen, He is not here" [sermon on Mark 16:6], 1.

[401] Ibid., 2.

[402] Gerhard Forde, review of "Theology and Proclamation: Dialogue with Bultmann," by Gerhard Ebeling, 302.

[403] Ibid., 302. Emphasis Forde's.

[404] Ibid., 302.

[405] Forde, "Outside the Gate," 252.

[406] Ibid.

[407] Ibid.

[408] Forde, "The Work of Christ," 56-57.

[409] Forde, "Christ and the teachers" [sermon on Luke 14:1-11], 4. Emphasis Forde's.

[410] Forde, "Outside the Gate," 252.

[411] Ibid.

[412] Ibid.

[413] Forde, "The Work of Christ," 49.

[414] Ibid., 50. See also Forde's first book, *Where God Meets Man*, chapter 1.

[415] Ibid., 51.

[416] Ibid., 52.

[417] Ibid., 52-53.

[418] Ibid., 55. Likewise, it is not clear how the accident translates into the curse and wrath of God. Perhaps God's placing him before the vehicle may be considered a curse, but then a curse in a different sense.

[419] Ibid., 61.

[420] Ibid., 52.

[421] Gerhard Forde, "In Our Place," in *A More Radical Gospel: Essays on Eschatology, Authority, Atonement and Ecumenism*, ed. Mark C. Mattes and Steven D. Paulson (Grand Rapids: Eerdmans, 2004) 112.

[422] Forde, "The Work of Christ," 51.

[423] Ibid., 52.

[424] Ibid.

[425] Ibid., 56.

[426] Ibid.

[427] Forde, "Karl Barth on the Consequences of Lutheran Christology," my unedited transcription of the original videotape, edited edition in *The Preached God*, 85.

[428] Gerhard Forde, "Robert Jenson's Soteriology," in *Trinity, Time, and Church: A Response to the Theology of Robert W. Jenson*, ed. Colin Gunton (Grand Rapids: Eerdmans, 2000.) 131.

[429] Gerhard Forde, "Response to James Nestingen's Article," *dialog* 31/1 (Wint 1992) 34-35.

[430] Gerhard Forde, "Justification by Faith Alone: The Article by Which the Church Stands or Falls?" 260.

[431] Gerhard Forde, "Justification," in *A New Handbook of Christian Theology*, ed. Donald W. Musser and Joseph L. Price (Nashville, TN: Abingdon, 1992) 271.

[432] Forde, *Justification by Faith*, 19.

[433] Forde, "Luther and the *Usus Pauli*," 276, and Gerhard Forde, "Martens on the Condemnations," 68.

[434] Gerhard Forde, "The Exodus from Virtue to Grace," 42.

[435] Gerhard Forde *et al.* "The Critical Response of German Theological Professors to the Joint Declaration on the Doctrine of Justification," *dialog* 38/1 (Wint 1999) 71. Italics are part of the document, which Forde joined others in signing.

[436] Forde, "Justification by Faith Alone: The Article by Which the Church Stands or Falls?" 262.

[437] Gerhard Forde, "The End of Theology," in *Mid-Winter Convocation: What Are We Up To? Systematic Theologians at Work* [sound recording], casssette 8 (St. Paul: Luther Seminary, 1997). Unpublished transcript of recording in Gerhard Forde file, Evangelical Luheran Church in America Region 3 Archives, St. Paul, MN, page 3.

[438] Forde, "Forensic Justification and Law," 288.

[439] *Smalcald Articles* III.3.2, in *Book of Concord: The Confessions of the Evangelical Lutheran Church*, ed. Robert Kolb and Timothy J. Wengert (Minneapolis: Fortress Press, 2000) 312, quoted in Forde, "The End of Theology," 3.

[440] Forde, "The Exodus from Virtue to Grace," 38.

[441] Forde, *Justification by Faith: A Matter of Death and Life*, 23.

[442] Forde, "Justification by Faith Alone: The Article by Which the Church Stands or Falls?" 260.

[443] Gerhard Forde, "Lutheranism," in *The Blackwell Encyclopedia of Modern Christian Thought*, ed. Alister McGrath (Cambridge, MA: Blackwell, 1993) 354.

[444] Gerhard Forde, "Romans 8:18-27," *Interpretation* 38/3 (Jul 1984) 281.

[445] Forde, *Justification by Faith: A Matter of Death and Life*, 23.

[446] Gerhard Forde, "Moses' Baccalaureate" [sermon on Exod 4:21-26], in *The Preached God: Proclamation in Word and Sacrament*, ed. Mark C. Mattes and Steven D. Paulson (Grand Rapids, MI: Eerdmans, 2007) 288.

[447] Forde, "My Sheep Hear My Voice," 1-2.

[448] Forde, "Proclamation: The Present Tense of the Gospel," 170.

[449] Forde, "Robert Jenson's Soteriology," 133.

[450] Forde, "The Work of Christ," 70-71.

[451] Ibid., 71.

[452] Ibid., 73. Mark Thomsen has written a classic reaction to this scandal, sharply criticizing Forde's "Annihilator God" in his *Christ Crucified: A 21st Century Missiology of the Cross* (Minneapolis: Lutheran University Press, 2004) 39-53.

[453] Ibid., 72.

[454] Notice that Forde doesn't that say God must cloth himself in flesh and blood or human nature or any other static characteristic of human existence. Rather, he is consistent in his emphasis on the function.

[455] Forde, "The Work of Christ," 73.

[456] In a sermon entitled "On God's Goodness" [sermon on John 1:43-51] Forde proclaims, "Why so little talk of this [electing] God? It is, I suppose, because we are afraid of him. He threatens us. He threatens to reduce us to insignificance. He does not really fit, I suppose, with what we like to call the modern consciousness of 'freedom.' We cannot really allow him to move too far into the center of the stage for fear he will seem to take too big a place."

[457] Forde, "The Work of Christ," 67.

[458] Chosen as title for his last book, *The Captivation of the Will: Luther vs. Erasmus on Freedom and Bondage*, ed. Steven D. Paulson (Grand Rapids, MI: Eerdmans, 2005).

[459] Forde, "The Work of Christ," 66. See also "Bound to Be Free," 74. Once again Forde's sense of the common plight of humankind in its fallenness is clear. There seems no room in this discussion for other treatment of those whose wills are not their own. See the comments on pp. 73-75.

[460] Forde, *Captivation of the Will*, 54.

[461] Ibid.

[462] Forde, "The Work of Christ," 66. Emphasis Forde's. These assertions do raise questions about the doctrine of creation and the created order's independent integrity alongside God. Forde is here describing the actual state of fallen humanhood in creation, not speculating about what it might be in some unfallen state. Nevertheless, the strength of his confession of God's sovereignty seems to affect negatively the way one should think about creation as such.

[463] Ibid., 66.

[464] Forde, *Justification by Faith: A Matter of Death and Life*, 1.

[465] Ibid., 2. Forde distinguishes strongly between knowledge and experience as agents of change for fallen

humankind in the old age. In discussing atonement theory he held out no hope for gnosis of whatever stripe, neither a legal theory or a loving example, to be an agent of the critical eschatological work (pp. 83-89), and now he holds no expectation that academic research will provide the impetus necessary to stage a recurrence of the reformation explosion.

466 Ibid., 2-3.
467 Ibid., 3. Emphasis added.
468 Ibid., 11.
469 Forde, "The Newness of the Gospel," 92.
470 Gerhard Forde, "The Cross as Sign of Faith" [sermon on Matt 27:46], 2-4.
471 Forde, "Christ and the teachers" [sermon on Luke 14:1-11] 5.
472 Gerhard Forde, "A Refuge for Beggars" [sermon on Luke 18:35-43], 2.
473 Forde, "The Power of Negative Thinking, 251.
474 Forde, "Bound to Be Free," 76.
475 Forde, "The Work of Christ," 58.
476 Ibid., 96.
477 Forde, *Justification by Faith: A Matter of Death and Life*, 19, with citation from "Lectures on Galatians" [1535], in *LW* 26:67-68. Emphasis Forde's.
478 Ibid., 17. Forde expresses similar concern about God talk in "Naming the One Who Is above Us," 113. Though he uses the term himself in another context, he resists the "collective sigh of relief" that might come with reducing speech about God or his justification to "only metaphorical."
479 Gerhard Forde, "Some Remarks on [Ted] Peters' Review of *Christian Dogmatics*," *dialog* 24/4 (Fall 1985) 299.
480 Forde, "On New Ideas and Old Traditions" [sermon on Matt 3:1-10], 2.
481 Gerhard Forde, "The Laborers in the Vineyard: Matthew 20:1-16," in *The Preached God: Proclamation in Word and Sacrament*, ed. Mark C. Mattes and Steven D. Paulson (Grand Rapids, MI: Eerdmans, 2007) 317. The emphasis is Forde's in the original manuscript.
482 Gerhard Forde, "The Newness of the New Testament," in *All Things New: Essays in Honor of Roy A. Harrisville*, ed. Arland J. Hultgren, Donald H. Juel, and Jack D. Kingsbury (St. Paul, MN: Word & World, Luther Northwestern Theological Seminary, 1992) 177.
483 Forde, "The Normative Character of Scripture for Matters of Faith and Life," 312.
484 Forde, "Once More Into the Breach," 12.
485 Gerhard Forde, sermon on Matthew 3:1-10 beginning with "The season of Lent is one which is traditionally . . . ," 1.
486 Forde, "The End of Theology," 16.
487 Forde, "Authority in the Church," 56.
488 Forde, "Seven More Demons!" [sermon on Luke 11:24-26], 3.
489 Gerhard Forde, "Is Invocation of Saints an Adiaphoron?" in *The One Mediator, The Saints, and Mary: Lutherans and Catholics in Dialogue VIII*, ed. H. George Anderson, J. Francis Stafford, and Joseph A. Burgess (Minneapolis: Augsburg, 1992) 336. A similar paragraph could be written about "reorientation" which occurs in the early sermon on Matthew 3:1-10 already noted, but is absent from his later writings. Certainly from the beginning of his ministry, and if anything, increasingly so, Forde preferred a strong approach to the eschatological moment.
490 Forde, "The End of Theology," 16.
491 Forde, "The Exodus from Virtue to Grace," 36. Emphasis Forde's.
492 Ibid., 37.
493 Forde, "The Lutheran View," 29.
494 Forde, "Christian Life," 407.
495 Ibid., 431.
496 Ibid., 437.
497 Forde, *The Law-Gospel Debate*, 185.
498 Gerhard Forde, "The Irrelevance of the Modern World for Luther," 77.
499 Forde, sermon on John 19:28-30 beginning "'It is Finished' In a world like ours . . . ," 4.
500 Forde, "The Power of Negative Thinking," 252.
501 Gerhard Forde, sermon on Luke 9:24, 2.
502 Forde, "Outside the Gate," 253.
503 Gerhard Forde, sermon on Matt 8:1-13, 4.
504 For a casual reference to this passiveness, see Forde, "Justification," 272.
505 See Forde, "The Work of Christ," 100: "The law, like the masks of God, only changes form, and in the end administers a death from which there is no resurrection." Or again, on p. 136, "[W]e may exchange this liberty for license, try desperately to realize some kind of destiny by a life of self-indulgence. But that only means that the Old Adam has not died to sin and so shall die the death of sin from which there is no return." See also Gerhard Forde, "Speaking the Gospel Today," in *The Preached God*, 189; and "The Lutheran View," 19-20. Occasionally one hears the position that Forde was a universalist. References like these to death without resurrection argue to the contrary. Forde himself distances himself from universalist language in a tight paragraph in "The Work of Christ," 92-93. See also a gentle mocking of a universalist position in "Whatever Happened to God? God Not Preached," in *The Preached God*, 47.

[506] Gerhard Forde, sermon on John 19:28-30 beginning "'It is Finished!' I suppose it might seem strange. . . ," 3.

[507] Forde, "The Irrelevance of the Modern World for Luther," 77.

[508] Forde, sermon on John 19:28-30 beginning "'It is Finished' In a world like ours . . . ," 4.

[509] Forde, "Justification by Faith Alone: The Article by Which the Church Stands or Falls?" 261.

[510] Forde, *Theology Is for Proclamation*, 137.

[511] Forde, "The Exodus from Virtue to Grace," 37.

[512] Forde, "Infallibility Language and the Early Lutheran Tradition, 130.

[513] Forde, "Unity without Concord?" *dialog* 20/2 (Spr 1981) 172. For a similar statements on the experience of the Word's work in the hearer, see Forde, "Law and Gospel as the Methodological Principle of Theology," 61-62, and "Infallibility Language and the Early Lutheran Tradition," 126. Here again is a reliance on the experiential aspect for definition of belief. See above, pp. 47-48.

[514] Forde, *Theology Is for Proclamation*, 146. Again, it is the use of an experience for definition.

[515] Forde, "Some Remarks on [Ted] Peters' Review of *Christian Dogmatics*," 298.

[516] Gerhard Forde, "A Gracious Neighbor or a Gracious God?" in *The Preached God*, 315.

[517] Forde, "Robert Jenson's Soteriology," 133. We have already remarked on both the overlap and the difference in emphasis between these two theologians (p. 243, n158). When Forde says promise, the present reality of the promised gift is emphasized by consciousness of firmness of the will of the God who stands behind it.

[518] Forde, "The Exodus from Virtue to Grace," 42.

[519] Forde, "Something to Believe," 233, 235, and sermon on Matt 26:29, 1. Forde knows how positively to consider love as a characteristic action of God, but its use is rare in the corpus. For the exceptional use, see his "Bound to Be Free," 76; "The Work of Christ," 60; and "The One Acted Upon," 55. But by and large, the idea of God's love is brought up as an abusable and abused term, a characterization of the age's sentimentality ["What's in a Name? Eucharist or Lord's Supper," *Word & World* 9/1 (Wint 1989) 54], "a pitable platitude, a meaningless cipher" that has been "endlessly drummed into us," ("Is Forgiveness Enough?" 305). A sign of Forde's uneasiness about the term might be his deletion of it from the first draft of a Lenten sermon where a first draft has God's first order words to the hearer, "I love you, in spite of everything and I mean to have you back," with "you are mine," pencilled in. In the second draft they become simply, "You are mine, in spite of everything and I mean to have you back." See Forde, "It Is Finished" [sermon on John 19:30], beginning, "It is finished. It is over. . . , " 2, and the second draft of the same beginning, "It is finished! Over," 1. For Forde it appears that the idea of the divine claim on us more effectively speaks the force of divine love for us. This contrasts sharply with Robert Jenson in *Story and Promise* where love's self-surrender through death and beyond constitutes an important element of God's identity in Jesus (pp. 55-56, 62-63, 120-128). It also becomes an important theme in describing relationships, human as well as divine, that create a future (pp. 96, 120-128, 140, 151-160) and the presence and consciousness that go with it (pp. 174-176). My particular lens in reading Forde did not address his awareness of "presence" and "consciousness" as significant theological factors, and I record only three instances of his use of "relationship." I tentatively propose, that, along with love, these are relatively less significant in Forde's theology, though this would bear further study.

[520] Forde, *Theology Is for Proclamation*, 141.

[521] Forde quotes Luther, calling it reason's "slaughter," in "Called to Freedom," in *The Preached God*, 261. See also Forde, "A Lutheran Response [to the Contemplative View]," 192. Forde preaches this "without-ness" in "A Word from Without" [sermon on Jer 23:29] in *The Captivation of the Will*, 92. This externality experienced as something "from without," from God, stands in tension, as we pointed out, with the proclamation as from one of us in the midst of us and therefore clothed in outward ambiguity of this-worldliness.

[522] Forde, "Something to Believe," 233.

[523] Ibid.

[524] Gerhard Forde, *et al* ., "A Call for Discussion of the 'Joint Declaration on the Doctrine of Justification,'" *dialog* 36/3 (Sum 1997) 228. For other uses of the term "relationship" by Forde, see "Justification," 271-272, and "Naming the One Who is Above Us," 116. See n519 above.

[525] Forde, "My Sheep Hear My Voice" [sermon on John 10:22-30], 4. See also Forde, *Theology Is for Proclamation*, 126.

[526] Forde, "Justification," 271. See above, pp. 100-101.

[527] Forde, *The Law-Gospel Debate*, 211. But for Forde's almost visceral censure of altar call versions of "receiving Christ" ("Yuk!"), see "Preaching the Sacraments," 13.

[528] Forde, "The One Acted Upon," 59.

[529] Forde, *Theology Is for Proclamation*, 14.

[530] Forde, "Proclamation: The Present Tense of the Gospel," 167-168.

[531] Ibid., 168.

[532] Ibid., 172.

[533] Forde's definition of proclamation here seems to fit only that of the gospel. One would think that preaching of the law, too, might be first order, present, and authorized by Jesus Christ or by the scriptural text, but conditional and accusing threat, not unconditional promise. If this definition is maintained, Christian proclamation, it appears, is defined, finally, by its gospel force.

[534] Forde, *Theology is for Proclamation*, 59

[535] Gerhard Forde, "You Are Witnesses (Ordination)" [sermon on Luke 24:44-49], in *The Preached God*, 301.

Emphasis Forde's.

[536] Gerhard Forde, "The Ordained Ministry," in *Called & Ordained: Lutheran Perspectives on the Office of the Ministry*, ed. Todd Nichol and Marc Kolden (Minneapolis: Fortress Press, 1990) 120-121.

[537] Forde, "The Word That Kills and Makes Alive," 5. Emphasis Forde's.

[538] Forde, *The Law-Gospel Debate*, 215.

[539] Forde, "The Exodus from Virtue to Grace," 40-41. Emphasis Forde's.

[540] Forde, "A Short Word, 91. Emphasis Forde's.

[541] Forde, "Preaching the Sacraments," 11, 26. See also Forde, "Law and Gospel in Luther's Hermeneutic," 248.

[542] Forde, *Theology Is for Proclamation*, 155. See "A New Approach to the *Communicatio Idiomatum*," pp. 151-153, above.

[543] Ibid., 156.

[544] Ibid. Here the hermeneutical task is at last examined. That task requires investment by the proclaimer — careful examination of the intent of the text historically and cultural and linguistic work to make that intent possible today. Yet it respects the goal of the text as well, seeking to permit/enable/free/empower the message intended.

[545] Forde, "Proclamation: The Present Tense of the Gospel," 172.

[546] Forde, "The Lutheran View," 17.

[547] Forde, *Theology Is for Proclamation*, 157. Here the proclaimer's task is again emphasized in terms of Forde's confidence in the power of the Word which must simply be released. Perhaps Forde would say the text does the task and the proclaimer holds the text to it.

[548] For some examples from the Gospels, see Forde, "The Other Side of Christmas" [sermon on Matt 2:13-15, 19-23], 3; "The Wedding Feast" [sermon on Matt 22:1-14], 1-2; "A God Who Acts" [sermon on Matt 22:1-14], 4; sermon on Matt 22:1-14 beginning "Our text today," 2; sermon on Matt 25:1-13, 4; sermon on Matt 27:46 beginning "'My God, My God...' Today, on Good Friday," 3; sermon on Luke 23:32-38 beginning "'Father, forgive them...' Well, he's at it again!" 2; sermon on Luke 23:32-38 beginning "'Father, for give them, for they know not...," 2; "On God's Goodness" [sermon on John 1:43-51], 2; "Food and Drink Indeed!" [sermon on John 6:53-60], 1; and Sermon on John19:29 entitled "'It is Finished!' It is finished, completed...," 2, all listed in *Register of the Surviving Sermon Manuscripts of Gerhard Forde*; "Go Away, Jesus!" [sermon on Matt 8:28-34], 104; "The Easy Yoke" [sermon on Matt 11:25-30], 85; "On Getting Out of the Way for Jesus," 98, all in *The Captivation of the Will: Luther vs. Erasmus on Freedom and Bondage* ; "The Laborers in the Vineyard" [sermon on Matt 20:1-16] 317, 318; "A Voice from the Darkness" [sermon on Mark 1:21-28], 310; "The Interrupted Party" [sermon on Mark 14:25], 279; and "The Doing of God" [sermon on John 1:18 and 5:19], 275, all in *The Preached God* .

[549] Forde, "The Wedding Feast" [sermon on Matt 22:1-14], 2.

[550] Forde, "The Doing of God" [sermon on John 1:18 and 5:19], in *The Preached God*, 275.

[551] Forde, "Go Away Jesus!" in *The Captivation of the Will*, 104.

[552] For all quotes in this paragraph, see Forde, "Something to Believe," 237.

[553] Forde, "Preaching the Sacraments," 13.

[554] Ibid., 23.

[555] Forde, "Something to Believe," 234.

[556] Ibid., 229.

[557] Ibid., 20. See also Forde, "A Refuge for Beggars," [sermon on Luke 18:35-43], 4; and "The Interrupted Party," 279, and "Abstractions Aside," 281, both in *The Preached God* .

[558] Forde, "Preaching the Sacraments," 19.

[559] Gerhard Forde, "The Apocalyptic No and the Eschatological Yes: Reflections, Suspicions, Fears, and Hopes," in *A More Radical Gospel: Essays on Eschatology, Authority, Atonement and Ecumenism*, ed. Mark C. Mattes and Steven D. Paulson (Grand Rapids: Eerdmans, 2004) 32.

[560] Forde, "Preaching the Sacraments," 18. Emphasis Forde's.

[561] Forde, "Indherred 125th Anniversary" [sermon on Ps 107:1-3], 4.

[562] Forde, "A God Who Acts" [sermon on Matthew 1:14], 3.

[563] Forde, "The Formula of Concord Article V," 187.

[564] Forde, "Infallibility Language and the Early Lutheran Tradition," 132. Emphasis Forde's.

[565] Gerhard Forde, "The Lutheran Response [to the Pentecostal View]," in *Christian Spirituality: Five Views of Sanctification*, ed. Donald L. Alexander (Downers Grove, IL: Intervarsity, 1988) 156.

[566] Forde, "Naming the One Who is Above Us," 113.

[567] Forde, "Christian Life," 400.

[568] Ibid.

[569] Forde, "The Newness of the Gospel," 90.

[570] Forde, "The Power of Negative Thinking," 251.

[571] "Discussion [between Gerhard Forde and Eric Gritsch]," following Forde, "Bound to Be Free," in *Encounters with Luther*, 81.

[572] Gerhard Forde, "Explosions and the Christian Faith" [sermon on Gen 3:1-5 and Col 3:3], 4.

[573] Forde, "Called to Freedom," in *The Preached God*, 257.

[574] Forde, *The Law-Gospel Debate*, 211.

[575] "Discussion [between Gerhard Forde and Eric Gritsch]," following Forde, "Bound to Be Free," 81.

[576] Forde, "Explosions and the Christian Faith" [sermon on Gen 11:1-9], 4.

[577] Forde, "The Viability of Luther Today," 31.

[578] Forde, "Seven More Demons!" [sermon on Luke 11:24-26], 3.

[579] On the other hand, see "On Losing One's Life" [sermon on Mark 8:35 and Col 3:3], 2, where the old Adam may also be pleased to feign such a concern about these things that the actions are ultimately ambiguous.

[580] Forde, "Called to Freedom," in *The Preached God*, 255.

[581] Forde, "Bound to Be Free," 69. Emphasis Forde's.

[582] Forde, "Called to Freedom," in *The Preached God*, 259. Emphases Forde's.

[583] Ibid., 264, but as it reads in the transcription of the original lecture, "Called to Freedom." In *Befreiung und Freiheit: Martin Luthers Beitrag: Eighth International Congress for Luther Research*, Tape 1. St. Paul: Luther Northwestern Theological Seminary, 1993, my transcript page 13. Emphases Forde's.

[584] Forde, "The Viability of Luther Today," 25. Spontaneity would here refer to the unbound potentiality of true freedom implicit in the Latin root, not a bubbliness or an expression of a vibrant emotional spirit common in modern speech.

[585] Forde, "The End of Theology," 3, 20.

[586] Forde, "Romans 8:18-27," 283.

[587] Forde, "The Lutheran View," 20.

[588] Forde, "The End of Theology," 24.

[589] Ibid., 19.

[590] Forde, "Caught in the Act," 27.

[591] Gerhard Forde, " *Exsurge Domine!* Psalm 74:22-23," in *A More Radical Gospel: Essays on Eschatology, Authority, Atonement and Ecumenism*, ed. Mark C. Mattes and Steven D. Paulson (Grand Rapids: Eerdmans, 2004) 208.

[592] Gerhard Forde, "Does the Gospel Have a Future? Barth's Romans Revisited," 77.

[593] Gerhard Forde, "Thought for Easter Sermon" [sermon on Matt 28:6], 1, later rendered more gentle in "He has risen, He is not here" [sermon on Mark 16:6] 1.

[594] Forde, "The Laborers in the Vineyard," in *The Preached* God, 317. Emphasis Forde's.

[595] Forde, "The Lutheran View," 30-32.

[596] Forde, sermon on Matt 25:1-13 beginning "There were ten maidens," 3-4.

[597] Forde, "Explosions and the Christian Faith" [sermon on Gen 11:1-9], 4.

[598] On Forde's discussion of tyranny, see above, pp. 80-81.

[599] A word he uses of it, for instance, in the closing sentences of his *Christian Dogmatics* Locus XI, "Christian Life," 469.

[600] Forde, *The Law-Gospel Debate*, 232-233. Emphasis Forde's.

[601] Forde, "The Revolt and the Wedding," 85.

[602] Forde, "Food and Drink Indeed!" [sermon on John 6:53-60] 1.

[603] Forde, "On Preaching Good News to the Poor" [sermon on Matt 11:2-5 and Mark 14:3-9] in *The Preached God*, 303.

[604] Forde, "Preaching the Sacraments," 25.

[605] Forde, "On Losing One's Life" [sermon on Mark 8:35 and Col 3:3], 2.

[606] Forde, "The Viability of Luther Today," 29.

[607] Ibid.

[608] Ibid. Emphasis Forde's.

[609] Forde, "Christian Life," 466.

[610] Forde, "Christian Life," 469.

[611] Examples of the appearance of one or both "expressions of freedom" in Forde's writings include *The Law-Gospel Debate*, 211, 215; "*lex semper accusat?*" 274; "The Revolt and the Wedding," 82, 85; "Discussion [between Gerhard Forde and Eric Gritsch]," following Forde, "Bound to Be Free," 81; "Fake Theology," 251; "Called to Freedom," in *The Preached God*, 262, 268; "Does the Gospel Have a Future?" 75, 77; "*Exsurge Domine!*: Psalm 74:22-23," in *A More Radical Gospel*, 209; and sermon on John 19:28-30 beginning "'It is Finished!' I suppose it might seem strange...," 3.

[612] For instance, Gerhard Forde, sermon on Rom 6:1-11, 2.

[613] Forde, "Proclamation: The Present Tense of the Gospel," 167-168.

[614] Josef Glazik, "Missiology" in *Concise Dictionary of the Christian World Mission*, ed. Stephen Neill, Gerald Anderson and John Goodwin (New York: Abingdon, 1971) 388.

[615] The Random House Dictionary of the English Language, 2nd ed. (New York: Random House, 1987) 1231.

[616] L. Nemer, "Mission and Missions," in *New Catholic Encyclopedia*, 2nd ed. (New York: Thompson Gale, 2003) 683; A. Scott Moreau, "Mission and Missions" in *Evangelical Dictionary of World Mission*, ed. A. Scott Moreau (Grand Rapids, MI: Baker, 2000) 636.

[617] Farris L. McDaniel, "Mission in the Old Testament," in *Mission in the New Testament: An Evangelical Approach*, ed. William J. Larkin Jr. and Joel F. Williams (Maryknoll, NY: Orbis, 2003) 11-16.

[618] Bernard J. Bamberger, "Proselytes," in *The Universal Jewish Encyclopedia* (New York: Universal Jewish Encyclopedia Co., Inc, 1943) 9:1.

[619] Joachim Jeremias, *Jesus' Promise to the Nations*, trans. S. H. Hooke (Naperville, IL: Alec R. Allenson, Inc., 1958) 11.

[620] Scot McKnight, *A Light among the Gentiles: Jewish Missionary Activity in the Second Temple Period* (Minneapolis: Fortress Press, 1991) 117.

[621] Clifford Bedell, "Mission in Intertestamental Judaism," in *Mission in the New Testament: An Evangelical Approach*, ed. William J. Larkin, Jr., and Joel F. Williams (Maryknoll, NY: Orbis, 2003) 26. Emphasis Bedell's.

[622] McDaniel, "Mission in the Old Testament," 11.

[623] I identify at least ten different categories of sending in the New Testament beyond daily and mundane human-to-human sending: references to the Father sending Jesus to the world as in John 17:18, God sending Jesus specifically to certain persons as in Acts 3:26, God sending an angel as in Luke 1:26, God sending chosen persons as in Matt 11:10, God sending a message or salvation as in Acts 28:28, the sending of the Holy Spirit or the Spirit's gifts as in 1 Pet 1:12, the Spirit sending people as in Acts 10: 20, God sending spirits out into the earth as in Rev 5:6, Jesus' sending his disciples in ministry as in Mark 6:7, and witnesses of Jesus sending word of him to others as in Matt 14:35. No doubt other nuances of sending in the New Testament could be discerned.

[624] Martin Hengel, *Between Jesus and Paul: Studies in the Earliest History of Christianity*, trans. John Bowden (Philadelphia: Fortress, 1983), 62, quoted in John D. Harvey, "Mission in Jesus' Teaching," in *Mission in the New Testament: An Evangelical Approach*, ed. William J. Larkin Jr. and Joel F. Williams (Maryknoll, NY: Orbis, 2003) 30.

[625] Harvey, "Mission in Jesus' Teaching," 32, 35.

[626] Jeremias, *Jesus' Promise to the Nations*, 11, 19, 25, 41, 46, 51-54, 71.

[627] Harvey, "Mission in Jesus' Teaching," 43.

[628] David J. Bosch, *Transforming Mission: Paradigm Shifts in Theology of Mission* (Maryknoll, NY: Orbis Books, 1991) 57.

[629] Ibid., 57, 83, 114.

[630] Harvey, 47.

[631] Don N. Howell, "Mission in Paul's Epistles: Genesis, Pattern, and Dynamics," in *Mission in the New Testament: An Evangelical Approach*, ed. William J. Larkin, Jr., and Joel F. Williams (Maryknoll, NY: Orbis Books, 1998, 2003) 65.

[632] Ibid., 70-91.

[633] Bosch, *Transforming Mission*, 172-178.

[634] Ibid., 181-182, 187-189. See Bosch's reference to Hans Küng on paradigms in "Paradigm Change in Theology," in Hans Küng and David Tracy, *Paradigm Change in Theology* (New York: Crossroad, 1989) 3-33.

[635] Ibid., 190-214.

[636] Ibid., 233. Emphasis Bosch's.

[637] Ibid., 245-255.

[638] Ibid., 274.

[639] Ibid., 286-296, 310-312, 313ff, 327ff, 334ff.

[640] Ibid., 349-362.

[641] Thomas Aquinas, *Summa Theologiae*, trans. T. C. O'Brien (New York: Blackfriars, 1976) 209-217.

[642] Ibid., 119-121.

[643] Ibid., 217-229.

[644] Timothy Yates, *Christian Mission in the Twentieth Century* (Cambridge: Cambridge University Press, 1994).

[645] Ibid., 19.

[646] Ibid., 31.

[647] Ibid., 35.

[648] Ibid., 36.

[649] Ibid., 42.

[650] Ibid., 46.

[651] Ibid., 49-50.

[652] J. C. Hoekendijk, *Kirche und Volk in der deutscher Missionswissenschaft* (Munich: Kaiser, 1967) 280, quoted in Yates, *Christian Mission in the Twentieth Century*, 54.

[653] Yates, *Christian Mission in the Twentieth Century*, 56.

[654] Ibid., 60-61.

[655] Ibid., 63, 65.

[656] Ibid., 67.

[657] Ibid., 71

[658] Hendrik Kraemer, *The Christian Message in a Non-Christian World* (Grand Rapids, MI: Kregel Publications, 1938, 1956) 48.

[659] Yates, *Christian Mission in the Twentieth Century*, 98.

[660] Ibid., 73.

[661] Ibid., 65

[662] Hendrik Kraemer, *The Christian Message in a Non-Christian World* 123-124, as summarized in Yates, *Christian Mission in the Twentieth Century*, 113.

[663] Yates, *Christian Mission in the Twentieth Century*, 122, referring to the International Missionary Council Tambaram reports, 3:372-373.

[664] M. A. C. Warren, "General Introduction," in A. K. Cragg, *Sandals at the Mosque: Christian Presence amid Islam* (London: Oxford, 1959) 9-10, quoted in Yates, *Christian Mission in the Twentieth Century*, 142.

[665] Yates, *Christian Mission in the Twentieth Century*, 145.

666 Ibid., 153.
667 Ibid., 159.
668 Ibid., 161.
669 Ibid., 180.
670 Ibid.
671 Ibid., 181.
672 Ibid., 182.
673 Ibid., 216-217.
674 Ibid., 227.
675 Ibid., 231-232.
676 Ibid., 233.
677 Ibid., 232-233.
678 Ibid., 234.
679 Ibid., 235.
680 Ibid., 242.
681 "Global Mission in the Twenty-First Century: A Vision of Evangelical Faithfulness in God's Mission," 5, available online at http://archive.elca.org/globalmission/policy/gm21full.pdf (accessed July 10, 2008).
682 Ibid., 6.
683 Ibid.
684 Stephen Neill, *Creative Tension* (London: Edinburg House Press, 1959) 81.
685 "Decree *Ad Gentes* on the Missionary Activity of the Church," Chapter 1, section 2, http://www.vatican.va/archive/hist_councils/ii_vatican_council/documents/vat-ii_decree_19651207_ad-gentes_en.html (accessed March 12, 2009), quoted in Bosch, *Transforming Mission*, 372.
686 Using terms from the five churchly types in Avery Dulles, *Models of the Church* (Garden City, NY: Doubleday, 1974) 31-57, quoted in Bosch, *Transforming Mission*, 368-369.
687 Bosch, *Transforming Mission*, 272.
688 Karl Barth, "Die Theologie und die Mission in der Gegenwart," in Karl Barth, *Theologische Fragen und Antworten* (Zollikon-Qürich: Evangelischer Verlag, 1932, 1957) 3:100-126.
689 Bosch, *Transforming Mission*, 389-393.
690 Ibid., 394-399.
691 Ibid., 403.
692 Ibid., 399.
693 Ibid., 403.
694 David B. Barrett, *Evangelize! A Historical Survey of the Concept* (Birmingham, AL: New Hope, 1987) 42-45, lists seventy-nine definitions, 42-45, quoted in Bosch, *Transforming Mission*, 409.
695 Bosch, *Transforming Mission*, 411-412.
696 Ibid., 413-420.
697 Ibid., 423-424.
698 Ibid., 434-435.
699 Ibid., 436, 444.
700 Ibid., 452-454.
701 Ibid., 460.
702 Ibid., 467.
703 Ibid.
704 Ibid, 472.
705 Ibid., 478-482.
706 Ibid., 491.
707 Ibid., 494-496.
708 Carl Braaten, *The Flaming Center* (Philadelphia: Fortress, 1977) 36, quoted in Bosch, *Transforming Mission*, 508.
709 Bosch, *Transforming Mission*, 508.
710 The title of chapter 9, Stephen B. Bevans and Roger P. Schroeder, *Constants in Context: A Theology of Mission for Today* (Maryknoll, NY: Orbis, 2004).
711 Ibid., 287, paraphrasing *Ad Gentes* 2.
712 "Go Forth in Peace: Orthodox Perspectives on Mission," in *New Directions in Mission and Evangelization 1: Basic Statements 1974-1991*, ed. James A. Scherer and Stephen B. Bevans (Maryknoll, NY: Orbis Books, 1992) 204, quoted in Stephen B. Bevans and Roger P. Schroeder, *Constants in Context*, 288.
713 Elizabeth Johnson, *She Who Is: The Mystery of God in Feminist Discourse* (New York: Crossroad, 1992) 223, quoted in Bevans and Schroeder, *Constants in Context*, 292.
714 Robert J. Schreiter, "Mission for the Twenty-First Century: A Catholic Perspective," in *Mission for the Twenty-First Century*, ed. Steven Bevans and Roger Schroeder (Chicago: CCGM Publications, 2001) 36-39, quoted in Bevans and Schroeder, *Constants in Context*, 293.
715 The title of chapter 10, Bevans and Schroeder, *Constants in Context*, 305.
716 Pope Paul VI, *Evangelii Nuntiandi*, 6, 8, http://www.vatican.va/holy_father/paul_vi/apost_exhortations/documents/hf_pvi_exh_19751208_evangelii-nuntiandi_en.html (accessed March 13, 2009), quoted in Bevans and Schroeder, *Constants in Context*, 305-306.

[717] Bevans and Schroeder, *Constants in Context*, 320.

[718] The title of chapter 11, Bevans and Schroeder, *Constants in Context*, 323-347.

[719] John Paul II, *Redemptoris Missio*, Chapter 1, section 4, http://www.vatican.va/holy_father/john_paul_ii/encyclicals/documents/hf_jp-ii_enc_07121990_redemptoris-missio_en.html (accessed March 13, 2009), quoted in Bevans and Schroeder, *Constants in Context*, 324.

[720] George Vandervelde, "Introduction," *Evangelical Review of Theology* 23/1 (January 1999) 9, quoted in Bevans and Schroeder, *Constants in Context*, 326.

[721] Adam Wolanin, "Trinitarian Foundation of Mission," in Sebastian Karotremprel *et al* ., eds., *Following Christ in Mission: A Foundational Course in Missiology* (Boston: Pauline Books and Media, 1996) 50, 53, quoted in Bevans and Schroeder, *Constants in Context*, 332.

[722] Bevans and Schroeder, *Constants in Context*, 338.

[723] Ibid., 326, referring to Vatican Council II, *Gaudium et Spes (Pastoral Constitution on the Church in the Modern World)*, Chapter 1, section 22, http://www.vatican.va/archive/hist_councils/ii_vatican_council/documents/vat-ii_cons_19651207_gaudium-et-spes_en.html (accessed March 13,2009).

[724] John Paul II, *Redemptoris Missio*, 55, quoted in Bevans and Schroeder, *Constants in Context*, 324, 326.

[725] John Stott, *Christian Mission in the Modern World* (Downers Grove, IL: InverVarsity Press, 1979) 35, quoted in Bevans and Schroeder, 335.

[726] Bevans and Schroeder, *Constants in Context*, 348, beginning chapter 12.

[727] Ibid., 348-349.

[728] Ibid., 349.

[729] World Council of Churches Sixth Assembly, "Witnessing in a Divided World" (1983), in *New Directions in Mission and Evangelization 1: Basic Statements 1974-1991*, ed. James A Scherer and Stephen B. Bevans (Maryknoll, NY: Orbis, 1992) 55-56, cited by Bevans and Schroeder, *Constants in Context*, 353.

[730] Bevans and Schroeder, *Constants in Context*, 353-357.

[731] Ibid., 357-361.

[732] Ibid., 361-362.

[733] Ibid., 367.

[734] Wayne Teasdale, *A Monk in the World: Cultivating a Spiritual Life* (Novato, CA: New World Library, 2002) 1, quoted in Bevans and Schroeder, *Constants in Context*, 368.

[735] Bevans and Schroeder, *Constants in Context*, 369.

[736] Ibid., 370.

[737] Ibid., 370-372.

[738] Ibid., 378.

[739] Ibid., 382. See Bevans and Schroeder's reference on p. 379 to Vatican II documents *Lumen Gentium* 16 ("the possibility of salvation for all people of good will, whether they have faith in God or not"), *nostra Aetate* 2 ("of other religious ways as possessing 'a ray of that Truth which enlightens all men'"), and *Gaudium et Spes* 22 ("the presence of the Holy Spirit who 'in a manner known only to God, offers to every man the possibility of being associated with this pascal mystery'").

[740] Andrew Walls, *The Missionary Movement in Christian History: Studies in the Transmission of Faith* (Maryknoll, NY: Orbis, 2005) xvii, quoted in Bevans and Schroeder, *Constants in Context*, 464, n120.

[741] S. Mark Heim, *The Depth of the Riches: A Trinitarian Theology of Religious Ends* (Grand Rapids, MI: Eerdmans, 2001), 138, quoted in Bevans and Schroeder, *Constants in Context*, 380.

[742] Bevans and Schroeder, *Constants in Context*, 383-384.

[743] Ibid., 385.

[744] Ibid., 386-388.

[745] Ibid., 389-390.

[746] Ibid., 393, referring to Robert Schreiter, *The Ministry of Reconciliation: Spirituality and Strategies* (Maryknoll, NY: Orbis, 1998) vi.

[747] Gustav Warneck, *Outline of a History of Protestant Missions from the Reformation to the Present Time*, ed. George Robson (New York: Fleming H. Revell Company, 1901) 9.

[748] Gustav Leopold Plitt, *Kurze Geschichte der lutherischen Mission in Vorträgen* (Erlangen, 1871), quoted in Gustav Warneck, *Outline of a History of Protestant Missions*, 10.

[749] Gustav Warneck, *Outline of a History of Protestant Missions*,10-11.

[750] Martin Luther, *Small Catechism*, Lord's Prayer 2, in *The Book of Concord*, ed. Robert Kolb and Timothy J. Wengert (Minneapolis: Fortress Press, 2000) 356, as English translation of the citation in Gustav Warneck, *Outline of a History of Protestant Missions*, 11.

[751] Gustav Warneck, *Outline of a History of Protestant Missions*,13.

[752] Martin Luther, *Sermons of Martin Luther*, ed. and trans. John Nicholas Lenker (Grand Rapids, MI: Baker Books, 1907, 1983, 1995) 209-243, an English translation of the citation in Gustav Warneck, *Outline of a History of Protestant Missions*, 14.

[753] Gustav Warneck, *Outline of a History of Protestant Missions*, 14

[754] Ibid., 15.

[755] Ibid., 17.

[756] Ibid., 15-17.

[757] Ibid., 17.

[758] Paul Wetter, *Der Missionsgedanke bei Martin Luther* (Bonn: Verlag für Kultur und Wissenschaft, 1999) 29, with respect to Gustav Kawerau; 31, with respect to Karl Sell; 31, with respect to E. Lachmann; 35, with

respect to Julius Richter; 37, with respect to Danish missiologists; 45, with respect to Herbert C. Jackson; 46, with respect to John Haward Yoder. My translations.

[759] Karl Holl, *Gesammelte Aufsätze zur Kirchengeschichte*, Band I [Tübingen: Verlag von J. C. B. Mohr [Paul Siebeck], 1932].

[760] Ibid., 234-236.

[761] Ibid., 236-237, my translation.

[762] Ibid., 238.

[763] Ibid., 239, my translation.

[764] Ibid., 239-242.

[765] Paul Wetter, *Der Missionsgedanke bei Martin Luther*, 47.

[766] Jaroslav Pelikan, "Forward," in Werner Elert, *The Structure of Lutheranism*, trans. Walter A. Hansen (St. Louis: Concordia, 1962) I:x.

[767] Ingetraut Ludolphy, "Elert, Werner," in *The Encyclopedia of the Lutheran Church*, ed. Julius Bodensieck (Minneapolis: Augsburg Publishing House, 1965) I:771.

[768] Elert, *The Structure of Lutheranism*, I:385.

[769] Ibid., 390. See also 402.

[770] WA, 13:541, line 17, quoted in Elert, *The Structure of Lutheranism*, I:386.

[771] Elert, *The Structure of Lutheranism*, 385.

[772] Walter A. Hanson, "Translator's Preface," in Elert, *The Structure of Lutheranism*, xix-xx.

[773] Elert, *The Structure of Lutheranism*, 385.

[774] WA, 41:594, line 22; 31 (I):285, line 12; 10 (I.1):1, 540, lines 5 and 12ff; 24:392, line 28; 10 (I.2):50, line 10, respectively, quoted in Elert, *The Structure of Lutheranism*, 386-388.

[775] Elert, *The Structure of Lutheranism*, 388.

[776] WA, 11:412, lines 11ff, quoted in Elert, *The Structure of Lutheranism*, 389.

[777] Wilhelm Löhe, *Three Books about the Church*, trans. & ed., James L. Schaaf (Philadelphia: Fortress, 1969) 59, quoted in Elert, *The Structure of Lutheranism*, 390-391.

[778] Elert, *The Structure of Lutheranism*, 393-394.

[779] Ibid., 393-402.

[780] Ingemar Öberg, *Luther and World Mission: A Historical and Systematic Study with Special Reference to Luther's Bible Exposition*, trans. Deal Apel (St. Louis: Concordia Publishing House, 2007).

[781] Ibid., 1-3. Scholars cited include J. Richter, H. W. Schomerus, E. Schick, L. Bergman, and Kenneth Scott Latourette.

[782] Ibid., 3.

[783] Ibid., 3-5. Scholars cited include Drews, Holl, Elert, Danbolt, Wingren, Dörries, Holsten, Maurer, Genischen, Scherer, Peters, Bunkowske, Aagaard, Heubach, Beisser, Forsberg, Hallencreutz, and Becker, besides Öberg himself.

[784] Ibid., 4-5.

[785] Ibid., 6-7.

[786] Ibid.

[787] Ibid., 8.

[788] Ibid., 199-205, 205-211, 211-218, 225-230, 232-253, 253-266, respectively.

[789] Ibid., 8-9.

[790] Ibid., 3.

[791] Ibid., 426.

[792] Ibid., 491.

[793] Julius Wiggers, Christian Kalkar, and others. See Paul Wetter, *Der Missionsgedanke bei Martin Luther* 27ff.

[794] Öberg, *Luther and World Mission*, 8-9.

[795] Forde, "The Place of Theology in the Church," *dialog* 22/2 (Spr 1983) 123-124.

[796] Forde, "Once More Into the Breach?" 10-11.

[797] Forde, "My Sheep Hear My Voice" [sermon on John 10:22-30], 1.

[798] Gerhard Forde, "The Minister as Ambassador: Reflections for a Revised Curriculum at LNTS" [paper presented before the Curriculum Revision Committee, August, 1990].

[799] Forde, "The Exodus from Virtue to Grace," 42.

[800] Forde, "The Place of Theology in the Church," 129.

[801] Forde, "My Sheep Hear My Voice" [sermon on John 10:22-30], 2.

[802] Forde, "The Ordained Ministry," 120-122.

[803] Forde, "The Minister as Ambassador," 12.

[804] Forde, "The Word on Quotas," *Lutheran Quarterly* 6/2 (Sum 1992) 124.

[805] Forde, sermon on Matt 23.37, 6.

[806] Forde, "The Exodus from Virtue to Grace," 42.

[807] One might speculate that the word may have entered Forde's vocabulary haphazardly here, coming as it does in a negative critique of an unrelated train of thought and added unto a more common term almost as an afterthought. It's almost as if it comes from without, from somebody else's conversation, maybe from the church's conversation where it was a popular concept in the aftermath of the American Lutheran Church's highly successful United Mission Appeal. It is almost as if, though it had not figured in his conversation

before, he found himself willing to talk about it in this focused sense, in terms of the proclamatory task.

808 Forde, "The Ordained Ministry," 121.
809 Ibid., 122.
810 Ibid., 136. Emphasis added.
811 Forde, "My Sheep Hear My Voice" [sermon on John 10:22-30], 3.
812 Ibid.
813 Forde, "The Place of Theology in the Church," 121-125.
814 Ibid., 126-127. Emphasis Forde's.
815 For another clear statement of this theological mission, see Gerhard Forde, "A Movement without a Move?" *dialog* 30/2 (Spr 1991) 83: "A confessing or a theological movement, to be true to itself, simply takes its confession or its theological witness before the world to be its mission, believing such witness to be its highest duty and calling — indeed the best thing it can do for the world."
816 Forde, "The Place of Theology in the Church," 128.
817 Ibid, 128-129.
818 Forde, "Radical Lutheranism," 17.
819 For example, Forde, "The Place of Theology in the Church," 123.
820 Forde, "The Word That Kills and Makes Alive," 3.
821 Forde, "Unity without Concord?" 171.
822 Forde, "Law and Gospel as the Methodological Principle," 59: "If you went to the mission field you most certainly would not begin this way" [with a doctrine of verbal inspiration].
823 Forde, "The Minister as Ambassador," 12. In a review of the thesis draft Marc Kolden recalls that Forde also included missiology as such in conversations concerning this point.
824 Forde, "Once More Into the Breach?" 9; "The Discipline of Silence" [sermon on Ezek 3:4-15], 2.
825 Forde, "Something to Believe," 238-239.
826 See pp. 141-144.
827 Bosch, *Transforming Mission*, 494. See above, p. 143-144.
828 Forde, "Outside the Gate," 250.
829 Forde, "Once More into the Breach?" 13.
830 See pp. 144.
831 Forde, "The Word that Kills and Makes Alive," 5-6.
832 Forde, *The Law-Gospel Debate*, 199.
833 Forde, "Once More Into the Breach?" 7-8.
834 Ibid., 13.
835 Ibid.
836 Forde, *The Law-Gospel Debate*, 233.
837 Forde, sermon on Matt 25:1-13 beginning, "There were ten maidens...," 4.
838 Forde, sermon on Mark 8:35 and Col 3:3.
839 Forde, "The End of Theology," 23. I have corrected the placement of his second quotation mark from before "sends" to its presumed proper place after "Headquarters."
840 Forde, "The Viability of Luther Today," 23-24.
841 Bosch, *Transforming Mission*, 424.
842 Forde, "Theology as Modus Operandi," 179.
843 Forde, "The Power of Negative Thinking," 251.
844 Forde, "Romans 8:18-27," 283. Emphasis Forde's.
845 According to the wording of the original presentation, Forde, "Karl Barth on the Consequences of Lutheran Christology," in *The Consequences of Christology* part 5 [videorecording] (St. Paul: Luther Northwestern Theological Seminary, 1990), p. 20 in my transcription. This is the source of the edited version, "Karl Barth on the Consequences of Lutheran Christology," in *The Preached God*, 83-84.
846 Gerhard Forde, "Behold and See!" [sermon on Lam 1:12], 2.
847 Forde, "The End of Theology," 23.
848 Forde, "Unity without Concord?" 2.
849 Forde, "The Lutheran View," 19-20. See p. 251, n505 on the death from which there is no rising.
850 For examples in Forde, see "Bound to Be Free," 69; and "The Lutheran View," 120.
851 Forde, "The End of Theology," 3.
852 Bevans and Schroeder, *Constants in Context*, 369.
853 Ibid., 387
854 Ibid., 390-393.
855 Öberg, *Luther and World Mission*, 7-8.
856 Elert, *The Structure of Lutheranism*, I:385.
857 Öberg, *Luther and World Mission*, 3-5.
858 Forde, "Lutheran Ecumenism," 446.
859 Forde, *The Law-Gospel Debate*, 224.
860 Forde, "Once More Into the Breach?" 11.
861 Forde, "The Word That Kills and Makes Alive," 4.
862 Forde, "The Irrelevance of the Modern World for Luther," 77.

[863] Forde, "My Sheep Hear My Voice" [sermon on John 10:22-30], 4.

[864] Bevans and Schroeder, *Constants in Context*, 369.

[865] Forde, *The Law-Gospel Debate*, 213.

[866] Bevans and Schroeder, *Constants in Context*, 323-324

[867] Warneck, *Outline of a History of Protestant Missions*, 14.

[868] Neill, *Creative Tension*, 81.

[869] Forde, "A Movement without a Move," 83.

[870] Apparently, for instance, it did not occur to musicians in medieval Europe to affix their name to the music they composed before the twelfth century. See Robert Greenburg, How to Listen to and Understand Great Music (Chantilly, VA: The Teaching Company Limited Partnership) part 1, lecture 3.

[871] See pp. 111-112.

[872] Ibid.

[873] See p. 124.

[874] Gerhard Forde, sermon on Is 11:1-5 beginning, "Das helle Licht der Weihnacht bricht wieder. . . ."

[875] Forde, "The One Acted Upon," 55. See above, p. 19.

[876] Forde, "Justification by Faith Alone," 261.

[877] Forde, "On Sin" [sermon on Gen 2:15-17, 3:1-13] 2; Forde, "Justification by Faith Alone," 264.

[878] Forde, "Romans 8:18-27," 282-284.

[879] Forde, "Called to Freedom," in *The Preached God*, 262, 268.

[880] Forde, "Does the Gospel Have a Future?" 75.

[881] Gerhard Forde, sermon on Matt 22:1-14 beginning "Our text today compares the Kingdom of Heaven . . . ;" and "The Wedding Feast" [sermon on Matthew 22:1-14 beginning "As an Advent message this day . . .]." The first is one of those rare sermons that actually carries a date, September 26, 1966. The second is handwritten on the backs of memoranda bearing the dates, September 3, 1975 and September 18, 1975.

[882] Forde, "Proclamation: The Present Tense of the Gospel," 170.

[883] Forde, "A Word from Without" [sermon on Jer 23:29], 93.

[884] Forde, "Something to Believe," 237.

[885] Forde, "The Exodus from Virtue to Grace," 42. For the subsection on justification by faith, see pp. 97-101.

[886] Forde, "The Irrelevance of the Modern World for Luther," 77.

[887] Forde, *Theology Is for Proclamation*, 137.